D1497888

THE POOR
—— AND THE ——
POWERLESS

THE POOR
——AND THE——
POWERLESS

Economic Policy and Change in the Caribbean

Clive Y. Thomas

Monthly Review Press
New York

List of illustrations

Cover photo taken from a painting by Ray Povey; cover design by Jan Brown. Credits for photographs in the text are as follows:

Introduction, Philip Wolmuth; Chapter 1, BBC Hulton Picture Library; Chapter 2, Royal Commonwealth Society; Chapter 3, A Costa; Chapter 4, Royal Commonwealth Society; Chapter 5, Philip Wolmuth; Chapter 6, Royal Commonwealth Society; Chapter 7, Belinda Coote/OXFAM; Chapter 8, Philip Wolmuth; Chapter 9, Roshini Kempadoo/Format; Chapter 10, Belinda Coote/OXFAM; Chapter 11, Philip Wolmuth; Chapter 12, Philip Wolmuth; Chapter 13, Philip Wolmuth; Chapter 14, Jenny Matthews/Format; Chapter 15, Jenny Matthews/Format

First published in Great Britain in 1988 by
Latin America Bureau (Research and Action) Limited
1 Amwell Street
London EC1R 1UL
Copyright © Latin America Bureau (Research and Action) Limited 1988

Library of Congress Cataloging-in-Publication Data

Thomas, Clive Yolande.
    The poor and the powerless: economic policy and change in the Caribbean/Clive Y. Thomas.
        p.   cm.
    Bibliography: p.
    Includes index.
    ISBN 0–85345–743–3. ISBN 0–85345–744–1 (pbk.).

    1. Caribbean Area—Economic policy—Case studies.
2. Economic development—Case studies.   3. States, Small—Economic conditions—Case studies.   I. Title.
HC151.T56   1987
338.9′009729—dc19   87–30159
                                                                      CIP

Monthly Review Press
122 West 27th Street
New York, N.Y. 10001

Manufactured in the United States of America

10 9 8 7 6 5 4 3 2 1

Contents

Contents

Contents

List of Tables

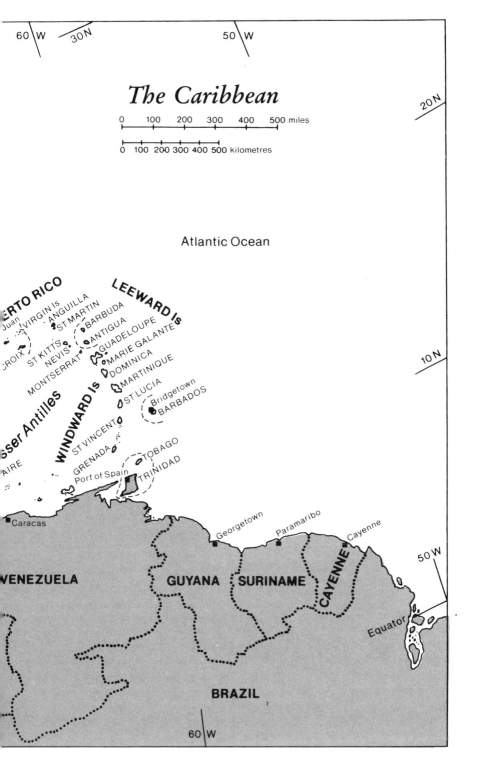

The Caribbean

Atlantic Ocean

Preface

Five centuries after the encounter of the Old World and the New World which Columbus's voyages heralded, the Caribbean region remains as much a focal point of global power struggles and momentous internal social upheavals as it was then. The result is that as we approach the 21st century, all layers, social classes and groups within these societies, as well as all the contending factions and nations involved in the wider struggle, view the region as a hotbed of crisis and a potential source of global warfare.

Behind this view, however, lies a remarkable variety of explanations as to why this is so, and an equally remarkable variety of offered solutions. A commonly held view is that the situation in the region is essentially a by-product of larger, global struggles and rivalries and that consequently nothing can be done *within* the Caribbean itself to chart its own destiny and future. Many representatives of the recently arrived business class see the problems of the region as essentially the product of too much state and political interference in the freedom of the market place. Echoing 'Reaganomics', their solutions are privatisation, deregulation, reduced taxation, an open house to foreign capital and the closest possible ties with the region's natural ally, the US. Many of the region's politicians, in and out of power, on the right and on the left, see the problems as due to a failure of ideology, and depending on whether or not they are in power, as due also to the incompetence, venality and corruption of those who hold state power. The intelligentsia and academics (particularly those in the humanities) see the crisis in terms of the collapse of old paradigms and the failure to discover new ones. Many naively assume that if the essential truth of the region's condition could be understood, then that understanding alone, without any concerted social or political action, would end the region's underdevelopment and lead to its successful transformation. Perhaps in sub-conscious reaction to this approach, academics in the so-called 'hard' sciences attribute much of the region's failure to the ascendancy of their counterparts (particularly the social scientists) in forming public opinion and policy.

Those of religious persuasion, particularly the recent evangelising groups, see in all this the handiwork of the Creator and a fitting retribution for societies in hasty retreat from the values of Christianity and perhaps (only perhaps) from Hindu and Muslim faiths, in token recognition of the more than one million East Indians who live in the English-speaking Caribbean. To foreign capitalists the region's problems are ultimately due to too little and not too much penetration of their technology, financial resources, marketing know-how and management expertise. Large sections of the US establishment see the Caribbean's situation as either the product of, or the fertile opportunity for, communist conspiracy and terror against western interests.

Finally, to the poor the crisis means more poverty, while to the powerless it is the harbinger of excuses for their further exclusion from the exercise of real power over their lives.

While there is an element of over-statement, if not caricature, in the presentation of these views, each in its own way contains an aspect of truth about the reality of the present-day Caribbean. The issue, however, which has to be engaged is that the present crisis should not mask the perpetual crisis in which the vast majority of the peoples of the region have lived for the past five hundred years. This study seeks to articulate the social rhythms which have given rise to this feature of Caribbean life and to evaluate the various public policies which have been developed in response to it. This, it is hoped, will not only raise our consciousness of these events, but also lay the foundations for social action, policies and programmes aimed at rectifying the mistakes of the past.

This work would not have been completed if I had not received considerable support from others. First of all, the Latin America Bureau created the occasion for this work by raising the idea of doing it with me at a time when, quite independently, I had come to consider it a vital necessity, given the paucity of educational materials in this area. However, without the timely material support of the International Development Research Centre (IDRC), Ottawa, I would not have been able to spend time at the Centre for Educational Research for Latin America and the Caribbean nor to visit countries in the Caribbean, acquiring needed materials and doing much of the writing. Over the past two years, while I was working on this book, many of my friends and colleagues contributed more than they might have realised at the time. This help took many forms: testing an idea, supplying research materials on request, facilitating a trip which would allow me to gain access to badly needed library materials, and even in one case helping me to proof-read and edit the manuscript. Among those whom I would like to mention here in deep appreciation for their help are: Maurice Odle, B (Vishnu) Persaud, Theo Gittens, Mike Kaufman, Tony Tillet and Chris Smart.

Often it is those closest to the author who bear the harshest burdens in seeing a work through to completion: silences, absences, and even unexplained grimaces as an insight or intuition arrives with the threat of immediate departure if any interruption occurs. There is no way that one can atone for these neglects, but there is always the hope that the creative enterprise is worth it all.

Introduction

The close of the 15th century was marked by the explorations of Columbus and the beginnings of systematic European penetration into the western hemisphere. While probably not appreciated at the time, this encounter heralded a new era of human development, variously described as the dawn of the modern period, 'the birth of capitalism', and 'the rise of the New World'. Today, five centuries later, the Caribbean is as important as any other region in determining whether we destroy ourselves as a species or advance to a more humane civilisation where, among other things, nobody would be poor and powerless. Situated in the geo-political backyard of the United States, the world's leading capitalist power, at a period when the US administration is engaged in intense confrontation with what it calls 'international communism', countries like Jamaica, Grenada, Cuba, Puerto Rico, Haiti, Suriname, Nicaragua, El Salvador, Honduras, Guyana and the Dominican Republic conjure up images of widespread and momentous social upheaval.

This book, which attempts to analyse and interpret the economic development of the region since the Second World War, is aimed at that fairly wide category of readers who, although not necessarily economic specialists, nonetheless recognise that to comprehend contemporary Caribbean reality, it is important to understand how the economic and material basis of the region is organised and reproduced. Because this book is written from a multi-disciplinary, or what is sometimes described as a political-economy approach, most readers will find from their own experience and/or training that they have at least one familiar vantage point from which to follow the various arguments.

As its title suggests, this book is essentially concerned with the interests of the poor and the powerless. The reason for this is simple. For the whole of the region's recorded history, the poor and the powerless have comprised the majority of the population. As the saying goes, 'the poor have always been with us'. While this is undoubtedly true, the poor have also taken on many different forms over the past five centuries: the indigenous inhabitants of the area, the early waves of European immigrant settlers, African slaves, indentured workers, peasants, urban and rural workers, as well as the unemployed of the post-slavery period. The powerless are all those who, under prevailing social and institutional arrangements, are or have been unable to exercise any control over the workings of the state, the machinery of production and all the other established institutions of social authority. In other words, they are the ones who are excluded from the dominant or ruling political groups or classes. With rare exceptions, the dominant classes have always, throughout the region's recorded history, comprised a small fraction of the population and the powerless the vast majority.

Within the region the poor and the powerless have invariably been the same people, but from this, one should not infer that the poor are incapable of acting as a powerful social group. On the contrary, because they have always comprised the bulk of the work force, the producers of wealth, they can command considerable social power. Nevertheless, except for a few very brief insurrectionary interludes, the Cuban revolution being the best known example, over the past five centuries and more they have failed to seize control of state power which is a necessary step towards reordering social priorities with a view to securing an eventual and permanent end to their poverty and subjugation.

Since the days of Columbus, the region has been colonised by the European powers, and, more recently, has fallen under the domination and sway of the United States. Thus powerlessness has to be conceived at both the *national* level (in the sense that the colonial and imperial powers have historically oppressed *all* groups and classes in a given territory, depriving them of effective control of the machinery of state) and at the *internal* social or class level, where some groups and classes are better placed than others.

The methodology employed in this book is explicitly oriented towards making the reader aware that there are other possible paths of development for the region. But before we can comprehend the present, let alone launch into plans for the future, it is necessary to gain a thorough understanding of the past. The historical method employed here attempts to infuse the analysis with a sense of historical direction rather than merely providing historical details or insights as ends in themselves. Hopefully such an approach will facilitate a deeper appreciation of the major continuities and discontinuities of the present and future and thus lessen the danger of repeating the mistakes of history as so many before us have done.

Our task is made considerably more difficult, however, by the fact that, while seeking to advance a regional or area approach, in reality no other part of the world can boast as much fragmentation or balkanisation as the Caribbean area. In addition, the almost continuous entanglement of the region as an actual war zone in the struggles between East and West (as well as North and South) adds further difficulties to our project. One example of fragmentation is the use of the term *English-speaking Caribbean* to include three broad categories made up of (i) the 13 CARICOM (Caribbean Community and Common Market) territories with a population of 5 million (Antigua-Barbuda, Bahamas, Barbados, Belize, Dominica, Grenada, Guyana, Jamaica, St Kitts-Nevis, St Lucia, St Vincent, Trinidad-Tobago and Montserrat); (ii) the UK dependencies of Anguilla, British Virgin Islands, Cayman Islands, the Turks and Caicos, and possibly Bermuda; and (iii) the US Virgin Islands. This linguistic grouping includes Guyana and Belize which are not islands but mainland territories of South and Central America. It also includes the dependencies of the US and the UK, whereas all the CARICOM territories (with the exception of Montserrat) obtained their independence from Britain during the two and a half decades after 1960. It also ignores the special status of the US Virgin Islands. For these and other reasons, the use of a rather loose linguistically determined definition of the area of social study is inadequate and other factors, such as the cultural, economic, geographical, political and historical elements need also to be taken into account.

A second example of fragmentation occurs when an attempt is made to determine the area of study *geographically*. This approach defines the Caribbean as the islands of the Caribbean Sea and, as such, includes all the islands listed above, as well as Cuba, the Dominican Republic, Haiti, Puerto Rico, the French overseas *départements* of Martinique and Guadeloupe and the Dutch Antilles. To these (22 countries and about 28 million people) it is conventional to add the four non-island territories of Guyana and Belize (part of the English-speaking grouping), Suriname and the French overseas *département*, Cayenne (in all 26 countries and approximately 30 million people). A problem with this definition, however, is that it ignores the different forms of political organisation in the region, which include socialist Cuba, non-socialist independent states, as well as some surviving European and US colonies.

At present the most widely used concept is that of the *Caribbean Basin*, which includes all the countries already mentioned, plus the whole of Central America (including Mexico and Panama), as well as Colombia and Venezuela – in all 36 countries and over 150 million people. This concept owes much to the US government's view of its strategic and geo-political concerns in the area. As we shall see later in the text, in its Caribbean Basin Initiative (CBI) the US government has systematically sought to give this concept an economic content through its external aid, trade and investment relations. The East-West conflict emerges through the CBI's exclusion of countries like Cuba and Nicaragua and bias in favour of places such as Jamaica and El Salvador.

In addition to these problems raised by the high level of fragmentation and balkanisation within the region, is that of the difficulty posed by one author handling such a large number of different societies and nation states within one volume without turning the study into a simple gazetteer and thus forfeiting any in-depth analysis. Yet another problem arises when one country develops in such a distinctively different direction from the others (Cuba is again a case in point here) that it becomes impossible to include it within a general analysis of the Caribbean as a region.

For the purposes of this book an attempt has been made to combine two elements. On the one hand, historical, cultural, linguistic and geographical features have been taken into account in defining a meaningful area of study, and on the other, the strength and direction of the regional consciousness of the populations in the various territories has also been considered. Despite its many weaknesses (which are identified later in the book) CARICOM's attempt at regional integration comes closest to providing a framework for this shared regional consciousness within the Caribbean. All the major classes, groups and strata in these territories have moulded into their social consciousness a particular view of the Caribbean, which they take into account in pursuing their interests and which directly influences their political behaviour. In no other significant grouping of territories in the region (except possibly Central America which I believe should not be treated together with the Caribbean for the purposes at hand) is this community of interest as far advanced.

This book therefore concentrates primarily on the CARICOM group of countries. Nevertheless, for comparative and analytical reasons, it sometimes becomes necessary to embrace wider definitions of the area. Examples of these include the treatment of the historical forces shaping the early formation of the region's economy, the pattern of the region's industrialisation, the role of plantation and peasant agriculture in the region's food systems, the dominance of transnational corporations, the militarisation of the area and the effects of the East-West confrontation. I should also stress that the argument in the previous paragraph is reinforced by the additional consideration that most of the countries in the core group identified here are recent post-colonial states. By this I mean much more than their formal subjection to 'colonial office rule' and recent acquisition of 'political independence'. The distinction is based on the treatment of colonisation as an inherently distinctive process which has shaped these societies and on the potential for a 'break' with this process, which is inherent in independence in so far as colonial domination can no longer legally mediate itself through all the important structures of the society.

Although this study is confined to a relatively limited area, it nonetheless combines territories of enormous complexity, with both unifying and disintegrating tendencies. Perhaps by definition an area study tilts the balance in favour of unifying tendencies, but the fact that these territories have evolved out of British colonialism into separate and independent nation states, however, means that local differences in resource availability and its management, economic opportunity, location, leadership, as well as factors such as historical accident, cannot be ignored. In the region a continuous tension exists between unity and further fragmentation and this is reflected in the tension between the unifying and disintegrating tendencies which form the theoretical basis of this book.

Before concluding this introduction, I would like to point to a couple of other recurring themes in this work. One of these is that, in evaluating the region's past, I identify four fundamental periods of transition: (1) the destruction of indigenous communal societies and the imposition of systems of forced labour (slavery and indenture); (2) the breakup of these systems of forced labour; (3) the liberation and independence movements of the Spanish and Portuguese speaking countries; and (4) the global economic and political crisis of the 1930s and of the Second World War, which had an enormous impact on the region in general and on the core-group of countries in particular.

The last of these was, of course, the immediate precursor to the independence movements in the countries under consideration. A further point however, is that fundamental transitions in the mode of production have not only been a constant feature of Caribbean life over the past 500 years, but I also interpret the *present* historical conjuncture as comprising elements with this potential. This has given my task a certain immediacy, if not urgency.

Another issue, referred to earlier in connection with the fragmentation and balkanisation of the region, is that of size and scale. In terms of population, geographical area and size of national market, all Caribbean countries are small, but within the CARICOM sub-group there are considerable variations. Guyana, for example, covers an area of 214,970 square kilometres, whereas Montserrat has a mere 104. Jamaica, with 10,992 square kilometres, however, houses 40 per cent of the group's population, while Jamaica and Trinidad-Tobago (5,128 square kilometres) together comprise almost two-thirds of its population. These are the only countries with a population of a million or more. Meanwhile, Trinidad-Tobago alone accounts for 60 per cent of the regional market. Relative income per head varies considerably, from a per capita GDP in 1985 of over US$7,800 in the Bahamas to US$584 in Guyana. In Trinidad-Tobago and Barbados the comparable figures are US$6,538 and US$4,894 respectively. Only Jamaica (US$858) and St Vincent (US$933) had, along with Guyana, a per capita GDP lower than US$1,000. In the larger region, the Dominican Republic (US$712) and Haiti (US$368) fell into this category. Meanwhile, the British Virgin Islands (US$7,101), the US Virgin Islands (US$9,280) and the Netherlands Antilles (US$6,110) all exceeded US$6,000. The variation in market size, per capita income, population and geographical area is dramatically revealed no matter which definition of the Caribbean is employed. In the entire region only nine territories have land areas in excess of 1,000 square kilometres and five currently possess a population of one million or more. Eight countries in the wider region have a GDP in excess of US$1,000 million and three (the Dominican Republic, Trinidad-Tobago and Cuba) in excess of US$8,000 million. Given such circumstances, it is hardly surprising that questions of size and scale should frequently crop up throughout the study.

Looking at the broad sweep of human history, migration, trade and investment have arguably been the three most powerful vehicles of cultural penetration and dissemination. Nowhere else in the world have these been as highly developed, in relative terms, as in the Caribbean. Although the text focuses more on trade and investment, the continuing importance of migration in shaping the area should always be kept in mind. The migration of Europeans to the region and the enforced movement of millions of slaves and indentured labourers are too well known to be overlooked. The abolition of legally enforced labour did not, however, end the movement of people. While occurrences such as the wave of West Indian migrants to Britain in the 1950s and 1960s, the Mariel boat-lift and the plight of the Haitian boat people have called attention to this from time to time, it has none the less been a continuous feature of the area ever since the abolition of slavery. Movement both within the region (e.g. the construction of the Panama Canal, employment in oil refineries in Curaçao and sugar plantations in Cuba, and the famed migratory movement of workers from Haiti to the Dominican Republic, the Windward Islands to Barbados, and Grenada to Trinidad-Tobago) and to countries overseas is an important characteristic of the area and has helped shape the theoretical structure of this study.

PART I:
Roots

Part I contains three chapters. Chapters 1 and 2 look at the major historical forces shaping the contemporary political economy of the region. The discussion is organised around four distinct periods – the European conquest, plunder and penetration between the end of the 15th and the middle of the 17th century; colonial settlement and the consolidation of slavery from the mid 17th to the early 19th century; the collapse of the colonial slave system and the rise of the peasantry throughout the 19th century; and the 20th century until the outbreak of the Second World War. This last period saw the consolidation of modern imperialism, the development of a clearly defined periphery and centre in the capitalist world economy and the rise of mass movements in the periphery, including the Caribbean. These two chapters aim to isolate the book's main interpretative and analytical themes, rather than attempting to offer a historical narrative or coherent history of the region. The third chapter looks at the socio-economic conditions in the West Indies shortly before the outbreak of the Second World War. Taken together, the three chapters indicate the roots of the contemporary political economy of the region.

1 Conquest, Settlement and Slavery: The Makings of the Colonial Economy

Before the Europeans penetrated and conquered the Caribbean, early forms of communal subsistence, based on fishing, hunting and shifting agriculture, dominated the area's economy. At that time the region was relatively underpopulated, although through the use of Amerindian canoes, there was a certain amount of movement of persons and commodities between the various islands and territories. There was no developed sense of private property or of possessions outside the group or tribe when the Europeans moved in and transformed the Caribbean forever. This chapter briefly identifies the main forces shaping the Caribbean economy during the period of conquest, plunder and early settlement and during the subsequent period of consolidating slavery and the colonial plantation.

I: The Treasure of the Indies: Conquest, Plunder and Rivalry

As Gordon Lewis has aptly remarked, what passes for Caribbean recorded history comprises a remarkable admixture of legend, myth and distortion.[1] From Columbus's so-called 'discoveries' to the 'earthly paradise' of today's tourist brochures, there has been a tendency to romanticise the area. But behind this romantic mask has always lain a brutal system of economic exploitation, both of the region and of the people associated with it. From its earliest recorded history, the Caribbean has witnessed some of the worst excesses of humankind: unrelieved plunder, genocide, slavery, indentured immigration and unspeakable barbarism. Thus, behind the myth of Columbus's 'genius and visionary character' lay an enterprise for commercial gain financed by the Spanish monarchs and their moneyed allies. As 'soldiers of fortune' the romantic *conquistadores* were actually promoting genocide and, as 'bearers of protestant liberty in the struggle against Catholic tyranny', the English buccaneers were really after a piece of the action – the slave trade and other people's territory.

The Caribbean was engulfed by the first wave of modern colonisation. Behind the voyages of exploration was a desire on the part of their financiers to find new sources of wealth

12

to compensate for the traditional Mediterranean routes to the East having been disrupted by the Turks, the Crusades and the strategic domination of that area by the city-states of Venice and Genoa. The early emphasis was on plunder and trade, in other words on reaping the benefits of the accumulated treasures of native peoples, either through 'exchanges' or force of arms. There was, however, a built in limit to this system of simply appropriating the produce of others – the stock of wealth already possessed and the capacity of these groups to produce surpluses. With the low level technology prevailing among the Amerindian inhabitants, further extortion depended on the colonisers installing a system of production in the region. Since the contemporary economies of the region grew out of this early system, it is important to understand its character. Certain features of this period played an important part in determining how the Caribbean economy developed, of which the following nine have been selected for the purpose of this study:

(1) The confrontation between Europeans and the original Taino-Arawak-Carib Indians, which resulted in the latter being decimated and their simple communal economies marginalised. This, as it were, gave the Europeans a 'clean slate' for, unlike places such as India, they did not have to build on indestructible indigenous bases or preserve indigenous economic forms. As Sidney Mintz puts it:

> The Caribbean colonies were not European imperial possessions erected upon massive indigenous bases in the area of declining great literate civilisations, as was true in India and Indonesia, they were not mere ports of trade, like Macao or Shanghai, where ancestral cultural hinterlands could remain surprisingly unaffected . . . they were not 'tribal' mosaics, within which European colonizers carried on their exploitation . . . they were in fact, the oldest 'industrial' colonies of the West outside Europe, manned entirely with introduced populations, and fitted to European needs with peculiar intensity and permissiveness.[2]

The newly installed system of production was, from the outset, oriented almost exclusively towards serving the needs of European expansion and development. This ultimately became possible through killing off large numbers of indigenous people and destroying their culture.

(2) Because so many of the original people were killed off, production and development within the region had to depend almost exclusively on imported labour. This eventually resulted in a labour force composed predominantly of Europeans (recruited from the North and South), Africans and Asians. Initially, Europeans fleeing religious and political persecution in Europe were expected to make up the bulk of the work force, along with the surviving Amerindians, but it soon became obvious that the expanding business of producing and exporting tropical staples to Europe required other sources of labour as well. Here, the Portuguese exploration and conquest of the West African coastline, which had already begun as early as 1415, came in useful – the slave trade would provide a solution to the labour shortage. The combination of immigrant and enforced labour thus became one of the most distinctive features of the early Caribbean economy. This meant that although the actual processes of penetrating and developing the region were initially fuelled by the capitalist momentum in Europe (which later became mutually reinforcing as the Caribbean stimulated further capitalist development in Europe), the Caribbean was developing differently from Europe in one fundamental respect, namely in the character and organisation of its work force. This feature was later to assume immense significance in the evolution of the modern Caribbean economy.

(3) The Caribbean was not, and indeed could not have been, conquered and settled in one go. In some instances centuries elapsed before a colonial power was guaranteed effective possession of a territory against the ambitions of rival colonial powers, which contributed towards creating the sense of continuously moving frontiers. The Spaniards engaged in plunder and exchange or initially discovering the islands, but later reserved these areas to protect their sea lanes as they pushed the frontiers of their colonisation onto the mainland. Because new territory promised inexhaustible riches – the gains of conquest were held to be high – Caribbean ventures fostered intense rivalries and even wars among the European powers. All these factors played a part in determining the shape of the area's economy, but of most enduring importance has been that they produced an unevenness in the region's development. Variations in geographical

position, size and resources, or even sheer accidents of history, would alone have ensured a certain amount of unevenness, but this was undoubtedly compounded by capitalism's proven tendency to develop unevenly through time and space.

(4) During the early periods of colonisation, the uncertainty of economic ventures in the region, along with the accompanying swings in the fortunes of the various territories, was further complicated by the high level of physical danger which characterised day-to-day life in the Caribbean until the end of the 17th century. The predatory activities of the buccaneeers, which continued throughout most of this period, made it impossible to consolidate any settled forms of economic life. Parry and Sherlock report that, during the six years of Morgan's ascendancy (1655–1661), as many as 18 cities, 4 towns and nearly 40 villages were sacked; several more than once. This estimate does not include English expeditions after 1670, nor French pillaging.[3] It was not until the end of the 17th century that such activities were more or less brought under control and settled forms of economic enterprise allowed to flourish.

(5) The social cleavages inherent in forced labour and in a system in which different racial groups have unequal access to the society's wealth and power, combined with the shifting fortunes of the territories, destroyed any possibility there might have been of creating societies with common consensual values. Force, terror, fear, fraud and ideology therefore inevitably played a major role in shaping the character of the region. Authoritarianism was essential to those in control. To enforce it they systematically tried to ensure that the beliefs, values and ideas held by most of the population, rationalised and supported their continued subservience and dependence. They could not, however, entirely prevent oppressed groups from resisting their servitude. Local militias were set up and back-up colonial military forces used to cope with the almost constant round of insurrections and revolts.

(6) Early capitalism in Europe and the 16th and 17th century drives to create a world market would have been less successful had the aspirations of the European merchants and monarchs not been matched by developments in science and technology. The explorations of the West African coastline,

the later crossing of the Atlantic and even the slave trade, only became possible because of improvements in nautical technology (maps, compasses, quadrants, ships, etc). To establish and sustain their domination, the Europeans were able to rely on a comparatively well developed armaments industry and systems of logistical support. Similarly, improvements in medical technology made it possible to transport millions of slaves under the inhumanly cramped conditions of a typical slave ship without losing too much of the cargo and crew to disease. Although the loss was still as high as three in ten on the journey and one third over a three-year period on the plantations, it would have been very much higher had it not been for advances in the medical sciences.

Having been central to the conquest of the region, European science and technology continued to play an important role in its subsequent development. For example, the fortunes of ports such as St Thomas (Virgin Islands) and Castries (St Lucia), which were built on the strategic geographical position of these islands for refuelling at the end of the Atlantic trade routes, were later lost when coal was replaced by oil. Similarly, the number of quick fortunes made in Barbados and the Bahamas diminished substantially when navigational and metereological advances reduced the number of shipwrecks. Perhaps of greatest importance, however, were the developments in the agricultural and animal sciences, which made it possible to produce sufficient indigenous plants and domestic animals to feed the growing populations and later to introduce new plants and animals into the region. As we shall see later on, the tendency to substitute indigenous plants and animals with imported varieties, had a marked effect on subsequent scientific and technological developments in the region. Thus, by the 16th century, sugar-cane (an import into the region) had become the most profitable agricultural crop and was being grown for export to Europe on plantations in Santo Domingo (in Hispaniola, now the Dominican Republic), Puerto Rico and Jamaica (then a Spanish possession).

(7) Because the territories were all colonies of one or other imperial power, positions taken by the imperial state were important to the fortunes of the individual territories.

The various imperial states sought to protect the interests of their own ruling classes in Europe and developed their colonies with this end in mind; they also implemented a number of devices, for example, Britain's infamous Navigation Acts in the 16th century, to ensure that they retained the benefits of colonisation for themselves. Intense rivalry developed over colonial possessions and this inevitably produced a remarkable succession of wars. Spain's initial monopoly was soon challenged by Portugal, and the Pope's attempts to arbitrate between these two colonising Catholic powers through a series of Papal Bulls had little real effect. Later, other lesser powers challenged both Spain and Portugal's claims in this region, but, despite these developments, the Spanish monopoly was still largely intact at the end of the 16th century, with the only fully settled colonies in the West Indies being Spanish. It therefore took more than a century before Spain's monopoly position began seriously to disintegrate.

Eventually, however, practically every European nation had fought for and controlled territory in the Caribbean, including such lesser powers as Denmark (which held the Virgin Islands until 1917) and Sweden (which held St Barthelemy until 1877), and the process of balkanisation was set in train. This tended to breed a rather insular outlook, which was reinforced by the imperial centre confining its sea routes (the most advanced form of communication at that time) to its own island possessions and thus discouraging the development of inter-territorial links in the area. The inter-island commerce and trade by canoes, which was practised by the original inhabitants of the area, was swept aside to meet the demands of European conquest and control. The continuous European rivalries and wars created a sense of insecurity among the local inhabitants who were never sure which power would be in control, for how long and what retributions would follow when a territory changed hands. Nevertheless, if only as a means of cementing ties with the mother country, each colonial power sought to import its own particular brand of European culture into its possessions. Hence the reference to Barbados as 'Little England', Martinique as the 'French Antillean jewel', and Cuba and Puerto Rico as the 'pride of Philip II of Spain'.

(8) While imperial powers fought to protect their own interests in the region, the new colonial states mediated these interests through local populations. Despite the apparent anarchy and lawlessness of the period of conquest and plunder, the colonising forces were quick to impose various governmental controls. Thus by the early 16th century, a rudimentary form of Spanish town government (the *cabildo*) had been set up in territories such as Jamaica (1509), Cuba (1511) and Puerto Rico (1512). What was striking about these territories at that time was how nakedly they promoted the interests of the imperial power and of the dominant local class of planters and colonists. This was ensured by denying the majority of the population any access to government; the colonial state thus played a vital role in shaping the characters of these societies. Conflicts arose later on when the local ruling classes tried to place their own interests over those of the imperial state. These sometimes led to open revolt and secession from Empire (as in the US) or at least fuelled the struggles for liberation from Europe (as in Spanish America as a whole).

(9) All these events took place during the commercial phase of capitalist development in Europe, when the emphasis was on market expansion, the simple exchange of commodities already produced and the seizure of treasure and surplus produce from others. In this phase the Caribbean provided an important source of primitive accumulation for the expansion and deepening of capitalist development in Europe. Profound changes were forced upon the New World: the decimation of the people and the destruction of their culture, the continued (if not systematic) loss of precious metals and tropical produce to Europe, the creation of white settler colonies (mainly in North America), the conversion of territory into trading posts and ports to facilitate European appropriation, and the growth of the slave trade and slavery. Although there is no doubt that *external* considerations took precedence in the development of the area, as local settlements were consolidated and local populations began to grow, *internal* factors began to assume more and more importance in the evolution of the territories. It is therefore a mistake to interpret the process as one-sided, for there was in fact a continuing and dynamic interaction

between *both* external and internal factors. Highly complex *internal* forms of economic exploitation and domination have always existed in the region, but because of the fluid way in which they could respond to local conditions and the potent admixtures of class and non-class factors (especially race and religion) which have shaped the development of the region, these have sometimes been difficult to detect. The complex configuration of religious issues created in the region when the struggle between Catholic and Protestant factors were combined with that of the slaves trying to preserve their ancestral religious heritage, is one case in point. Similarly, the ideologies of racism, which were developed to justify the economic enterprise of capitalism and slavery in the Caribbean, became so deeply interwoven into the fabric of the society that they assumed a life of their own, often against the ruling group's best economic interests.

II: Colonial Settlement: Slavery and the Rise of the Plantation

While the period covered in the previous section coincided with the commercial phase of capitalist development in Europe, that of this section (from the middle of the 17th century to the early 19th century) covers the industrial revolution in Europe, which saw capitalism advance to a new stage. Inevitably this development imposed new demands on the business of empire building. Within the Caribbean there was a change in land and property relations from a system based on the communal/tribal structures of the indigenous inhabitants to one based predominantly on private ownership. This development provided a legal basis for the emergence of plantation agriculture as the major form of activity in the region. The commercial basis for this development derived from the links between territories and the rapidly growing industrial needs of Europe. In that plantation agriculture was a commercial enterprise in which the systematic production of products for export (and the reproduction of the conditions for further production) took place, it created the basis for the introduction and widespread use of money in the region, both as a means of exchange and as a store of value. Nonetheless, because very little commerce or industry existed in the subsistence economies of these pre-colonial societies (which mainly produced corn, potatoes, and bread, some tobacco, cotton, tropical fruits and no domestic animals), the introduction of commercial farming was less disruptive to native producers here than in other colonised areas.

Also during this period the Dutch and later the English emerged as the most important colonial powers. The commercial agriculture they established was initially based on a succession of tropical staples, with sugar eventually assuming dominance in the English and French territories by about the middle of the 17th century. In the Spanish Caribbean, though, other products remained important: tobacco, cotton, cocoa, spices, dyes, meats and hides. Everywhere, however, production was principally based on forced labour. The pace of this development was fastest in the British territories, with the islands being more important than the mainland possessions.

While the phenomenon of slavery is too familiar for there to be any real need in a work such as this to elaborate on details, there are nonetheless a few points worth emphasising. First, the sheer scale of the operation should be fully recognised. The slave trade lasted for nearly four centuries and, although estimates vary, involved the movement of no less than 13-15 million people to the Caribbean and North America. This colossal venture was principally undertaken by four European countries: Britain, France, Holland and Portugal, all of which held slaving bases in West Africa. The object of these bases was to secure a monopoly of slaves, both for their own possessions and for sale to the Spaniards. The slave trade was organised around an annual triangular movement of people and products. Ships stocked with 'trade goods' (textiles, weapons, tools, pots, pans and trinkets) would leave Europe on a four-month journey to West Africa, where the 'trade goods' would be exchanged for slaves. The slaves were then transported as quickly as possible along the infamous Middle Passage to the Caribbean islands. Here several weeks would be spent selling slaves, resting and recuperating as well as acquiring cargoes of sugar, hides, tobacco and cotton to take back to Europe.

As Eric Williams pointed out:

> The slave trade kept the wheels of metropolitan industry turning; it stimulated navigation and shipbuilding and employed seamen; it raised fishing villages into flourishing cities; it gave sustenance to new industries based on the processing of colonial raw materials; it yielded large profits which were ploughed back into metropolitan industry; and, finally, it gave rise to an unprecedented commerce in the West Indies and made the Caribbean territories among the most valuable colonies the world has ever known.[4]

Williams also pointed out that between 1714 and 1773 approximately one-fifth of Britain's imports came from the British West Indies and that these territories absorbed one-sixteenth of Britain's total exports. In Britain, triangular trade accounted for 21 per cent of imports, 8 per cent of exports, and 14 per cent of total external trade. A Royal Commission of Inquiry noted that:

> In the eighteenth century. . . the ownership of sugar estates in the West Indies was the main foundation of the fortunes of many wealthy British families. West Indian Colonies were regarded by the state-craft of the day as an asset of the first importance, hence the prominent part played by expeditions to the Caribbean in the naval warfare between France and Britain.[5]

When settlement did take place, it was mainly around the tropical plantations and this led many scholars of the region to believe that the key to understanding it lay in an appreciation of the plantation's internal structure and dynamics. Today the terms 'plantation economy' or 'plantation society' are still widely used in describing West Indian society. While acknowledging the importance of the plantation, however, it is a mistake to overestimate its significance. Since this issue is central to later interpretations of the region's history, the remainder of this section will be devoted to a discussion of this topic.

From the outset, it is important to recognise that several factors lay behind the choice of the tropical plantation for cultivating sugar. First, costly overheads were required to produce sugar commercially in the Caribbean. For example, land had to be prepared, water control systems set in place, factories established near the fields (the loss of sucrose in the sugar-cane is rapid once it is cut) and transport laid on for moving the sugar-cane from the field to the factory and the sugar from the factory to the point of export. Second, outlays were necessary in learning to control the technology of sugar production. For example, cultivating sugar-cane required a detailed knowledge of the plant and its ratoon system, as well as of the various soil types. Extracting the sugar also involved fairly elaborate processes, from milling and crushing, through clarification, filtering and crystallisation to drying, bagging and weighing. Third, because these outlays were costly, the scale of operations had to be large to be profitable. This in turn required investments in slaves, not to mention all the buildings, agricultural implements, machinery, livestock and food necessary to feed and house them. Fourth, in that large-scale operations were possible only because sugar was produced for sale to the rapidly expanding markets of Europe, the industry was, from the outset, exclusively export oriented. And fifth, the sheer size of operations allowed for economies of scale in areas such as land utilisation, access to credit, and freight and shipping costs.

Because of the scale of operation and the need for a large proportion of relatively unskilled workers, under the close supervision of a small skilled labour force, slavery was an obviously attractive solution to the work-force problem. The planters pursued the production of sugar with single-minded fervour and, in the process, a mono-crop agricultural export economy was consolidated in many territories. Because sales were taking place in overseas markets, some form of control over these markets was always implicit to the arrangement. This frequently took the form of a colonial power giving preference to the produce of its own colonies – a practice that conformed to the mercantilist view of trade and external economic relations among countries.

It would be an error to deduce from these considerations that the plantation's main significance to the region at the time lay in the fact that it could, and did, provide the large amount of skill, technology and capital outlay required for commercial agriculture. What is more significant is that the plantation was itself a capitalist institution. This was expressed in its internal structure as well as in its dependence, as an institution, on the development of capitalism on a world scale. In the latter regard, it is important to remember that the development of capitalism in Europe created a large work force divorced from agriculture, which was to constitute the mass consumption outlet and, hence, market for the profit-able disposal of large-scale sugar production. Also, the concentration of wealth in the hands of a few in Europe meant that large amounts of surplus became available for overseas investment in the industry. Besides providing the equipment, machinery and raw materials needed for producing sugar, industrial, scientific and technological developments in Europe also created a smaller, but increas-ingly significant market for the industrial uses of sugar. Finally, Europe's industrial base made it increasingly possible to develop and apply science and technology with a view to funding cheaper ways of producing tropical staples.

While the process of capitalist transformation on a world scale and its impact on the region were dominant in consoli-dating the plantation as an institutional form, the plantation did not in itself constitute a separate and historically distinct 'mode of production'. It neither grew out of the communal or slave forms of production which preceded it, nor was it derived from the feudal origins of Europe. The plantation was no more and no less than the institutionalised expression of the dominant form of production. In other words, it was the basic producing unit and, as such, was one socio-econ-omic form of the period which, like others, existed both during slavery and after – albeit with important changes in its characteristics. The distinction made here is not purely semantic. To define Caribbean economy as a plantation economy because of the dominance of the plantation as the producing unit for sugar would be to leave the analysis at a primarily institutional level. To understand the essential mode of producing the means of livelihood in society we need to know more than the institutional form of production. Thus no one today would think of equating capitalism simply with the joint-stock company or the transnational corpor-ation. If to do so would be methodologically incorrect, so too would be to restrict the definition of Caribbean society to the plantation, even at that time.

As I have argued elsewhere, a more accurate specification of the region at this time would be to define it as a 'colonial slave mode of production' situated in the larger system of global capitalism.[6] Two reasons were given. 'First, despite the existence of a small number of petty commodity producers and the survival of a natural economy among the indigenous Amerindian inhabitants, slave labour was the legal and customary status of the overwhelming majority of direct producers'.[7] And second, the process of colonisation itself mediated the ways in which capitalism in Europe affected the region and produced distinctive forms. Generally extensive rather than intensive methods were preferred and this was rational because the extra-economic appropriation of the surplus diluted the economic impact of payments to the direct producers on costs and profits. It is therefore in the combination of forced labour (slavery) and colonisation as an all pervading process that we find the key to what determined the mode of production at that time. Hence the description 'colonial slave mode of production'.

If the distinction between the plantation and the determination of the prevailing mode of production is appreciated, we can then conclude this section with some further comments on the plantation, *qua* institution, as this would aid our understanding of points developed later in the text. It is important in interpreting the role of the plantation against the background of a dominant 'colonial slave mode of production' that certain features of this institution be kept to the forefront. First, the plantation must always be placed within the larger context of colonisation, where its link with the mass consumption of sugar in Europe and the simultaneous integration of the local planter class into the merchant classes and later into the emerging industrial bourgeoisie of Europe becomes clearly evident. As we shall see, it was out of this link that today's modern forms of dependency grew. Second, this integral tie with Europe was reinforced by and reflected in the *direct* colonial administration of territories in the region and this, in turn, meant (a) that the high degree of centralisation of political authority associated with colonial rule was mirrored in the political power of the planter class, which came to dominate these economies; and (b) that the sugar export trade was highly dependent on economic policies in Europe. In the early mercantilist phase an elaborate system of colonial preference was administered to protect the interests of the planter class. Later, however, as Europe industrialised and the industrial capitalists of Britain rose into world prominence, they clamoured for free trade, with the result that a Sugar Act, which led to the eventual abolition of preferences, was passed in 1846. The whole movement away from mercantilist policies to free trade created severe crises in the region, forcing alterations in major aspects of plantation activity. In the process, however, the vulnerability of local sugar interests to the dominant tendencies in the international economic system was exposed – and remains exposed to this day.

A third feature is that, where it took hold, sugar-cane cultivation was pursued to the exclusion of virtually all other productive activities, with the result that many of these territories developed overspecialised mono-cultural cropping systems. The demands of sugar-cane production brooked no alternatives. Not even marginal crops such as perennial fruit were permitted, even although the trees could be left unattended and utilised estate lands which would otherwise have remained idle. For whatever reasons, the planters were wholly committed to the single-minded pursuit of sugar-cane cultivation and processing. One flimsy excuse was that the 'absence of trees upon the "dams", or walks, and particularly in the extensive frontlands, was attributable to the fact that the slaves systematically robbed the original mango and other fruit trees, which were in consequence abolished by the planters'.[8]

Fourth, the plantation labour force was highly stratified. Dominated as it was by capital, there was a sharp distinction between owner-supervisor and worker. The former, through controlling of capital, virtually monopolised political, economic and social authority. The latter was at worst, a slave and at best, a 'freed' labourer in a system with a long and all pervasive authoritarian tradition. The sharp and rigid class distinctions were integrated into an equally severe system of racial differentiation, in which the various ethnic groups were physically separated. Initially all the slaves were Africans and all the supervisors European. It was not until after emancipation that other racial groups were added in large numbers to the work force.

Fifth, ideology and culture have played important roles in rationalising the obvious defects of the system. For example, the notion of 'white supremacy' was given ideological legitimacy to justify placing humans in bondage and to sustain inequality on the plantations. The dispossessed classes also created elaborate social mechanisms for coping with their situation, including the occasional 'flight from reality'. Patterson sees the current reluctance to work on sugar estates, even in areas of high unemployment, as the cultural remnant of an earlier time:

> Do we ask the Jew to live and work in the concentration camps in Germany? Do we ask a recently released prisoner who has been unjustly imprisoned for the better part of his life to continue living in his cell? Do we expect him to like it? Is it not natural for him to loathe it and despise it? Why then is it that when the ex-slaves and their descendants express an abhorrence for the sugar estate we do not accept the obvious explanation?[9]

Sixth, the physical hardship of sugar cultivation, combined with the high incidence of malnutrition and debilitating disease associated with the poverty of the rural population, cannot be overstated as aspects of plantation life. On the arduousness of cane cultivation Adamson noted that a 'disturbing reflection on the exhausting conditions of field labour emerges from a report that an attempt was made to use horses for ploughing, but it was found that they had a short life span and could only work a few hours per day'.[10]

Seventh, in the context of the extreme brutality, physical hardship and bare survival which characterised slave existence on the plantation, the plight of women, particularly slave women, was horrific in the extreme. They suffered from the consequences of the sexual division of labour, from sexual aggression by the masters and their sons on the plantation, while also carrying the major burdens of child rearing, that is the reproduction of the estates' direct producers.

The final feature of the plantation concerns its general pattern of accumulation and resource use. Although requiring heavy investments in slaves and water-control systems, the

early planters had a largely speculative outlook towards
sugar. They were always waiting for the big bonanza when
prices would skyrocket and they could make a 'killing',
which would then compensate for the leaner intervening
years. As we shall see more clearly in the next section, there
were three important components to this approach to investment. First, it emphasised the extensive exploitation of
labour. Instead of seeking to raise the productivity of each
man hour, the planters merely acquired more labourers.
Slavery and later indentured immigration made this possible.
Secondly, it emphasised the extensive exploitation of land.
Increased acreage rather than new and better farming practices accounted for most of the increase in output right up
to the Second World War. And thirdly, this extensive use of
land and capital was reflected in the relatively low level of
development and application of technology.

Some of these tendencies were also reflected in the plantation's ownership structure. By the early 19th century most
of the resident sugar farmers in the West Indies were being
replaced by absentee landlords, who relied on managers sent
on contract from Europe to run their estates. The owners
themselves were then free to develop other interests, for
example in shipping or in procuring supplies. These interests
eventually provided the basis for diversifying plantation
activity, although not unfortunately to the benefit of the
region.

The 'colonial slave mode of production', which became
fully formed during the period under consideration, was
essentially the product of the impact of colonialism on the
Caribbean. It took root in the specific geographic environment and cultural adaptation to a new world of African slaves
and European slave masters locked in deadly antagonism with
each other. In practice, it oriented these economies towards
serving the capital expansion requirements of Europe and
thus prevented the development of an internal momentum
strong enough to ensure that surpluses were ploughed back
into the region. One of the main characteristics of modern
dependency, namely the bias towards the utilisation of
domestic resources in the production of primary exports and
the widespread importation of products consumed locally
(food, clothing, housing, intermediate materials, machinery

etc) emerged during this period. The separation of consumption from production was further accentuated by the large discrepancy which existed between what was actually consumed and the basic needs of the broad mass of the population. In such a context there was no scope for indigenous technological development, for neither social pressures (to satisfy domestic demands) nor material incentives (because of the foreign ownership and management of resources) were enough to generate a 'necessity' for domestic invention. Consequently, because the rhythm of discovering and using resources was dictated by the imperatives of capitalist expansion in Europe, the true resource structures of the region remained largely unknown.[11]

2 *Transition: From Colonial Slave Economy to Centre-Periphery Relations*

Two fundamental transformations of the Caribbean political economy have occurred over the past 200 years. The first is associated with the disintegration of the colonial slave economy and the spread of independence movements, particularly in the Spanish possessions. This process started early in the 19th century with the abolition of the slave trade and later led to the abolition of slavery itself, which began with the British territories in the 1830s. At the same time, following the successful war of independence in the USA and Haiti's declaration of independence from France (1804), a number of independence movements sprang up in the Spanish possessions of Argentina (1816), Colombia (1819), Peru, Mexico and Venezuela (1821).

The second transformation took place during the 20th century, in the period leading up to the Second World War, when the capitalist world system was reaching its maturity and the roots of what is now known as modern imperialism were being firmly implanted. This was a time when the Caribbean economies began to conform more and more to the classic configurations of underdevelopment and its associated dependency. While the seeds of underdevelopment were sown during the first European encounters with the region, the period under consideration can be regarded as the turning point between the old colonial forms of economic domination and the neo-colonial forms which prevail today.

I: The Collapse of the Colonial Slave Economy and the Rise of the Peasantry

In 1803 Denmark ended the slave trade, followed by Britain in 1807, France in 1817, Holland in 1818 and Sweden in 1824. Slavery itself was abolished in the British colonies in 1833. Sweden abolished it in 1846, France in 1848, Holland in 1863, Puerto Rico in 1873 and Cuba in 1880. While much controversy surrounds the causes of these events, there is no doubt that although the slave trade and slave production in the Caribbean contributed substantially to the formation of capital in Europe and thereby helped to finance the industrial revolution, the rise of industrial capitalism in Europe in turn undermined the advantages of slavery as a system of economic organisation. This is not intended to suggest that external factors, either alone or principally, accounted for the collapse of slavery, but rather that the limitations within the 'colonial slave mode of production' interacted with external factors at all phases of its existence, particularly in the period culminating in its final disintegration.

The internal limitations of the slave-based system of production in the Caribbean were many sided. Despite being integrated into a rapidly evolving world capitalist system, the planters remained remarkably pre-capitalist in their approach. Instead of trying to increase productivity by improving the efficiency of either the individual or the combined factors engaged in production, they invariably responded by merely acquiring more and more land, slaves, equipment, machinery or buildings. Such extensive cultivation led to loss in overall soil fertility and, with more and more marginal lands being brought into production as output increases were sought, yields also went down. This approach set in train a constant search for newer and larger territories to colonise, thereby raising the costs of colonial enterprise. Furthermore, although sugar production was a scientifically based activity, the speculative, consumption-oriented approach of the planters of the period did not meet the requirements of careful attention to research and development or even the early application of technological innovations and advances developed elsewhere.

Of overriding importance, however, was the constant pressure on costs created by the slaves' struggles to free themselves. Since most of their capital was invested in slaves, to protect their investment the plantation owners were forced into carrying military overheads to contain the population, especially in areas where the slave numbers were increasing disproportionately fast. Each revolt disrupted production and sometimes ruined years of work. In addition, through sabotage and the slaves' indifference to their own productivity, levels of output were failing to rise. At the same time, the cost of maintaining slave labour was increasing, both because of the need to bribe potential agitators with extra rations and because of demographic changes in the slave population in which the percentage of child, elderly and female slaves had increased. As Fraginals points out:

> At first, the demographic structure of the slave-based plantations was eminently efficient: 70% male, and all slaves, male and female, between the ages of 15 and 45, that is, optimally productive. But when the plantations, as was inevitable, developed into a society in spite of low fertility and high mortality rates, the numerical imbalance between the sexes, then the productivity per slave fell, and the cost of his upkeep increased. Barbados offers a typical example: towards the end of the 18th century, it was producing about the same amount of sugar as a hundred years before, but using almost twice as many slaves to do so. The same held true for Nevis, Montserrat, Antigua, St Kitts. . .[1]

Thus on the eve of emancipation, sugar productivity was declining in all the Caribbean countries except Cuba, which had become the world's largest sugar producing area. Suppliers of cheaper cane sugar from India and Brazil and European beet farmers were making serious inroads into the traditional Caribbean markets. Although the planters fought hard to protect their traditional markets, it was by then too late – slavery was no longer a viable system of production. For a start, the Caribbean was less important to the rapidly industralising Europe of the 19th century than it had been in the 17th and 18th centuries. Also, now that the British could out-compete the rest of the world in manufactured goods, they were more in favour of free trade than of the protectionist mercantilism of old. Even key sugar interests in Britain – shippers, refiners, or important ports like Liverpool – were eager to acquire cheaper sugar imports and therefore backed free trade against the continued subsidisation of planter interests in the Caribbean, which by that time had become necessary.

At the political level, three important developments were also taking place in Europe, most noticeably in Britain. The first, the transfer of political power from the landed aristocracy to the industrial bourgeoisie, is attested by the French Revolution, the reform bills in Britain and even the defeat of the South by the North in the US Civil War. The second was the growth of an industrial proletariat producing new champions for the cause of democracy at home and, to a lesser extent, abroad. Many historians have highlighted the role played by the industrial towns of Britain and France in the political agitation against slavery with Eric Williams in particular, quoting Joseph Sturge the Quaker abolitionist as saying in 1833 that: 'the people must emancipate the slaves for the government never will'.[2] The third was the humanitarian agitation for emancipation which infused much of the consciousness of the period.

Internal and external, socio-economic and political factors thus interacted to break up a Caribbean economy founded on colonial slavery and in the process, laid the foundations of the 20th century Caribbean economy. Several elements were involved in the transition but the most important of these were undoubtedly those associated with the birth of the Caribbean peasantry, the progressive growth of local labour markets and the conversion of the planter class into first an absentee proprietor group and then a genuinely capitalist class.

Immediately after the abolition of slavery an important phase of rural development, in which the movement of freed slaves from the estates led to a rapid growth in African villages, began in many terrritories. In Guyana, for example, it is estimated that the number of Africans living in villages increased almost threefold from 16,000 in 1842 to 44,000 six years later.[3] The freed slaves acquired their lands either through communal purchase or individual proprietorships. In the absence of adequate overheads and a marketing capacity to export sugar successfully, peasant production was largely reliant on the emerging domestic market. The small size of this market, however, combined with poor communications and the inaccessibility of some areas, meant that some peasant producers were unable to generate enough income and so had to enter the labour market as wage earners on the very plantations from which they had been freed. This tendency was not uniform throughout the region, but was generally encouraged by the fact that land-owning peasants had to pay rates and taxes, which they could meet only if they participated in the cash economy. In Jamaica, for example, a marked differentiation emerged between those peasants who were forced into the labour market in a part-time way and those who remained completely independent.

Despite the compensation Britain paid to the slaveowners on abolition (although not to the slaves), the immediate impact of abolition was to plunge the plantation economy into an even deeper crisis. A rise in wage levels in response to the labour shortages caused by the slaves abandoning the sugar estates, was combined with a fall in the price of sugar, as the protectionist pricing system of the mercantilist period gave way to free trade. A Sugar Duties Act passed by Britain in 1846 had effectively brought an end to the protection previously given to the British West Indian sugar planters in its domestic markets. Caught in a spiral of rising costs and declining prices, the planter class responded in two basic ways. The first was to replace any remaining paternalist resident planters still living in the Caribbean with an absentee landlord class which, in turn, eventually gave way to limited liability or joint-stock companies as the main form of ownership of Caribbean plantations. The second was a process of land and capital consolidation. To take the example of Guyana again, the number of separate estates dropped from 400 just after abolition to a mere 46 in 1904, with the four largest of these controlling nearly 60 per cent of the industry.

The planters did not, however, accede to these economic changes readily. They used all the influence they could muster over the colonial state to wage a bitter campaign, which eventually succeeded in considerably protracting the period of transition. Through a combination of taxes and changes in landholding policies, they hindered the development of the peasantry by denying the freed slaves access to land. The planters' direct onslaught on the purchase of communal lands, where this did occur, caused an uneconomic fragmentation of peasant holdings and placed the peasants at a disadvantage *vis-à-vis* the plantation. It also fostered among the peasants an aggressive and often irresponsible individualism. In areas where land was available yet the planters were unable to prevent the flight of labour from their estates, indentured labour was introduced as a substitute for slavery. Most of the labourers were brought in between 1837 and 1917, mainly from India but also from Germany, Malta, Brazil, China, Madeira, Mauritius, Europe, Africa and other Caribbean territories.

Of the total of 750,000 East Indians, 234,205 were sent to Guyana, 144,000 to Trinidad-Tobago, 78,000 to the French territories of Martinique and Guadeloupe, 36,000 to Jamaica, 34,000 to Suriname and various numbers under 5,000 to St Lucia, Grenada, St Vincent and St Kitts. These migrants were compelled by their contracts to work for long hours on low pay. Worse still, the legal constraints of their servitude stopped them from forming any working-class associations.

The planters also used their influence to get legislation passed to protect their privileged control over land and labour. Thus laws were passed to prevent joint land purchase and to force those already owning land communally to break up their holdings if ten or more people were involved, as well as to increase the price and minimum size of prospective plots for sale. Laws were also passed to allow for the financing of indentured migration from public funds. In addition, stringent labour regulations were introduced which progressively limited the producers' freedom of movement and association, particularly where indentured labour was available. These measures were, of course, all designed to restrict the operation of a free labour market and to protect the planters' extra-economic means of appropriating the wealth of these societies.

In that abolition forced the planters to write off the bulk of their capital (slaves), it is hardly surprising that it also heralded the first systematic attempts to use the productive factors more effectively. Plantation machinery and techniques were improved significantly – steam-run iron mills were introduced into Cuba and other improvements, especially in the factory and transport systems of the estates, could also be found. The result was that the sugar industry took on a dual character in which an increasingly mechanised system of sugar-cane processing combined with a comparatively backward system of sugar-cane plant cultivation. This dichotomy survived well into the 20th century and still impedes the transformation of the agrarian system in the region and the ending of its underdevelopment.

The great struggles to abolish the colonial slave mode of production were not the only struggles in the Caribbean in the 19th century. Many territories also fought heroically to

35

free themselves from European domination – the liberation of Haiti in 1804 representing the most complete victory for slave resistance to colonialism and slavery. Haiti's example, together with the white settlers' opposition to continued European domination, was an important factor behind the creation of the independence movement, which later gained liberation for the Spanish territories. The white colonials, who outnumbered the slaves, had many grievances. They resented the autocratic way in which the mother country drained wealth from their territories to serve royalist interests in Europe. They resented the various licences and contracts each colonial power imposed to retain its monopoly over the slave trade and campaigned tirelessly to get them abolished, for they felt they kept up the price of slaves. Similarly, they felt frustrated by the way in which religious decrees imposed constraints on how they treated the Indian migrants, as well as by restrictions on the movement of non-slave foreigners from one territory to another, as this hampered their access to skills and capital. They also bitterly resented the various duties and levies imposed on them to finance the Royal Exchequers. As the earlier revolt in the American colonies showed, this group's desire for political autonomy constituted a powerful source of resistance to Europe. Although the same grievances and resentments were shared by white colonists in the British, French and Dutch territories, in their case their fear of the black masses (who far outnumbered them), was greater than their desire for independence and thus stood in the way of a final resolution of the conflict. This had to wait for the emergence of mass movements during the next period of our historical survey.

II: Imperialism, Dependency and the Rise of Mass Movements

The major developments in the Caribbean economies after the break up of slavery – the rise of the peasantry, the emergence of wage labour, the transformation of the planter class and the qualitative shift in the role of the colonial state – all underwent dramatic transformations during the past few decades of the 20th century, which were propelled by both external and internal forces.

Externally, capitalism as a world system had turned into a global system of imperialism. This happened because a new stage of capitalism had been reached in Europe, particularly in Britain, where a highly monopolistic industrial structure created the basis for the emergence of the post-Second World War oligopolistic transnational corporations which now dominate its economy. National capital was increasingly invested in global operations and its surplus peasantry became almost entirely proletarianised. The growth of the industrial working class had led to the formation of well-established worker organisations and trade unions. As the landed gentry's tenacious hold over the state and political system was broken, political power was placed firmly in the hands of the economically dominant financial and industrial bourgeoisie. There was a rapid increase in the amount of capital Britain and the rest of Europe were investing abroad to finance the development and export of primary, agricultural and mineral produce overseas. Through these developments the overseas countries helped to produce food for Europe's expanding working classes to provide raw materials for its industries and to open up markets for its industrial exports.

Not unexpectedly, this development led to a scramble for overseas possessions and set in train a new wave of colonisation. This created intense political and commercial rivalries which contributed to two world wars. Apart from the scramble for new colonies, a fundamental shift in Europe's relationship to empire now placed the emphasis on indirect as well as direct control of foreign resources and markets. Traditional colonial control over a territory, although a sufficient basis, was no longer a prerequisite for its exploitation. Trade, investment, technology and finance, operating through the normal mechanisms of the capitalist world market, were becoming increasingly effective as channels for appropriating surpluses from abroad. Legalised sanctions of one form or another and the exaction of a 'national tribute' through direct political control were no longer the primary mechanisms of global exploitation. Many people envisaged this period as the time when a comparatively small group of countries emerged at the 'centre' of the world capitalist system and became its main beneficiaries, while the other much larger group remained on the 'periphery'. The rhythm of growth and development in the system as a whole are seen to be dictated by the course of accumulation at the 'centre'. The 'periphery', by contrast, is wholly dependent on the system because its growth is largely a reflex of developments internationally. This dependent relationship was not political in any formal sense of the word. The British, French and Dutch colonies in the West Indies, as well as independent states such as Cuba and the Dominican Republic, all functioned as integral elements of the 'periphery' during this period.

Internally, it became obvious to the ruling class of the region that the production system could not be sustained on variants of enforced labour and other forms of servitude. Thus, with indenture finally ended in 1917, the planters, without abandoning their efforts to prevent former slaves becoming a socio-economic force, set about in a more or less systematic manner to adapt the plantations to the new requirements of a 'free' labour market. With the introduction of innovations and new techniques on a far wider scale than ever before, both field and factory sugar production witnessed many major changes. Using fertilisers in the field, steam pumps for drainage and irrigation, steam power in the factories, evaporators, centrifugal driers for separating molasses from sugar and juice clarifiers, as well as employing chemists in the factory and changing the layout of the cane fields, were some of the many innovations introduced during this period. In short, sugar production became more industrial and more capitalist in its orientation. At the same time, the concentration and centralisation of land and capital in the industry continued. Acreages were expanded on each estate as economies of scale were sought and consequently more and more of the smaller estates disappeared. In many instances, private ownership was transferred to a corporation, reflecting the decisive shift away from the old speculative venture approach of earlier planters who saw in the Caribbean a source of quick fortunes. In this context, estates linked to the mercantile houses in Europe were the best placed to introduce the changes early on: they also emerged as the most dominant estates in the region.

The strengthened link with the mercantile houses also provided the first opportunity to diversify plantation activity. Some of these corporations thus extended their interests into areas such as shipping, insurance, finance and providing estate supplies. Although initially merely intended as a safe-guard against the lean years when prices fell, the nucleus of the transnational corporation was being formed as these companies widened their investments and began to diversify, not only within the region but also in Europe itself and in other countries in the 'periphery'. At the same time, other new industrial and agricultural activities were being developed in the region, the most important of which were bauxite, petroleum, bananas and rice. These new industries created fresh openings for the region's population and led to a certain degree of differentiation in its employment, exports and output.

This transformation, which was paralleled by the development of labour markets in the region, produced innumerable labour-capital conflicts which led directly to the formation of trade unions and other working-class organisations. In the long run, this development was crucial to the growth and vitality of the mass movements which sprang up across the region. Although the peasantry was also continuing to develop during this period and some major new crops such as rice, bananas, citrus fruit, cocoa and coffee had been introduced, the peasants as a group were less inclined to diversify. In addition they remained poorly organised and made comparatively little impact on developments in the region. With the rise of political parties, however, they eventually found a vehicle through which to redress their grievances.

One important consequence of these developments was the growth of a certain degree of differentiation in the class structure of the Caribbean. We have already noted the rise of the working class and the emergence of a peasantry. The growth of the labour market brought with it open unemployment as a social category. The expansion of the peasantry was accompanied by increasing stratification, creating in its wake, indigenous forms of landlordism, exploitation and extensive peasant indebtedness. In addition to these, a local class of merchants and traders who dealt in retailing, wholesaling and the provision of transport and financial services was brought into existence. While as a class these groups shared property interests with the economically dominant plantation interests, ultimately they were excluded from it on racial grounds. This period also witnessed the formation of a group of educated people who achieved much social mobility through their education. While concentrating on professions such as teaching, public service, law and medicine, this group constituted the corps from which the local political elite came to be drawn. In pursuit of its political interests it forged an alliance with the masses to struggle for constitutional reform under a widened franchise, which eventually, after the Second World War, merged into the larger demand for independence.

By the 1930s, the Caribbean formed part of the capitalist 'periphery' and bore its specific characteristics. First, along with Latin America, Africa and Asia, the region was politically dominated by countries from the 'centre'. And second, because its patterns of resource use, production, exchange, consumption and class relations had been (and continued to be) mediated through colonial domination, a self-centred, autonomous development of its productive factors was impossible and the systemic divorce of domestic output from consumption became more accentuated than ever. Indigenous resources were brought into use exclusively at the dictates of capital accumulation in the 'centre'. What was consumed through the market was, by and large, imported and did not reflect the basic needs of the broad mass of the community. No indigenous science and technology existed and the continued dependence of the region on a few primary products made it extremely vulnerable to the vagaries of world trade.

The imperialist division of labour was thus reinforced by an internal class structure and pattern of social relations in which the reproduction of the system of domination was the main, but not exclusive, purpose. In summary, two basic features characterised the underdevelopment of the region's economy, namely the perpetuation of distorted economic structures and a rhythm of economic expansion dependent mainly on the expansion of capital in the 'centre'. Examples of the former include the lack of industrial development, the limited agricultural differentiation, the secondary role played by internal markets in determining how resources were used, the pattern of domestic consumption failing to reflect the needs of the broad mass of the population, low levels of indigenous technological development *combined* with the import of high-level technology for those sectors most integrated into the centre and, as a consequence, marked disparities in labour productivity in the two sectors. In the latter case, the absence of autonomous, internally regulated sources of capital accumulation ensured that development within the region was, more often than not, essentially a reflection of the pace and direction of accumulation in the 'centre'.

Also during this period certain changes were taking place in the colonial state which were to have a considerable bearing on the subsequent evolution of the Caribbean economy. The most important of these were the abandonment of *laissez-faire* ideology and the development of a concern for economic production and organisation. Thus the state assumed responsibility for social services like health and education which had previously been performed by private institutions such as the churches and plantations. In addition, improvements were made to its existing functions, whether these were to provide postal services, a legal framework for joint-stock company operations, regulations governing banking and commerce, or to frame laws to guide the operations of associations and trade unions. In some territories, the state took over responsibility for infrastructural works (roads, drainage, irrigation, etc) which, more often than not, had previously been provided by the plantations. The result of all this was that, of the local institutions, the state was becoming by far the most important for the organisation and development of the Caribbean economies.

There was a continuous movement of peoples within and between the various Caribbean territories, particularly between 1885 and 1920, when labour was required to build the Panama Canal, to construct railroads and banana plantations in Central America and to build the Bermuda dry docks. In addition, many sought new opportunities in the United States. Between 1920 and 1940, however, the outlets for migration became more limited and the movement of persons was substantially reduced. What movement that did take place was confined mainly to the oil fields in Venezuela and the oil refinery in Curaçao. Available data shows that between 1885 and 1920, the net population loss from the British West Indies was 130,000. Between 1902 and 1932, 121,000 Jamaicans went to Cuba, between 1900 and 1920, 10-12,000 Bahamians went to Miami and between 1904 and 1914, 60,000 Barbadians went to Panama.

Although still the leading capitalist nation, during the early part of the 20th century, Britain's relative decline was starting to become evident as new powers such as Germany and, especially, the US were rising into prominence. Thus, while in 1870 Britain's share of world industrial production was 32 per cent, it was down to 14 per cent shortly before the First World War and to 9 per cent immediately preceding the crisis of the 1930s. Over the same period, the share of the US was 23, 38 and 42 per cent respectively. Similarly, Britain's share of world trade fell from one-fifth in 1880, to one-sixth in 1913 and down to one-eighth by the Second World War. The US, however, had grown substantially during the period of the First World War.

This expansion and growth of the US provided for the investments in the region which occasioned much of the Caribbean migration of that time. The rise into prominence of the US and Germany brought changes to the 'centre' of the capitalist world system.

Reflecting its newly acquired economic might, the US began to articulate its own policies within the region. These were basically governed by two primary considerations, namely to neutralise the European influence and presence in the hemisphere and to promote the development of client states. The scores of military interventions and occupations which took place to keep 'friendly' governments in power, as well as the seizures of land for US bases (in Cuba, Haiti and the Dominican Republic) had a tremendous impact on the formation of the Caribbean economy. The ultimate aim of these strategies was to create full freedom of movement for US capital in the area and to develop its trade. Attempts to neutralise Europe's influence during this period were not entirely successful, for there were still many European colonies in the area. The Second World War, however, dramatically changed the balance of power in favour of the US and, as the contest between East and West intensified, the US grew more and more determined to protect its own backyard by maintaining the *status quo* and squashing any externally or internally impelled movements for change.

In concluding this section, it is important to recognise that although strong class distinctions remained in the region, these were being offset by increased cultural and racial mixing. Alongside the antagonisms and conflicts was also emerging a more or less indigenous system of values and thought processes, a characteristic way of looking at and perceiving the world. In other words, a regional social consciousness was beginning to appear which was reflected in the area's art, literature, scientific writings and folk religions. In the latter case, the mix of Catholic, Protestant and African religions produced a number of original indigenous religious forms: shango, tamboo bamboo, camboulay, pocomania, voodoo and santería.

3 Revolt and War: The Caribbean Around the Time of the Second World War

Before embarking on the main body of this chapter, which takes a brief look at the Caribbean before and during the Second World War, it is important to place it in its true context by recalling the significance of the original encounter between the Europeans and the native inhabitants of the New World. As Wong points out, the fathers of both 'orthodox' and 'radical' economics were in agreement over the monumental significance of this event.[1] Adam Smith regarded the 'discovery of America and. . . a passage to the East Indies by the Cape of Good Hope. . . [as] the two greatest and most important events recorded in the history of mankind'.[2] Karl Marx claimed that:

> The discovery of gold and silver in America, the extirpation, enslavement and entombment in mines of the aboriginal population, the beginning of the conquest and looting of the East Indies, the turning of Africa into a warren for the commercial hunting of black skins, signalised the rosy dawn of the era of capitalist production. These idyllic proceedings are the chief momenta of primitive accumulation. On their heels treads the commercial war of the European nations, with the globe for a theatre.[3]

Throughout its history, the capitalist world system, which grew up alongside colonialism, has always combined expansion with crisis. In addition, the crises tend to conform to definite periodic patterns of recession (short waves) and depression (long waves) which occur at crucial phases in the process of capitalist accumulation. Although these crises are the product of a number of different conflicts and circumstances inherent in capitalist growth, as Beaud points out, they mostly stem from four fundamental contradictions, namely:

— the contradiction between capital and labour, ie, between capitalist companies and the working classes;
— the contradiction between capitalists (either in the same sector or between sectors);
— the contradiction between national capitalisms;
— the contradiction between dominant capitalisms and dominated peoples, countries, or regions.[4]

During the last quarter of the 19th century these contradictions converged to produce a protracted economic depression which eventually led to the outbreak of the First World War. By the 1930s, an even more serious crisis was at hand and this also ended in a world war. Of the many economic factors underlying the latter crisis the following five are probably the most important.

First, the decline of the industries on which Europe's industrialisation had been based and the rise of new industries (chemical, automobile, electrical, mechanical), new industrial companies and new industrial nations, particularly the US. Second, and as a direct consequence of the above, the intensification of national rivalries as ascending powers jockeyed to improve their stakes in a world already carved up into carefully demarcated and jealously guarded zones of commercial influence: the US zones, the British Commonwealth, the French, Dutch and Belgian empires, the Japanese sphere of influence in Asia, and the USSR. Third, the more effective organisation and militancy which had developed in workers' organisations and which was putting pressure on profits. (This militancy was reflected in the advances of the communist parties and in the revolution in the USSR.) Fourth, the absence of international institutions to provide guidelines for world and global movements of finance and capital, or to deal with foreign exchange and currency management. With national rivalries at a peak there was a proliferation of 'beggar-my-neighbour' policies such as competitive devaluation, dumping and protectionism. And fifth, the damage done to the world economy by the victors of the First World War attempting to exact tribute and reparations from a defeated Germany and thereby promoting a complicated and unprecedented era of price inflation.

The period of the Great Depression of the 1930s and of the Second World War was one of crisis everywhere, but nowhere more so than in the Caribbean. The integration of the world's productive system, which started with the commercial expansion of Europe in the 15th and 16th centuries, had produced a situation in which no country could isolate itself from the cataclysmic changes taking place in Europe. There was widespread revolt and rebellion throughout the then British West Indies – between May and July 1934 on the sugar estates in Trinidad; in January 1935 in St Kitts; in May 1935 in Jamaica; in September and

October 1935 on several sugar estates in Guyana; in October 1935 in St Vincent; in June 1937 in Trinidad; in July 1937 in Barbados; in May and June 1938 in Jamaica and in February 1939 in Guyana. The British government responded to this so-called 'hurricane of protest' by appointing a Royal Commission of Inquiry (the Moyne Commission). Its report, published after the Second World War, contains an excellent description of the social and economic situation in the region at that time.

Because the disturbances in the 1930s were so quickly followed by the outbreak of the Second World War, it becomes virtually impossible to separate their respective influences on the subsequent evolution of the post-war Caribbean economy. This task becomes even more impossible when the disturbances are placed in the context of the Great Depression – itself a major element in the disintegration of Europe and the movement towards war. Indeed, so entangled was the association between these events that the first national election to be held in Jamaica in which there was universal adult suffrage took place in the midst of the war in 1944. This election, which arose out of the disturbances and in effect conceded the right of the West Indian people to manage their own affairs, is often taken to mark the beginning of the Caribbean's modern period.

Although there was a long-established and growing US influence in the region – in fact ever since the Monroe doctrine of 1823 US foreign policy had been based on the assumption that any interference by a European power in the hemisphere would be taken as an 'unfriendly act' – it was only through the Second World War that US military forces gained a legal entitlement to enter the British West Indies. Once this was acquired, successive US governments arrogated to themselves the right 'to protect' the region both from outsiders and from those hostile to the *status quo* within. This was the basis for numerous invasions, threats and forced treaties which were used to further US interests in the hemisphere. While the 'big stick' period of Theodore Roosevelt gave way to the 'dollar diplomacy' of William Taft (1912), the purpose of substituting 'dollars for bullets' was the same – to consolidate US hegemony in the hemisphere. Thus, although the propaganda behind Franklin Roosevelt's 'good neighbour' policy renounced armed intervention, the threat and use of force by the US continued. As the war between Britain and Germany advanced, the British government entered into lend-lease arrangements with the US in which military bases in some of its Caribbean territories were given to the US in exchange for war materials.

The war itself had a major impact on the British West Indian economies. The construction of the US bases and other wartime facilities, in particular, gave a tremendous filip to economic activity in the region. Apart from the employment and income it generated, it also provided an important means of training the labour force in a wide range of construction skills. In addition, by disrupting colonial exports and imports, the war shifted the focus of domestic production towards serving the local market. For example, food production in Trinidad-Tobago at the end of the war was two-and-a-half times higher than it had been in 1939. A wide range of local industries and a number of import-substituting activities were established during this period, including some large-scale secondary industries, both producing for the domestic market and exporting regionally (lime and limestone, matches, industrial gases); some secondary industries serving the local market (food, drink, tobacco, clothing, household items, etc), as well as some local handicraft and artisan output.

All the traditional export industries, however, were very badly hit by the disruption of trade in the region. The major export, sugar, was in such serious difficulties that, at the end of the war, the British government had to introduce massive rehabilitation schemes to save the industry. Also of great importance to the future of the region was that, because of Germany's threat to UK shipping and the diversion of British industry to the war effort, North America began to replace the UK as the main supplier of imports to the region and provided a sizeable market for its exports.

To return to the labour disturbances, it is worth noting that, while specific circumstances in each territory undoubtedly affected the timing, nature and course of revolt in the region in the 1930s, there were common underlying factors which gave rise to the situation. The most important of these were: (i) the colonial economy's collapse in the wake of the

Depression. (This underlined the extreme vulnerability to world events of an economy dependent on exporting one or two primary products to a few metropolitan markets); (ii) the peasants' longstanding grievances against plantation interests; (iii) the growth of working-class consciousness, organisation and agitation for better pay and working conditions evident throughout the 20th century, but particularly so in the 1930s with the decline in real incomes and further drop in already subhuman living standards; (iv) an increase in nationalist, pro-independence sentiment among the local population countering the autocratic, repressive authoritarianism of the Crown Colony's unresponsive and unrepresentative system of government; (v) the raised expectations of some sections of the population who had returned from periods abroad only to find that the entrenched colonial system was incapable of meeting their newly acquired socio-economic aspirations. The impact of these persons was particularly noticeable in the leadership of industrial, social and political organisations; (vi) the more widespread provision of education which sometimes, instead of merely inculcating loyal empire values, opened students' minds to other values and possibilities; (vii) the rise of unemployment – a new social phenomenon brought about by the Depression, the growth of towns in the 20th century and by the capitalist wage system which had by then become firmly entrenched in the region. As their numbers grew, so the unemployed tended to join the ranks of the protesters and those agitating for improved conditions of life; and finally, (viii) the conflicts produced by these various factors, combined with a woefully inadequate system of social welfare in which there was virtually no relief for the broad mass of the population exposed to these unrelenting pressures.

Some of these factors were identified in the Moyne Commission Report. Although a truly remarkable document for its time, and unparalleled in its detailed description of the poverty and powerlessness of the West Indian masses in the 1930s, in its recommendations, it consistently failed to address the root causes of the people's distress and, as such, was unfortunately neither revolutionary nor radical. In keeping with the Fabian tradition of the time, it recommended improving social services, sending more financial aid to the region from London, ensuring that the region's agricultural produce became more readily available in Britain and introducing land settlement schemes to prevent confrontations between the peasants and the planters over access to land and other resources. As a package, these recommendations paved the way for the paternalistic Colonial Development and Welfare Committee, which was established by the British government after the Second World War to cope with the region's difficulties.

As the Moyne Commission's Report noted, the rapid *population* increases, which began at the turn of the century and which had been brought about by a decline in the death rate through marginal improvements in public health, put pressure on public and social services, intensified the pressure on the land and contributed to the rise in unemployment. In *industry*, the Report noted very little development. What little there was, was confined to mining (oil in Trinidad-Tobago; bauxite, gold and diamonds in Guyana); agro-processing (the use of coconut in products such as oil, lard, margarine and soap, biscuit and bread manufacture, fish preserving and aerated drinks); a limited range of consumer goods (cigarettes and matches) and services (tailors, carpenters and printers); transport and utilities (electricity plants, horsedrawn carriages, canoes and small wooden boats) and processing export staples (mainly sugar).

Agriculture formed the subject of a specialist report in which it was asserted that:

> The general level of agriculture in these Colonies is low in technical knowledge, business organisation and management efficiency; systematic agriculture, by which is meant mixed farming on a plan suited to the inherent circumstances of the area, is unknown. The basic types of agriculture in the West Indian Colonies are shifting cultivation, under which land may be used for, perhaps, two years in every eight or ten, and the continuous growing of one crop on the same land over a long period. Livestock are never the effective complement of crops and the connection between them is frequently adventitious or totally absent. So long as these methods continue it will be impossible for agricultural production to provide even the essentials of life for the growing population of the West

Indian Colonies and comprehensive reform of existing agricultural methods is therefore inevitable.[5]

An equally gloomy picture was painted of export agriculture:

> It will be apparent from this survey that the present outlook for the export agriculture of the West Indies, apart from the sugar industry, is extremely discouraging. Only the citrus industry offers a reasonable hope, and that a highly uncertain one of material expansion. A diminishing volume of employment is the prospect in most of the other branches of agriculture, and the outlook for the two most important of them, the Jamaica banana industry and the cocoa industry of Trinidad and Grenada, is grave in the extreme.[6]

Paradoxically, these conclusions led to a renewed emphasis being placed on sugar and, after the Second World War, a major process was set in train to rehabilitate the region's sugar industry.[7]

In its section on *social conditions* the Report was particularly scathing about the system of *education*:

> Secondary schools exist in the West Indies many of which provide an excellent classical education, but they provide for only a very small proportion even of the children who pass through the primary schools. As it is, unemployment is rife among the products of secondary education, owing to the lack of suitable 'white collar' jobs and the disinclination of the pupils to take employment in agriculture as at present organised.[8]

This educational system had evolved from slavery, which offered virtually no education at all. After emancipation, the churches were mainly responsible for providing some kind of education to the former slaves, but this was in overcrowded classrooms in inadequate buildings with poor facilities and with far too few trained teachers. Vocational training was badly neglected and there was no university or other provision for tertiary education. No attempt had been made to integrate the system and virtually no Caribbean materials were available, let alone used in the schools.

The *health* situation was also distressing, with high infant and maternal mortality rates in most territories, especially in Guyana. Also, many of the diseases could have been prevented – hook worm, dysentry, enteric fever, malaria and deficiency diseases such as rickets, scurvy and beri-beri – had more money been spent on preventive medicine. The statistics on medical expenditure cited in the Report reinforce this gloomy picture (see Table 3.1). The root causes of the situation lay in the broad mass of the population's poverty and lack of education in health and hygiene, as well as in the public services' failure to provide a safe water supply or adequate sanitation. In all the territories, the situation was worse in the urban than in the rural areas.

Table 3.1
Health Statistics: British Caribbean 1945

	1	2	3
Barbados	11.3	8	92
British Guiana	10.2	12	88
British Honduras	8.9	–	–
Jamaica	9.8	18	82
LEEWARD ISLANDS:			
Antigua	17.1	22	78
St Kitts-Nevis	18.6	31	69
Dominica	15.6	8	92
Montserrat	8.9	25	75
Virgin Islands	16.9	–	–
Trinidad-Tobago	9.2	18	82
WINDWARD ISLANDS:			
Grenada	16.9	9	91
St Lucia	12.7	10	90
St Vincent	19.6	15	85

1. % of medical expenditure to total expenditure
2. % of preventive to total medical expenditure
3. % of curative to total medical expenditure
Source: West India Royal Commission Report, 1945, CMND 6607, p. 141.

The following information was presented in the Report on *housing*:

It is not an exaggeration to say that in the poorest parts of most towns and in many of the country districts, a majority of the houses is largely made of rusty corrugated iron and unsound boarding; quite often the original floor has disappeared and only the earth remains, its surface so trampled that it is impervious to any rain which may penetrate through a leaking roof; sanitation in any form and water supply are unknown in such premises, and in many cases no light can enter when the door is closed. These decrepit homes, more often than not, are seriously overcrowded, and it is not surprising that some of them are dirty and verminous in spite of the praiseworthy efforts of the inhabitants to keep them clean. In short, every condition that tends to produce disease is here to be found in a serious form. The generally unsanitary environment gives rise to malaria, worm infection and bowel diseases; leaking roofs, rotten flooring and lack of light encourage the spread of tuberculosis, respiratory diseases, worm infections, jigger lesions and rat-borne diseases; overcrowding which is usually accompanied by imperfect ventilation, is an important agent in contributing to the high incidence of yaws, tuberculosis, venereal diseases, and, to a certain extent, leprosy.[9]

The tradition of poor housing went back to the slave plantations where the planters sought to minimise the costs of keeping slaves. With emancipation and the later development of large villages and towns, migration to these areas led to a certain amount of overcrowding, made worse by the complete absence of a coherent policy on public housing.

With the virtual absence of any government-sponsored social welfare programmes, those provisions that did exist were sponsored and administered by the church, or by voluntary organisations like the Salvation Army, YWCA and YMCA. There was no place for leisure and recreational activities in the social life of the times. The orphaned child, the indigent, the mentally ill, the physically handicapped, all lived off the crumbs of the society – and there were few of these. Women were systematically discriminated against and, as mothers, left to carry a disproportionate share of the burdens of parenthood:

> Little can be said for the social conditions which exist in the West Indies today. The child, so often reared in an ill-built and overcrowded home, passes from it to what is, all too frequently, an overcrowded school. If he has been fortunate

enough to continue his education until school-leaving age,
which is usually 14 in the towns and 12 in the rural districts,
he enters a world where unemployment and under-employment are regarded as the common lot. Should he find work
as a manual labourer, his wages often provide only for bare
maintenance and are far from sufficient to enable him to attain
the standard of living which is set before him by new contacts
with the outside world. If he is fitted by education and intelli-
gence for clerical posts, competition for which is intense, he
will have the prospect, at best, of a salary on which, even in
Government employment, he will find it a serious struggle to
keep up the social position and appearances which he and his
friends expect. He will have leisure hours but few facilities
for recreation with which to fill them.

The position of women is more unfortunate. . . Generally
she has a large family, and whenever employment is available,
must work to support them or to eke out the slender earnings
of her man. Most commonly her work is in the fields; after
feeding her family she must start out from her home in the
early morning, often leaving little or no food in the house for
her children whose main meal may have to wait for her return
in the evening. Her difficulty in securing work is at least as
great as that with which the West Indian man is faced. If she
alone is responsible for the support of a family, her position
is indeed difficult and there can be little cause for wonder
that a combination of economic circumstances and natural
irresponsibility so often leads a woman, even if she already
has the sole responsibility for several illegitimate children, to
seek the uncertain help afforded by association with yet
another man, although she must realise only too well the
temporary nature of that assistance and that eventually,
perhaps after her responsibilities have been increased, she may
again be abandoned.[10]

The report also gave a detailed description of *labour*
conditions. As expected, the bulk of the work force was
agricultural or rural based, with a significant percentage of
the female work-force employed as domestic servants – 25
per cent in Barbados and 15 per cent in Guyana. Payment
by piece-rates rather than by the length of time worked –
one of the legacies of slavery/indenture – meant that there
were constant disputes between employers and employees
over the size of the tasks and the length of time needed to
perform them. Most of the work force was underunionised,

often because there were legal restraints against trade union activity. Only in Guyana were trade unions protected from paying damages for strikes and in Jamaica was peaceful picketing accepted as legal. Housing employees in quarters owned and provided by their employers and subjecting them to the possibility of eviction without notice, served as another powerful weapon for keeping labour intimidated.

Large sections of the labour force fell into the categories of unemployed, underemployed and seasonally employed. Given that there were no social welfare programmes to fall back on, the 'plight of the unemployed, aggravated as it. . . [was] by the seasonal character of employment. . . [was] serious to the point of desperation'.[11]

The whole situation was, of course, made worse by the colonial domination of the region. Although there was some measure of internal self-government, its effectiveness was reduced by the extremely narrow franchise which existed until the end of the 1930s. For example, in 1938 only seven per cent of the population in Trinidad-Tobago had the vote and in Barbados it was only three per cent.

The Moyne Commission Report has been cited at some length because its detailed description of social life in the pre-war British Caribbean colonies is unmatched. The intrusion of poverty into all aspects of social life – work, housing, education, medical services, access to land, even leisure and recreation – and the powerlessness of a barely franchised and unrepresented population to act in the face of the established authorities, are all vividly portrayed in the Report. None the less, despite their poverty and lack of representation, the power of the masses as a social group soon made itself felt everywhere in the area as revolts, riots, strikes and disturbances shook the very foundations of Britain's colonial power. Four and a half centuries after the first encounter with the Europeans, the Caribbean had moved into the phase of its modern history.

PART II:
Independence and the Nationalist Alternatives

The second part of this book takes a look at how the impact of the independence movements forced a change in the economic strategies of the old colonial order. It shows, however, that by the late 1970s – towards the end of the period under consideration – despite rapid expansion in some sectors (such as manufacturing, tourism and off-shore finance), the region was in the grip of a serious economic crisis. This was caused by the impact of the world economic crisis on a still basically vulnerable area and by the exhaustion of the possibilities inherent in the nationalist economic strategy. The nationalism which had fed the independence movements had lost its capacity to withstand over four and a half centuries of colonial rule in the Caribbean. By the end of the 1970s, therefore, despite some important changes having taken place, the dispossession of the majority of the people in the region, the poor and the powerless, continued.

Chapter 4 outlines the Colonial Office view of development and explains the nationalist alternative. Chapter 5 looks at one of the main pillars of this alternative, namely 'industrialisation by invitation'. Chapter 6 examines the policy of natural resource development, while Chapter 7 looks at the competition between plantations, peasants and the state for land and other resources and its impact on the rural economy. Chapter 8 investigates the region's search for new 'poles of growth' – tourism and off-shore banking. Chapter 9 concludes this part of the book with an examination of the role of the state in organising and administering the region's economy. The period ends with the crisis of the 1970s.

4 Colonialism and Nationalism: Alternative Economic Strategies

In this chapter an attempt is made to examine and compare post-war colonial development strategy with the evolving nationalist model of development which accompanied the struggle for independence and, at least until the crisis of the 1970s, formed the bedrock of government policies in the region.

I: The Colonial Office View of Development for the British West Indies

In attempting to provide a concise presentation of the Colonial Office's view of development in the region, I run the risk of suggesting a greater coherence of understanding and purpose on the part of the major actors than might have been the case at the time. More frequently than not, participants in a historical process do not see their actions with the 20-20 vision offered by hindsight. It is therefore important for readers to bear in mind that this is a synthesised and somewhat idealised view of the Colonial Office's role in the region.

The Colonial Office generally portrayed its colonial mission as one of 'trusteeship' – a view in which the aim of a good colonial administration was to foster and encourage a progressive and orderly movement towards representative self-government. But for the West Indies, at least until the Second World War, independence was regarded as definitely beyond the horizon of the time. The policy of trusteeship was thus administered amidst constant protest and agitation. While the main supporters of this resistance were the poor and powerless masses, its leadership (when organised) was invariably recruited from the educated professional middle classes or other intermediate strata that had developed under colonial tutelage. These leaders usually channelled the protest into demands for more local self-government and a wider franchise than the Colonial Office was willing to concede. In fact, the Colonial Office tended to reverse the direction of constitutional advance if the struggles intensified or became too violent. When, for example, the first Guyanese election based on universal adult suffrage produced the first freely-elected Marxist government in the Empire in 1953,

Guyana's constitution was suspended after only 133 days of rule and the country occupied by British forces. Given this type of response and, more importantly, the four centuries of slavery, unrest and even genocide preceding it, it is difficult to believe how anyone could have been anything but cynical about the trusteeship ideal. Despite this, however, it still persisted in the formal colonial administration of the region and quite a few of the major participants in the drama of those times came to believe in it.

The wealth of the Caribbean fed the first waves of conquest and colonisation. The entrenchment of industrial capitalism in Europe brought with it new demands on colonies and overseas possessions which aided the latter's transformation into peripheral societies. But by this time, the view had gained ascendancy in Europe that the region had exhausted its potential. Small tropical countries, peopled in the main by non-Europeans, could never be industrialised and hence there was an already exhausted limit to their growth and development.

Several theories were advanced to justify this view. First there were the *racial theories*, based on the alleged 'inferiority' of non-European peoples, which condemned them to live in (and reproduce) backward social systems. Thus, as a partial explanation for the absence of industrial development, the view was expressed by an industrial expert (who visited the area to advise on industrial development) that the temperament of the West Indian worker was 'easy going, unambitious and casual'.[1]

Second, allied to the first, was the *over-population theory*. This explained poverty and backwardness in terms of high population-to-land ratios in small economies which, when combined with rapid demographic growth (high birth rates and rapidly declining death rates) and a highly dependent population structure (large numbers of people outside the working age of the population), rendered them incapable of faster growth and development.

To this was later added a type of *geographical determinism* which argued that poor soil types, a debilitating climate (at least for Europeans) and unknown natural resources meant that growth was virtually impossible in tropical countries. In small economies these arguments were expected to hold even more strongly, since, given a random distribution of resources, the smaller the country, the more limited its natural resources were likely to be.

In addition, there were the Ricardian-type *comparative advantage theories* of trade, which argued in favour of the region focusing on what it already had, namely tropical staples and minerals. That these endowments were themselves the historical remnants, first of early mercantilism and later of the British concept of an integrated Empire, was a possibility that was never raised. The deterministic approach was also often expressed in cultural terms. The societies' institutions were described as traditional, stagnant and unchanging and, as such, resistant to the modernism the colonial authorities and Europeans sought to introduce. This led to a rather dualistic conception of the area's economy as containing a growing (modern) part and a stagnant (traditional) part.

All these theories imply a certain philosophical acceptance of the enduring state of underdevelopment in the area. The 'pragmatists' put forward their various claims about what was holding economies back (for example, a lack of capital, skill, entrepreneurship or work ethic), but whatever their individual lines of argument, they all purported to explain underdevelopment as a phenomenon independent of the historical process. In other words, these were fundamentally ahistorical theories which explained poverty and powerlessness in terms of the innate characteristics of people and their environments or self-perpetuating cycles of poverty. Given that Europe was initially attracted to the Caribbean because of its wealth, this was indeed an ironic historical development.

Views such as these obviously discouraged any serious efforts at industrial development in the region. More and more people, including those in the Colonial Office, began to believe that a country could only break out of the 'vicious circles of poverty' or 'the disequilibrium traps of underdevelopment and dependence' if it diversified and became differentiated through developing a broad-based manufacturing sector. From the more positive standpoint, however, these views did at least encourage the Colonial Office to pinpoint the following key areas for attention in fostering expansion and growth in the Caribbean.[2]

(i) Population control:

As we saw in Chapter 3, the Moyne Commission identified rapid population growth as a serious source of pressure on the region's resources and a major cause of the alarming increase in open unemployment. The rapid growth of population in the area was held to be caused by the non-white peoples' cultural and temperamental inclination to be reproductively prolific. Thus, to facilitate the demographic transition to smaller families, 'family planning' policies were advocated and implemented.

(ii) Agricultural production:

Agriculture was seen as the sector best suited to the region. The agrarian structure had, however, developed a certain duality, with a high concentration of large-scale plantations on the one hand and numerous small and landless peasants engaged in a mix of subsistence agriculture, food production for the domestic market and participation in the export cash-crop economy, on the other. To overcome this, several measures were proposed and adopted. The first was to introduce land settlement schemes. This was an old proposal, originally advanced by the Royal Commission of 1897 as 'the *only* way of meeting the fundamental requirements of the British West Indies' and, according to the Moyne Commission, ' the Sugar Commission of 1930 endorsed their views'.[3] Economically, it was held that land grants, particularly of unused lands, would help relieve population pressure on the land and, by opening up occupational opportunities in the rural areas, would not only halt migration to the towns but also encourage a reverse flow of people back to the countryside. Additionally, they would broaden the agricultural base if in this process export cash crops other than sugar were encouraged, for example, bananas, coffee, cocoa and citrus. In this way, open unemployment, as well as underemployment in the rural areas, would be reduced. At the social level, this policy was generally expected to iron out the more extreme inequalities in the distribution of landholdings and encourage improvements in the area's complex land-tenure arrangements. More particularly, it was seen as a means of correcting an obvious abuse, namely the plantations' practice of operating a system of 'tied houses', whereby labourers lived on the plantations in overcrowded, patently subhuman conditions, with poor sanitation, inadequate ventilation and without any drinking water on the premises.

In an attempt to ensure adequate regulation and supervision of land use and proper distribution of output, wherever possible, peasant production was linked to cooperatives or to newly created state marketing agencies. In practice, however, this tended to foster the development of 'outside leadership' in the rural areas, which negated rather than promoted cooperation, self-help and self-reliance in the rural economy.

The Colonial Office also recommended giving a certain amount of technical help to those engaged in agricultural production. Thus, in many parts of the region, government departments concerned with agriculture and land policies were either established or, where they already existed, reorganised. These agencies developed extension networks through which they supervised, aided and advised the farming communities. Institutions were also established for providing credit and for ensuring that steady flows of fertilisers, machinery and technical advice were channelled into the peasant producing areas. To counteract the plantation's dominance, great efforts were made to rehabilitate, modernise and reorganise these producing units. However, this often meant giving the plantation owners huge subsidies with which to replace their run-down capital stock and implement the kind of wage and employment policies that would stabilise the flow of labour to the estates. In the case of sugar, for example, after the Second World War special funds were set aside for rehabilitating the industry, for supporting a stable wage policy in it and for protecting it (through a system of buffer or stabilisation funds) against the wildly fluctuating price of sugar on the world market. In addition, the region's sugar had protected entry into the UK market and this also helped to support this relatively high-cost producing unit, into which the plantation in the region had developed.

The main focus of the agricultural economy was on the

plantation-exporting sector. Thus, even in cases like Guyana, where the colonial authorities promoted large-scale production of rice as a peasant crop, this was done in such a way as to ensure that labour and other inputs of the crop complemented, rather than competed with, the requirements of the plantation-producing sector.

(iii) Infrastructural facilities:

In that the colonial authorities had identified an inadequate infrastructure as a major deficiency, much emphasis was placed (through state financing) on ensuring that private producers were supplied with the services they needed. Included among these were land reclamation schemes, drainage and irrigation works, roads and communications, as well as the usual public utilities such as electricity, sanitation and a pure water supply. This development envisaged the state taking over much of the responsibility for creating favourable conditions for private enterprises in the region.

(iv) Foreign capital inflows:

The Colonial Office believed that the level of development attained would depend a great deal on an inflow of foreign finance, enterprise, skills, know-how and technology, which could be supplied either on a private basis or through international agencies. It was felt that integrating the markets of individual territories (as far as this was possible) with that of the UK, would provide a major incentive to the flow of capital – a view shared by the British Colonial Office's counterparts in France and Holland. Given that the integration was envisaged on a vertical rather than a horizontal basis – horizontal exchanges within the region were merely a by-product of the arrangement – the currency and banking facilities already established in the region's British territories provided an effective channel through which to implement the policy. Later, however, the inconveniences of having to administer so many small and mini-states encouraged the view that some form of West Indian integration might serve the purpose of all concerned.

In the Colonial Office's attitude to foreign capital there was a rather quaint blend of the old mercantilist views on promoting empire and the more exploitative strategies inherent in the Ricardian theories of comparative advantage. In practice, however, Britain's policies encouraged increasing domination of the region's economy by transnational corporations (TNCs) and reinforced the 'centre/periphery' legacy of the Second World War. In this sense, therefore, the Colonial Office's approach sought to reverse the tendency (which had started to develop during the Second World War) towards severing Britain's commercial ties with the region.

(v) Colonial development and welfare:
As Chapter 3 noted in discussing the Moyne Commission Report, a certain concern for welfare (in part an adjunct to the trusteeship view) was elaborated, particularly in 'liberal' and labour circles of the Colonial Office. This led to some emphasis on reform and the better provision of social services, investments in public utilities and the promotion of trade-union legislation in the area.

(vi) Trade:
The emphasis in trade was on reciprocal preferences. The region was a high-cost producer and without protected access to the UK market its factor endowment, which was supposed to favour agriculture, did not yield competitive prices. The subsidy required was to be borne by the British consumer. In return, Britain maintained preferential access for her manufacturers and other exports to the region. It was hoped, if not expected, that the protection of the UK market would provide a transitional means of support for the region and, in this sense, the policy was not a simple reversion to the old mercantilism. The emergence of North America as the major trading partner for several of the territories was tolerated because the US and Canada were expected to share the costs of subsidised production in the region by giving preferential access to Caribbean exports. In view of this, a policy of officially discouraging Canadian and US exports to the region could not have been vigorously pursued.

(vii) Migration:
One of the paradoxes of empire was that citizens of the UK and of the colonies theoretically enjoyed the same rights of citizenship. With the pressure on living standards in the

region and the attraction of relief in the UK, large waves of poor and powerless West Indians sought refuge in Britain. During 1953 and 1954, a total of 168,000 entered the UK and between 1955 and 1959 they entered at the rate of between 20,000 and 30,000 a year. Migration to Britain was effectively halted by the Commonwealth Immigration Act of 1962. It did, however, take place to other areas, especially the US which took in 200,000 West Indians between 1951 and 1960 and as many as half-a-million between 1961 and 1970.

(viii) Industry:

Despite the bias against industrialisation mentioned earlier, it is pertinent to note that an important phase of industrial development had in fact occurred in the region, largely because access to the UK market had been closed off by the Second World War. Although the range of industrial development was quite considerable (see Table 4.1 for Trinidad-Tobago), the colonial authorities remained unconvinced of its significance and continued to hold the view that industry should largely be confined to local craft production and small-scale manufacturing activities most of which were to rely on overseas capital, organisation and ownership.

Taken as a whole, these various policies adopted by the colonial authorities had three major consequences. First, they reinforced a particular rhythm of production, which I have described elsewhere in terms of there being:

> . . . a crucial feature of the combination of smallness and underdevelopment [which] when dynamically applied and expressed in terms of objective, material phenomena. . . consists of the fact that the conjunction of production relations and productive forces is of such a character that the measure of structural dependence, underdevelopment, and the economic backwardness of the process of production which is important above all others is *on the one hand*, the lack of an organic link, rooted in an indigenous science and technology, between the pattern and growth of domestic resource use and the pattern and growth of domestic demand, and *on the other*, the divergence between domestic demand and the needs of the broad mass of the population.[4]

Table 4.1
Industries in Operation in Trinidad–Tobago 1942–43

PART I:	Large Scale Secondary Industries Manufacturing Goods Both for the Domestic Market and for Export:	
	Angostura Bitters	
	Carbon Dioxide Manufacture	
	Industrial Gases	
	Matches	
	Lime and Limestone	

PART II: **Secondary Industries of an Advanced Kind Producing Goods for Local Consumption but not to any Substantial Extent for Export**

1. Food, Drink and Tobacco

Aerated Waters	Coffee	Jams and Jellies
Beer	Coconut Oil (Edible)	Lard & Lard
Biscuits	Coconut Meal (animal	substitutes
Bread	food)	Liqueurs
Chocolate and Cocoa	Confectionery (sweets)	Margarine
Powder	Grapefruit (canning)	Pipe Mixtures
Cigars	Ice	Stout
Cigarettes	Ice Cream	Wines

2. Clothing and Footwear

Alpargatas (sandals)	Hats	Suits
Dresses	Pyjamas	Underclothing
	Shirts	

3. Household Equipment

Candles	Mattresses	Washing Soda
Furniture	Soap	

4. Medicines, Toilet Preparations, etc.

Alcohol	Medicinal Preparations	Perfumed Spirits
Bay Rum	Methylated Spirits	Toilet Preparations
Herbal Extracts		

5. General Industries

Acetylene	General Engineering	Steel Barges
Boats & Launches	Laundries	Steel Drums
Book-binding	Motor Car Repairing	Storage Tanks
Bricks	Oxygen	Tanneries
Building	Packages	Tombstones
Clay Products	Printing	Tyre Repairing
Concrete Products	Saw-milling	(re-treading) and vulcanising)

▶

Table 4.1—Continued

PART III: **Minor Industries and Crafts Conducted Principally in the Homes of the Workers**		
Basketry	Dress-making	Novelties (including
Boots and Shoes	Engraving Gold and	wooden toys)
Brooms and Brush	Silver Work	Pottery
making	Jewellery	Preserves (fruits
Charcoal Burning	Lampshades	chutneys, sauces)
Coconut Fibre	Barrels	Tinware
Mats		

Source: Industrial Development in the British Territories of the Caribbean vol. II, pp. 10/11.

This produces an economic system in which the lack of *material* linkages (between labour, resources, technology, demand and needs) reflects a set of *social relations* in which the ownership and use of the productive factors and the pattern of consumption/yield/output are not oriented to domestic consumption (as expressed through the market), or to the domestic needs of the population (as reflected in the continuing shortages of food, clothing, shelter and recreational goods).

The colonial authorities accepted this condition as inevitable and irreversible – in fact more or less 'naturally ordained'.

The second consequence was that, until independence, the local state did very little to mediate in the rhythm of production. With the approach of independence, however, it began to play a more and more important role in economic organisation and production, with the eventual result that by the 1980s it had become the dominant internal institutional factor in the region's economy. This should not be taken to mean that the Colonial Office had a strictly *laissez-faire* view of the state. On the contrary, the state did act at this time, but lacking the political and social influences produced by the nationalist movement, its mediation of colonial policies was less effective than in the later period.

Finally, the region's economic structures became increasingly poverty stricken, underdeveloped and dependent, with the following characteristics:[5]

— overspecialised production of a narrow range of primary products produced mainly for export, with sales confined to a few overseas markets;
— unstable prices for products sold abroad leading to wide fluctuations in domestic levels of income, employment and prices;
— an open economy (produced by the combination of the two features listed above) and a heavy dependence in the region on imports and foreign capital inflows to feed the population, service industry and finance internal capital expansion;
— a predominance of foreign decision-making in economic activity;
— sophisticated mechanisms for siphoning off the domestic surplus abroad (for example, the Currency Board, the commercial branch banking system in operation at the time, strict adherence to the sterling exchange standard and an absence of any form of regulation or control over the movement of capital in and out of the country);
— a predominance of agricultural and mining economies, with limited diversification of output and occupations;
— widespread poverty, malnutrition, inadequate housing and social services such as education, health and sanitation;
— backward agrarian systems with marked inequalities in ownership and access to land;
— no real presence of the major classes of the period (the industrial proletariat and a local industrial/financial bourgeoisie) and, as a result, the underdevelopment of their particular institutions (political parties, trade unions, etc).

To the above listing, which is more indicative than exhaustive, should also be added the complications produced by the small size and scale of these economies and by the racial stratification of economic functions in the area.

Because colonial policies were basically designed to perpetuate colonial domination, they ultimately stood in opposition to the interests of the broad mass of the region's peoples, despite some benefits being produced here and there. The large plantation owners and foreign capital were invariably the main beneficiaries. Attempts to redress the twin scourges of peasant dispossession and widespread unemployment were largely tentative and, in the main, politically motivated with a view to defusing pressures and agitation for independence. In this sense, therefore, such measures were designed to demobilise rather than release the people's creative energies and they certainly ensured that the broad mass of the population remained poor and powerless.

II: National Independence and Economic Strategies

The growth and spread of the national independence movement was the most characteristic feature of the region immediately after the Second World War, but, as in other areas of social life, its development was uneven. By the 1960s, however, some territories had gained their independence: Jamaica, Trinidad-Tobago, Guyana and Barbados. Although the broad mass of the population (particularly the peasants, workers and unemployed) produced the main pressures against the colonial system, the leaders of the mass movements, in other words those who negotiated the mechanics of the independence settlements, came from petty-bourgeois, professional or other intermediate strata. None the less, there was no doubt that the struggles for a broader franchise, more local autonomy, improved access to resources for the local population, better pay and labour conditions, better prices for agricultural produce, more security of living standards and, ultimately, the struggle for independence itself, represented an exceptionally important period in the development of populist politics in the region.

Two very important considerations arise from this period of Caribbean development.[6] First, the growth of mass politics (and the mobilisation of the population this entailed) legitimised politics and the state to an unparalleled degree in the history of the region. The inference of this was that the post-colonial state was qualitatively different from its predecessor, despite the continuation of certain real constraints to its growth such as economic structure, geopolitical context and size. The period up to and after independence therefore marked a *real*, as distinct from a merely symbolic, turning point in the state's role in the economic life of the area. While this often led people, especially on the left, to overestimate the state's capacity to change inherited structures and to alleviate poverty and powerlessness without actually undergoing a complete transformation itself, as an economic institution the state did play a decisive part in improving the prospects for local development.

Paradoxically this coincided with another development, which significantly affected the way in which the state's potential was exploited. Having taken over state power, the leaders of the independence movements sought to *demobilise and de-politicise* the masses to prevent any further entrenchment of mass politics in the society at large. The most extreme examples of this were seen in Eric Gairy's Grenada and Forbes Burnham's Guyana. This development occurred because the petty-bourgeoisie (along with the other intermediate strata from which the mass movement's leaders were recruited) was essentially a colonial creation with limited objectives. The members of this group – which had grown up through limited sections of the population having been given preferential access to education, the professions and, to a lesser extent, land – resented their second-class status in colonial society and expected, with independence, either to be consecrated by the colonial authorities or seen by the masses, or both, as the logical inheritors of the Colonial Office's 'right-to-rule'. Their struggles were not therefore oriented towards a revolutionary reversal of power relations in favour of the poor and powerless. For them, the independence settlement provided a means of excluding the masses from effective power.

Given this background, it is hardly surprising that while leading to certain important changes, the policies pursued by the nationalists all fell far short of bringing any real economic independence to the area. These policies, each of which forms the substance of a separate chapter, basically followed six major lines of development:

(i) Industrialisation based on a capital import model (allegedly derived from the Puerto Rican experience), in which there is an emphasis on protection, capital subsidisation and a leading role for TNCs in alliance with the emerging local business elite (Chapter 5).

(ii) Natural resource development through TNCs (Chapter 6).

(iii) A restructuring of the traditional agricultural export sector and of domestic agriculture (Chapter 7).

(iv) Diversification of the economy, with special emphasis on developing a significant service sector (particularly tourism) and creating off-shore financial havens (Chapter 8).

(v) The introduction of new economic institutions and the restructuring of existing ones (Chapter 9).

(vi) The promotion of a certain form of economic integration in the region to overcome the limitations of small size (Chapter 12).

5 *Puerto Rico to the Rescue:*
Industrialisation by Invitation

The boom in economic activity experienced in several of the Caribbean territories from the early and middle 1950s to the late 1960s was, in large measure, fuelled by unprecedented developments in three sectors, namely manufacturing, mining (oil and bauxite-alumina) and tourism. The development of the manufacturing sector forms the substance of this chapter. Its links with the other two sectors should, however, be constantly borne in mind, for in at least one crucial area – foreign-exchange availability – the manufacturing sector was able to grow to the extent that it did only because the other two sectors supplied much of the foreign exchange it consumed.

I: The Rationale

As we noted in the previous chapter, at the end of the Second World War the Colonial Office viewed the possibility of industrial development in the small tropical colonies of the Caribbean as uneconomic and undesirable, if not impossible to achieve. This was an old view dating back to 1897 when the West Indian Royal Commission had stated that 'there was no prospect for manufactured industries being established on any considerable scale'.[1] Although conceding certain exceptions, such as cement, if British firms could be persuaded to participate, the Moyne Commission reinforced this same view by denouncing 'speculative industrial enterprises' in the region.[2] But when the war stimulated economic activity in the Caribbean, particularly in mining, construction and domestic food production, there was also a noticeable expansion of manufacturing activity. This, combined with nationalist denunciations of colonial rule on the grounds that it stifled the growth in the area, led to the belief that industrialisation was possible in the region provided the right combination of circumstances could be created. As it turned out, the theoretical rationale for these aspirations was found in the work of the St Lucian-born economist, Sir Arthur Lewis. Although perhaps not altogether deservedly, his is the name most closely associated with the policies which were put into effect.

The theoretical basis of Lewis's approach was built on

the work of two earlier economists, David Ricardo and Colin Clark. Clark's empirical work had indicated that there was a positive relationship between the wealth of a nation and its share of manufacturing output. In addition, Lewis's own observations of the region had led him to recognise that primary agriculture was incapable of providing enough jobs, let alone the sustained development of the area. Ricardo had also arrived at a similar conclusion about 19th century Britain and, from these two streams of thought, Lewis decided that 'the policy which seems to offer most hope of permanent success is for the islands to follow in the footsteps of other agricultural countries in industrialisation. . . No other policy seems to offer such permanent prospects as the development of local industries'.[3] Ricardo's arguments against the possibilities of development and transformation through agricultural activity, from which Lewis drew so much inspiration have, however, been criticised for seriously underestimating the role of international trade and for focusing almost exclusively on the effective *home* demand for agricultural products.

Be that as it may, Lewis's arguments were more guarded than is popularly assumed. Certain elements in his rationale were later ignored by policy makers and it is important that these are recognised if his work is to be evaluated fairly. First, Lewis saw industry as playing the *pivotal transforming* role in the process of development and viewed this *not as an alternative* to agricultural diversification and development but as its *complement*. The failure to recognise this element of his formulation led, as we shall see in Chapter 7, to the serious neglect of West Indian agriculture. Second, Lewis's model was based on the coming into existence of a *dynamic class of industrialists* (much as in Ricardo's time) who would control and utilise the surplus, as well as play a leading role in the political development of the region. But, as we shall see, a new kind of business class was in fact created which, although making a substantial political impact, lacked the necessary command over financial resources, science and technology, skills and know-how and, consequently, has grown into a junior partner or surrogate of the transnational firms. Third, Lewis insisted that industries pinpointed for development should reflect resource availabilities/factor endowments/comparative advantages. For the region, this meant *labour-intensive industrial activities* based on the relative abundance of labour (and consequently low wage rates) and the relative shortages of natural resources and capital. But the policies which were pursued subsidised capital and not labour. Finally, problems of size and scale were recognised by Lewis and, from the outset, he had advocated a *regional* approach to industrialisation and an *export-oriented* industry. These suggestions were also ignored, with the result that the opposite characteristics emerged in the industrial structure of the region.

As events turned out, Puerto Rico's much touted industrial 'successes' in the late 1940s and early 1950s provided the practical model for industrialisation strategies in the West Indies. As one author aptly put it:

> Since 1947, Puerto Rico has been transformed into a laboratory of corporate organisation, pinning its hopes for development and gearing its social and economic policies to one objective; attracting US capital. Using the unique circumstances of the island's colonial relationship with the United States and its condition as a relatively poor Third World country, a succession of Puerto Rican administrations have offered investors a corporate paradise where wages are low, government docile and taxes virtually nonexistent.[4]

The Puerto Rican model should not, however, be interpreted as fixed or static, for it has evolved through several stages since the Second World War. Here we are concerned with its first phase of evolution which aimed to attract US investors and, to do so, depended on two major factors. One was an industrial incentives law passed in 1947 which gave tax exemptions and other subsidies to foreign industry. The other was the activities of its development agency (FOMENTO), which were directed towards luring foreign investors to the country with the promise of cheap labour, unlimited trade with the US market, weak unions and political stability guaranteed through its colonial relationship with the US. The strategy attracted a number of small and medium-sized labour-intensive companies with an average investment of under US$1 million per plant in such areas as textiles, clothing, food-processing and leather goods.

This model became exhausted in the 1960s when a

number of factors inherent in Puerto Rico's colonial relationship with the US created obstacles to further expansion. One of these was the extension of the US federal minimum wage to Puerto Rico in response to the US labour movement's fear of 'cheap and underunionised labour competition' from Puerto Rico. As a result, between 1950 and 1960 the median wage in Puerto Rico more than doubled (from 42 to 94 cents per hour), while in the US it grew by only 53 per cent. Another was the significant increase (29 per cent in 1958) which occurred in maritime tariffs for US/Puerto Rican shipping. As part of the US, Puerto Rico could not resort to cheaper foreign carriers and had to maintain its US carriers which had won the increase in rates. Finally, a growth in union activity which was taking place in Puerto Rico (partly in imitation of similar developments in the US) put pressure on wages and decreased Puerto Rico's attractiveness as a 'docile labour market'.

To combat these developments, the policy of capital imports was further intensified as a new incentives law was passed in 1963. This law increased the tax exemption period from 10 to 16 years – more in certain circumstances, particularly for heavy industry which was assumed to be oriented towards long-term profits. This gave some impetus to the shift towards a heavy-industry stage of development, a process accelerated by the US administration's approval of special quotas expanding cheaper foreign oil imports to Puerto Rico, as well as providing an incentive to expand the local petrochemical industry. As events turned out, this industry became the centrepiece of expansion in the second phase of the Puerto Rican model, which lasted until the mid-1970s. As Portojas García observed:

> The new petrochemical complex became the fulcrum of industrial development through the mid-1970s. . . the years after 1965 saw the arrival of an entirely new group of multinationals linked to the petrochemical sector, as well as other representatives – such as pharmaceuticals and electronics – of big monopoly capital. The focus of accumulation shifted, as light labour intensive industry was displaced by heavy capital intensive operations. . . by 1974, 110 of the Fortune 500 were operating in Puerto Rico. They ran a total of 336 subsidiaries, of which 333 had received special (and free) factory construc-

tion, training, financing, or legal assistance from FOMENTO.[5]

He goes on to point out that by 1979 as many as 139 of the Fortune 500 firms operated there. Of the total of 1,720 FOMENTO-promoted factories on the island in 1974, 994 were US owned, which meant the US effectively controlled the most dynamic industrial sectors in the island.

Despite the model's popularity, it has been (and continues to be) the subject of many trenchant criticisms. For example, it has been pointed out that, over the course of time, it increased the colonial dependence of Puerto Rico on the US. The new business/capitalist class, which developed under it and replaced the older rural oligarchs, was neither more nationalist in outlook nor more concerned with the poor and the powerless than its predecessors. Moreover, in the process of creating this class, indigenous entrepreneurship was destroyed, traditional crafts, skills and technical know-how became marginalised and the society became more oriented to the consumer ethic of its metropolitan patron. It is true that a relatively better-off industrial proletariat came into existence, but this was amidst high unemployment and a steady stream of migration of Puerto Ricans from their homeland to the US. As much as one-quarter of the population migrated out of Puerto Rico during the 1950s, while unemployment throughout this period stood above 20 per cent of the labour force. Foreign domination of the country's tangible and reproducible assets was such that only 44 per cent of it was held by Puerto Ricans. Its orientation to the US market was so complete that in 1974 it produced '40 per cent of all paraxylene consumed in the US, as well as 30 per cent of the cyclohexane, 26 per cent of the benzene, 24 per cent of the xylene, 23 per cent of the propylene, and 12 per cent of the vinyl chloride. Forty-four per cent of all electrodes used in the US came from Puerto Rican factories'.[6] All in all, Puerto Rico was the most important site of direct US investment in the whole of Latin America.

Finally, corporations attracted to Puerto Rico began to adopt two practices. One was to close companies when the tax exemption period expired and the other was to invest tax exemption profits in liquid assets in Puerto Rico rather than to reinvest them in manufacturing. The latter course was encouraged by the system's orientation towards exempting profits from tax. Portojas García, citing the Tobin Report, argued that a typical subsidiary maintained as much as 80 per cent of its assets in financial form. About one-half of all investments in Puerto Rico (including company operations outside the country) were composed of financial assets, with the result that the rate of return on physical assets ranged from between 35 and 60 per cent. Thus it was possible in 1977 for a group of multinationals (Pepsi Cola, Union Carbide, Digital Equipment, Abbott Laboratories, Eli Lily, Smith Kline, Motorola and G D Searle) to have their Puerto Rican-registered subsidiaries record more than one-fifth of their global profit. In fact, with the exception of Eli Lily, Union Carbide and Pepsi Cola, the proportion of profit recorded by these Puerto Rican subsidiaries exceeded one-half.

This brief outline of the Puerto Rican model is provided as an aid to understanding the theoretical rationale behind the nationalist leaders in the West Indies pursuing their particular line of industrialisation. The next section shows how this policy was put into practice and the third section evaluates its performance.

II: The Practice

In practice, the West Indian approach to industrialisation closely approximated to the first phase of the Puerto Rican import capital model. Incentives were offered to both local and foreign investors (with the emphasis on the latter) and, by 1960, all the territories had incentive legislation and schemes, along with industrial development corporations, in operation. These usually comprised: (i) state provision of basic infrastructural services such as harbours, airports, roads and telecommunications. In all the territories it was seen as the government's duty to finance these and, where local funds were insufficient, recourse was made to secure grants and loans from overseas; (ii) protective import tariffs and quota restrictions on imports to protect local operators from foreign competition; (iii) the adjustment of income and property taxes to provide accelerated depreciation allowances to firms that invested locally; (iv) income tax holidays for new investors or for those expanding their operations; (v) the state-financed construction of factory shells which were then put on sale or lease in the form of industrial parks. These sites usually included the provision of site roads, water supply, sewerage, layout, electricity, refuse-disposal, landscaping, maintenance, as well as postal, telephone and telex services; (vi) state-supported training facilities for the local work-force in the form of technical or polytechnical institutes and universities; and (vii) the so-called Industrial Development Corporations (IDCs), which the various governments set up to regulate the programme.

A typical example of an IDC is found in Barbados, where one was created to provide the following eleven functions:

— supply socio-economic information to prospective investors;
— explain the operations of the fiscal incentive legislation and give assistance in the preparation of applications for these;
— advise investors on factory erection;
— provide factory space on a lease, purchase, or rental basis;
— undertake pre-feasibility studies for prospective investors;
— provide assistance in coordinating joint ventures between local and foreign interests;
— liaise between prospective investors and appropriate government departments;
— act as a consultant to investors during the initial phases of negotiations with private-sector organisations;
— assist in recruiting and training suitable labour;
— assist in making applications for work permits for personnel brought in by firms established under this programme.

In Barbados, income tax and customs duty exemptions are based on a three to ten year period of grace on the following terms: (i) if local value added is 50 per cent, the grace period is 10 years; (ii) if local value added is between 25 and 50 per cent, the grace period is 8 years; or (iii) if local value added is between 10 and 25 per cent, the grace period is 6 years. In cases of what have been termed enclave and highly capital-intensive industries, a ten-year grace period is provided. In the mid-1980s the IDC in Barbados was administering ten parks and based the operation of its incentive schemes on the Fiscal Incentives Act passed in 1974, which suspended the Industrial Incentive Act of 1963 and the Industrial Development (Export Industries) Act of 1969.

The rest of this section is devoted to a brief review of the experiences of Jamaica and Trinidad-Tobago, the two most highly industrialised countries in the West Indies, as well as of St Lucia which is one of the smaller territories in which the process is fairly far advanced.

Given the small size of Jamaica's population, industrialisation brought a surprisingly large variety of products. White rum, sugar and molasses accounted for 28 per cent of value added in manufacturing in Jamaica in 1950; by 1970 a whole range of new industries had brought this figure down to two per cent.[7] Included among these were food, beverages, tobacco, textiles, footwear, garments, furniture, fixtures, wood products, printing, publishing, paper products, cement and clay products, metal products and chemicals. Also in 1950 manufacturing accounted for only 11 per cent of GDP, but by the late 1970s a burst of activity had taken this close to 20 per cent. In real terms, annual growth in the manufacturing sector between 1950 and 1968 was 7.6 per cent, after which its declined to 5.2 per cent (1969–73) and 3.8 per cent (1974–78). In 1978, 79,000 people (about 10 per cent of the employed labour force) were employed and 10 per cent of total merchandise exports were provided by manufacturing.

Between the 1950s and the mid-1960s, incentives played a critical part in achieving this result. In the early years, these were mainly in the form of income-tax exemptions, duty-free imports of raw materials and machinery, tax-free dividends and generous depreciative allowances, but increasingly these came to be overtaken by quantitative restrictions on imports and other trade and exchange policies. At the time of independence there were 50 items on the restricted list in Jamaica – by 1979 these had risen to 334. But, in that a number of different products often appear as one item (for example, clothing), even a numerical increase as large as this understates the full extent of this new policy development.

Ayub points out that most of the items on the restricted list were consumer items, in view of which the 'incentives now appear excessively generous'.[8] He also thought that the period of tax exemption was too long in Jamaica and that exempting dividends from tax discouraged profit retention for reinvestment. 'In short, quantitative restrictions and the accompanying import quotas have provided an unusually generous incentive for import substituting firms, the benefits of which far exceed those accruing from the industrial incentives and other policy measures.'[9] Between 1970 and 1973, 40 per cent of all the companies established were wholly owned or controlled by foreigners. This comprised 33 per cent of the firms established under the industrial incentives legislation and 68 per cent of the firms under the export industry encouragement legislation. Joint ventures were significant, accounting for 35 per cent of the former and 9 per cent of the latter category.

While the need to encourage the export of manufactured goods was recognised in theory, in practice very little concrete support was given. As a result, two lines of export activity developed. One was to export the manufactured goods to the CARICOM market. This occurred largely because the CARICOM treaty had been generous in the way in which it defined the origin of goods for the purposes of regional export. In addition, the very existence of CARICOM meant that there was a commitment to the phasing in of a common external tariff and free intra-regional trade. This regional market also demanded the least effort in terms of promotional activities (for example, packaging and description of contents) because cultural and social links were already established. Until the disruptions of the CARICOM market, brought on mainly by the economic crisis after the mid-1970s, this was by far the most important of the Jamaican manufacturing sector's export outlets. The other export effort was in the form of industrial sub-contracting within the export-processing zones. Under this arrangement (and located in factory space provided by the Jamaica Industrial Corporation) a number of firms in electronics and clothing were encouraged to set up shop and exploit the low wages prevailing in Jamaica. These firms assembled products imported into Jamaica with the sole intent of re-exporting them to the parent firms. In practice, however, these firms were rather footloose, so when the political situation in Jamaica deteriorated after the mid-1970s and the wage advantages began to erode, they were quick to flee to greener pastures, often in other parts of the same region.

The experience of Trinidad-Tobago was broadly similar. Incentive legislation passed in 1950 with the usual tax exemption, accelerated depreciation allowances, and duty-free imports formed the cornerstone of the system. This was subsequently stepped up through a series of government five-year plans which stressed:

— development of infrastructure and supporting facilities for industry;
— the creation of technical schools to train labour and (in 1968) a Management and Productivity Centre to train management; research was also catered for through the establishment of the Caribbean Industrial Research Institute (in 1971);
— the establishment of an industrial development corporation (in 1958) to secure institutional supports for the industrialisation process;
— the creation of a Bureau of Standards (in 1972);
— the raising of protection to levels 'prevailing in competing countries'.

In addition, a series of special measures were introduced to cater for large investments. These included the Cement Industry Development Ordinance (1951), the Nitrogenons Fertilisers Industry (Development) Ordinance (1958), the Lube Oil und Greases Development Ordinance (1961), the Petrochemicals Industry Development Act (1962), the Tyre Manufacturing Industry Development Act (1967) and the International Marketing Corporation (1971).

As in Jamaica, there was a spurt of new business and a manufacturing sector, albeit of a special type, began to emerge. While in February 1959 there were 56 'pioneer industry' establishments with an investment of TT$40.2 million and 2,713 employees, by 1968, during the second five-year plan (1964–68), the number had risen to 139 with an investment of TT$257.8 million and 6,921 employees. Between 1951 and 1961 the annual rate of expansion in the manufacturing sector was 9.7 per cent. During the third five-year plan, the sector grew by seven per cent per annum.

Again, as in Jamaica, most of the growth in manufacturing was in textiles and clothing, food processing and in the assembly of consumer durables, such as cars, radios and refrigerators. Also, as in Jamaica, import substitution was given priority over export promotion, which created certain difficulties once the domestic market had passed through its initial relatively 'easy phase'. When this happened, export promotion was discussed more seriously and here again the starting point was the fairly captive CARICOM market. The process of industrialisation in Trinidad-Tobago was, however, complicated by the country's oil resources. Prior to 1973, between 25 and 30 per cent of the GDP in current prices was supplied by oil. In 1975, after the oil boom when prices quadrupled, this had gone up to 48 per cent. The consequence of this was that although manufacturing continued to grow (it had been averaging between 9 and 10 per cent of GDP from 1950 to 1970) its share of GDP had fallen to six per cent by 1975 and has hovered in the range of 6–8 per cent ever since.

With favourable resources at its disposal (mainly natural gas and petroleum) and readily available foreign exchange, the government believed it could overcome the inherent limitations of the simple assembly of consumer goods and food processing by developing a heavy-industry complex at Point Lisas on the south-west coast of Trinidad. A major operation involving several complex joint-venture arrangements, consultancies, marketing and technology deals with foreign transnationals was set in train for the production of iron and steel, natural gas, electricity, fertilisers, methanol and other industrial chemicals. Still in the planning stages (in the mid-1980s) are an aluminium company, utilising Guyanese and/or Jamaican bauxite and Trinidad-Tobago's natural gas, and a liquified natural-gas enterprise. As Eric St Cyr puts it:

> For more than 30 years the cream of the nation's intellect and the vast bulk of its public investment have been concentrated,

first on the development of import substituting industries based on imported inputs, and most recently on resources in the energy based industries at Point Lisas. This effort we hasten to state, has been carried out with tremendous success in the sense that what it was stated would be done has been done. However, the hoped for dynamic has not come about: the economy still functions very much as it did historically being export staple propelled, and most of its basic problems remain.[10]

As events turned out, the Point Lisas project was plagued by a number of bad business decisions. These included over-optimistic market forecasts, weak cost estimation leading to huge cost overruns and unwise involvements in pre-feasibility, feasibility, production and market arrangements with TNCs whose interests were different from those stated or indeed expected of a 'partner'. One major difficulty has been that the new industries are constructed on such a large scale that they have no option but to be export oriented. Other problems also arose, the most daunting in its implications being the charge by US steel companies that steel exported to the US by Trinidad-Tobago was being 'dumped'. After that, the US authorities put the imports on 'hold'. So disastrous was the decline in oil revenues that by 1986 the government was seriously considering pulling out of these investments altogether.

We shall return to this issue later in the text, but it is clear from all the circumstances that one motivating factor in this venture was the desire of the authorities to find a path of development (and hence industrialisation) which could free them from their traditional dependence on exporting staples. The Point Lisas project offered a way of transforming an abundance of raw materials into heavy industry products within the same economy.

Although the favourable circumstances created by the oil boom in Trinidad-Tobago were unprecedented, Jamaica's industrialisation was also associated with the rapid expansion of a major mineral, in this instance, bauxite-alumina. The relatively buoyant economic conditions created by these circumstances yielded large surpluses and abundant foreign exchange with which to finance this wave of industrialisation.

But, as we shall see later, when the boom in these commodities ended, the process ground to an abrupt halt.

Other parts of the West Indies have undergone experiences similar to those of Jamaica and Trinidad-Tobago. Apart from the constraints of its smaller size and less favourable foreign-exchange situation (tourism was less buoyant than oil or bauxite), the pattern of industrialisation in St Lucia has in many respects been very like that of the two larger territories. St Lucia's industrialisation began with the simple processing of raw materials into rum, copra products, pottery, furniture and soft drinks. When in the early 1970s the governments of the four Windward Islands entered into a joint venture with a Venezuelan firm (Papelera Industrial) to establish a corrugated carton manufacturing plant, this led to a spurt of new investments. Over 80 enterprises were established to produce items such as plastic, beer, industrial gases, toilet paper, batteries, garments and electrical components. In addition to passing the usual incentive legislation, the government also established a development corporation in 1972 through which to channel loans to build industrial estates and to develop factory skills. By the late 1970s, this corporation was operating four estates, comprising 230 acres with 150,000 square feet of factory space. Export processing firms were also established in textiles (Hong Kong and US investors), diving suits (US) and electronic components (US). At the end of the 1970s the new sector was employing approximately 3,000 people and earning about US$12 million in foreign exchange.

As in the other territories, however, political uncertainty, the economic depression and the world crisis brought much of this activity to a standstill. Table 5.1 gives a general indication of the size of the manufacturing sector in the various countries in the region.

While overall the data show quite modest levels of industrialisation for the West Indian countries, ratios of manufacturing activity to GDP should be interpreted with caution as there are several inconsistencies. To begin with, some territories include certain slightly processed agricultural products such as sugar and rice among their manufactured goods, whereas others do not. In Guyana, for example, the ratios in Table 5.1 include this type of processing as well as the

Table 5.1
Manufacturing as a Percentage of GDP

	1975	1980	Most Recent Year
Antigua	9.1	6.1	4.9 (1984)
Barbados	10.3	10.9	10.0 (1985)
Belize	13.7	10.5	9.2 (1985)
Cuba	31.2	32.1	33.1 (1982)
Dominica	4.2	5.0	7.3 (1984)
Dominican Republic	20.9	15.2	17.8 (1983)
Grenada	4.5	3.0	3.1 (1984)
Guyana	6.8	8.1	10.3 (1986)
Haiti	13.7	17.8	16.0 (1983)
Jamaica	17.1	16.1	19.6 (1986)
Montserrat	6.1	6.1	8.8 (1984)
St Kitts	2.3	14.9	14.2 (1984)
St Lucia	7.1	8.9	10.5 (1984)
St Vincent	6.6	14.4	12.2 (1984)
Suriname	6.2	8.6	10.0 (1983)
Trinidad-Tobago	5.5	5.6	8.2 (1986)

Source: UNECLA, *Agricultural Statistics*, Vol. VI, 1984 LC/CAR/G, 132, and government statistics of the various territories.

operations of public utilities like water and electricity, while in other countries these are left out. Secondly, a high ratio in a particular year may principally reflect a decline in GDP brought about by low sales for a particularly unstable mineral or export crop. The ratios also mask the comparative depth and variety of manufacturing activity. Thus the low ratio of 8.2 per cent in Trinidad-Tobago partly reflects the heavy weight given to petroleum exports in its GDP, but also conceals the fact that Trinidad-Tobago has far more industries and is very much more industrialised than a country such as St Kitts, where the ratio is twice as large. In some of the territories, however, such as Barbados, St Lucia and Jamaica, the ratios are more representative of the importance of the manufacturing sector in the national economy. The high ratio for Cuba (33 per cent) does indeed reflect a qualitatively higher level of industrial development then elsewhere in the Caribbean.

III: The Results

This section attempts to identify some of the major weaknesses which have emerged from the process of industrialisation in the region over the past three decades. As it will be observed, the weaknesses are many; the order of presentation, however, does not reflect any form of ranking.

(i) Import-substitution and export discouragement:
As already noted for Jamaica and Trinidad-Tobago, the industrialisation process was essentially oriented around captive domestic markets. These markets were limited, concentrating on the consumption requirements of a small minority in the high income, largely urban sectors of the population. Since these groups were small and well placed to bring in consumer durables after visits abroad, it was hardly surprising that these markets were quickly exhausted. CARICOM then became an important outlet for larger producers, who saw an advantage in its common external protective policies and in the willingness of the TNCs to facilitate the regional exports of their products. It also slightly inhibited the TNCs from duplicating facilities in other parts of the region. In practice, however, import substitution proved to be very import intensive (often more so than the product it sought to replace), thus making the availability of foreign exchange a critical factor in the sector's survival. Export was only considered acceptable if it was linked to the operations of the export-processing zones.

(ii) High capital intensity:
So committed were those who subsidised the industrialisation process to capital-intensive, as opposed to labour-intensive industry, that by 1965, after the policy had been in effect in Jamaica for 14 years and over 150 new industries had been established, only 9,000 jobs had been created.[11] In Trinidad-Tobago fewer than 5,000 jobs were created between 1950 and 1963.[12] Over the same period, the labour force in Jamaica was increasing at the rate of 20,000 people a year, while in Trinidad-Tobago it had expanded by 100,000 over the same 13-year period. The new manufacturing sector therefore only absorbed between one-tenth and one-eighth of the labour

force increase. Contrary to its early optimistic promises, industrialisation has been unable to cope either with the natural increases in the region's population and labour force or with the backlog of unemployment which existed at its commencement. In fact, it has not even been able to absorb the labour displaced from other sectors by mechanisation (for example, sugar) or by the ruinous effect of these new industries on traditional craftsmen such as shoemakers, carpenters, seamstresses and cooks.

The bias in favour of capital and the rich becomes even more apparent when account is taken of the pitiful levels of relief afforded to the poor in the form of sick-pay, old-age pensions or unemployment benefits. Indeed to obtain what few benefits do exist, the poor are required to make far more disclosures about their circumstances than investors have to about their operations, despite their being the beneficiaries of large amounts of relief financed by West Indian taxpayers. Even after they have been established, these companies still fail to provide the minimal disclosures required by law and custom. They are able to do this through having only one large stockholder who in effect controls the company. This reduces annual meetings to simple rituals and the election of directors and other office bearers to a mere charade. As the *Jamaica Daily Gleaner* of 12 May 1985 reported: 'Most companies listed on the Stock Exchange have one larger stockholder that controls each company. . . Because of this situation, annual general meetings are clear cut, directors are re-elected unopposed and the old ways continue to keep stockholders abreast of company developments. They send out financial statements when they feel like it.'

(iii) Capacity under-utilisation:

Surveys have shown that many of the industries established under these programmes operated with significant excess capacity. Ayub, for example, found that 80 per cent of the firms in Jamaica operated on the basis of a single shift, reflecting both the small size of local markets as well as TNC restrictions on export sales, at least outside the CARICOM area.

(iv) Domestic value added and linkages:

The industries established in the early years tended to be organised around the final assembly of imported components and involved little technology other than an ordinary screwdriver. The result was that the value created locally by these products remained very low, thus reinforcing this sector's critical dependence on foreign exchange. Because of the extensive reliance of this sector on imported inputs, linkages with the internal economy were never developed to any significant degree. The growth effects of this sector for the national economy were therefore largely confined to the wages received by the workers in the sector and to the profits received by the local business persons.

(v) Monopoly:

As Ayub points out, the 'degree of industrial concentration in terms of the number of firms in each subsector indicates that production is monopolistic or oligopolistic'.[13] This has produced a number of disastrous results. First, the levels of protection afforded to these industries is extremely high. Because domestic value added is so low, the effective protection conferred by tariffs is much higher than the nominal rate of the tariff. This therefore gives these companies excessive scope to pass off inferior quality products, to institute a usurious system of consumer financing and to maintain poor after-sales servicing facilities. This was also facilitated by the absence of any meaningful statutory or other regulatory agencies concerned with the standards of products in these industries. As a result, the products of the TNCs that produce in the area are of a poorer quality than their counterparts at home or in other industrialised countries. This has led to a certain amount of consumer resistance and preference for imports. Second, because the level of protection was so high and the monopoly power so great, the pressure to find export outlets was reduced. Third, the same combination of circumstances makes for high profitability despite high costs due to uneconomical scales of production. Rates of return on US investment in the region are considered to be substantively higher than elsewhere. For 1980, Barry *et al* reported a rate of return of 30.5 per cent, compared with a Latin American average of 15.8 per cent and a world average of

14.3 per cent. For the six countries for which they had data, they showed that between 1976 and 1981, TNCs withdrew four times the amount they imported in the form of new investments (Bahamas, Barbados, Dominican Republic, Guyana, Jamaica and Trinidad-Tobago).[14]

(vi) Export-processing zones:
Caribbean governments have tried to counter the limitations of their reliance on this kind of import-substitution industrialisation. One such attempt has consisted of promoting the setting up of export-processing zones in which investment takes place either through TNC subsidiaries or as joint ventures. Typically, the TNC/joint venture enters into a subcontract with either a local firm, one of its own subsidiaries, another foreign firm specialising in the same line of business, or a local agent who further subcontracts to operators who work from their own homes. This pattern of investment is different from the direct investment in agriculture, minerals or manufacturing for the home market (which preceded it) and depends on the TNCs ability to fractionalise its production lines and to manage its production in different locations by taking advantage of advances in transport and telecommunications. By the 1980s, the preferred industries had become those with high product standardisation (which facilitated fractioning) and those with different levels of labour intensity at different stages of production (which facilitated the exploitation of wage cost differences). The best examples are electrical goods, electronic material, clothing, toys, sports goods, office machines and, increasingly, information processing.

Export processing relies heavily on marketing arrangements which allow the TNCs to minimise on taxes and levies they would have to pay if they were producing in their home country. Marketing arrangements between the African/Caribbean/Pacific group of countries and the European Economic Community, the provisions of regulations 806.3 and 807 of the Import Regulations of the USA and, more recently, the CBI and CARIBCAN (a Caribbean/Canadian trade agreement) have been decisive in encouraging this development in the region. (Regulations 806.3 and 807 place duties only on the value added to products from overseas production operations, while the CBI expands the range of duty-free items from the area.)

These zones are literal enclaves set aside exclusively for processing imported inputs for direct re-export to Western Europe, North America and Japan and, as enclaves, they fall outside the jurisdiction of the various national customs authorities. Many of these firms are owned and managed by foreigners attracted by the low wages, adequate infrastructure and location near the US market. The gross exploitation of the work force, which is often composed predominantly of women is the order of the day. Some of the most ferocious industrial onslaughts against trade unionism, frequently with the connivance or tacit support of the governmental authorities in the region, have come from this sector. These industries are usually able to close down and move elsewhere in a matter of days and, with so many other countries in the region competing to offer them hospitality, they get away with the most backward industrial practices in the region. In April 1985, five major unions in Jamaica wrote to their government alleging that workers in these zones were being treated as 'indentured labourers'. Frank Long highlights a whole list of abuses, including the frequent failure to recognise unions, poor safety standards in hazardous working conditions, pollution of the work place and the immediate environment, poor medical facilities and in several cases, no medical record keeping, limited formal training provisions with almost all training done on the job, restricted mobility and career prospects and, finally, despite appearances to the contrary, frequently lower pay than in other industries. Long observes that 'with respect to wages, it is sometimes held that overseas MNEs offer better pay packages than local enterprises. We have found that it is difficult to uphold this proposition entirely'. He cites examples in which, 'the weekly pay for unskilled, semi-skilled and skilled workers tends to be lower than a large number of non-enclave enterprises', but goes on to point out that 'managers in MNEs are paid higher than elsewhere in the manufacturing sector'.[15] For this sector, Long's study shows that:

(i) there is a high net transfer of resources abroad. The

       outflow of profits and dividends is as much as 40 per cent in excess of equity capital inflow;

(ii) the net foreign-exchange contributions to the local economy out of current operations is negative;

(iii) very limited inter-industry linkages exist;

(iv) there is foreign domination of the sector, with 90 per cent of the firms owned by TNCs;

(v) the employment level as a percentage of national employment is insignificant – in the case of Jamaica and Trinidad-Tobago less than one per cent and in the case of Barbados four per cent. The rate of increase (1981-84) is high and, given the failure of employment levels to expand in other areas, its relative importance in the future will be enhanced;

(vi) technological diffusion to the rest of the economy is virtually non-existent, a feature which reflects the enclave character of these operations.

As a result of these various factors, many of the hoped for advantages of these firms (such as increased export earnings, significant increases in employment and development of skills among the population) have failed to materialise.

    One interesting feature about the export-processing zone is that a particular type of regional specialisation has developed through twin-plant and international subcontracting arrangements. Typically, these regional operations use Puerto Rico as the US base, with certain elements of the production process being parcelled out, or further subcontracted, to other Caribbean territories where wage rates and costs are even lower or environmental regulations less stringent. The subcontractor agrees to supply the factory, the management and the employees and undertakes to produce agreed quantities with approved specifications. An enormous amount of work has been subcontracted out of Puerto Rico to Haiti and the Dominican Republic in this way. In fact, Haiti is second only to Mexico among the US's subcontracting territories in the western hemisphere.[16] Overall, an estimated 20,000 people, mainly women, work in 750 garment factories in the English-speaking Caribbean and are producing mainly for the US market.[17] With these arrangements the TNCs are able to relieve themselves of the problems of day-to-day management and control of operations. While local or smaller foreign enterprises could do the job as well in theory, in practice subcontracting is usually favoured because of the higher level of specialism invariably acquired by a foreign operator with experience elsewhere.

The export-processing zone constitutes a further aspect of the foreign capital domination model of exploitation of the regional economies. In this regard, it is significant how it has developed as an offshoot of the international restructuring of capital process, in which the TNCs have been engaged in recent years. The aim of restructuring is to reduce assembly costs, as well as the costs of repetitive operations, which would be too expensive if they were located in the industrialised countries because of their high wages. Also, the contract method reduces some of the risks of locating abroad (rising wages, militant unionism, or political upheaval) by shifting them onto the subcontractor. He in turn finds partners or advisers from among the local business elites and selects host governments that are prepared to police or even deactivate the labour movement should this prove necessary.

(vii) Regional industrial programming:

The second strategy to circumvent the limitations of small, uneconomic, import-substituting activities was to promote industries at the regional level. The idea was to take advantage of the larger regional market, as well as to pool skills, technology, resources, finance and enterprise within the region. This, it was hoped, would reduce the dog-eat-dog competitive pressures to attract foreign capital. This strategy began with Brewster and Thomas's proposals for the dynamic integration of the West Indian economies in the 1960s.[18] These placed the emphasis on fusing the resources, production structures and markets of the various individual countries of the region so as to reap economies of scale with a view to creating an industrial sector capable of producing the goods (wage goods and industrial materials) needed directly and indirectly for the production of all other goods. A number of critical industries were identified as appropriate for the region: iron and steel, textiles, plastics, wood, paper, glass, industrial chemicals (mainly the alkalis, chlorine and sulphuric), cement, leather, rubber, aluminium and fuel.

Although there was no actual development along these lines in the sphere of regional industrial programming, the ghost of these proposals continued to haunt regional discussions and efforts, particularly under the CARICOM arrangements. What tended to happen was that TNCs operating in the area would seek in a rather haphazard way to rationalise production and, as far as possible, to avoid duplicating establishments. But unfortunately, as Payne points out, 'a decade and a half after Brewster and Thomas published their formidable tome, nearly a decade since the Caribbean Community treaty was signed not a single "integration industry" exists in the Commonwealth Caribbean'.[19] This sentiment was echoed in the Report of a special Group of Experts who examined the workings of the CARICOM arrangements when they wrote that 'efforts to programme industrial production on a regional basis have been slow and disappointing'.[20]

(viii) Technology:

Another weakness of the industrialisation process has been its negative effect on technology. As we noted above, the technology is usually limited to assembling fabricated inputs. It is also highly capital intensive and this is encouraged by the favourable state subsidisation of capital. This capital intensity is generally inappropriate to the needs of these economies with their high levels of unemployment. The technology arrangements under which the transnationals operate preclude any real transfer to the local economy. There are strict conditions attached to patenting rights and in the licensing arrangements for local production. Maintenance, replacement of equipment and innovation are also strictly regulated in these arrangements. The overall consequence is that the technology utilised in this sector is not rooted in the development of an indigenous technological capability based on the use of local skills and local resources. There develops, therefore, a relation to technology in which people use it but do not produce it. There is no creative social interaction between the local people and the machinery and techniques with which they produce.

(ix) Urbanisation:

The pattern of industrialisation has resulted in an urban concentration of these industries. This has encouraged a flow of people from the rural areas to the cities in the hopes of obtaining a job. With the disintegration of traditional agriculture, the urban drift pushes the underemployed in the countryside into the open. The cities become distinguished by their *barrios*, ghettos and large numbers of young people who have never worked. The earlier periods of this phase of industrialisation coincided with high rates of external emigration. This reduced some of the pressure on urban unemployment, but later, as stricter migration quotas were adopted by the receiving countries, this effect was diminished. In addition, as only the relatively skilled were able to obtain residency visas, this, combined with the flight of professionals out of the region, has led to a serious brain drain.

(x) Infrastructure:

Industrialisation inevitably placed a strain on the region's infrastructural facilities. Although huge airports, deep-water harbours and roads were built – mostly with financial aid or soft-loans from the major capitalist countries and multilateral lending institutions such as the World Bank, Inter-American Development Bank and the Caribbean Development Bank – as the manufacturing sector became more firmly established and the urban population more concentrated, most of the state-owned public utilities failed to keep pace. Electricity breakdowns, improperly functioning telephone and postal systems and public transport incapable of moving the labour force to and from its places of work, became the rule rather than the exception. These problems compounded the difficulties encountered by the state in its efforts to promote industrialisation along these lines.

(xi) Uneven development and crisis:

Industrial development occurred in the region in an uneven manner and thereby widened the gap *between* countries and among social groups *within* countries. Uneven development is inherent in capitalistic modes of production where the market principally determines output, resource allocation, the appropriation of the surplus and other benefits of production. Proportionality in growth and an equitable distribution of benefits, at the minimum, require planned social intervention in the system. In the absence of this, the larger territories, mainly Jamaica and Trinidad-Tobago, became the principal beneficiaries of the regional market. At one stage a group of business people tried to dismantle national market protective barriers within CARICOM countries, but the economic crisis (which began in the mid 1970s) undermined their efforts. The collapse of the regional payment mechanism in 1983 and the failure to replace it with a workable alternative led to the stagnation of intra-Caribbean trade. In addition, the macro-economic and balance-of-payments policies, which were introduced into the region partly with a view to curtailing imports, also affected regional trade. Restricting home demand (for example, through wage restraint policies and curtailing imports, especially industrial inputs and spare parts) seriously disrupted industrialisation in the 1980s. The critical dependence of the new manufacturing sector on the region's capacity to earn foreign exchange through the traditional export sector was also exposed by the adverse situation facing these industries. The neglect of agriculture, which accompanied the focus on the new manufacturing sector, was then bitterly regretted everywhere in the region.

Decades of industrialisation and the huge commitment of resources this entailed have brought no real progress towards eliminating poverty and powerlessness among the broad mass of people, or improving the quality of their care and protection. The limitations of the Puerto Rican model have been known for a long time. 'In a practical sense the most disillusioning experience has been that of Puerto Rico, which, lying in the midst of the region, is as much the showpiece of industrialisation, as of unemployment and maldistribution of wealth and income'.[21] In retrospect, the slavish imitation of the Puerto Rican model, without recognising how much it depended on Puerto Rico's colonial relationship with the US, was doomed to fail in that part of the region aspiring towards independence and a break with its colonial past. Indeed, as the model spread and the territories slavishly began to imitate it, they inevitably had to compete with each other to attract overseas investors. In this sense also, the model undermined the drive towards regional integration, which in itself is an aspect of the move towards independence.

The dependence of this new sector on foreign technology, finance, enterprise, raw materials and components, and the consequent drain of surpluses in the form of profits, royalties, dividends, interest, licensing fees, sales charges and management fees, bound the region more and more firmly into the very metropolitan sources of domination it was ostensibly trying to get rid of in its pursuit of independence. Even in the large, mature, highly industrialised capitalist countries in the centre, attempts to stimulate investment through public subsidies in the form of tax breaks, have rarely achieved their objective. R S McIntyre shows that in the US tax breaks 'do not spur investment – the companies receiving the largest benefits from the Reagan tax program have actually decreased their investment and retained the windfall or used it for dividends. The heaviest new investments, by contrast, have tended to come from companies that pay more in taxes'.[22] Thus, given the constraint operating in the region of a small market, continuing this flow once the industry is already established rarely leads to the kinds of new investments governments anticipate. Instead it is diverted elsewhere – into dividends, larger cash reserves, higher executive salaries, extra fees or other charges to the parent company and larger advertising budgets.

While the process of industrialisation in the region has created many new industries and a certain degree of differentiation in the region's productive structure, it has fallen far short of structurally transforming Caribbean economy and society. It has, however, created several new layers of business people who have exercised a growing influence over the state and whose views of the world have tended to play an increasingly important part in shaping the views of other strata and classes. As the beneficiaries of the process they have developed a collective self-interest in its preservation. By their reckoning, the process has done well, it has given them profits and status even if unemployment, extreme inequalities and social distress continue. Their objections or criticisms, if they have any, stem largely from vague nationalist concerns about foreigners dominating industry and society. This, however, is not the enlightened nationalism of a developed bourgeoisie; it is the expectation of a colonially-cultured petty bourgeoisie to inherit the colonial legacy and to adapt it to its own interests.

6 *The Caribbean in Boom: Oil and Bauxite*

This chapter presents a broad outline of nationalist policies on natural resource development in the region up to the 1970s. Developments after this period are discussed in Part 3, where issues of TNC control and government responses are taken up.

I: Survey

The boom conditions, which most West Indian economies experienced in the mid-1950s and 1960s, depended quite heavily on the expansion of three sectors, namely manufacturing (discussed in Chapter 5), tourism (discussed in Chapter 7) and mining, particularly of petroleum in Trinidad-Tobago and bauxite-alumina in Jamaica and Guyana. The importance of the mineral sector to these countries' national output is shown in Table 6.1. Despite the wide annual fluctuations observed in these data, at their peak oil accounted

Table 6.1
Percentage Contribution of Mining and Quarrying to GDP

	Guyana	Jamaica	Trinidad-Tobago
1960	11.0	9.6	31.0
1970	20.4	12.6	20.0
1974	13.5	9.1	45.0
1975	13.0	8.5	48.0
1976	13.7	8.7	46.0
1977	16.1	10.4	46.0
1978	15.7	13.6	38.0
1979	13.3	14.5	36.0
1980	16.5	14.3	42.0
1981	7.5	10.2	35.0
1982	7.0	5.9	29.0
1983	1.4	4.1	22.7
1984	4.6	7.1	25.7
1985	3.1	5.0	25.6
1986	6.4	–	21.0

Source: UNECLAC, *Agricultural Statistics*, vol. V, 1984, LC/CAR/ G, 132 and government statistics for recent years

for nearly half the GDP in Trinidad-Tobago and bauxite-alumina more than one-fifth of the GDP in Guyana, and about one-seventh of the GDP in Jamaica. While petroleum and bauxite-alumina in the three territories listed in the table are the major products of the region's mining sector, other mineral production also takes place: gold and diamonds in Guyana and petroleum in Barbados.

In the post-war period there have been two watersheds in the development of these industries. The first started in 1952 when Jamaica (and to a lesser extent Guyana) began producing bauxite-alumina on such a large scale that by 1957 Jamaica had become the world's largest producer. The second started in 1974 with an oil boom in Trinidad-Tobago which was so large that it soon doubled this sector's contribution to GDP. Although mainly concerned here with the CARICOM group of countries, the region as a whole (including the wider Caribbean) has been an important mineral-producing area. At the end of the Second World War Guyana and Suriname were supplying two-thirds of the world's bauxite. By 1965 other territories had also started producing bauxite and the world's share supplied by the region as a whole (Guyana, Jamaica, Dominican Republic, Haiti and Suriname) fell to 56 per cent. While the growth of the industry in Brazil, Australia and Guinea substantially reduced the region's share, by 1970 it was still producing 48 per cent of the world's bauxite and 17 per cent of its alumina. It was only after the 1970s that these industries plunged into crisis and output fell so dramatically that by 1982 the region was producing only 18 per cent of the world's bauxite (14 million tonnes) and 10 per cent of its alumina (3 million tonnes). In 1982 Suriname and Venezuela were the only countries in the region producing primary aluminium and even this was only 317,000 tonnes of the world's total output of about 14 million tonnes. Jamaica currently produces 6.7 million tonnes of bauxite (1985–86). This is 55 per cent of the already low output of 1980. It also produces about 1.5 million tonnes of alumina (1985–86), just over 60 per cent of the 1980 output. In Guyana, alumina production has ceased since 1983. Dried bauxite produced in 1986 was one million tonnes, less than half the output of 1970. Calcined bauxite production was just over 441,000 tonnes in 1986, about 60 per cent of 1970 output. In Suriname, the bauxite/alumina/aluminium plants have been closed in the wake of civil violence.

Traditionally the Caribbean has been the principal supplier of bauxite and alumina to the US and Canada, but its stake in the oil trade is also considerable. In the mid-1970s export intermediate refineries (that is, facilities for the importation of crude oil for refining and export) in the Caribbean region constituted the largest concentration of such facilities in the world. The net exportable capacity of the Caribbean islands was more than two million barrels per day (bpd), with the major facilities in the Bahamas (432,000 bpd), the Netherlands Antilles (653,000 bpd), Trinidad-Tobago (394,000 bpd), and the US Virgin Islands (606,000 bpd). At the same time, the trans-shipment capacity of the region was 2.7 million bpd. By the mid 1980s, however, both the export intermediate refineries and the trans-shipment facilities were in considerable jeopardy. The combination of conservation policies in the USA and the encouragement given to US-based refineries has reduced the need for both these facilities and significant overcapacity and dislocation have ensued.

It is estimated that one-sixth of the oil consumed in the USA is refined in the Caribbean. The dependence of the US on the region for this strategic mineral is further strengthened by the fact that about one-half of the oil shipped to the US passes through Caribbean shipping lanes. In the English-speaking Caribbean, only in Trinidad-Tobago is there a significant domestic output of crude oil and natural gas. Barbados produces small amounts of these products but not enough to cover its domestic needs. In 1985 Trinidad-Tobago produced over 10 million cubic metres of crude oil and 8,000 million cubic feet of natural gas. In Barbados for the same year, output of oil was only 679,000 barrels (about one-half its domestic requirements) and natural gas output just under 14 million cubic feet. Recoverable crude oil reserves in Trinidad-Tobago have been estimated at 580 million barrels, or about 10 years' output at 1983 levels. Output of natural gas is projected to rise to 1,000 million cubic feet per day.

The importance of the Caribbean has not been as an oil producing region, but as a major refining centre. The refineries located there have all been financed by European or North American capital. The attraction of the region for

these investments has depended on four major considerations, namely (1) the region's proximity to the US market
and to the Panama Canal routes; (2) the existence of easily
accessible deep-water harbours; (3) political stability (based
on the assumption that, as former colonies, these countries
would be amenable to host governments and unlikely to
engage in revolution); and (4) the existence of regulations
and incentives offered in the US market to regional suppliers.
As events turned out, several of these territories witnessed
major social and/or industrial upheavals during the 1970s
and 1980s. In addition, new regulations concerning oil
imports into the US and new incentives for domestic
producers in the US, reduced the attractiveness of the region
as a refining location. As we shall see later, this created many
difficulties for the area.

The region's most important refining centre is in the
Netherlands Antilles, where Shell first built an installation in
1917 for refining up to 80 per cent of Venezuela's crude.
Later, Standard Oil constructed a large refining facility in
Aruba for refining Middle Eastern and Venezuelan crude for
shipment to the US market. Eventually, oil refining
accounted for over one-fifth of the GDP of these territories
and five per cent of their employment. In 1966 Amerada
Hess Oil started building an oil refinery in the US Virgin
Islands. The incentive here was provided by an old legal
provision in the US, which exempted US oil companies
located on the islands from having to use US flag ships for
their domestic trade. The wider Caribbean, especially the
Netherlands Antilles, Trinidad-Tobago and St Lucia, also
provides an important trans-shipment facility for oil carriers.
The spread of multinational petroleum interests in the region
is indicated in Table 6.2.

In concluding this section two points should be noted.
One is that many of the region's territories depend on oil
imports to service their domestic needs. The post-1974 rise
in petroleum prices therefore meant that until well into the
1980s, these deficit countries suffered considerable pressures
on their foreign-exchange budgets, with oil imports often
exceeding one-third of their total import costs. The impact
of this on these national economies and its role in the post-
1970s crisis in the region will be taken up in Part 3. The basic

Table 6.2
Oil in the Caribbean – Production, Refining, Trans-shipment

Location	Company	Ownership	Functions
Antigua St John's	West Indies Oil (temporarily) closed 1983)	National Petroleum Antigua-Barbuda Government	18,00 bpd* refinery
Bahamas Freeport	Bahamas Oil Refining Co (BORCO)	50% Charter Oil 50% Chevron (SOCAL)	500,000 bpd refinery 60,000 bpd desulfuriser 350,000 bpd crude oil distribution facilities
Freeport	Burmah Oil	Apex Oil Bahamas Government	Trans-shipment
Barbados St Michael	Mobil Oil Barbados	100% Mobil Oil	4,000 bpd refinery
Bridgetown	Barbados National Oil	100% Barbados Government (formerly Mobil)	production
Cuba	Instituto Cubano del Petroleo	100% Cuba Govt (formerly Shell Exxon & Texaco)	3 refineries totalling 68,750 bpd 120,000 bpd refinery under construction
Dominican Republic Bonao	Falconbridge Dominicana	100% Falconbridge	16,500 bpd refinery
Haina	Refinieria Dominicana de Petroleo	50% Royal Dutch Shell 50% DR Govt	30,000 bpd refinery
Jamaica Kingston	Petroleum Corp of Jamaica	100% Jamaican Govt (formerly Exxon)	33,000 bpd refinery
Martinique Fort de France	Societe Anonyme de la Raffinerie des Antilles	24% Royal Dutch Shell 14.5% Exxon 11.5% Texaco 25% CFP 25% Erap	13,000 bpd refinery

▶

Table 6.2—Continued

Location	Company	Ownership	Functions
Netherlands Antilles			
Aruba	Lago Oil and Transport	100% Exxon	480,000 bpd refinery trans-shipment
Bonaire	Bonaire Petroleum	Northville Industries Paktank	trans-shipment
Curaçao	Curaçao Oil Terminal		1.2 million bpd trans-shipment
Curaçao	Shell Curaçao	100% Shell	370,000 bpd refinery trans-shipment
Puerto Rico			
San Juan	Caribbean Gulf Refining Corp	12% Gulf Oil 88% others	40,000 bpd refinery
San Juan	Petrolane of Puerto Rico		LP gas producer
Yubacoa	Yubacoa Sun Oil	100% Sun Oil	85,000 bpd refinery
Penueles	Clark Oil (formerly Commonwealth Refining)	Apex Oil	161,000 bpd refinery
Penueles	Peerless Petrochemicals		10,000 bpd refinery
Guanyanilla		PPG Industries	Bulk terminal
St Kitts-Nevis		planned by Canadian investors	10,000 bpd refinery
St Lucia			
Cul-de-Sac	Hess Oil	100% America	trans-shipment
Trinidad-Tobago			
Point-a-Pierre	Texaco Trinidad	77% Texaco Oil 23% Others	355,000 bpd refinery
Brighton	Texaco Trinidad 23% Others	77% Texaco Oil 23% Others	6,000 bpd refinery
Port of Spain	Amoco Trinidad	Standard Oil of Indiana (Amoco)	oil and gas production
Port of Spain	Trinidad-Tesoro Petroleum	50.1& T–T Govt 49.9% Tesoro (formerly British Petroleum)	oil and gas production

▶

Table 6.2—Continued

Location	Company	Ownership	Functions
Port of Spain	Trinidad-Tesoro Agriculture	Trinidad-Tesoro Petroleum	
Port Fortin	Trinidad & Tobago Oil (Trintoc)	100% T–T Govt (formerly Shell)	100,000 bpd refinery
	Trimmar	Standard Oil of Indiana (Amoco) Trinidad-Tesoro Trintoc	oil and gas production
Port of Spain	Occidental of Trinidad	100% Occidental Petroleum	production
US Virgin Islands St Croix	Hess Oil-Virgin Islands	100% Amerada Hess	700,000 bpd refinery (largest in world)

*bpd = barrels per day

Source: The Resource Centre, Compilation of Corporations, 1984 Cited in T. Barry *et al*, pp. 96–9

paradox, however, remains. It is that of an oil exporting region in which many territories are suffering acutely from balance of payments pressures induced by rising import prices for oil. The second point is that the decline in the region's export intermediate refining capacity is quite considerable. Thus, Trinidad-Tobago no longer refines imported crude oil, but uses its own domestic crude output. The huge refinery in Aruba (440,000 bpd) was closed, and deals are now under way to process Venezuelan crude at far reduced levels of output. In the US Virgin Islands, current capacity usage is only 40 per cent of the potential total.

II: Policy

Until the 1970s, the various Caribbean governments approached the problem of developing the region's natural resources by inviting foreign capital to exploit them. They did this because they believed it would be impossible to generate sufficient capital domestically to develop these resources themselves. In addition, they felt that the constraints of a small domestic market meant that the industries would have to be export-oriented to be profitable and that the only way of ensuring this was through foreign ownership and control. As a consequence, by the time the 1970s approached, the bulk of North American (if not worldwide) capital investments in the area consisted of TNC investments in this particular sector. At the end of the 1960s, all West Indian bauxite-alumina production was controlled by six American and one Canadian TNC, with 98 per cent of the region's bauxite and 57 per cent of its alumina being remitted to North America.

In 1972, when Jamaica was the world's second largest producer of bauxite, US investments in this industry in Jamaica were valued at over US$500 million. As a result, the US was dependent on the region for a strategic military mineral resource, as well as for fuel and consequently sought to play a major role in ensuring the flow of these products. In the case of bauxite, this was done by stockpiling the ore which, in turn, gave the US government undoubted leverage over the market. The purchase of ore at a time when stocks were high to ease the foreign-exchange pressures on Seaga's Jamaica, is a good example of the use of this power. The publicity attending this, together with the more or less open admission of both parties of the intention behind the Reagan administration's purchases, can leave no doubt about the significance of this leverage and the willingness of the US authorities to use it to protect its interests.

A number of the usual incentives were offered to encourage foreign capital into this sector, including peppercorn rents for the large tracts of state lands from which the TNCs extracted their ore or prospected for new sources of supply. Environmental and health regulations were also deliberately kept lax to make the area comparatively more attractive than the industrialised countries, where progressively tighter regulations on pollution were raising the costs of these types of operations. This was particularly applicable to oil refining and storage.

By the 1970s, however, the initial spurt of import-substituting industrialisation began to taper off and a new (more militant) nationalist phase began, in which governments now feeling the pressure on their revenues and foreign-exchange earnings, struggled to increase their control over developments. This phase was also prompted by political and industrial agitation by some trade unions in the area and by the emergence (at the national level) of the first post-war left-wing or socialist movements. The rallying point of this opposition was the proportionately small contribution the bauxite and oil companies were making to national employment, tax revenues and foreign exchange. The criticism was based on the consideration that the vertical integration of the local mineral TNC subsidiaries into their parent organisations allowed them literally to fix the price at which they 'transferred' the local product out of the region. This transfer price was invariably devised in such a manner that it minimised the overall tax liabilities of the parent company, as well as the costs of its entire operations. The view was also advanced that the global operations of these TNCs were highly oligopolistic in structure and that this encouraged the individual corporate groups to collaborate in market sharing, to rationalise the rate at which they introduced new technology into their operations in order to minimise costs, to hide the true quantity of local reserves and to exploit any *single* government or trade union with which they negotiated. The last of these was made easy because the producing countries stood in competitive relation to each other and did not act as a group. It is hardly surprising, therefore, that in Jamaica in 1973, at a time when the companies there were producing the world's second largest amount of bauxite ore, only US$24.5 million was paid in taxes.

By 1970, the Guyanese government had begun to make moves towards nationalising the local bauxite-alumina industry. In 1974, Jamaica's Prime Minister, Manley, began to demand a fairer return from these companies to the Jamaican economy and, to this effect, introduced a levy on all ore mined or processed in Jamaica. This was a novel approach, for the levy was set at 7.5 per cent of the selling price of aluminium ingot, in other words of the final product rather than the ore produced locally. The effect was dramatic. In one year government revenues jumped almost sevenfold to US$170 million. As we shall see later, Manley also encouraged the formation of an International Bauxite Association to reduce the cut-throat competition which existed among the ore-bearing countries, to get better returns on the ore that was mined and to create an independent body for the world-wide gathering and sharing of data on the industry. In 1968 and 1974, British Petroleum and Shell sold their operations to the Trinidad-Tobago government.

The companies reacted to these developments swiftly. They pressured their home governments to intercede on their behalf – much of the destabilisation of the Manley regime in Jamaica stemmed from this episode. They also began to diversify out of the region and, as we saw, the region's output declined rapidly as a proportion of the world's total. By the mid 1980s, the benefits of these nationalist moves were all but gone. World depression and the glut and collapse of the oil and aluminium markets had placed the boom economies in deep depression. So-called prosperity was at an end and a new phase of crisis was once again confronting the Caribbean region. By 1986, issues such as local ownership and control, relations to TNCs, regional and international collaboration towards securing a new international economic order, all of which dogged discussions on economic policy in the region after 1970, had turned out to be far more complex than was at first realised. This, however, anticipates the discussion in Part 3, where this phase of development and the companies' reactions to it are elaborated in somewhat more detail.

7 *Foreign Plantations, Peasants and the State: The Struggle for Land*

I: Introduction

The genocide and institutionalised slavery which accompanied European penetration of the region has meant that the Caribbean peasantry is a modern phenomenon, rather than the timeless agent of older European, Asian and African cultures. Not only is the Caribbean peasantry a comparatively recent transplant from other continents, but the plants and animals which were and still are the source of its livelihood, are also recent transplants. Many of the region's grains, fruits, export cash crops, vegetables and domesticated animals originated elsewhere and were diffused through Europe. From Asia and Oceania came rice, chickens, mangoes, coconuts, bananas, sago, bamboo and breadfruit. From Africa came the watermelon and okra. Even sugar-cane and many of the ground provisions making up the bulk of domestic agriculture were originally imported into the area. When these factors are taken into account, it becomes obvious that the development of the capitalist system on a world scale played a crucial part not only in shaping the economy of the Caribbean in general, but even in such specific matters as what land was used and by whom, what was produced, who consumed it and in what form.

The lush green vegetation, extensive forest cover and deep blue seas which characterise the Caribbean and form its tourist appeal have always been held in the popular imagination as proof that nature has endowed the region with immense agricultural potential. Yet this is not the case and, when the early development of the region's agriculture is examined, it is evident that a system of settled agriculture became possible only because of important scientific, technological and institutional changes introduced at the time. In fact, the clear blue seas which attract tourists betray the absence of sufficient nutrients in the water to darken it and so support concentrated levels of marine life. Similarly, the extensive forest cover of Guyana and Belize gives only the illusion of high fertility, since once the forest is cut and the landscape's natural cover removed, the fertility maintenance cycle of the soil is broken and nutrients have to be added from outside the system to replace those which are lost.

A brief sketch of the region's resources would show that

not only is the total land area small and unequally distributed, but the area in agriculture is correspondingly small and unevenly distributed, with the major concentrations in Guyana and Belize (Table 7.1). The discrepancy in the Bahamas figures reflects the inhospitable nature of that land mass for crop cultivation. Additionally, the island land masses are located in a relatively undifferentiated climatic area, with their soil resources differing relatively little in capabilities. The combined effect of these two circumstances is to reduce the variability of crop growing conditions in the region, despite the comparatively long distances it covers. It is only within Guyana and Belize that truly significant variations occur, although these land masses cover a smaller geographic span than the island chains. In Guyana, a striking variation exists between the low-lying alluvial soils found in the coastal and fluvial areas, the hilly sand and clay belt soils, those of the intermediate savannahs, and those found in the mountainous hinterland regions. Despite the reduced variability of resource conditions in the island territories, it is still often noted that there are three broad geographic and soil categories. These comprise the low island territories composed mainly of coral reef rocks (The Bahamas, Barbuda, Antigua and part of Barbados) which are unsuitable for fruit trees, coffee, cocoa or bananas; the high islands of volcanic origin (Dominica, Grenada, St Lucia, St Vincent, St Kitts and part of Antigua) composed mainly of young volcanic rocks with high fertility; and the high islands created mainly by tectonic uplift and composed mainly of sedimentary and ancient batholitic rocks (Jamaica, Trinidad-Tobago and part of Barbados), where the soils are more varied and complex, dependent on whether they are located on interior plains, coastal plains, wider river valleys, foothill zones or plateaux.

Much of the agricultural land has been, and continues to be, reduced by both natural and social processes. Natural processes include the continuous soil erosion caused by wind, sea and rivers. Social processes usually refer to the comparatively widespread practice of removing (and not replacing) existing vegetational cover in exposed areas. The hilly topography of many cultivation zones and the pressure on land resources leading to the removal of forest cover on hill sides often encourage this. In addition, there is the little

Table 7.1
Population Density

Country	Population '000 (1985) (A)	Area Sq. Km (B)	Agricultural Area Hectares (C)	(Density) A/B	A/C
Antigua-Barbuda	80	440	11	183	7
Bahamas	230	13,935	17	17	12
Barbados	250	430	37	581	7
Belize	170	22,963	125	7	1
Cuba	9,846	110,860	4,992	89	2
Dominica	84	750	19	112	4
Dominican Republic	6,247	48,734	2,730	128	2
Grenada	96	311	16	309	6
Guyana	788	214,970	1,378	4	0.6
Haiti	6,103	27,750	1,395	220	4
Jamaica	2,346	10,992	475	213	5
Montserrat	12	104	2	115	6
Netherlands Antilles	266	960	8	277	33
St Kitts-Nevis	44	269	15	161	3
St Lucia	137	616	20	222	6
St Vincent	110	389	19	283	5
Suriname	368	163,265	59	2	7
Trinidad-Tobago	1,181	5,128	169	230	6

Source: UNECLAC *Agricultural Statistics*, vol. VI, 1984 and government statistics of the various countries.

Figures for Suriname, Netherlands Antilles, Haiti, Dominican Republic, Cuba, are for the year 1982.

controlled, but extensive alienation of land for non-agricultural purposes such as housing, speculative development, tourism, building and transport.

Despite its tropical location, the most severe natural constraint to Caribbean agriculture is possibly water availability at the correct time, place, amounts and conditions needed for good yields. In some territories (for example Antigua and Jamaica), water shortage is a perennial problem. In several of them, because of the region's location in the hurricane belt, the threat of water innundation and wind damage to crops is immense. In Guyana, the combination of topography, location and soil type has forced from the very inception of its settled agriculture, the construction of complex and costly hydraulic systems to sustain agriculture; the natural drainage and irrigation are woefully inadequate. Thus it requires 50 miles of a complex network of waterways to drain and irrigate each square mile of land under sugar-cane in Guyana! In all the territories, flash flooding is an ever present danger to agriculture.

Because of these circumstances, water management has emerged as a crucial factor in the region's agriculture. Indeed, it is probably the most crucial aspect of natural resource management. Increasing concern has been expressed in recent years over the drastic changes which have been observed in micro-climates. This is partly due to the serious alteration of the vegetation cover in several of the territories and in nearby regions such as Brazil and Venezuela. Given the importance of water management, it is noteworthy that, over the years, specialists have commented on the decline in climatological data collection. Most of this now takes place at airports (which are not necessarily in agricultural locations). The older practice of estates systematically recording data on rainfall, temperature and humidity seems to have stopped.

If water availability is probably the most severe natural constraint to the region's agriculture, pests and diseases consume an unknown, but in all likelihood considerable, quantity of actual produce, as well as being responsible for severely reduced yields. The estimated pre- and post-harvest loss is on average 60 per cent. The loss to some fruit and vegetable crops is considerably higher. Because of the mono-crop cultivation practices employed in many areas, the vulnerability of the region's agriculture to pests and diseases is further heightened. As a result, increasing reliance is being placed on chemical means to combat it. However, the prac-tice of using pesticides and fungicides to deal with these problems has raised concerns about their foreign exchange cost, the potential toxicity of locally produced foods as well as the danger they pose of long-run damage to soil nutrients. Additionally, it is feared that this practice may lead to the development of resistant species.

These various issues have to be juxtaposed with the consideration that average yields in almost all the region's principal agricultural crops show a land productivity significantly below other producing regions and the world average. While resources management and cultivation practices have contributed to this result, the combination of available land and water and the effects of pests and diseases are also major contributory factors to this poor outcome.

Prior to emancipation, small-scale farming was limited to the ventures of a few runaway slaves such as Maroons and independent blacks, who squatted on Crown Lands. It was only after emancipation that there was any substantial growth among this group and that the various different individual and collective forms of tenancies, sharecropping and freehold arrangements emerged. This new peasantry existed within a larger rural social system which was effectively dominated by the plantation. Its relationship to the plantation, however, was never that of a mere adjunct, nor was it a simple dualistic one. From the outset there was a dynamic interconnection in which the peasantry formed the core of a counter-plantation system. Because the plantation depended for its survival on an assured supply of cheap (usually seasonal) labour, the development of a peasantry (and hence an alternative set of activities for the producers) always posed a threat to its prosperity. Throughout its history, therefore, it always sought to ensure that the system could produce and reproduce an adequate supply of labour. To achieve this, however, it was sometimes necessary to resort to brute force and, as Thorne observes, 'it was at one time a common occurrence for military and para-military expeditions to be launched to destroy crops that were not grown on plantation-controlled lands; to prohibit plantation workers from rearing cows, pigs and the like and seize animals reared without permission'. This was, of course, in contrast to 'policies of accommodation and encouragement adopted in non-plantation or "settler" colonies such as America, Canada, Australia and New Zealand. In these colonies families were stimulated and assisted to expand inwards and "settle" '.[1]

The counter-plantation system, which grew up alongside the peasantry, is one of relatively long usage, based on economic as well as social and cultural factors, such as kinship structures and religious practices. It therefore follows that a broader and deeper social analysis than that represented in the idea of an alternative agricultural system or set of agricultural practices is needed for a proper understanding of it. It is only through a relatively deep analysis that we can really grasp the inner core of the peasantry and understand the mechanisms through which it has been marginalised, excluded from the political process and denied social mobility. As a group, the peasantry has always *possessed* land (albeit in small, uneconomic quantities) and has worked it with a variety of instruments it has *owned and controlled*. Overall, however, most of the input has been in the form of family or household labour, which traditionally produced much of what the peasants themselves consumed and continued to do so even once the peasantry became engaged in export cash-crop production. This self-sufficiency, which pertained not only to food but also to clothing and shelter, did not, however, preclude the peasantry from becoming strongly associated with the introduction and development in the region of new export crops such as bananas in Jamaica, cocoa in Grenada and rice in Guyana.

Woodville Marshall identifies three major stages in the development of the West Indian peasantry – the two or three decades after abolition when many former slaves were attempting to acquire land; the second half of the 19th century, when peasant numbers grew and many moved into export production; and from 1900 onwards when the peasantry reached a point of 'saturation', with numbers remaining static and in some territories even declining.[2] It seemed clear, however, that by the Second World War a variety of peasant structures had emerged in the region, which basically fell into four categories, namely (i) rural wage earners working on estates or in public works programmes who also rented and/or leased small plots of land, often with very insecure tenure; (ii) smallholders owning less than 5 acres (who may also have rented other small areas away from their homes), producing food for family consumption, some cash crops, livestock, and perhaps also engaged in fishing and timber extraction; (iii) smallholders specialising in cash crops and producing very little in the way of domestic food crops and owning virtually no livestock; and (iv) intensive small farmers, particularly of vegetables, who lived near urban areas and sometimes combined this activity with occasional wage labour and/or craft sales in the cities. These four structures indicate not only a 'pure' peasant type, but also the transitional nature of the group as a whole. Many of the peasants in the first two categories would be on their way towards becoming proletarianised as wage labourers outside the domestic group, whereas a minority in the second two categories would be acquiring more and more land and becoming comparatively better-off farmers.

In general, however, poverty and destitution were the lot of those who fell into this system. This, combined with their exclusion from the political process through which otherwise they could have used their numbers to seek redress through the state, was one of the major elements in the explosive confrontations of the 1930s. The Moyne Commission recognised this when it remarked that:

> Serious discontent was often widespread in West Indian Colonies during the nineteenth century, as is indicated by the occasional uprising that occurred, leading sometimes to considerable loss of life. But the discontent that underlies the disturbances of recent years is a phenomenon of a different character, representing no longer a mere blind protest against worsening of conditions, but a positive demand for the creation of new conditions that would render possible a better and less restricted life. It is the co-existence of this new demand for better conditions with the unfavourable economic trend that is the crux of the West Indian problem of the present day.[3]

II: Colonial and Nationalist Strategies in Agriculture

As we saw earlier, one of the two central planks of colonial strategy in agriculture was to implement the Moyne Commission's recommendation to introduce land-settlement schemes. The other aimed to rehabilitate the plantation sector, especially sugar, which had suffered such serious neglect during the war, mainly through the disruption of shipping and the strain this put on the sector's attempts to acquire the financial and material inputs it needed to keep its capital stock efficient, that by the end of the war a massive infusion of outside funds was necessary to put the industry back on its feet. As we also noted earlier, the land-settlement schemes were intended not only to distribute land, but also to restructure the peasantry and create a new social order for the rural areas. These reforms ultimately aimed to stem the tide against any revolutionary assault on the old colonial order and, for this reason, the policy's major objectives were always explicitly expressed in economic as well as social terms. Hence the stress on relieving agricultural pressure on the land, on finding ways of checking unemployment, on cooperatives and rural restructuring, on the need for fairer access to land and, especially, to support the rise of a vibrant, independent class of peasants. Even the purely economic objectives aimed for more than simply making a better living. They emphasised the need to move away from over-dependence on one staple export and to develop a system of mixed farming in the region.

As events turned out, these objectives never did materialise. Outside leadership stifled the cooperative movement and land distribution was on too small a scale to have any noticeable impact on the gross inequities in landholdings and on the plantation's control over rural resources. The plantations continued their effective monopoly over the land with the best soil types, in the best locations and served with the best infrastructures in the country, particularly access roads, drainage and irrigation. Many of the new crops which the colonial authorities encouraged on these schemes, such as bananas, were intended for export rather than home consumption. This not only meant that resources were diverted away from domestic food production, but also that the country was made precariously dependent on earnings from one or two agricultural staples. The effect of all this, however, was to drive more and more of the traditional subsistence farmers into the cash economy. After the banana boom in Dominica, for instance, nearly 70 per cent of the farmers who previously produced for subsistence no longer did so.

Another effect of the land-settlement schemes was to reduce distributed lands to uneconomic sizes. The main cause of this seems to have been the general failure to come to grips with the variety of customs and laws governing intergenerational transfers of land in the region. Many of the schemes also only gave out marginal lands. In Jamaica, for example, only four per cent of the settlements were estimated to have been situated on the country's most fertile type of soil[4], which made it very difficult for the peasants to earn an adequate living. Also, since much of the land distributed was of an uneconomic size, very often less than five acres, the peasants were forced to seek supplementary forms of income. In Jamaica, 13 per cent of the peasants on these schemes supplemented their income with seasonal work and as many as 24 per cent had regular part-time jobs.[5]

The land-settlement schemes generally involved significant capital outlays. In Guyana as much as US$30 million was spent on such schemes between 1954 and 1964. Under these schemes, the government would clear the land, provide drainage and irrigation facilities and build access roads and housing sites. In the case of the rice development schemes in Guyana, the lands were ready for immediate cultivation when they were allocated.

The colonial administration attempted to rehabilitate the sugar plantation in two ways – by introducing protected entry of the product into the UK and later the Canadian and US markets, and by raising an export levy on all sugar exports. The levy was designed to create three separate funds; the first to finance rehabilitative investments, the second to finance plantation expenditures on social amenities for its work force, and the third to provide funds to stabilise wage earnings in the industry by putting aside resources to finance wage payments at times of low earnings and prices. Once these funds came into operation, the sugar estates commenced massive mechanisation programmes and restructured their operations to increase labour productivity. Many of the existing factories for processing sugar-cane were scrapped and replaced with new, more efficient ones. Transport was mechanised, as was much of the land preparation through use of diggers, bulldozers and trucks. Bulk loading stations were established to facilitate the storage and export of sugar. Cultivation practices were improved and reorganised to make more effective use of the land. And finally, time-and-motion studies were applied to the labour-intensive planting and reaping operations. This all resulted in a rapid displacement of labour, which served to exacerbate social tensions.

Between 1950 and 1960, employment in the sugar industry in Guyana fell by approximately one-third, even although output was expanding.

As the movement towards self-government and later independence gathered momentum, the leaders of the nationalist movement became increasingly capable of exercising an influence over state policies. On rural and land problems and on agricultural questions in general, however, they were surprisingly lax in their approach which, at best, sought improvements through various adjustments here and there. No attempts were made to implement, or even to articulate, any real alternatives. Even the Marxist government of the Peoples Progressive Party (PPP) in Guyana approved of the land-settlement measures and actively sought to implement them. The nationalist phase thus constituted no qualitative break with the past. What improvements were attempted can be summed up under the following five general headings:

(1) Support for the *land-settlement schemes*, while seeking to introduce other measures to encourage the beneficial occupation of Crown Lands. In many instances, this policy was self-serving as it was seen as a means of passing out patronage to particular constituencies of voters.

(2) Support for the *rehabilitation of export crops*. This comprised two major initiatives, namely to entrench the level of protection for sugar in the UK market and to advocate the extension of this kind of protection to other export cash crops such as coffee, cocoa, bananas and coconuts. The period immediately before Britain joined the European Economic Community (EEC) was one of great upheaval with desperate efforts being made to secure the extension of the protection afforded by the UK into the EEC arrangements. The situation was eventually satisfactorily resolved at the Lomé Convention and the regional approach to the issue of resolving the sugar problem and the UK entry into the EEC adopted.

(3) Support for the *diversification of export cash crops*, with the government playing a major role in developing alternative crops through land policies and marketing and credit arrangements.

(4) *Incentives to agro-processors* under the rubric of an industrialisation drive. As a consequence a number of TNC subsidiaries, either alone or in joint-venture arrangements, entered into such areas as canning juices, processing milk and making sweets, preserves, chocolates and other confectionery.

(5) The most significant improvements during this period were in the area of *institutional reform and development*. The major changes included the creation of land and/or cooperative departments in the government; the setting up of statutory marketing boards to regulate the sales of both domestic and export crops; the creation of state-supported financial agencies to facilitate the flow of credit to small farmers; the use of public funds for constructing processing and related facilities such as silos, warehouses and bulk-loading apparatus for export crops; and the construction of infrastructure, especially water-control systems, access and feeder roads and rural electrification. In addition, various extension services, agricultural advisory agencies and grading authorities were established.

Taken as a whole, this approach was neither revolutionary nor radical, for it failed to address the root causes of the problems confronting the rural economy. In fact no really serious land reform programme has ever been attempted anywhere in the West Indies. Throughout the period between the end of the Second World War and the 1970s, most of the emphasis was placed on industry, tourism and off-shore finance, with agriculture being effectively neglected. As a result it remains in a poor state throughout the West Indies.

III: The State of Agriculture

The Moyne Commission's Report on the state of West Indian agriculture immediately before the Second World War (see Chapter 3) showed that the general level of agriculture was low 'in technical knowledge, business organisation and managerial efficiency' and that 'systematic agriculture . . . suited to the inherent circumstances of the area' was unknown. It predicted that if these methods continued, it would 'be impossible for agricultural production to provide even the essentials of life for the growing population of the West Indian Colonies'. The comprehensive reforms in agricultural methods the Report deemed necessary were not, however, implemented and the situation did not greatly improve.

Nearly half a century later the region was still largely producing high-cost export products organised on a more or less monocrop basis in each territory, with the plantation or large estate still of preponderant importance in the region's agricultural economy. The net result was that although much of the region's human, financial, technical and land resources were tied up in agriculture, the sector had been so badly neglected that by 1970 the food balance sheet of the area had gone into deficit. Over 50 per cent of the food consumed in the area was being imported (in Barbados, Antigua and Trinidad-Tobago this estimate was over 80 per cent) at a cost of approximately US$1,000 million, in other words the equivalent of Barbados's total national output, five times Guyana's and double that of all the Leeward and Windward Islands combined. Of the nine major food groups used in the classification of imports (meat and meat preparations; dairy/eggs; fish/fish preparations; cereals/legumes; fruit/ vegetables; sugar/sugar products; coffee/cocoa/spices; oils and fats; and miscellaneous foods), in only two categories (sugar/sugar products and coffee/cocoa/spices) is the region as a whole in surplus. Taken together, imports exceed exports by US$300 million. This amount is 13 times the value for the average of the years 1970-73.

This situation reflects several developments. First is the real neglect at all levels of peasant domestic agriculture (scientific, organisational, credit and marketing) which was touched on in the previous section. Second are the changes in the population's tastes in favour of imported foods. These have been reinforced by tourism, migration and the region's proximity to the US and Canada and to the access this provides through the media to their consumer advertisements. Thus apples, salted cod and grapes became highly prized in the area, although it was in the expansion of fast-food outlets, franchised from TNCs, such as pizza parlours, 'Kentucky Fried Chicken', ice cream and hamburger outlets, that this development was most dramatically seen. A third development has been the movement of the population away from agriculture. Thus, whereas in the 1950s approximately half the region's economically active population was engaged in agriculture, three decades later, the proportion had dropped to about a quarter. The decline in agriculture was general, affecting both the export and domestic markets. While in the early 1960s the region was producing more than 1.3 million tonnes of sugar, by the mid-1980s output had fallen to just under 0.8 million tonnes. This trend was the same in all the major territories. Overall indices of per capita food production in the region for the period 1961–84 are shown in Table 7.2. They reveal the extent to which current output is below peak levels achieved in the 1960s and 1970s.[6]

The region's agricultural exports fall into six basic categories, namely (i) sugar – overall the most important export and produced mainly in Barbados, Belize, Guyana, Jamaica, St Kitts-Nevis and Trinidad-Tobago: the decline in production here has been noted; (ii) bananas – with an output of approximately 250,000 tonnes and directly and indirectly employing about half the working population of the Windwards. Other important producing areas are Jamaica and Belize, but the former's output is currently about 22,000 tonnes; (iii) citrus fruits, produced principally in Belize (half the region's output), but with Jamaica, Trinidad-Tobago, Dominica and Grenada producing some quantities. Output is currently about 100,000 tonnes (that is, 40 per cent of the average output for the period 1970–74); (iv) grain – produced mainly in Guyana, with smaller crops in Trinidad-Tobago, Jamaica and Belize. Although the industry in Guyana has a capacity of about 400,000 tonnes, regional output is only about 350,000 tonnes, of which Guyana produces about 200,000 tonnes and Belize 100,000 tonnes. Cereals and legumes form the largest category in the value of food imports (about 25 per cent of the total value); (v) tree crops – which together constitute the so-called 'minor-export' staples (coffee, cocoa and coconuts) and produce approximately 16,000 tonnes of copra (little more than half the annual output of the period 1970–74), 9,000 tonnes of cocoa beans (about two-third of output levels between 1970 and 1974) and 6,000 tonnes of coffee; and (vi) a variety of speciality crops – these include sea-island cotton, the production of

Table 7.2
Indices of Per Capita Agriculture and Food Production   (1974–76 = 100)

Country	1961		1970		1975		1982		1984	
	Agric:	Food	Agric:	Food	Agric:	Food	Agric:	Food	Agric:	Food
Antigua & Barbuda	118	116	98	98	99	99	98	99	97	99
Bahamas	64	64	169	169	97	97	128	128	120	120
Barbados	119	119	132	132	95	95	101	101	95	95
Belize	–	–	–	–	–	–	–	–	–	–
Dominica	91	91	95	95	98	98	94	94	96	96
Grenada	79	79	117	116	95	95	97	97	96	96
Guyana*	–	–	–	104 (1971)	–	102	–	88	–	85
Jamaica	103	102	103	103	97	97	94	94	93	93
Montserrat	–	–	–	–	–	–	–	–	–	–
St Kitts-Nevis	–	–	–	–	–	–	–	–	–	–
St Lucia	110	110	104	104	94	94	94	94	94	94
St Vincent and the Grenadines	132	132	99	99	97	97	106	106	108	107
Trinidad and Tobago	118	119	113	114	98	97	63	63	56	56

Source: FAO, *Problems Affecting Agricultural Development in the Small Island States of the Caribbean,* LARG 86/6, June 1986.

* Note: Guyana estimate from IADB, Annual Report 1960–61 and 1964 estimate from FAO data in *Background Paper on Food and Agricultural Situation in Latin America and the Caribbean.* LARG/86/INF/4, June 1986.

which has declined from over 1,250 tonnes of lint in 1957/ 58 to less than 10 per cent of that total, arrowroot which has declined from 3,000 tonnes in the 1960s to about one quarter of that total today, and ganja or marijuana. To those in control of the region's supply, ganja probably yields more foreign exchange than all other agricultural products combined. As an illegal and therefore unrecognised activity however, it does not appear in the region's official accounts. Jamaica is reputed to be the second largest supplier of ganja to the US, after Colombia. Exports are estimated at US$1,500 million of which about US$250 million remains in Jamaica. About 3,000 farmers are involved in its production.

Apart from these export crops, a number of local products are grown – sweet potatoes, yams and cassava, which currently average about 220,000 tonnes (10 per cent lower than output a decade ago). Other vegetables and fruits are increasing in output and, although small quantities are exported, these are almost entirely for domestic consumption. A certain amount of livestock is kept for both beef and dairy purposes. Most of the milk consumed in the region, however, is imported reconstituted milk solids. Meat, meat preparations and dairy imports account for one-third of the value of all food imports in the region. The poultry industry has expanded enormously, but is based on imported feeds and other inputs which, according to present estimates, account for 80–90 per cent of production costs.

The organisation of export agriculture is characterised by two broad features, namely the predominant role historically played by TNCs in the export sector and the high cost and lack of competitiveness of the products. For example, the banana industry in the region is dominated by two major TNCs (Geest plc and United Brands), which control the purchasing, shipping, distribution and sale of bananas. Even where small growers produce the bulk of the output, the sales from their local associations go to one or other of these companies. Besides controlling the crops in St Lucia, St Vincent, Grenada and Dominica, Geest also buys citrus fruit, coconuts, mangoes and egg-plants from these territories. Fyffes, a UK subsidiary of United Brands, purchases from Belize, Jamaica and Suriname. (A French subsidiary of

United Brands controls banana production in the French departments of Martinique and Guadeloupe.)

The TNCs' hold over sugar was somewhat loosened in the 1970s with the nationalisations in Guyana, Trinidad-Tobago and Jamaica. Despite this, however, they continued for some time to exercise considerable leverage through their control of marketing and of the production and sale of the machinery, equipment and spares used in the industry. The mid-1980s then brought signs in Jamaica of a move towards divesting the sugar installations taken over by the state. TNC control over West Indian agriculture is also expressed by its presence in agro-processing and in the convenience and fast-food outlets in the region. About 35 TNCs operate in the food system of Jamaica and 19 in Trinidad-Tobago. Using imported machinery, these industries basically assemble imported inputs with the domestic value added derived almost entirely from the local work-force's contribution to these machine-intensive operations. The domestic value added is further reduced by the absence of any real link being set up with domestic agriculture. In Barbados and the Eastern Caribbean, 81 per cent of the value of agricultural inputs to this sector is estimated to come from outside the CARICOM market. Indeed some products, such as corn, spaghetti and bread, rely 100 per cent on imported agricultural inputs.[7] Included in agro-processing are all the beverage industries, which operate either as TNC branch plants or as locally-franchised or joint-venture arrangements of one sort or another. TNC domination also extends to the feed industry, which is important in poultry production. Here, local inputs vary from one territory to another, but usually comprise a mixture of coconut meat, citrus meal or molasses. They never, however, make up more than half of the feed mixes used in the region.

In keeping with post-Second World War trends, these TNCs have become highly diversified. Thus, although Geest's growth was closely tied up with the Windward Islands' banana industry, by the 1980s it had become the largest distributor of fresh fruit and vegetables in the UK market and had diversified into exotic and unconventional items (flowers), value-added foods (prepared salads) and distribution to the UK multiple retail chains. Similar diversification occurred with such well known sugar TNCs as Tate & Lyle and Booker Bros McConnell.

The second feature about export agriculture is that all the major export crops are high cost and uncompetitive in world markets. As a result, they depend on protective marketing arrangements which offer premium prices and/or domestic subsidies. Thus banana exports to the UK and the EEC, sugar exports under the ACP-EEC Sugar Protocol and quotas to the USA, as well as Guyanese rice exports to the other CARICOM territories, enjoy some measure of protection. These protected prices have not, however, risen as fast as the increases in costs which have occurred as Caribbean agriculture has become less and less efficient, with the result that the region is caught in a serious price-cost squeeze. The general inflation of prices since the mid-1970s has turned the terms of trade against the region, partly on account of rising input prices into agriculture – fuel, fertilisers, chemicals, machinery, equipment and services (such as freight and insurance). This undesirable situation is made even worse by the marked fluctuations in export earnings, which is a well-known consequence of reliance on agricultural export staples. Finally, the devastation of crops and agricultural infrastructure by periodic hurricanes has considerably worsened the plight of the region's farming population.

Tables 7.3 to 7.7 highlight some of the features of the region's agricultural economy. Table 7.3 shows what percentage of the economically active population was engaged in agriculture for the period 1970/71 and for the most recent year for which data are available. In the latter period, the data indicate a variation of between 4.5 per cent (in the Bahamas) and 43.1 per cent (in Guyana). The 1982 figure for Guyana, however, reflects the special circumstances of economic collapse and is therefore more an indication of declining activity in other areas of the economy than of any real expansion of output and employment opportunities in agriculture. The sharp decline in Trinidad-Tobago reflects the rapid growth of the petroleum sector, as well as the neglect of agriculture in that country during the oil boom. Over the period in question, the ratios in Barbados, Belize and Jamaica remained stable, with the only other significant movement being the decline brought about by the develop -

ment of the tourist industry in St Lucia, Grenada and Montserrat. Table 7.4 shows the contribution of agriculture to GDP at factor cost, measured in current prices for the period 1974/75 to the most recent year for which data are available. In five of the countries shown, agriculture contributed less than 10 per cent to GDP. These, together with three other territories (St Lucia, St Kitts-Nevis and St Vincent) had ratios of 20 per cent or less. In Belize and Dominica, the ratio exceeded 30 per cent, with agriculture in the latter country contributing as much as 35 per cent. When data on the economically active population are compared with the contribution of agriculture to GDP it can be seen that the

Table 7.3
Percentage of Active Population in Agriculture

Country	1970	Most Recent Year
Antigua-Barbuda	8.7	9.0 (1982)
Bahamas	9.7	4.5 (1983)
Barbados*	16.7	8.4 (1984)
Belize	34.1	35.9 (1982)
Dominica	38.1	30.8 (1981)
Grenada	55.0	27.6 (1982)
Guyana	28.1	43.1 (1982)
Jamaica	24.5	24.9 (1982)
Montserrat	25.0	10.0 (1982)
St Kitts-Nevis	30.8	35.7 (1980)
St Lucia	37.0	29.5 (1983)
St Vincent*	15.4	20.3 (1980)
Trinidad-Tobago	22.8	8.6 (1984)
Suriname	22.4	11.6 (1982)
Netherlands Antilles	1.6	n.a.
Haiti	74.2	64.9 (1982)
Dominican Republic	61.2	55.0 (1982)
Cuba	30.6	21.9 (1982)

Source: UNECLAC, *Agricultural Statistics*, vol VI, 1984
* Labour force in agriculture

Table 7.4
Percentage Contribution of Agriculture to GDP
at Factor Cost

Country	Average for 1974–75	Most Recent Year
Antigua-Barbuda	7.5	5.4 (1984)
Bahamas	n.a.	4.6 (1984)
Barbados	12.0	6.5 (1985)
Belize	27.0	20.0 (1985)
Cuba	13.3	13.6 (1983)
Dominica	35.0	30.2 (1983)
Dominican Republic[1]	21.5	17.4 (1983)
Grenada	26.8	22.8 (1983)
Guyana	30.5	24.5 (1986)
Haiti	40.9	33.0 (1983)
Jamaica	7.2	5.9 (1985)
Montserrat	7.8	4.8 (1983)
St Kitts-Nevis	24.7	22.3 (1983)
St Lucia	17.6	13.7 (1984)
St Vincent	13.6	15.5 (1983)
Suriname[1]	11.5	9.4 (1983)
Trinidad-Tobago	3.3	5.4 (1986)

(1) Year 1975

Source: UNECLAC *Agricultural Statistics*, vol. VI, 1984, IADB, *Annual Statistics Digest 1987* and government statistics

former is higher. This indicates (other things being equal) that income per agricultural worker is only a fraction of the average for the other urban-oriented sectors. This is sometimes treated as an 'index of relative poverty'. When the ratios are calculated in all the countries, this relative impoverishment is revealed, except in the cases of Dominica and Barbados. Trinidad-Tobago's and Jamaica's data reveal the worst situations.

Tables 7.5 and 7.6 show the area of agricultural holdings by size groups and numbers. Two points are obvious from these tables. The first is the paucity of the data. In view of the socio-economic importance of the region's rural economy, it is amazing that no territory collected data suitable for analysing meaningful changes in the rural areas. These tables are therefore as revealing for what they omit as for what they contain. The second point is the manifestly uneven distribution of land. Although the data are not strictly comparable, they do suggest that just under 150,000 hectares of land, of a total of about 1.1 million hectares, or about 14 per cent of the total land in farms, is held by small farmers with up to two hectares of land. These farmers own about two-thirds of the total number of holdings registered in these tables. It is also widely acknowledged that a high proportion of the land on large farms (of 40 hectares or more) is idle. As this is usually the better-quality land, the land pressures are greater than these data at first reveal. In addition, many of the small farms are held in widely scattered holdings, often with marked variations in the quality of the land and this also increases the land problems for the small farmers.

Tables 7.7 and 7.8 show the contribution of food imports and exports to total merchandise trade. In 1972, food accounted for over 20 per cent of the imports in seven out of a total of 13 countries and, in the 1980s, six countries spent over 20 per cent of their import bill on food.

In interpreting these data, it should be borne in mind that the real importance of food imports has often been masked over the years by the rising fuel costs of imports which were noted in the previous chapter. Except for Guyana (where there were special economic circumstances), no territory has shown any significant decline in its food imports. The export data for 1972 show that in seven of the countries food exports accounted for over two-thirds of export earnings and in two others for just under one-half. In the 1980s, in only two of the countries were export earnings from food in excess of two-thirds of total export earnings. As we pointed out earlier, although the region developed as an exporter of food, there is currently a sizeable deficit on the trade account. Despite the high level of food imports, the claim has been made (and repeated by the Group of Experts who examined CARICOM prospects for the 1980s) that 44 per cent of the region's population consume less than the

Table 7.5
Area of Holdings by Size Groups

Country	Year	Total ha	0–0.4 ha	0.4–2 ha	2–4 ha	4–10 ha	10–20 ha	20+ ha	20–40 ha	40+ ha
						Size Groups				
Antigua-Barbuda	1961	14,003	—	3,885	...	...	...	...	1,942	8,176
Bahamas	1978	36,267	188	1,894	1,646	1,843	1,959	28,737	—	—
Barbados	1961	34,197	—	4,573	...	...	...	...	1,700	27,924
Dominica	1961	30,835	354	3,715	—	8,217	...	18,549	—	—
Grenada	1975	18,897	1,016	4,255	1,987	1,915	1,055	8,669	—	—
Jamaica	1968/69	602,674	—	92,764	...	...	...	...	189,385	320,525
Montserrat	1975	2,372	88	382	177	173	75	1,477	—	—
St Kitts-Nevis	1975	16,766	281	1,139	570	—	14,776	—	—	—
St Lucia	1973/74	29,150	702	3,430	2,862	2,589	2,550	17,018	—	—
St Vincent and the Grenadines	1972	13,909	533	2,738	1,645	834	418	7,740	—	—
Suriname	1969	93,383	407	43,928	—	—	49,498	—	—	—
Trinidad-Tobago	1957/58	190,452	—	23,837	...	...	...	...	76,448	90,167

Source: UNECLAC, Agricultural Statistics, vol VI, 1984.

Table 7.6
Number of Holdings by Size Groups

Country	Year	Total	Landless	Number of Holdings / Size Groups							
				0–0.4 ha	0.5–2 ha	2–4 ha	4–10 ha	10.1–20 ha	20+ ha	20–40 ha	40+ ha
Antigua-Barbuda	1961	5,747	...	5,233 ———			...	...	...	476	38
Bahamas	1978	4,246	...	931	2,063	626	357	164	105	–	–
Barbados	1961	18,803	...	——	18,313 ——		...	...		292	193
Dominica	1961	8,667	...	2,115	4,290 ——		2,087	——	175	–	–
Grenada	1957	14,039	...	——	12,265 ——		...	...	...	1,675	99
Jamaica	1968/69	193,359	...	——	151,705 ——		...	...	...	40,662	992
Montserrat	1975	1,247	88	551	496	66	28	6	12	–	–
St Kitts-Nevis	1975	3,535	...	2,036	1,222 ——		161	——	106	–	–
St Lucia	1973/4	10,938	502	4,730	3,828	1,082	475	199	122	–	–
St Vincent and the Grenadines	1972	7,088	706	3,032	3,171	659	161	28	37	–	–
Suriname	1969	16,078	...	1,461	——	14,266 ——		——	351	–	–
Trinidad-Tobago	1957/58	91,116	...	——	14,800 ——		...	...	...	14,800	313

Source: UNECLAC, *Agricultural Statistics*, vol VI, 1984.

Table 7.7
Percentage Contribution of Food Exports in Total Exports

Country	1972	1975	1978	1980	1981	1982
Antigua-Barbuda	1.3	0.6	5.3	4.6	2.9	. . .
Barbados	63.7	58.2	38.9	41.2	28.7	. . .
Belize	79.1	89.8	78.2	. . .	. . .	. . .
Dominica	81.7	88.4	75.8	51.4	56.0	51.4
Grenada	98.5	97.2	. . .	84.2	86.9	83.4
Guyana	49.0	61.3	48.1	43.0	45.2	49.3
Jamaica	21.3	25.6	14.6	10.6	9.5	. . .
Montserrat	47.5	69.4	14.5	11.3	11.4	3.1
St Kitts-Nevis	66.5	63.9	77.2	64.3	68.6	69.8
St Lucia	65.2	60.5	57.7	38.9	43.0	47.6
St Vincent	82.5	91.6	93.4	83.3	80.0	72.0
Trinidad-Tobago	8.4	5.9	2.7	1.8	1.8	1.7

Source: UNECLAC, *Agricultural Statistics*, vol VI, 1984.

Table 7.8
Percentage Contribution of Food Imports in Total Imports

Country	1972	1975	1978	1980	1981	1982
Antigua–Barbuda	18.1	16.9	28.8	24.2	26.2	. . .
Bahamas	10.6	2.4	. . .	. . .	. . .	. . .
Barbados	24.2	23.3	22.1	17.6	17.0	16.8
Belize	24.8	28.3	24.3	23.2	. . .	. . .
Dominica	25.9	31.6	29.0	20.0	. . .	. . .
Grenada	31.1	34.8	. . .	28.9	28.2	27.5
Guyana	13.9	5.9	8.8	6.2	5.9	8.4
Jamaica	14.5	11.6	19.0	6.2	15.6	16.0
Montserrat	21.5	27.3	23.0	20.9	25.3	25.9
St Kitts–Nevis	24.5	20.8	24.5	19.1	19.5	19.5
St Lucia	19.2	25.1	20.6	18.0	20.4	21.1
St Vincent	29.0	32.3	32.7	30.0	27.5	29.2
Trinidad–Tobago	9.1	8.8	9.3	9.3	11.2	10.2

Source: UNECLAC, *Agricultural Statistics*, vol V1, 1984.

minimum requirements of *protein* and that 56 per cent have an insufficient intake of *calories*.[8] This same report projected food imports at US$1,600 million by the end of the decade.

To take the specific example of Barbados, for instance, sugar occupies 85 per cent of the country's arable land and employs about one-sixth of the labour force. Sugar exports and the processing of sugar-related products yield approximately 36 per cent of the foreign exchange earned on the merchandise trade account. This situation yields the following self-sufficiency ratios: beef (six per cent), mutton (nine per cent), dairy products (44 per cent), fruit (56 per cent) and vegetables (61 per cent). In the farming system, over 98 per cent of the landholders own less than five acres and 75 per cent of the agricultural population farm on a part-time basis.

IV: Conclusion

Their neglect of agriculture has probably been one of the most distinguishing and disastrous consequences of the nationalists' approach to economic and social policy in the region. The bias in favour of industry has created a legacy of unattended problems, including inadequate water-control systems, far too few feeder roads, a lack of research and development in local agriculture, the absence of land reform, a continuing drift of the population from the countryside to the cities (or to other countries) and land wastage. 'Amid pressures for foreign exchange and the need to promote employment and generate incomes, the countries of the Caribbean Community. . . announced a Regional Food Plan, to activate agriculture. After nine years', Long laments, 'the impact of regional efforts to boost agriculture remains negligible'.[9] Long felt that his 'study would be incomplete without reference to the continued bias facing agriculture in the Caribbean. . . [and that this bias was] *probably the greatest single factor affecting regional efforts to stimulate food output*'.[10]

Through such neglect a number of under-reported and little-discussed problems have arisen in the region's agricultural sector. One of these is soil erosion. In March 1985, it was claimed that 'soil erosion [was] probably the most serious single cause of a loss of agricultural land in the Caribbean'.[11] Another of these is the increasing alienation of agricultural land, particularly in the smaller territories where property developers and land speculators have bought up agricultural land for housing developments. In Barbados, for example, property speculators are estimated to have taken over about one-quarter of the land previously in sugar. The so-called 'developers' rush in with their plans for residential developments, but in the meanwhile, thousands of acres of alienated land remain idle.[12] If to this we add the land alienated for tourist development, the spoliation of land through urban development, port development, quarrying and mineral extraction, then the impact of these factors on a small country is indeed very great.

The low rewards of 'risk-taking' in agriculture and the disproportionate share of the value of output going to intermediaries and sellers of the final product have considerably reduced the attractiveness of agriculture as a choice of occupation. This has caused small farmers to abandon agriculture altogether and to accord it such low status in the occupational hierarchy that unemployment and hustling in the streets is often considered preferable to farming. The predicament of the small farmer could hardly be worse.

To sum up, then, with traditional export staples becoming increasingly uncompetitive on the world market and without any significant new export crops with which to replace them, coupled with the poorly developed facilities which exist for producing and marketing food and raw materials for local consumption, it is hardly likely that palliative measures will be of much avail. What is needed are radical land reforms, fundamental changes in the legal and institutional structures of the agrarian system, a science-based form of mixed farming, a technically trained agricultural work force, marketing and distribution arrangements that cater for the needs of the broad mass of the population, credit and infrastructural provisions (such as drainage, irrigation, feeder roads and various other facilities to minimise post-harvest losses). Until such far-reaching measures, which actually tackle the root causes of the problem are introduced, the reversal of the historical dispossession of the poor and powerless peasants will never be attained. What is needed is another kind of development, an alternative to the developing underdevelopment so characteristic of post-Second World War Caribbean history.

8 *The Search for New Poles of Growth: Tourism and Off-Shore Banking*

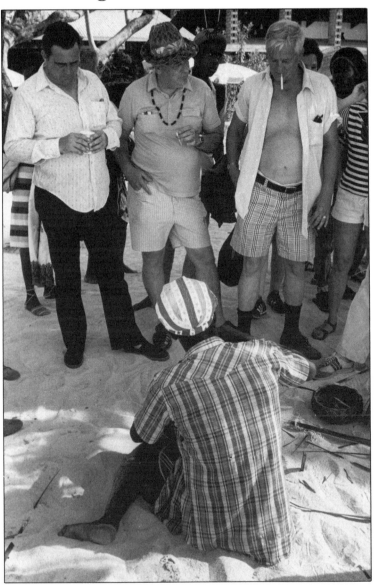

I: Introduction

After the Second World War, the main thrust of nationalist economic policy was directed towards building up a manufacturing sector of sorts. Although the pursuit was not entirely single-minded, most governments in the region, particularly in the smaller territories, were eager to promote a service sector comprised mainly of tourism and off-shore banking.

The stated objectives of this policy were to exploit the region's natural advantages with a view to expanding employment opportunities, raising incomes and sustaining foreign-exchange inflows into the local economy. As we have seen, despite the original import-substitution motivation underlying the industrialisation policy, it in fact turned out to be import intensive and consequently heavily dependent on the continuous availability of foreign exchange. Whenever this flow was interrupted, a crisis of accumulation (with its negative income, employment and growth consequences) always ensued. Tourism offered a partial solution to the problem and was particularly welcomed in view of the declining performance of the traditional export staples sector. The extent to which tourism could ease the situation, however, depended on the import-intensity of accumulation and current expenditure flows in the sector. The employment problem stemmed from the slow growth of export agriculture in the region, combined with the increasing mechanisation and low labour absorptive capacity of the new manufacturing sector which was being created. The rate of increase in the labour force was high and this, together with the migration from rural to urban areas (particularly among the youth), resulted in open unemployment, destitution, slums, ghettos and all the other distinguishing characteristics of third-world cities. These features stood in sharp contrast to the affluent suburbs which were springing up in the wake of the new manufacturing sector. It was obvious that these considerations would have impelled the search for new ways of keeping the region's people gainfully employed. To the nationalists, off-shore finance and tourism seemed to offer this opportunity, especially since the region was relatively abundantly endowed with the resources required to develop these services.

The natural advantages tourism sought to exploit consisted of a tropical climate, soothing winds, sandy beaches, blue sea, and attractive and relatively varied scenery. The advantages for off-shore banking included a location in the time zone of the north-eastern seaboard of the US, proximity in terms of travel time to the US, accessible communications, the widespread use of English and a highly literate population and, apart from the occasional hurricane, good weather throughout the year (which made it attractive for business trips). In addition, it was hoped that both these services would appreciate the added assets of the region's political stability (derived from its longstanding colonial links with Europe) and the legal and financial reliability of its institutions.

II: Tourism Policy

Government action to develop the tourist industry was first taken in the mid-1950s. Although none of the territories had yet attained their political independence, there were varying degrees of internal self-government in existence at the time, which meant that the nationalist movements could exert quite a strong influence over the direction of economic policy. To this group (and to the colonial authorities) tourism seemed to offer a solution to the pressing problems of the day. Throughout the region, however, the policies adopted to promote tourism tended to veer rather strongly towards subsidisation. For a start, a series of legislative acts was passed to provide the framework for the operation of a system of incentives such as income-tax exemptions, accelerated depreciation allowances and duty-free imports. The Hotel Aids Act passed in Barbados in 1956 is a good example of such legislation. Tourist Boards were established and made responsible for the overall regulation of the industry. The duties of the Barbados Tourist Board (formed in 1958), for example, included advertising and publicising the country and its tourist industry, ensuring adequate shipping and airline facilities to cater for the flow of tourists, providing training facilities for hotel employees, classifying and grading hotels, restaurants, tour operators and car rental or taxicab agencies, conducting surveys and monitoring services, improving the image and acceptability of the industry among the local population and generally helping to develop and improve the efficiency of the industry as a whole.

The Jamaican Tourist Board was similar except in so far as it acquired a number of specialised subsidiaries, including the Tourist Product Development Company (responsible for hotel standards and worker attitudes) and the Jamaica Attractions Development Company (responsible for devising schemes, programmes and advertisements for attracting tourists). In addition, the Tourist Board owns, leases and operates various tourist-related facilities (such as marketing and advertising companies, car rental firms and travel agencies) and supports a hotel training programme. It is also responsible for ensuring that there is sufficient investment in the industry's infrastructure – for example, airports, telecommunications, roads, harbours and foreshore developments.

In promoting the tourist sector, all the governments in the region adopted essentially foreign-oriented policies. Not only were the tourists encouraged to come from outside the region and the finance for infrastructural developments sought from multilateral and bilateral aid donors, but the hotel industry, the tour operators and the airlines were principally attracting investment from the major TNCs. In all instances, colonial relationships were exploited, with the English-speaking Caribbean turning to Britain, the French overseas departments to France and the Dutch colonies to Holland in their attempts to lure visitors seeking holidays in warmer climes. It was only later that the US and the Canadian markets were approached.

Since all the territories were basically trying to market a similar product, they soon found themselves locked in antagonistic competition with each other.

This situation was only resolved when steps were taken to collaborate regionally and it was through this concern that the Caribbean Tourist Association (CTA) and its research arm (the Caribbean Tourism and Development Research Centre) were founded in 1972. The research arm developed out of an initiative by the Caribbean Conference of Churches' development agency (CADEC), the association of Caribbean Universities (UNICA) and the CTA itself. By the mid-1980s,

29 governments were participating in these groupings and were managing to maintain reasonably amicable relations, despite the competitive pressures they obviously all felt.

As early critics had anticipated, the industry soon came to be dominated by the TNCs, with 13 Holiday Inns, 9 Hiltons, 9 Sheratons, 8 Trust House Fortes, 7 Club Méditerranée de Paris and 5 Grand Metropolitan (Inter-Continentals) operating in the region in 1984.[1] Apart from all these hotels, many of the airlines, tour operators and other associated services are also under TNC control. The TNCs often function as integrated units, running hotels, owning shares in airlines, providing tourist services and serving as tour operators. Sun Tours of Canada, for example, moved 400,000 visitors on 3,000 flights into the West Indies in 1979 – in other words, more people than any individual country in the Eastern Caribbean contains. Another example is the British firm, Inta Sun, which apart from bringing over 100,000 visitors to the region each year, also operates its own airline (Air Europe) which, with a fleet of six B747s and two B737s, is certainly larger than any West Indian-owned airline. On the whole, the movement of the TNCs into hotel operations has been a comparatively recent development, with nearly two-thirds of those presently in the region having arrived after 1970. A fairly significant number of small businesses, family and individually-owned hotels and boarding houses therefore coexist with the TNCs, creating a certain kind of dualism in the tourist industry.

The dominance of TNCs in the Caribbean is not, however, entirely a product of local policies, but is also a reflection of an overall world trend. Tourism is the world's second largest international business and, with its worldwide structure and dispersion of location, is an attractive proposition to enterprises with the resources and flexibility to operate globally. The links between Trans World Airways (TWA) and the Hilton Hotels, or between ITT and the Sheraton subsidiaries speak for themselves.

III: Statistical Profile

The tables in this section highlight the main features of the region's tourist industry. Table 8.1 shows the number of tourist arrivals in the Caribbean and worldwide for the period 1970–85. As these data show, between 1970 and 1985 the region's tourist arrivals increased at a slightly higher rate than in the world as a whole, with nearly eight million arrivals in 1985, the Caribbean region accounted for about 2.6 per cent of the world total. This percentage was almost identical for 1970. While the data do show fluctuations from year to year, these have been fairly minor, with only two years (1975 and 1981) showing negative growths (−3.0 and −4.0 per cent respectively) in the region as a whole. The highest growth rate (11.6 per cent) was achieved in 1978.

Table 8.1
International Tourist Arrivals in the World and the Caribbean

	All Countries		Caribbean	
	Million	% Change	Million	% Change
1970	168		4.24	
1971	182	+8.3	4.62	+9.0
1972	198	+8.3	5.05	+9.3
1973	215	+8.6	5.41	+7.1
1974	209	−2.8	5.65	+4.4
1975	213	+1.9	5.48	−3.0
1976	218	+2.3	4.77	+5.3
1977	242	+11.0	6.22	+7.8
1978	260	+7.4	6.94	+11.6
1979	273	+5.0	7.16	+3.2
1980	284	+4.0	7.21	+0.7
1981	288	+1.4	6.92	−4.0
1982	287	−0.1	7.12	+2.9
1983	294	+2.2	7.37	+3.5
1984	312	+6.1	7.62	+3.3
1985	325	+4.2	7.90	+3.7

Source: Caribbean Tourism Research Centre (CTRC).

Tables 8.2 and 8.3 give a breakdown of the regional data for 1980 and 1985. They show that the CARICOM countries (including the Bahamas) accounted for 38 per cent of the arrivals in 1985. Of those, however, the Bahamas alone accounted for nearly half the total (in other words more than

Table 8.2
Tourist Arrivals in the Caribbean (Thousands)

	1980	1985
OECS COUNTRIES	314.5	428.8
Anguilla	5.7	15.4
Antigua-Barbuda	86.6	139.7
Dominica	14.4	21.5
Grenada	29.4	52.0
Montserrat	15.5	16.5
St Kitts–Nevis	32.8	47.1
St Lucia	79.7	94.5
St Vincent and the Grenadines	50.4	42.1
OTHER CARICOM	1028.1	1215.2
Barbados	369.9	359.1
Belize	63.7	93.4
Jamaica	395.3	571.7
Trinidad–Tobago	199.2	191.0
NETHERLANDS ANTILLES	577.8	755.8
Aruba	188.9	206.7
Bonaire	25.2	24.0
Curaçao	184.7	127.6
St Maarten	179.0	397.5
BAHAMAS	1181.3	1368.3
BERMUDA	491.6	405.9
FRANCE (DOM)	314.9	341.2
Guadeloupe	156.5	150.9
Martinique	158.5	190.3
US TERRITORIES	2007.4	1943.8
Puerto Rico	1627.4	1532.3
US Virgin Islands	380.4	411.5
OTHER COUNTRIES	1277.1	1446.7
British Virgin Islands	97.0	129.9
Cayman Islands	120.2	145.1
Costa Rica	345.5	261.6
Dominican Republic	301.1	425.0
Haiti	138.0	141.0
Suriname	48.4	36.0
Turks & Caicos Islands	11.9	69.1
Venezuela	215.0	239.0

Source: Caribbean Tourism Research Centre (CTRC)

Table 8.3
Tourist Arrivals in the Caribbean by Region

	Percentage Share of Total		Percentage Change
	1980	1985	1980–1985
OECS	4.4	5.4	+22.7
Other CARICOM	14.3	15.3	+ 7.0
Netherlands Antilles	8.0	9.6	+20.0
Bahamas	16.4	17.3	+ 5.5
Bermuda	6.8	5.1	−25.0
French Territories	4.4	4.3	− 2.3
US Territories	27.9	24.6	−11.8
Other Caribbean	17.8	18.4	+ 3.4
Total	100	100	

Source: Caribbean Tourism Research Centre (CTRC)

17 per cent) and the OECS just over 5 per cent. Within the latter subgroup, Antigua and St Lucia together accounted for well over half the total. The Jamaica data show a substantial increase of nearly 45 per cent between the low period of Manley's rule (1980) and 1985. In 1985 Jamaica received less than half as many tourists as the Bahamas, although it still had the second largest total in the CARICOM grouping. With its 359,000 visitors, Barbados received about one-quarter of the number going to the Bahamas.

If the non-CARICOM territories are also taken into account, then Puerto Rico becomes the largest receiving country in the region, bringing in nearly one-fifth of the total number of tourists. Tourist arrivals in the Dutch territories account for about 9 per cent of the regional total and the French territories about 4 per cent.

Table 8.4 shows arrivals by country of origin. In 1985, the US accounted for 66 per cent of the total, followed by Europe (with 10.2 per cent), the Caribbean (with 9.2 per cent) and Canada (with 6.5 per cent). Annual data (not included in the text) show that every year since 1980, the US's share of the total has been increasing, while that of

Table 8.4
Tourist Arrivals in the Caribbean by Country of Origin

	1980	1985[2]
	thousands	*thousands*
US	4152	5210
Canada	556	511
Europe	962	800
Caribbean ([1])	596	725
Other	947	636
Total	7213	7882
	percentages	*percentages*
US	57.6	66.0
Canada	7.7	6.5
Europe	13.3	10.2
Caribbean[1]	8.2	9.2
Other	13.2	8.1
Total	100	100

Notes: (1) Excludes Venezuela, The definition of 'Caribbean' varies from country to country.
   (2) Preliminary estimate.
Source: Caribbean Tourism Research Centre (CTRC)

Canada and Europe has been going down. Of the five million US tourists who have visited the region, approximately 29 per cent went to the US territories of Puerto Rico (23 per cent) and the US Virgin Islands (6 per cent) and 39 per cent to the Bahamas (23 per cent), Jamaica (9 per cent) and Bermuda (7 per cent). The region's dependence on the US market is also revealed in Table 8.5, which shows that only Dominica and Suriname are less than 20 per cent dependent on the US market. In all the leading tourist areas, (the Bahamas, Bermuda, Puerto Rico, Jamaica and the US Virgin Islands), the US's shares of the market is in excess of 70 per cent. European tourism, however, has been most important in the two French overseas départements in the region, Guadeloupe and Martinique, which together received over a quarter of the total number of European tourists. Most of the Canadian tourists went to the Bahamas, Barbados and Jamaica, which together accounted for about half the total number in the Caribbean region. As Table 8.4 shows, there is a significant amount of intra-Caribbean tourism, with Barbados and Trinidad-Tobago being the most popular destinations. In some of the smaller territories, a significant proportion of the tourists (52 per cent in St Vincent and the Grenadines and 42 per cent in Dominica) come from within the Caribbean. It should be noted, however, that through the structure of regional communications, Barbados and Trinidad-Tobago have become the two main gateways to the Eastern Caribbean and that this factor has played a role in determining the pattern of this sector of the region's tourism.

Table 8.5
Tourism's Dependence on US Market 1985[1]

US Tourist arrivals as a percentage of total Tourist arrivals in the Caribbean	
Percentage Range	
less than 20	Dominica, Suriname
20–30	Costa Rica, Curaçao, Grenada, Guadeloupe, Martinique, St Lucia, St Vincent and the Grenadines, Trinidad-Tobago, Venezuela
30–40	Barbados, Belize, Bonaire, St Kitts-Nevis
40–50	Montserrat
50–60	Antigua-Barbuda, Haiti
60–70	Anguilla, British Virgin Islands
70–80	Aruba, Dominican Republic, Jamaica, Puerto Rico, St Maarten, US Virgin Islands
Over 80	Bahamas, Bermuda, Cayman Islands

[1]Or most recent year for which information is available.
Source: Caribbean Tourism Research Centre (CTRC)

If we exclude travel by US citizens to the bordering states of Canada and Mexico and to US territories abroad, then about one-third of US travellers went to the Caribbean in 1985. Their expenditure in the region, however, was comparatively low, accounting for less than one-fifth of the total. For Canadians, visits to the Caribbean represented 18 per cent of all visits abroad to countries other than the US. Expenditure in the region at 19 per cent of the total was slightly above the average for all regions visited.

Table 8.6 shows the region's capacity to handle tourists measured in terms of available accommodation in 1984. In all 30 territories together, the estimated capacity was 133,900 rooms, of which over one-third were in Venezuela. Next in ranking were the Bahamas, with 10 per cent and Jamaica, with 8 per cent of the rooms. The distribution of hotel by size reveals that in the Bahamas just over two-thirds of the accommodation available was provided by 29 hotels each of which had 100 or more rooms. Excluding Venezuela, Costa Rica and Suriname (for which data were not available) hotels with 100 or more rooms on average accounted for 40 per cent of the total number of rooms available. Table 8.7 gives a breakdown by country. Room occupancy ratios, which indicate the level of utilisation of these facilities, show that in the region these range from between 46 and 80 per cent. Not unexpectedly, the ratio fluctuates from year to year, but is usually taken as a measure of performance. Obviously not all tourists stay in hotels, but some with friends and family. The available data show that visitors in this category range from 7 per cent of the total in Aruba to 53 per cent in St Kitts-Nevis. In Barbados, Montserrat and St Vincent and the Grenadines, this percentage exceeds one-third.

The prosperity of the tourist industry depends not only on how many tourists arrive in the region but also on how long they stay and how much they spend when they are there. Data for 1984 show that, on average, tourists tended to stay between three and five nights in Puerto Rico, but between eight and nine nights in places like Jamaica, Grenada, St Lucia and St Vincent and the Grenadines. On average, tourists from Europe stay longest, followed by Canada and then the US, which is hardly surprising given the differences in costs and distances. About half the tourists arrive on cruise liners, of which 25 per cent go to the Bahamas, 18 per cent to the US Virgin Islands and 12 per cent to Puerto Rico.

Table 8.8 shows that in 1985 tourists spent a total

Table 8.6
Tourist Accommodation by Country 1984

Country	Number of Rooms	
	Total	In hotels with 100+ rooms
Anguilla	390	–
Antigua-Barbuda	2560	853
Aruba	2460	1983
Bahamas	13790	8766
Barbados	7400	2556
Belize	1490	–
Bermuda	4850	1540
Bonaire	460	225
British Virgin Islands	1150	121
Cayman Islands	2010	339
Costa Rica	3580	n.a.
Curaçao	1760	964
Dominica	340	–
Dominican Republic	4300	3203
Grenada	580	184
Guadeloupe	3340	1760
Haiti	3600	455
Jamaica	11280	5497
Martinique	2750	1131
Montserrat	280	–
Puerto Rico	7420	5724
St Kitts–Nevis	710	138
St Lucia	1700	820
St Maarten	1910	1516
St Vincent and the Grenadines	700	–
Suriname	640	n.a.
Trinidad-Tobago	1750	918
Turks and Caicos Islands	330	–
US Virgin Islands	4370	2191
Venezuela	46000	n.a.
Total	133900	

Source: Caribbean Tourism Research Centre (CTRC).

Table 8.7
Number of Rooms in Hotels with 100 or More Rooms as a
Percentage of Total Number of Rooms in Country

Percentage range	Country
70 per cent or more	Aruba, Dominican Republic, Puerto Rico, St Maarten
60–69 per cent	Bahamas
49–59 per cent	Bonaire, Curaçao, Guadeloupe, Jamaica, Martinique, St Lucia, Trinidad-Tobago
20–39 per cent	Antigua–Barbuda, Barbados, Bermuda, Grenada
10–19 per cent	British Virgin Islands, Cayman Islands, Haiti, St Kitts-Nevis
Nil	Anguilla, Belize, Montserrat, Dominica, St Vincent and the Grenadines, Turks and Caicos Islands

Source: Caribbean Tourism Research Centre (CTRC)

of US$5,000 million (compared with US$3,286 million in 1979). Of this, 18 per cent went to the Bahamas (US$870 million), 11 per cent to Puerto Rico (US$689 million), 9 per cent to Jamaica, 8 per cent to the US Virgin Islands and about 6 per cent each to Barbados and the Dominican Republic. Data on employment generated by tourism for selected countries are shown in Table 8.9. While on average only 3 per cent of the total regional labour force finds employment through tourism, in individual territories the percentage ranges from 49 per cent in the Bahamas to 1 per cent in Venezuela. In six of the countries for which data are available employment generated by this sector exceeded one-eighth of the total labour force.

The contribution of tourism to the GDP of selected countries is shown in Table 8.10. This indicates there are wide variations of between 5 and 36 per cent, thus suggesting an uneven dependence on tourism among the various territories. Although data are not available for all the countries, they tend to fall into one of three broad groupings. The first consists of countries such as Jamaica, the

Table 8.8
Tourism: Estimates of Visitor Expenditure (US$ million)

	1979	1985
Anguilla	1.0	8.9
Antigua-Barbuda	36.3	83.6
Aruba	108.7	120.8
Bahamas	561.7	870.0
Barbados	201.5	309.0
Belize	7.4	11.1
Bermuda	240.1	356.7
Bonaire	3.4	4.4
British Virgin Islands	38.6	19.7
Cayman Islands	36.2	85.5
Costa Rica	72.9	113.6
Curaçao	119.9	70.6
Dominica	2.3	4.5
Dominican Republic	130.8	297.4
Grenada	14.3	24.4
Guadeloupe	72.3	95.0
Haiti	62.8	69.2
Jamaica	194.3	406.8
Martinique	71.5	92.8
Montserrat	3.7	7.7
Puerto Rico	560.9	689.2
St Kitts–Nevis	6.0	31.0
St Lucia	33.0	55.7
St Maarten	87.2	150.0
St Vincent and the Grenadines	10.5	23.0
Suriname	18.2	20.0
Trinidad–Tobago	110.0	197.3
Turks & Caicos Islands	3.4	12.2
US Virgin Islands	299.1	531.5
Venezuela	178.0	197.0
Total US$ million	3286	5031.0

Source: Caribbean Tourism Research Centre (CTRC)

Table 8.9
Employment in Tourism

Country	Employment generated by tourism as percentage of employed labour force
Antigua-Barbuda	23.6
Dominica	5.3
St Kitts-Nevis	13.1
St Lucia	18.2
Barbados	14.0
Jamaica	2.3
Trinidad-Tobago	1.5
Puerto Rico	5.2
US Virgin Islands	32.6
Bahamas	48.7
Costa Rica	1.7
Venezuela	1.0

Source: Caribbean Tourism Research Centre (CTRC).

Table 8.10
Percentage Contribution of Tourism to GDP (1)

Country	Per cent
Antigua-Barbuda	36
Bahamas	23
Barbados	10
Bermuda	9
Grenada	5
Montserrat	7
St Kitts-Nevis	5
St Lucia	19
US Virgin Islands	32

Source: Caribbean Tourism Research Centre (CTRC)

(1) These estimates are not strictly comparable due to different methods of compilation. The data are from 1979, except for Barbados (1985).

Dominican Republic, Trinidad-Tobago, Venezuela and Puerto Rico, where although tourism is important as a foreign-exchange earner (in Jamaica it is the largest source of foreign exchange) or generator of income and employment, the country also possesses some prized mineral resources which has enabled it to attain a significant level of industrial diversification and has retained a fairly important agricultural sector. Second, is the group of countries such as the Bahamas, Bermuda and the Cayman Islands, where the dependence on tourism is very high and where other economic activities, with the exception of services like off-shore banking, are insignificant. Between these two groups is a middle range of countries (including Barbados) in which, although tourism contributes significantly to employment and foreign-exchange earnings, its overall importance to the GDP is lessened by a modest development of light industry and the existence of at least one important agricultural staple.

IV: The Results

The unevenness of tourist development in the region and the individual countries' varying levels of dependence on the industry should be borne in mind in evaluating tourism's regional achievements. None the less, because all the territories have tried to market the same product in roughly similar ways, the absence of properly coordinated development has resulted in increased social costs for the region as a whole, despite cooperation through the Caribbean Tourism Research Centre (CTRC). These increased social costs have arisen from the under-utilisation of infrastructure and other capacity at the regional level and from the relative disadvantage at which the smaller territories are placed by their less accessible airline links to the major markets and by having fewer resources with which to promote and market tourism in the expensive cities of Europe and North America. In the early years of the industry, Antigua, Barbados and Trinidad-Tobago had an advantage over the other territories because their airports could accommodate large jets, whereas those of the other territories could only accommodate very much smaller propellered aircraft. So greatly did the so-called 'gateway' territories benefit from this situation that smaller countries like St Lucia, St Kitts-Nevis and Grenada were eventually forced into upgrading their airports to retain their competitive standing.

For much of the period under review, there was a single-minded focus on marketing the industry in Europe and North America. The main points of promotion were sun, scenery, beaches, water sports and other outdoor pursuits, which were targeted specifically at the up-market cruise liners, conventions, business travellers and leisured classes who could afford holidays in the sun. In its early years, the industry catered predominantly for these high-income leisured groups (often seeking to escape the harsh winters in the north) and it was only with the increase in incomes in Europe and North America and the advent of cut-price travel that tourists in the middle-income brackets were attracted to the region. From the increasing numbers of holiday-makers who started pouring into the region despite minimal efforts at promotion, it soon became apparent that there was tremendous untapped potential and that if this was to be fully exploited, the industry would have to abandon its colonial and cultural bias.

Although TNC domination of the industry has been continual, some attempts have been made to modify its character, particularly in the hotel sector. These have taken the form of governments entering into joint-ventures with TNCs and, in some cases, as in Jamaica during Manley's period of office, even nationalising them. In general, the TNCs have not resisted these developments, for the joint-venture/management-contract types of arrangements which tend to be preferred seem to work to their economic advantage. Where nationalisation has occurred, the assets have been purchased rather than confiscated and even in cases where the TNCs have not directly owned the concern, care has been taken to avoid the possibility of complications arising while the TNCs continue to receive income. In addition, with the government as a partner, the TNC is protected from the somewhat negative social image the big hotel operations have in these countries and by the incomes these arrangements inevitably ensure to the management. It is hardly surprising that such arrangements have a negative effect on efficiency. Barry and his associates note that 'in almost every case in which a TNC operation has been unsatisfactory in the Caribbean, the TNC had no direct financial involvement in the hotel. In contrast, in all cases where the hotel keeping experience was satisfactory, the TNC had direct financial input'.[2]

One of the principal reasons why governments have consistently supported and promoted tourism in the region has been the expectation that it would generate scarce foreign exchange. Experience has shown, however, that there are a number of major leakages out of this sector, of which the most important have been (1) the high foreign-exchange content of the original investment in the hotel and infrastructure, caused largely by the incapacity of local industries to supply the various construction materials, furnishings, heavy-duty equipment and other machinery needed for building the hotels, airports, harbours and telephone systems. Sometimes this leakage has been partly eased through investment in infrastructure, for tourism has been a popular source of grants and aid by both bilateral and multilateral donors to these countries; (2) the high import content of transporting tourists both into and within the area. Most of the airlines and all the aircraft and cruise liners are either foreign owned or purchased from abroad. In terms of local travel, with a few exceptions such as Trinidad-Tobago, both the vehicles and the fuel they use are imported; (3) the huge amounts of foreign exchange used to pay for the various consultants, architects and builders who routinely win the contracts to build and service these facilities and for the management recruited from abroad to run the enterprises or to train those who will run them; (4) the repatriation abroad of profits, fees and other locally-earned incomes which governments have facilitated through their wish to keep the high foreign participation in local industry intact; (5) the high import content of food and beverages served to tourists. A study conducted by the CTRC in Grenada, St Vincent and St Lucia shows that 54 per cent of the food, 62.5 per cent of the beverages, 70 per cent of the meat, between 20 and 25 per cent of the fruit and vegetables and almost all the dairy products consumed by tourists were imported; and (6) the high foreign-exchange cost of promoting the industry abroad, particularly on television.

Leakages also occur through a number of illegal channels, the most important of which are the movement of foreign exchange through the black market (or at least outside the banking system) and the paying of hotel bills and other expenses to tour operators in Europe and North America who then fail to remit the full amount required by law. In Antigua, for example, 95 per cent of all hotel reservations are made from abroad and in the Bahamas (according to a study cited by Barry *et al*) 81 cents out of every tourist dollar spent there are leaked out of the economy.

Despite the leakages, however, some local earnings, derived mainly from construction and maintenance work, are retained in the economy. A certain amount of employment and income is also generated by tourist-related services (night clubs, taxis, banks, shops and restaurants) and by the maintenance of the tourist infrastructure (aircraft, motor vehicles and pleasure boats). In Jamaica, for example, the ratio of direct to indirect employment in this sector is estimated at 1:1.25. In addition, a number of different taxes are levied – company taxes (although these vary depending on what incentives are in operation), personal taxes on those who derive direct and indirect income from the industry, import duties, airport taxes and taxes on hotel rooms and services. While it has been claimed (and with some justification) that the tourist industry has placed enormous budgetary pressure on the West Indian governments which have had to provide the infrastructure, the local population often benefits as well and territories in which the tourist industry is well developed tend to have comparatively high levels of public services.

In addition to questions of ownership and control, the marketing of the product and foreign-exchange earnings, there are a number of miscellaneous economic considerations which have also to be taken into account in evaluating tourism in the region. One of these is the inflationary impact of tourism on local economies. Although no precise measurements have been made, it appears that the prices of services and food in the tourist sector on average rise faster than other prices, largely because it is assumed that the incomes of tourists at home rise faster than those of the local population and therefore the tourist traffic can bear more. When this occurs it also raises the prices of items such as food, transport and clothing for the local population. A related practice is that of pricing products in the tourist sector in US dollars, which tends to induce inflation when the US rate rises against the local currency exchange rate. Where, as in the West Indies, local currencies are tied to the US dollar, a rising US dollar relative to other currencies acts as a disincentive to tourists coming from Europe, Canada and elsewhere. Given that between 1979 and 1984 the British pound depreciated against the US dollar by about 58 per cent, the Canadian dollar by 11 per cent, the French franc by 105 per cent and the German mark by 56 per cent, the impact of this factor is obviously quite considerable.

Another consideration is that, having been built early on, the TNC-controlled hotels have taken over some of the best beaches and scenic locations in these territories. In addition, they have given an impetus to new ventures by other TNCs, which seem to support the industry as a whole. Examples of these include fast-food chains, car-rental agencies and restaurants. In all of this, however, the hotel industry remains the most central element in the performance of the region's tourist industry. Table 8.11, which is based on an article by Bell, is particularly instructive in this regard.[3] These data indicate that of the 13 geographical areas listed in the world survey, the Caribbean had the lowest net income per room (US$150 against a world average of US$2,913) while the second lowest of the 13 regions had a net income six times larger; that the Caribbean's productivity index (2.54) was also the lowest, with the world average being one-third larger (3.38); that of the 13 regions, the Caribbean had the highest cost of electricity, the second highest cost of water and a well above world average cost of fuel; and that maintenance charges per room at US$2,076 were the highest in the world, compared with a world average of US$1,526.

The poor performance indicators revealed here must, however, be seen in the context of two further features, first that the industry is a major buyer on the local market as well as an importer and second that the tourist industry charges excessive commissions. Bell refers to numerous complaints about overcharging by local distributors and manufacturers.[4]

Table 8.11
Operational Factors in the Hotel Industry

	Sales Per Avail. Room	Net Income Per Avail. Room	Productivity Index	Admin. & Gen. Per Avail. Room	Marketing Per Avail. Room	Maint. Per Avail. Room	Fuel Cost Per Occup. Room	Elec. Cost Per Occup. Room	Cost of Water Per Occup. Room
World Average	26,267	US$2,913	3.53	US$2,796	US$877	US$1,526	US$1.04	US$3.24	US$0.49
Caribbean	23,619	150	2.54	3,015	941	2,076	1.28	7.55	0.83
USA	25,933	1,383	2.98	2,769	1,223	1,355	0.91	3.09	0.31
Canada	25,769	1,762	2.76	2,233	1,257	1,506	0.80	1.71	0.32
Northern Africa	30,874	3,932	5.60	2,392	827	1,918	0.48	1.57	0.04
Southern Africa	20,428	1,648	3.54	3,233	575	1,578	1.15	3.94	1.09
Middle East	35,183	5,532	3.14	4,273	1,086	2,006	0.80	2.60	0.73
Asia	21,732	3,797	4.65	2,295	780	1,264	0.80	4.97	0.47
Far East	33,181	9,273	6.07	3,379	1,022	1,545	1.03	6.01	0.28
Pacific	34,157	3,589	3.24	3,138	1,110	1,714	0.97	3.03	0.30
Continental Europe	22,542	1,049	2.63	2,382	809	1,294	1.25	2.05	0.58
Scandinavia	20,184	903	2.73	1,364	380	996	1.51	1.14	0.53
United Kingdom	20,178	1,967	2.91	2,791	395	1,011	1.87	1.87	0.32
Latin America	27,692	2,889	3.16	3,065	1,002	1,586	0.67	2.57	0.57

Source: Cited in J. Bell, 'The Operational Constraints Facing Caribbean Tourism Establishments and the Resulting Impact on the Financial Visibility'', Caribbean Hotel Association, Document No. CTMC/6, December 1983.

In the case of local distributors, middlemen and import regulations are identified as the major reasons for overpricing, while in the case of the manufacturers it is the inefficient scale of operations in the manufacturing sector and the monopoly status of many of the producers. On excessive commissions Bell cites the time 'not too long ago' when the hotels paid 10 per cent to the retail travel agent, an override of a further 5 per cent to the wholesaler and a negotiated flat fee to the representative. By 1983 these charges had gone up to 13, 20 and 5 per cent respectively. In addition, the cost of credit-card handling and commission had risen to between three and five per cent, with the result that, on average, the Caribbean hotel industry was paying out between 25 and 30 cents in every dollar in the marketing of its product.

Although this high-cost inefficiency of the tourist industry is also apparent in other areas of economic activity in the Caribbean, such as export cash crops and the manufacturing sector, the industry's negative economic features are further complicated by several socio-political factors. One of these derives from the industry's original upper-class colonial bias, which promoted the region as a winter retreat for the rich. Even when its orientation shifted towards the US market, the emphasis was not on mass marketing as such. It was not until later, with the arrival of package tours and cheap cruises that a serious cost-consciousness developed, but by then the industry was already locked into high-cost structures it could not easily break out of without drastic consequences for the returns to resources currently invested in the industry.

A second socio-political factor affecting the industry is its excessive concentration on the US market. Not only has this made it vulnerable to the vicissitudes of the US economy and to changes in fashion, but has also enabled the US government and media to destabilise particular Caribbean countries through adverse publicity and hostile foreign-policy statements. The best-known examples of such conduct occurred during Manley's period in Jamaica and Bishop's period in Grenada.

The third factor is environmental. The industry inevitably generates a certain amount of pollution, for tourists are bound to leave litter on the streets and beaches. While attempts have been made to keep these areas tidy, the most important of all tourist attractions, the Caribbean Sea, is itself under threat. As one commentator has observed:

> The tourist image is still valid: white sand beaches, fringed with palms, cooled by lucid blue water. But another reality is creeping up on the vision of paradise. On any given day, 100 loaded tankers carrying 5 million barrels of crude are likely to be churning their way through the narrow shipping lanes of the Caribbean. An estimated 6.7 per cent of the regional oil production ends up in the sea.[5]

The author goes on to point out that in 1977, 77 million barrels of oil were spilled from oil platforms. If to this we further add the 7 million or so barrels which are lost through washing and emptying tankers, all the waste 30 million people dump into the sea, the spillage from hotels and other establishments on the sea fronts, the untreated discharges from cement works and from chemical and fertiliser plants, we get some idea of the scale of the problem.

These environmental dangers do not exist only in relation to the sea. Over 50 per cent of the region's forests have been lost since colonisation, with the rate of forest depletion currently running in excess of ten times the rate of replacement. The consequences which include soil erosion, flooding, land slips and marine pollution, are increasingly being brought to the public's attention by concerned persons and organisations and, in 1981, 27 countries in the region agreed to participate in a Caribbean Action Plan under the auspices of the United Nations Environmental Programme. This has led to two treaties – the one dealing with oil spills was signed in Colombia in 1983.

The final factor is concerned with the industry's image. In the past, the local population was always portrayed as menial and servile, living for the tourists and willing to do anything to make them happy. Because the tourists were overwhelmingly white, this tended to reinforce negative racial stereotypes among both parties and, as a consequence, although important to the region, tourism was not easily accepted by the population at large. While glad of the opportunity to earn an income, local people also resented the second-class status it seemed to confer on them. In recent

165

years, governments have tried to offset this negative association by developing 'courtesy corps' and emphasising the
importance of the industry to the local population through
the media. On the whole, however, the results have been
disappointing and in its *Economic and Social Survey* of 1984,
the Jamaican Government acknowledged that it had had to
launch 'an aggressive campaign on local radio and television
against tourist harassment as a number of surveys had shown
that this was the major complaint of visitors to the island'.[6]
Also, throughout the region, tourism and its associated entertainment industry have caused a significant growth in male
and female prostitution, but governments and other social
agencies have generally turned a blind eye to this development, with only occasional public outcries. Finally, there is
much concern over the continued seasonality of the tourist
trade, which, reflecting its earlier orientation as a winter
home for northerners, shows a marked division between a
high season (mid-December to mid-April) and a low season.
Efforts to even out these swings have not been particularly
successful.

In the late 1970s it became popular to promote the
industry in terms of the region's local culture and artifacts,
which gave rise to a number of publicity campaigns on local
foods, art, sculpture and literature. The overall approach,
however, essentially remained one of promoting Caribbean
exotica, with heavy emphasis on winning favourable journal-
istic comments in the foreign press.

> During 1984, the Jamaica Tourist Board diversified its promo-
> tional strategies to include not only the promotion of tourism
> features but also cultural, historical and economic aspects of
> Jamaica, through joint promotions with such organisations
> as Jamaica National Export Corporation, the National Trust
> Commission and Things Jamaican. In this regard, in addition
> to the regular familiarisation tours for travel writers, special
> familiarisation trips dealing with Jamaica art and culture were
> arranged for foreign journalists.[7]

The Report went on to cite as an example of this type of
promotion an exhibition at Macy's department store in California where 'over a one-week period. . . not only Jamaica's
tourism products but also [its] art, crafts, foods, fashion and
manufacturing industries were on display'.[8]

Nevertheless, as Kaufman observes:

> Tourism is based on a radical disjuncture between the local society and the tourist setting. Visitors in Jamaica cling to a narrow enclave. . . live in conditions unheard of by Jamaican standards. . . Rather than reduce the gap, enclave tourism draws a sharp distinction between tourist and local people. The coastline between Ocho Rios and Negril is a *cordon sanitaire* where North America is recreated in a tropical setting serviced by those of another world.[9]

The harsh reality therefore remains. Plush tourist facilities coexist with depressed rural areas, unemployment, poverty and urban slums. The contrast is a constant reminder that enclave tourism is mutually negative – negative in terms of its local impact and negative for tourists themselves. The result is that the development of the industry, at huge financial and social cost, has in the long run contributed little towards the permanent eradication of the widespread poverty and powerlessness of the West Indian people.

V: Off-Shore Banking

Just as tourism was developed on the principle of selling the Caribbean's natural advantages to Europe and then later to North America, so too was off-shore banking, only this time the natural advantages were a location in the eastern-seaboard of the US time zone, proximity to North America, convenient locations for building communications directly linked to US networks and good weather throughout the year. To these were also added the man-made advantages of an absence of financial regulations and laws (which was an inducement for certain types of transactions) and the security of the region by virtue of its political and cultural orientation to North America and Europe.

Contrary to popular belief, overseas banking is not new to the area, but has long been a part of its history. The Currency Board systems, which operated in the region until the 1960s, linked the currencies of these countries to the pound sterling at fixed and unchangeable exchange rates and also required the currency issuing authorities to back each unit of currency it issued with its equivalent in sterling. Such an arrangement ensured that banks in Britain carried no more risks for their operations in the British territories of the area in terms of exchange-rate movements and inconvertibility of their profits than they did at home. Britain's decline in the area and the increased influence of North America, other parts of Europe and Japan, together with the new activities being promoted by the nationalist governments of the area, combined to attract a number of new banks into the region, including the Chase Manhattan, Bank of Nova Scotia, Bank of Commerce and Southern and Citizens. These principally, however, came in to exploit local credit opportunities and to make profits from the financing of the region's external trade.

These financial havens are not, however, formally or directly integrated into the territories' internal credit structures or international trade. Local law usually distinguishes between resident and non-resident banking activities, with the latter not being subjected to the same controls on reserve requirements or foreign-exchange remittances as the former and being taxed, if at all, at very low rates. Controls only exist where non-residents deal in local currency. Some territories have passed legislation which exempts all or certain categories of wealth and income from tax. The rest tax income and wealth, but at much lower rates than those pertaining in the USA, Canada, Japan and the West European countries of the EEC. These arrangements are normally backed up by institutional and/or legal regulations which enforce rules of secrecy and confidentiality on commercial transactions conducted through or in foreign countries. Sometimes, as happened in the Cayman Islands, criminal penalties are imposed on those who breach local laws enforcing secrecy and confidentiality. These laws are intended to deter the courts of other countries from trying to force officials who work in the Caribbean to make disclosures without the prior approval of the local courts. Sometimes, the country wanting to operate as a haven enters into a tax treaty with another country. The Netherlands Antilles, for example, entered into such an agreement with the US when it agreed to exempt certain interest remitted from the US to persons resident in those territories.

The Bahamas and the Cayman Islands are the most active

of the off-shore financial centres in the region. The Bahamas handles over US$150,000 million in funds and hosts about 370 banks. On some days, more funds pass through Nassau than through London and it has been claimed that the Bahamas is the second largest loan-syndication centre in the world, with London being the largest. In 1964 the Cayman Islands had virtually no off-shore business and only two banks; by 1977 they had 218 licensed banks and trust companies and by 1985 they were hosting 13,600 companies and 360 banks. The Cayman Islands are particularly favoured by Canadian companies. Bermuda is also a major centre and at the forefront in the field of insurance.[10] The Dutch territories have been important for US corporations seeking a tax haven for in-house financing, but the tax treaty referred to earlier is unlikely to be allowed to continue in the wake of certain legislation which was passed in the US in 1984. Barbados was a more recent addition to the region's list of off-shore banking territories. Started in 1979, there are currently over 500 companies registered there with total assets of US$2,000 million. This activity has been combined with developing Barbados as a port of registry for international shipping (1982). Overall, the region is believed to host over a quarter of the banks located in financial centres around the world.

The huge expansion of off-shore financial centres had nothing to do with the needs of the region, but was rather a reflection of the restructuring of world finance which was taking place in the capitalist system as a whole in the 1950s, particularly the development of what have been termed Euro-currency markets. Although so named, the market in effect depended on the growth of banking transactions in any currency other than that of the country in which the bank involved was located. It first evolved in Europe where the banks dealt in deposits denominated in US dollars. Today such dealings are widespread and embrace several major currencies on a world-wide basis. The market is currently estimated at over US$3,000,000 million, of which 80 per cent is held in US dollars. It was therefore in an effort to exploit this development that the Caribbean became involved. Each of the territories spent large amounts of public funds on promoting their country as an attractive haven and, as with tourism, there was considerable intra-regional competition to outbid each other in their appeal. Because of the emphasis on secrecy and tax avoidance, the industry has developed strong connections not only with the questionable activities and possibly large-scale white collar crimes committed by TNCs, wealthy families and individuals, but with well-organised crime and drug trafficking. There have been several scandals involving the higher echelons of the political and police administrations of the Bahamas, the Cayman Islands, the Turks and Caicos Islands, Jamaica, Trinidad-Tobago and Barbados.

Although these off-shore financial centres operate predominantly as entrepots in the movements of finance, the local territories do derive some economic benefits from their presence. For a start, the governments receive revenue from the fees and licences these companies pay prior to engaging in business. Although small in comparison with the benefits of a tax-haven status (exemption from taxes on income, profits, earnings, capital gains or distribution, inheritance, succession, withholding and death duties) and in relation to the magnitude of the funds the banks handle and even to revenue raised by the governments, they none the less constitute a fair sum, averaging for instance, between three and five million US dollars annually. A second benefit is employment. Here again, the amount involved is quite small since very little of the actual bookkeeping in these transactions takes place locally. In 1979, 270 of the 300 banks located in the Bahamas had no physical presence on the islands other than 'a plaque, a walk-in closet, a desk, a file cabinet and a telephone'.[11] At the end of 1983, it was estimated that the activities of all the off-shore centres in the Bahamas provided employment for about 3,000 people, namely between 2 and 3 per cent of the labour force.[12] A third benefit is the spill-over effect into other services. In this respect, local lawyers and accountants have benefited most and some have developed specialist reputations in particular areas, usually associated with the legal red tape and bookkeeping involved in starting up operations and coping with any changes that might occur in local laws and procedures. Since the banks have no Bahamian dollar incomes, all local expenses are financed from foreign-exchange inflows. A final benefit is that the territory is promoted as an attractive place for tourists and hopefully also investors with an interest in the local market. There is no doubt that frequent references to these countries in the financial press, through the electronics media and on film do help to raise their profile and that occasionally someone doing business in the territory forms an attachment to the area and possibly invests some funds there. It is difficult to find many concrete examples of this, although people do buy holiday and retirement homes on the islands.

There are also, however, certain costs to be considered. First, governments have to provide the infrastructure, the airports, local transport, hotels, telex and telephone links so that the territory will be regarded as a feasible choice. Although this cost is eventually offset by the extra tourism it stimulates, the initial financial outlay is none the less considerable. Second, given that the entire venture is founded on tax avoidance and that there is a grey area between legal tax avoidance and illegal tax evasion, a number of dubious people and operations are attracted to the area, including organised crime and drug trafficking. This has inevitably corrupted many of the rich and powerful in the region, who have been tempted into selling the birth rights of the poor and powerless.

Public concern has, however, been growing in Europe and North America over these tax havens unfairly increasing the tax burden for citizens without the knowledge and/or resources to exploit such arrangements themselves. The link these activities have with crime and drugs reinforces this concern and increases the pressures being placed on governments to eliminate these loopholes. While there is no immediate threat to the future of this new West Indian enterprise, a note of uncertainty has started to creep in, particularly in the US. While initially contributing to the growth of these centres with legislation such as the Interest Equalisation Tax of 1963 (deterring US citizens from investing in non-American securities) and Regulation Q (deterring non-Americans from buying American domestic dollar bonds by limiting the interest rates on these bonds below international rates), recent moves by the Reagan administration, particularly in exempting from taxation interest earned by non-residents holding accounts in the US, have encouraged a considerable movement of funds into the US. Similarly, the Reagan administration's high-profile attacks on drug trafficking have opened many of these havens to systematic investigation. It has been alleged that it is as a result of this type of investigation that the tax treaty between the US and the Netherlands Antilles was terminated by the US in 1987. Under this treaty, Americans paying interest to foreigners were exempt from paying a 30 per cent tax if they borrowed in the Netherlands Antilles. Several thousand millions of US dollars in loans were raised by US corporations through this source.

The State and Institutional Reform

In Part 1 we examined the main contours in the development of the colonial state in the Caribbean over four broad historical periods – the conquest, the colonial slave mode of production, its disintegration during the transition to free labour in the 19th century and, finally, in the 20th century until the Second World War, the emergence of a more or less definitive peripheral capitalist formation. Until the 20th century, the ruling planter class was able to use the state to wield its economic and political power. The state demonstrated its support by backing slavery and later, when abolition became inevitable, by thwarting the growth of a free labour market and of a local agriculture oriented towards serving a domestic market and the needs of an emerging peasantry.

By the end of the Second World War, however, the continuous resistance of the dominated classes to planter rule (along with the momentous transformation which had taken place and which were still taking place in the capitalist world in general and in Europe in particular) had forced important changes on the colonial state. These could be seen in a number of areas. First, confronted with the strength of nationalist sentiment and popular resistance to colonial rule, those in control of the local state were being forced to abandon their old *laizzez-faire* policies in support of an increasingly active role for the state in laying the foundations of what was then described as a modern economy. Under the guidance and patronage of the Colonial Office, the state became more and more an institution of economic reproduction, eclipsing in the process its earlier and cruder emphasis on repression. The ultimate aim of this exercise was to facilitate a new imperial division of labour at the global level and to entrench market relations into the internal process of accumulation, thereby irretrievably putting the capitalist stamp on the local economy. The existence of a restricted franchise at the end of the Second World War ensured that there were enough colonial officials and planter representatives with access to state power to promote this design. Later, when the franchise was widened to include universal adult suffrage and the local educated, professional, business and landed elite came to exercise more control over the state machinery, the pursuit of this grand design became much more complicated.

The state also made some important ideological and cultural changes. As access to education grew, the merits of a bourgeois political democracy were increasingly promoted, particularly of the so-called Westminster model of parliamentary rule. The Westminster model, with its notion of 'orderly constitutional advance' was based on the premise that although the masses at that time were incapable of self-rule, they could eventually be brought to the appropriate stage of development. In the meanwhile, however, the Colonial Office would be the 'trustee' of their interests. By orderly constitutional advance was meant the progressive widening of the franchise and devolution of functions from the Colonial Office to the local government, as well as the creation of a multi-party political system capable of bringing about orderly changes in government based on honest electoral practices, the rule of law and the independence of the judiciary. So great was the hold of this ideology over the population that virtually every prominent local personality subscribed to the approach, with only perhaps minor differences in emphasis. The practice, however, fell far short of the ideal. In retrospect, it can be seen that limited self-government reflected a deep-seated fear of the masses on the part of both the Colonial Office and the economically important plantocracy, which constituted a very small minority of the population. It was hardly surprising therefore that when a Marxist government was freely elected to office in Guyana in 1953, under the pretext of a 'communist subversion', the British government invaded the territory and suspended the constitution.

A careful analysis of the region shows that until the Second World War, constitutional advance depended basically on the state of social struggle and the capacity of the nationalist forces to press for concessions from the Colonial Office and the local plantocracy. After the Second World War, however, the leaders of the struggle more readily accepted the Colonial Office's outlook and, as a consquence, social struggle as the basis of constitutional advance was replaced by the concept of a 'partnership of interests', as it was put, 'to advance the masses to full independence'. The result of this was that on the eve of independence in the 1960s a number of negative features became obvious. One was that nowhere in the West Indies was the colonial state going to be 'smashed'. The petty bourgeoisie, which viewed itself as the group best constituted to lead in the development of these societies, opposed any revolutionary transformation of internal class relations. Another was that the independence settlements would inevitably exclude the masses from real political power and that this exclusion was neither accidental nor shortsighted, as some have argued, but fully in accordance with the long-term interests of the colonial power. A third was that the rise of mass politics prior to independence and the proliferation of mass organisations (especially political parties and trade unions) served to legitimate state activities and reinforced the increasing gap between imperialism and direct colonisation.[1]

Although linked to wider social struggles, the constitutional struggles against the colonial state did not, in the end, result in many significant economic or social victories for the poor and powerless. Many crucial struggles had therefore to be carried over into the independence period. Among the most important of these were the struggles against the colonial division of labour (with its emphasis on primary commodity production, export specialisation and minimal industrialisation), the struggles against the forced trade and financial links with Britain (through currency boards, tariff policies and imperial preferences designed to reproduce the world market internally), the struggles against foreign personnel filling key executive and management positions in the upper echelons of the state and private sector and, above all, the struggles against the limited autonomy of local economic, social and political institutions.

It is from this perspective that we should seek to interpret the economic functions of the state in the region between the Second World War and the 1970s. Apart from the roles it played in industry, agriculture, mineral production, tourism and off-shore banking, the post-colonial state also established a considerable number of institutional and administrative arrangements in the region which can be organised into the following six categories:

(1) Institutions and agencies through which national economic processes were guided and regulated. Among the most important of these were the rudimentary national planning authorities, often with support from statistical agencies which systematically collected and assembled data on the national economy. In collaboration with the University of the West Indies, these bodies were responsible for the preparation of the area's first set of national economic and social accounts, the local organisation of the population censuses in 1960 and 1974, a number of social and economic surveys on employment and unemployment, household-expenditure surveys, as well as various studies on the balance-of-payments and financial performance of the region.

The work of these agencies was also responsible for currency boards being replaced by Central Banks in some territories and for foreign-exchange authorities being brought into legal existence. They also regulated the development of commercial banking, non-banking financial intermediaries (like insurance companies, mortgage companies and hire-purchase arrangements) and exchange-control regulations.

(2) New developments in the area of trade and foreign relations. Initially these were activated by Britain's long, drawn-out decision to join the EEC. Later, the countries that became independent in the 1960s sought membership of the UN and its related organisations (IMF/World Bank, UNCTAD), participated in the non-aligned movement and echoed the call for a new international economic order. These activities brought a certain diversification to foreign relations and foreign trade, which can be witnessed by the establishment of new embassies in Eastern Europe, Asia and Latin America. The customs departments (which had long existed in these countries but been passive for most of their history) became active as new import and quota arrangements were put in place. The creation of the Caribbean Free Trade Association (CARIFTA) in 1968 and then CARICOM in 1975 gave a further impetus to these changes. Finally, import licensing, which became universal as the system of incentives was elaborated, transformed the Ministries of Trade into relatively active institutions.

(3) The increased regulation of labour. This took many forms, including the creation of labour exchanges (sometimes

called employment exchanges) to facilitate the matching of supply to demand. Since unemployment remained staggeringly high during this period, however, their effect was largely cosmetic. Also various departments of labour in the state bureaucracy were allocated the task of preserving harmony in worker/employee relations, with the Ministers responsible for these departments being given conciliatory and arbitration powers over employer/employee disputes. They were also expected to oversee existing legislation in so far as it affected trade unions and workers (especially in such areas as trade union recognition), the implementation of minimum wages, hours of work and, where these existed, apprenticeship provisions. In Trinidad-Tobago, for example, income policies were institutionalised by legislation and backed by industrial courts, thus constituting a new and significant form of state intervention.

(4) The placing of certain utilities, such as electricity in Guyana, under the direct ownership and control of the state. In some territories both private and state-owned utility boards were subjected to scrutiny by agencies with the authority to regulate their rates and quality of service. In addition, a number of government agencies and/or parastatal institutions were established in the wake of governmental decisions to supply the infrastructure for industrialisation and the development of tourism. Consequently, in many territories new harbours, airports and shipping terminals were constructed during this period and placed under the control of special parastatal authorities.

(5) The provision of new or improved welfare services, which included health, education, community development, old age pensions and national insurance. Although the level of benefits from these services remained pitifully low and as major an area of social need as unemployment was not provided for, these departures were new in the region, for such functions were historically provided for by plantations, churches and other private groups.

(6) Finally, the introduction of local company legislation, patterned after the British model and aiming to provide a clear legal framework for the operation of private capital in its corporate guise.

The overall aims of these institutional and administrative developments were to minimise the social costs and social disorganisation inherent in foreign investment in the region's national economies being constituted as the 'engine of growth'; to correct the distorted and biased colonial production structures in so far as they were seen as an inadequate basis for the development of indigenous capital; to enhance the position of local capital *vis-à-vis* foreign capital, particularly in the fields of resource control, technology, marketing and skills; and generally to enhance state control over the society by seeking to control the use and disposition of the means of production and the work process. When considered in this light, it can be seen that the state had started its interventionist role in the region's economic life even before political independence had been attained. This intervention was never intended to be hostile to the interests of either local or foreign capital. On the contrary, it was advanced as essential to its survival and success. If it were otherwise, how could it have been promoted by the colonial authorities?

Another manifestation, which although only of token importance in 1970 later became a major distinguishing characteristic in the region, was the rapid growth of state ownership. This phenomenon will be discussed at greater length in the next chapter, but it is useful to draw attention to it here in that it grew out of the thrusts identified in this chapter. During the period under consideration, state ownership was considered justifiable only under certain limited circumstances. One of these was where the product or service offered was a natural monopoly (such as a pure water supply, electricity or telephone) and state ownership was seen as a means of preventing consumer exploitation and guaranteeing services to investors. It was also acceptable for governments to own certain essential services to ensure that in the interests of promoting greater equality in the society profit did not become the only criterion in their provision. Yet another was when an industry or enterprise was under threat of immediate closure and it was felt that the state should take it over to prevent the loss of incomes and jobs and the accompanying social dislocation. At best these views favoured the development of a strong public-utilities sector.

Later, however, ideological and other socio-political considerations came to the forefront and it was in the name of such objectives as 'developmental imperatives', 'improved regulation of economic activity', 'control of the commanding heights of the economy', 'anti-colonialism', 'anti-imperialism' and 'socialism' that an expanded state property sector was established in the region – the best example of this being the 'cooperative socialism' of Guyana. At the same time, a similarly rapid expansion of the state property sector was occurring in other parts of the region but in this case, however, unheralded, without any trumpeting or fanfare, but justified solely on 'pragmatic' and 'non-political' grounds. The best example in this respect was Trinidad-Tobago.

The actual foundations of this tendency towards state expansion/intervention lay in the organic and structural relations these states had with the colonial division of labour and the internal accumulation requirements these historically imposed on the countries of the region, rather than in any voluntary development on the part of those in control. Because the expansion of the state property sector followed immediately after the period of mass politics and popular agitation for independence, the post-colonial state was able to acquire a level of legitimacy unparalleled by the colonial state. The potential inherent in this, however, did not play itself out because those in control of the machinery of state had no fundamental interest in a radical or revolutionary alteration of internal social relations. To the ruling groups, the state was there to protect them and the interests of their class. This had important consequences. For a start, all the independence settlements reached between Britain and the individual territories excluded the masses from effective power. So important was this that a precondition for Guyana's independence was the removal of the People's Progressive Party (PPP) from office – a feat achieved through the manoeuvres of the British government, the US government, the CIA and Guyana's own opposition forces, particularly Burnham's People's National Congress (PNC). Also, once independence was attained, those in political power sought increasingly to demobilise and depoliticise the mass of the population. How otherwise could they have been kept in such poverty and powerlessness? As I have written elsewhere:

> . . . despite the different degrees of importance which. . . these various policies attach to the freedom of private owner- ship of property and the freedom of markets, they are all fundamentally characterised by the deliberate intention of using the state apparatus as a principal instrument of devel- oping a strong class formation, capable of assuming the responsibility of raising the level of development of the productive forces. Traditionally, in the context of highly developed class societies. . . the state [is] the *object* of class conquest and the *instrument* of class rule. In the historical situation that prevails in these countries, it is more correct to argue that the state has become, as it were, an *instrument* of *class creation*.[2]

It is because of considerations such as these that this book is based on the premise that it is virtually impossible to separate economic policy from socio-political factors in the region's development. While not exactly unswervingly and single- mindedly pursuing the class interests of those in power, the state's economic policies do nevertheless reflect the interests of the dominant groups, although these are perhaps watered down somewhat by the conflicts which develop from time to time with those who oppose them. It was solely to serve planter interests that the major source of tax receipts consisted of import duties and that no significant export duties or income taxation existed in the region until the period of internal self-government in the 1950s. Historically, these interests were served through a regressive tax structure which ignored the ability to pay but was none the less a useful device in the 19th century for forcing former slaves into the market economy, either as wage labourers on the estates or as producers of export cash crops.

Thus, despite the increasing range and proliferation of state functions and institutions, the period of nationalist strategy cannot be said to have yielded any real or lasting relief to the poor and powerless. In fact, even in local hands, the state was no less an agent of their domination. This is borne out by the neglect of domestic agriculture, the lack of opposition to the plantation system, the development of a class of local businessmen, as well as the import substitution

industrialisation built at huge social costs on the backs of the
unemployed and landless. For most of the period under
review, not only did the distribution of income and wealth
become more skewed, but much of it was also drained out
of the country through the various surplus-extraction mechanisms perfected by the TNCs and further facilitated by
the growth of a class of entrepreneurs, most of whom held
residency or citizenship rights in one or another North
American or European country. As more and more of the
local population's social wealth became concentrated in the
hands of this group, so the TNCs consolidated their control
over agriculture, commerce, banking, mineral development,
agro-processing, tourism and manufacturing, thus even
further alienating the masses from the region's decision-
making, income creating and reproductive systems. Associated with these developments was the growing importance
in the region's economic life (particularly as expressed
through state activities) of multilateral institutions such as
the World Bank, IMF, Caribbean Development Bank, Inter-
American Development Bank and European Development
Fund and bilateral institutions such as USAID, the UK's
Overseas Development Association and the Canadian International Development Agency. The movement into tourism
and off-shore tax havens also served to expose the political
directorate and several key professionals to international
criminal elements. In the process, the economically-active
state spawned a group of criminal marauders, like the buccaneers of yore, just as the new manufacturing elite promoted
functions like the absentee landlords of the past.

Part III:
Crisis of the Nationalist Models and Social Experimentation

By the early 1970s the nationalist strategies of economic development seemed to have exhausted their possibilities. The global crisis of capitalism, the oil crisis and calls for a new international economic order had interacted with local developments in the various territories of the region to produce a more or less generalised crisis. Everywhere in the region there was evidence of deep ferment and the desire for fundamental social change. At the grassroots level this erupted into strong direct action, culminating in the Rodney riots in Jamaica and the black-power protests in Trinidad-Tobago. At the same time new political, civic and social organisations were coming into existence. The New Jewel Movement in Grenada, the Working Peoples' Alliance in Guyana, the Antigua Caribbean Liberation Movement, Monali in Barbados and the Workers' Party of Jamaica, were all established during this period and all put forward programmes promising to open up new directions of social change and political development in the region.

Signs of resistance were also evident in many areas of cultural life – in the renaissance of the calypso, the new thrust and direction of reggae music, the growth of West Indian literature and even in the rise of Rastafarianism among the youth. Civic organisations like the Caribbean Conference of Churches and its local councils, human-rights organisations, friendly societies and solidarity organisations sprang up all over the region to give a voice to the concerns of the poor and powerless. New bold efforts were made to implement grassroots' forms of self-organisation and cooperation in such diverse areas as the arts, agriculture, education and recreation, often with support from other like-minded organisations. There was also lively intellectual activity in the region as the various theories (for example, the idea of dependency and Marxist theories of social change) were embellished and enriched by local experiences. Behind this, Cuba's image as a new kind of Caribbean society played an extraordinarily potent role. These developments set the stage for such major national experiments as Jamaica's democratic socialism, Guyana's cooperative socialism and Bishop's endeavours in Grenada.

This part of the book begins by outlining some of the basic issues affecting the economic strategies in Chapter 10 and is followed by a brief examination of national experiments in Jamaica, Grenada, Guyana, Trinidad-Tobago and Barbados in Chapter 11. The period ends during the crisis of the late 1980s.

10 *Social Structure, Ownership and Control: The Basic Issues*

I: Social Structure and Class

By the 1970s, the Caribbean's social structure (ie the sum total of classes, social strata and groups and their interconnections), had acquired certain distinctive characteristics. The historic classes (proletariat and industrial/financial bourgeoisie) and their respective organisations (trade unions, political parties and business lobbies) were relatively underdeveloped and, with further development impeded by various economic and structural factors, the class structure of the region has remained weaker and more complex than in the developed capitalist economies of Europe and North America.[1]

The region's employed *working class* is concentrated in four major areas – in the mineral-extractive sector, in the large-scale plantation-type agricultural enterprises, in the emerging import-substitution sector and in the services sector. The first two are the traditional colonial forms of wage labour which emerged in the late 19th and early 20th centuries. The third, which is oriented to the manufacture and/or assembly of consumer goods for local, high-income, urban markets, consists mainly of enterprises that are either branch-plants of, or operate under joint agreements with, TNCs. The fourth, the service sector, employs a large proportion of the labour force, although the government and tourism are the only components within it that are effectively organised. Some jobs in this sector, such as street vendoring and domestic service, really constitute an informal subsector within this category, while many other enterprises offering employment in the service sector are small and frequently concentrated in the urban areas.

The working class is typically distributed among enterprises that are both large and small, foreign and local, highly concentrated in urban settlements and in isolated communities. A significant proportion of the female labour force is concentrated in lowly-paid domestic work in individual households and in the more recently-established sweat-shops in the export-processing zones, where firms show an overwhelming preference for female employees. In only a few of the territories, for example Jamaica, are household domestic servants covered by any social or industrial legislation. The

complexity generated by the employment situation is compounded by the lack of unionisation of much of the labour force. Typically only about one third of the labour force is unionised and, even then, the unionised sector is frequently concentrated in the larger establishments.

The fact that employment is spread among a large number of small establishments has hindered not only the unionisation of the work force, but also the development of a sense of class identity and solidarity, both of which are necessary for united class action. The fact also that small-scale employment frequently predominates even in an urban environment, means that working-class organisations are weak in politically-sensitive areas such as those housing the seat of government, the administrative headquarters of political parties, trade unions, civic and social organisations and large concentrations of students. There is also consider-able geographical mobility in the work force, often with workers living and working in one area (a city, mining town, tourist resort, or plantation) and maintaining a household in another, usually in a distant rural community. Sometimes this migration is international with households split over huge distances. In other instances, seasonal migratory move-ments of the work-force occur internationally, as when sugar-cane cutters from the Leeward and Windward Islands go to Barbados, or agricultural workers go to North America as short-term contract labourers.

In addition, it should be noted that substantial sections of the working class in the region have some access to private property in the form of self-operated taxis, small landhol-dings or small stores from which they supplement their incomes. Significant sections also exploit their skills as higglers (street vendors), carpenters, seamstresses, elec-tricians or plumbers on a part-time, spare-time basis. These links to small property inevitably complicate working-class perceptions and behaviour. Another important complication is the seasonality of employment, with two of the region's major sources of employment (agriculture and tourism) being seasonal activities. This inevitably infuses the work-force with a sense of insecurity, for seasonal employment has generally been treated as temporary employment, thus making it possible for a sugar-cane worker to work seasonally all his working life and end up being a temporary employee.

The rapid expansion of the lower-level salariat paid by the state – clerical workers, teachers, nurses, messengers, drivers and other such service workers – has added a significant new dimension to the class structure of the region. With the growth of state functions and state property and with it the development of state productive enterprises in manufacturing, export agriculture and mining, this section of the work-force has developed close links with workers in the more directly productive sectors of these economies.

Finally, a large proportion of the working-class labour force (particularly among the youth) are long-term structurally unemployed. Unemployment rates in the region typically range between 12 and 30 per cent and can often represent as high as two-thirds of the labour force between the ages of 18 and 26.

Similar complexities exist among the *propertied classes*. For example, close family ties within the manufacturing bourgeoisie have enabled 21 families in Jamaica (usually with residency or citizenship rights in North America or Europe) to dominate the locally-controlled sections of manufacturing, construction and distribution developed since the Second World War. In addition, it is customary in the region for the traditional landed oligarchy (representing 'feudalism in the countryside') and the emergent manufacturing bourgeoisie (representing 'capitalist relations in the cities'), as they are classically defined, to have no clear demarcation, in fact to overlap in one person or in one family, thus creating a complex intertwining of semi-capitalist and capitalist property relations.

The landed oligarchy developed out of foreign penetration and settlement and as such had no indigenous roots in the pre-conquest class structure. The structure of the *peasantry* as a landholding class is equally complex. The category includes a wide variety of landless, small and medium peasants, any or all of whom may earn a substantial proportion of their income as wage labourers on state projects, private plantations, or in a number of artisanal and craft-type activities.

The concept of the *middle class* is especially vague, in

that it usually comprises a complex array of the lower ranks of the landholders, professionals, teachers, middle-level management in state and private enterprises and in small-scale commercial operations, and shopkeepers, artisans and traders working on their own or with family labour. This vagueness is compounded by the fact that certain elements of the middle class can fall into other groupings. For example, the lower ranks of the landowners can also be classified with richer peasants, while certain professionals can be included as part of the bourgeoisie. The middle class is sometimes equated with what is called the 'intermediate strata', which is a term used to describe the middle ground or gap between the relatively clearly-defined peasantry and working class and the large propertied classes.

By the 1970s, the most significant development in the region's class structure was the emergence of various petty-bourgeois groups and strata associated with the expansion of state ownership. In the post-war period petty-bourgeois elements sought to confirm their social position as a ruling class through assuming control of state power, albeit within the wider context of their relationship to the metropolitan power and its superordinate ruling class. This group of people, who essentially took on the political roles and managerial positions in state enterprises, is one of the specifically post-war, perhaps even post-colonial, manifestations of this period. It has variously been described as the 'state petty bourgeoisie', the 'state bourgeoisie' or the 'bureaucratic bourgeoisie', but whichever term is used, its essential features are control of state property, its 'non-antagonistic' relationship to the capitalist class in the metropole and its re-enforcement of the continued reproduction of capitalist relations both locally and on a world scale. Some writers have tried to handle the complexity of the petty bourgeoisie by distinguishing between a 'politico-administrative' element (comprised of heads of government ministries, top civil servants and top party leaders) and an 'economic' element (comprised of heads and higher functionaries of public corporations and other state-supervised economic enterprises).[2] This is not, however, a particularly useful formulation, because although these people are identifiable members of the petty bourgeoisie, they have strong kinship and other social ties with the more traditional petty-bourgeois elements, including the army, in which there has also been rapid expansion.[3]

An important consideration emerging from this development of state ownership and its associated petty bourgeoisie, is the *reversal of the classical relations of economic power to political power* manifested in the development of capitalism. Historically, in the developed capitalist countries the bourgeoisie aimed its political power only after it had consolidated its economic power. Thus, in the United Kingdom, the political influence of the landed gentry continued long after the economic ascendancy of the manufacturing bourgeoisie. In the Caribbean, however, the consolidation of economic power was consolidated *after* political power and the state machinery had been seized. This development suggests the notion of a 'state for itself', in other words, a situation in which those controlling the state use it to promote the economic interests of their own group of family, friends, and political allies. State power is therefore being used to form the nucleus of an indigenous bourgeoisie. It should be noted here that the expansion of state ownership in the region has seldom been opposed by local private capital because it has been directed against the dominance of foreign capital, via nationalisation, and not against capital as such. This is not to suggest that there were no conflicts between local private capital and the state over such issues as internal regulation of the economy, foreign-exchange and foreign-debt policies, or the desirability of IMF-type stabilisation programmes. Such disputes have occurred, particularly during interruptions and crises in the process of capital accumulation nationally and internationally. On the whole, however, private capital has benefited from the expansion of the state and more often than not maintains close links with the state petty bourgeoisie. Indeed members of the business class frequently move into the state sector when the state needs employees with entrepreneurial and managerial skills to run the nationalised enterprises.

Another distinctive feature of the region's social structure is that its classes are more fluid, not only in the movement of individuals from one class to another, but also in the changing nature of the classes themselves and their relative size. One such example is in the rapid development of new urban-based groupings, often of people such as higglers and unemployed youths, which result from the continuing migration from the countryside to the cities. Also, the development of a bourgeoisie and proletariat in the cities occurs within older, more established contexts, such as ethnic groupings, which serve to mediate in relations among the new urban classes. The mediation process, in turn, adds to the fluidity of class relations and, at the same time, makes these even more complex than would otherwise be the case. Furthermore, the rapid growth of urban centres is linked to the growth of two areas of economic activity, namely the expansion of the import-substituting industry and the proliferation of small businesses and trading establishments.

Yet another feature lies in the multi-structured way in which the region's economies combine numerous forms of production and types of economic relations – TNC branch plants, state ownership, peasant subsistence holdings, share-cropping, wage labour, individual/family traders, artisans, commercial houses and local manufacturing enterprises. Each in its own way affects national production, accumulation, employment and foreign-exchange earnings, thus counteracting the dominance of monopolistic industrial and commercial corporations. This is not, however, enough to prevent a pattern of specialised production of one or two commodities for sale on the world market and a heavy reliance on foreign skills, technology and financing, despite the specialised production embracing many different forms of enterprise. As we noted, the predominant role of production for the world market led to a very special type of capitalist relations. In the case of classical European, American and Japanese capitalism, production was initially impelled by the requirements of the internal market and internal resources were developed to satisfy that market. The world market then developed as an extension of the domestic market, thereby ensuring that the predominant economic relations were kept within the local economy. This has not, however, happened in the Caribbean.

A further element in the region's social structure is the dominant role played by foreign capital, whether resident or not. This development underlines a broader historical phenomenon, namely that of all the classes, only the bourgeoisie has historically been able to organise itself at the global level. However, although the region's ruling class has a foreign section, it is not a legitimate part of the nation state because neither its members, nor their resident representatives, are citizens. As a result, this section of the ruling class has to find ways and means of ensuring its continued influence and this inevitably complicates social relations and affects the structure of the Caribbean states.

Finally, there is far more interaction between class-based and non-property-based structures in the region than in the countries of the capitalist centre where class structures are more clearly defined. The greater interaction of class with ethnic, sex, colour, religious, rural/urban and even language divisions in the region makes the social structure even more difficult to analyse. The coexistence and interaction of non-property and class relations is the product of the particular stage of development of these societies and until class structures, class consciousness and class outlook become more defined, any attempt to understand the social structure of the region must take the nature and character of this interplay into account.

By way of concluding this discussion of the social structure, let me make a number of observations of direct relevance to the study. The first is that it is crucial to take colonialism and external capitalist domination (particularly their class and economic structures) into account in formulating any theories on how these societies operate. This point, which was implicit in the earlier discussions on how a specific type of colonial domination facilitated the development of petty-bourgeois control of state power and on how the independence settlements reached in the 1960s and after were predicated on excluding the masses from political power, constitutes a continuing thread of the analysis. Unless it is kept in mind there can be no real comprehension of the dynamics of the crisis after the 1970s.

The second observation is that in a region where both traditional capitalist classes (workers and capitalists) are underdeveloped and where both these classes are numerically small and qualitatively weak, there is no *clear hegemonic ruling class*. Although the weaker of the two, the proletariat has existed for longer and so demonstrates the existence of an original contradiction between the local working class and foreign capital, despite the local bourgeoisie and proletariat having developed under the domination of expatriate capital. This phenomenon is a particular feature of peripheral capitalist societies.

The third observation is that the social and cultural conditions under which the working class developed in the region have produced deep divisions within it. This fracturing of the working class – whether along sexual, ethnic, cultural, or religious lines has led to racial, religious and other aspects of a 'caste' outlook playing important roles in forming class consciousness in the region. This has frequently made it difficult to delineate class lines. Thus, while it may be possible to predict on the basis of past experience that class consciousness will develop in its own local forms as capitalist relations deepen, at the moment the situation in these societies is too complicated for easy prediction.

The fourth observation is that the petty bourgeoisie presently in control of state power is not a homogeneous group but is composed of several factions (professional, political, administrative, state-economic and private) and that although factional conflict exists, in the absence of an entrenched ruling class it has through its own self-interests developed closer relations with national private capital. The state thereby assumes the characteristics of a 'state for itself' and, unencumbered by any bourgeois-democratic constitutional restraints, rapidly proceeds to institutionalise all forms of corruption. This is probably the main reason behind the rise in corruption in the region and the fact that it has become one of the ways in which this class consolidates its economic base and increases its property.

The final observation is that, despite the complexity and fluidity of the class structure and non-capitalist influences on class outlook, class struggle nevertheless continues no less sharply than elsewhere. In fact the growth in state ownership and the state's consequent role as a major employer of wage labour has *enhanced* class struggle. The reason for this is that in developed capitalist societies, where private capital is dominant, the link between worker/capital conflicts and state power is not easily perceived by the general population, but where there is a significant state sector combined with a major structural crisis of world capitalism, the impact on employment and incomes is sufficiently great to allow employees to see the relationship between the state and the dominant economic interests in the region more clearly.

II: Ownership and Control

Having examined certain features of the social structure in the previous section, we are now better able to understand the crisis confronting nationalist policies in the early 1970s. These policies, we observed, aimed to adapt the then existing colonial model to the requirements of countries moving towards formal political independence and, as such, they depended on four key measures, namely:

(1) Capital importation. Although increasing colonial dependence on foreign capital, this did represent an important source of economic expansion in that it created opportunities to diversify local economic activity through import substitution, the development of mining in new areas and the promotion of tourism and off-shore financial services.

(2) Diversifying the source of capital and trade dependence through exploiting geographical and strategic links with Canada and the US. This process was facilitated by Europe's, and particularly Britain's, decline in the world economy and the rise of the US.

(3) Tightening the region's ties with the world market. It was felt that this would be best achieved by giving the TNCs (which effectively controlled technology, skills, finance, markets and management) a dominant role in diversifying the region's production structures.

(4) The introduction of a minimal range of social services. These were rather minor measures as no explicit policies were actively promoted to tackle poverty as a social problem. In general, the distressed sections of the population were expected to continue relying on relief from friends, family and social agencies, such as the Salvation Army, Child Boards and the churches. Implicit in this approach was the assumption that the benefits of economic growth would eventually trickle down to the poor and so ensure the development of the whole society.

Several economies including Jamaica, Barbados and the Bahamas, experienced high per capita growth during the post-war period. While this often depended on the development of special sectors under largely fortuitous and unexpected circumstances, (for example bauxite-alumina and tourist development), by the 1970s even these countries had begun to experience a range of economic, political, social and cultural problems. Unemployment in the region ranged between 12 and 40 per cent.

In Guyana, for example, only 15 per cent of peasant households were solely dependent on farming and, according to a survey conducted by the Pan-American Health Organisation/World Health Organisation (PAHO/WHO), as many as 57 per cent of such households had to rely on sources other than farming for more than half their income.[4] The survey also revealed the existence of a complex system of land titles under which over a third of the farmers surveyed had no *bona fide* titles to their land. Only 48 per cent of the farm lands surveyed had irrigation and 62 per cent had drainage facilities. Farmers were so poor that as many as 57 per cent applied no regular fertilisers and 56 per cent no insecticides. The survey also showed that as many as three to four people slept in the same room at night, only 53 per cent of the families had piped water running into their homes or yards and one-eighth of the rural housewives had to travel 100 yards or more for water. Pit-latrines were used by 90 per cent of the rural families, while only 23 per cent had refrigeration. A study of eating habits showed that rural diets were low in energy, protein, riboflavin and niacin, with 77 per cent of rural households consuming less than the recommended daily intake of energy and 65 per cent less than the recommended daily intake of protein. Indeed, as many as 54 per cent of the sample received less than 80 per cent of the recommended intakes of energy and protein respectively. It is hardly surprising that whilst the survey showed that one-third of the labour power available on these farms was underemployed and that the average farm worker worked only seven hours per day, one-fifth of these did so because they claimed that they were 'too tired to work'. The evidence on malnutrition was confirmed by anthropometric data. Approximately 18 per cent of the children in all households in Guyana suffered from malnutrition. However, 'malnutrition is more severe in the rural areas where 22 per cent more infants and children under 5 years old are in Gomez Grades II and III than in the urban areas'.[5]

In Jamaica, the evidence of poverty and inequality is no less striking.[6] Stone portrays the Jamaican class structure in terms of three major categories and seven sub-categories.

A. *Upper and Upper-Middle Class*

1.	Capitalists (owners and managers of large and medium businesses)	0.5%
2.	Administrative class	0.5%

B. *Lower-Middle Class*

3.	Independent property owners and middle-level capitalists	5.0%
4.	Labour aristocracy (technicians, white collar, skilled workers. . .)	18.0%

C. *Lower Class*

5.	Own-account workers or petty capitalists (small farmers, street vendors)	28.0%
6.	Working class (low-wage manual workers)	23.0%
7.	Long-term or indefinitely unemployed	25.0%

The stratification is reflected in unequal consumption levels and access to social amenities. As Kaufman points out, the data from Stone and other government sources indicate that in the Kingston area only 10 per cent of lower working-class and 21 per cent of working-class homes had a refrigerator or stereo set. Only 40.6 per cent of urban dwellings and 6.4 per cent of rural dwellings had piped water. As many as 45 per cent of urban dwellings had only one room. Using an estimate of J$30 per week and J$50 per week for the poverty-line of peasant and working-class categories respectively in 1977, he points out that Stone's data show that 84 per cent of small farmers, 94 per cent of the lower working class and 50 per cent of the working class earned below their respective poverty lines. The poorest 70 per cent of the population consumed only 37 grams of protein per day (a figure less than the recommended daily allowance) even although an average of 68 grams of protein per day was available to the population at large (in other words, one and a half times the recommended daily allowance). It was estimated then that one in three pre-school children received insufficient food energy and protein and that almost half the pregnant and lactating women were anaemic.[7]

This crisis became even more acute when, after a period of capitalist expansion lasting from 1945 to 1970, the global capitalist system itself entered into a period of crisis. This was caused by a number of factors, the most important of which were the ending of US hegemony in the capitalist world economy (established after the Second World War) and the emergence of a number of different growth centres, particularly in the EEC and Japan; the rapid growth of Eastern Europe, especially in terms of gross world output, manufacturing, technology and armaments; the emergence of the oil-producing states as a major economic force brought about by the oil crisis and its impact on the global division of income; and the growth of nationalism in peripheral countries eager to alter the terms of their engagement in the world division of labour.

The sluggish demand for imports, international inflation, persistent balance-of-payments crises in several important capitalist countries and the development of nationalist and 'beggar-thy-neighbour' policies, which put severe pressure on international regulatory mechnisms, are all evidence of the structural crisis of world capitalism. The generalised foreign-exchange crisis and the slow growth in the demand for exports of the non-oil-producing countries of the periphery have also forced growing indebtedness (with its attendant risks of default) and restrictions on demand for imports. These in turn have led to lower domestic consumption and a shortage of consumer goods, raw materials and spare parts and, because of the high import content of domestic output and consumption, to reduced domestic production. Not surprisingly, there was also considerable ferment and agitation. Popular resistance to all forms of foreign domination was widely expressed and these peaked in a number of social explosions, including the Rodney Riots in Jamaica, the Black Power revolt in Trinidad-Tobago (1970) and the crisis in the Dominican Republic in the late 1960s. A number of left-wing political parties also grew out of this increasing consciousness of foreign domination and the need for change. The question of the extent of foreign ownership and domination of the region's economy became a key issue in the ideological struggle which ensued. And, in that it questioned the very basis of the colonial and later the nationalist strategy for regional development, it turned out to be an issue of immense significance in the pursuit of a means to overcome the crisis.

Arguments against the existing strategy were based on the belief that regional ownership was a *necessary* and, misguidedly, a *sufficient* condition for indigenous control of the region's resources and that only with such ownership and control could models of economic development produce policies oriented to the needs of the poor and powerless majority. When put as crudely as this, as they frequently were, these arguments tended to overlook a number of complex considerations. For example, did regional ownership and control refer to state control or control by indigenous private capital? Was ownership and control indifferent to everything but the nationality of those in control? In other words, were these class-related categories? Was local ownership and control, in whatever form, capable of producing rates of material progress comparable to those of earlier periods *and*, therefore, in keeping with the *expectations of the masses* in whose name such control was being sought? What were the domestic political implications of these choices? What international ramifications did they entail and how far could small, vulnerable economies in the backyard of the world's most powerful imperialist state pursue policies in contradiction to the historical evolution of imperialism itself?

With the vision of hindsight, the importance of these considerations seems self-evident, but at the time they were less obvious and, as a result, a number of serious errors were made. These will be discussed later in the book, but for the meanwhile I would like to confine the discussion in the remainder of this chapter to examine the broad characteristics of the major approaches to the issue of ownership and control which, as events proved, were to be pursued in the region. Before turning to this, however, let us briefly recall some of the changes which had occurred in the pattern of TNC domination in the region, as these have an important bearing on the discussion. First, North American companies were challenging the exclusive dominance of UK firms. And second, TNC control was no longer confined to plantation, agriculture and raw materials. These sectors did remain important and were even developed with new crops such as bananas and new raw materials, such as bauxite-alumina in Jamaica and manganese in Guyana, but more important were the newer areas of tourism, banking, finance and other related services, as well as import-substitution manufacturing and agro-processing activities. Large-scale TNC capital projects in joint-venture arrangements with local governments (such as steel and fertilisers in Trinidad-Tobago), as well as in the more traditional manufacturing areas (such as the dairy and seafood business in Barbados and flour-milling in Trinidad-Tobago) were also important.

The policy responses to regional ownership and control were to take four major forms. These were (i) localising the management of foreign enterprises; (ii) requiring foreign firms to localise their ownership by raising a substantial part of their capital through local equities; (iii) state participation through joint-ventures; and (iv) nationalisation or compulsory acquisition. In broad terms, these four policies either reflected stages of evolution of policy or the degree of radicalism in the approach of governments to the problem.[8]

Localising Management

From the mid-1960s onwards, a great deal of state effort throughout the region went into trying to persuade foreign-owned companies to allow nationals to participate in the higher levels of management and decision-making. Besides finding attractive employment outlets for local skilled personnel, the strategy was based on the assumption that an infusion of indigenous people into key management positions would serve to localise the operations of these companies. Inasmuch as such localisation was believed to offset dramatically one of the main means of perpetuating dependency, progress tended to be measured simply in terms of how many foreigners' jobs were taken over by local personnel and, judging from claims all around, such progress was considerable. There are, of course, very serious limitations to this approach. For a start, while undoubtedly a logical extension of the dismantling of the administrative apparatus which began during the struggle for constitutional independence, it underestimates the power of these institutions and the degree of their control over the lives of individuals. Pursuing such a policy in the context of a drive to establish an indigenous capitalist class can contribute very little to the struggle to transform the mode of production. This is because when local people are appointed to positions in these companies they inevitably move into an institutional structure with its own ethos, values, life-styles and ways of doing things to exploit local resources for the benefit of metropolitan capital. These nationals therefore function in an institutional situation in which there are strong built-in pressures to conform to patterns of behaviour dictated by the enterprises. The pressures inevitably continue for as long as the individual is a functioning part of the corporate entity.

As this socialisation continues, it becomes evident that instead of the company becoming more and more national in its outlook, character and purpose, the nationals become more and more integrated into the foreign system and usually end up as extensions of the exploiting corporation. In this conflict between localisation and integration into the company, the enterprises are indirectly aided by public policies that seek to encourage capitalism. These policies create a contradictory situation in which the national bourgeoisie, which they themselves seek to create, becomes denationalised through being required to operate as a peripheral force to international capitalism. The fact that many of these personnel possess residency status in North America or Europe reinforces this trend.

It was because of their confidence in this acculturation process that many TNCs decided not to resist pressures for localisation but instead to appear to welcome nationals into their operations. It is now a well-accepted part of corporate practice to acquire a national image this way, knowing full well that the true nationality of the corporation will not be endangered. People living in the region have ample proof of this through the striking frequency with which the news media refer to these various promotions and appointments, often made to very public positions so as to maximise their publicity value. There is a pattern of appointments to directorships on boards with little authority or with only a minority of local appointments, of appointments to public relations offices and, of increasing strategic importance, of local appointments as personnel officers, which has the added advantage of being able to divert the hostility of the workers by concealing the true identity of the enterprise. Whatever the particular stratagem employed, these companies seek, as indeed they must, to undermine the significance of this strategy to take over their operations. They naturally hope to be able to exploit the dynamics of cultural and psychological dependence. They have the sheer weight and power of international capitalism on their side.

Another limitation of this approach is that it fails to take account of the technique of organisational substitution which has been facilitated by the technological possibilities of computerisation and virtually instant communication. This process permits the companies to let nationals nominally fill managerial positions while at the same time depriving them of any decision-making significance by referring to the head office decisions that would normally and routinely be made locally if the head office had the uncontrolled and uncontested right to appoint management. Of course, in so far as the previous argument holds (namely that local management is acculturated to the values of the enterprise and is also assumed by the head office to be efficient), the need for this form of organisational substitution is diminished. The degree of substitution can be seen as a useful gauge of the importance of cultural and psychological dependence in the development of the local managerial class.

The managers of localised corporations are meant to constitute the embryo of an indigenous capitalist class. They are supposed to acquire from their jobs and their positions in the multinational firms the technical and managerial skills to enable them to play a pioneering and innovative role in the transformation of their economies. But, being dependent on the multinational corporations and on local nationalist sentiment to ensure their mobility, it is unclear how they are supposed to get the capital for indigenously owned enterprises even should they acquire the necessary entrepreneurial capabilities. Although some run small businesses, as a side-line, usually in housing or land speculation, the returns on such ventures are clearly marginal to the capital needs of the society. Objectively this class is basically a dependent offshoot of the multinational firm and is unlikely to develop into much more than yet another agency for internalising the dependency characteristics of the society.

Localising Ownership

The second policy response of issuing local equities to ensure local private participation in the ownership of the enterprises also contains a number of fundamental limitations. First, when compelled to incorporate locally these companies always manage to issue shares in such quantities and in such a way as to avoid putting any real control of their companies into jeopardy. They are often encouraged in this by generous timetables set by the local governments for achieving stated levels of local private participation in their activities. The governments argue that these generous timetables are necessary to minimise disruptions of the local capital market. Second, this device is strongly reinforced by a tendency for these shares to be taken up by psuedo-local enterprises (for example, a financial company that has been similarly localised or by a particular group of local businessmen who specialise in partnering local and foreign capital).

A third difficulty with this policy derives from the familiar technique companies employ of ensuring that local share issues raise sufficient funds from the local capital market to finance the physical construction costs of the enterprise, but exchanging the remainder of the shares for patent rights or technical services from the parent firm. Furthermore, where the enterprise is long-established and already a going concern, the issuance of local shares to enable participation in this way simply provides the firm with funds that it may then choose to invest elsewhere, particularly if the fear of local incursion into its control is taken seriously. If, in the context of issuing local shares, foreign capital comes in, woos local capital, uses it and controls it for foreign ends, it becomes impossible to sustain any belief in its ability to augment national resources.

While the clamour to issue shares on the local market is often directed towards foreign-owned enterprises, at the same time there remain many locally-owned firms that are not very public in their ownership structures and that remain in the firm and uncontested grip of particular families and business cliques. While of lesser importance than their foreign counterparts in terms of capital employed, this failure to implement positive policies aimed at diluting their ownership structures none the less serves to emphasise that the strategy is based on creating a new local capitalist class to replace the foreign capitalists and in no way seeks to contest the legitimacy of the capitalist structure itself.

Joint Ventures

The third strategy, whereby the state is the majority shareholder (the 51 per cent formula), is the most common among the region's more progressively-inclined states. While the regional struggle to contain the TNCs is implicitly anti-imperialist, when pursued in the context of generating an indigenous capitalism, there are at least three basic reasons why it is incapable of leading to effective control of local resources.

First, given an absence of local confidence regarding knowledge of the technical, marketing and managerial processes of the firm, such participation in ownership has been frequently counteracted by the practice of simultaneously entering into management contracts with foreign capitalists. To the extent that this practice prevails, it is possible for these arrangements not to diminish the power of foreign decision-making in these enterprises. Moreover, when pursued in the context of generating a local capitalist class, this policy does not provide a dynamic basis for phasing out these foreign decision-makers.

Second, experience has shown that contracts made for these services often constitute a significant income drain. Thus, as both Guyana and Manley's Jamaica demonstrated, where there was a socialist programme for phasing out this foreign dependence, management contracts were concluded on bases such as the firm's total rate of sales (turnover). Since such expenses are prior to profits, this leads to firms with persistent commercial losses being forced to carry the income drain of foreign management contract payments. In other instances, either full profit repatriation is guaranteed or the state implicitly, or occasionally explicitly, accepts the obligation to 'manage' and 'stabilise' the labour situation. All these in effect provide these firms with guarantees they would never have had without state regulation.

This strategy's third weakness lies in the basic misunderstanding of what a multinational corporation, and particularly an exporting corporation, represents locally:

> It is essentially a plant. It is not a firm. It is true that there are titles such as Directors, Managers, Managing Directors, etc. But the local expression. . . makes no decision as regards prices. . . output. . . levels of investment, or the markets. All these are done at the head office, where decisions which normally define a firm are made. The apparatus which exists locally is just a participation in a multi-plant firm. Therefore, when we seek meaningful participation, it is not simply to acquire a share in the local apparatus, but to ensure that inroads are made into the decision-making centers which exist in the North Atlantic.[9]

If this point is not fully grasped and if the thrust of state policy is confined simply to legal ownership of part of the expatriate enterprise, there will inevitably be little change in the content and methods of production.

Nationalisation

Nationalisation has been heralded as the most radical of all the approaches, but it should not be confused with the kind of expropriation that occurred in Cuba after the revolution. In every known instance, firms that have been nationalised in the region have always been bought from their owners by the government concerned through a negotiated purchase-and-sale agreement. There are also no known instances of firms disapproving of any of these final settlements. At least none of them have said so publicly or pursued lines of redress, either through referring the matter to the government of the country concerned or through international legal arbitration.

One immediate consequence of such a purchase has been

to increase the foreign indebtedness of these countries and so add to foreign-exchange and balance-of-payments pressures which later emerged as the national and international crisis deepened. Guyana is a good example of this. The strategy also has a number of other defects, one of which is the existence of management contracts after nationalisation and the income drain this constitutes. Another is that in the absence of qualitative changes in the character of the state, a certain amount of degeneration occurs, especially with growing bureaucratisation of economic enterprises proving costly in terms of efficiency. Where the state and/or its functionaries are corrupt, the way is opened up for clientilism, nepotism and graft to become institutionalised. Later, confusion develops over the objectives and criteria for efficiency evaluation in these enterprises. This is particularly noticeable in situations where, as with bauxite-alumina in Guyana, nationalised concerns previously undertook responsibility for certain social functions traditionally within the purview of the state, or alternatively where world-wide downturns in economic activity impinge themselves on the markets for these firms' output. Once these developments are manifested in management, economic rationality quickly disappears.[10]

Because buying TNC assets under nationalisation programmes involves a fixed charge for the enterprise, companies in the region have never resisted these developments. Indeed, cases can even be cited where they have precipitated their own 'buy out' by the government as a means of shifting to the no less profitable but far less risky reliance on management, technology, marketing and licensing agreements with the government as the new owners.[11]

As the crisis in the region has deepened, local governments have tended to reverse many of their earlier positions for they now believe they need the TNCs more than the TNCs need their resources. This has opened the way for divestment policies, particularly in Guyana and Jamaica, which is a subject to which we shall return in the final section of this book.

11 *National Experiments: The Radical Options*

This chapter looks at three countries in the West Indies which tried to find radical or socialist solutions to the crisis they faced in the 1970s. Because so many issues are surveyed in this text, it would be unrealistic to attempt to provide detailed analyses or case studies of the various countries in the area. Instead I propose to focus on the major policy thrusts with a view to evaluating their general success (or lack of it) and the potential for success (if any) inherent in the approaches. The references given from time to time will enable interested readers to pursue the rapidly growing literature on the subject.

I: Democratic Socialism and Conservative Reaction: Jamaica

As social experiments, it is difficult to determine which of the three countries (Jamaica, Grenada or Guyana) has engendered the most interest. There is no doubt, however, that in terms of international propaganda on the merits and defects of 'socialism' and 'free enterprise' as models for third world development, Jamaica has attracted a considerable amount of attention. This is partly because successive US administrations have played an active role in Jamaica's internal affairs (particularly in destabilising Michael Manley's socialism in the 1972-80 period and since then in supporting Edward Seaga's free-enterprise approach) and partly because Manley himself has played a leading role on the world stage, particularly in the Non-Aligned Movement and the Socialist International. In Ambursley's view:

> The fall of Michael Manley, the Socialist International's most important representative in the Third World, dealt a serious, if not fatal, blow to the gradualist strategy of social change advocated by broad sectors of the Caribbean left and endorsed in recent years by the Cuban leadership. At the same time the restoration of the stalwartly anti-communist JLP provided the Reagan administration with an invaluable collaborator in its crusade to contain and roll back the wave of revolutionary mobilisation that has swept the Caribbean and Central America since 1979.[1]

Payne, however, felt that although in 'the last few years

Jamaica [had] aroused more interest in the eyes of the world than any other country in the Commonwealth Caribbean. . . the whole Manley experiment constituted dramatic evidence of the problems and possibilities that attach to 'democratic socialist' strategies of reform in trying to overcome dependency in the Third World'.[2]

Policies

To appreciate the nature of the solutions offered by Manley's democratic socialism, it is necessary to bear in mind that between the Second World War and 1972, Jamaica (more than perhaps any other West Indian territory), epitomised the classic forms of the colonial-nationalist strategies discussed in Part 2. During this period there was rapid growth in Jamaica's domestic output as the bauxite-alumina and tourism sectors expanded in response to large foreign capital inflows. Between 1950 and independence (in 1962), nominal GDP grew sevenfold and per capita national income and foreign trade, eightfold. In real terms, GDP had grown at a compound annual rate of 5-6 per cent while real per capita GDP had grown at 3-4 per cent per annum. Foreign savings financed about one-third of total investment in this period. The extent of the growth of these new sectors is reflected in the fact that at the end of the Second World War the traditional exports of sugar, bananas and other agricultural products accounted for 96 per cent of merchandise trade, whereas by the mid-1960s their share had been reduced to 37 per cent.

Despite the rapid growth in national income, the country was in a state of severe crisis in 1970. Between 1962 and 1972, unemployment rose from 13 to 24 per cent of the labour force. The situation became even worse with the closure of migration outlets, especially to the UK where governments were trying to stop the flood of West Indian immigration into the country. Income distribution also worsened as personal income earned by the poorest 40 per cent of the population declined from 7.2 per cent of the total in 1958 to 5.4 per cent in 1968. In absolute terms, the annual income of the poorest 30 per cent of the population fell from J\$32 per capita in 1958 to J\$25 in 1968, measured in constant

1958 dollars. At the same time, there was evidence of continued consolidation of the society's traditional hegemonic groups, with 21 families accounting for 125 of the 219 directorships in corporations registered in Jamaica. These same families also supplied approximately 70 per cent of the chairpersons of the various corporate boards. Not one of these firms was in black hands, although blacks made up 80 per cent of the population. Of the 219 directorships only six were held by black people and, of these, two were government appointments in joint-venture arrangements.[3] There was also extensive foreign ownership in the major sectors of the economy, with 100 per cent of mining, 75 per cent of manufacturing, 66 per cent of financial services, 66 per cent of transport, over 50 per cent of communications, storage and tourism and 40 per cent of sugar in foreign hands. The Jamaican bourgeoisie was thus economically subordinate to North American and British capital.

The Manley government had five main aims, namely to reduce the dependence of the economy; to create a mixed economy with the commanding heights under state control; to reduce social inequalities; to deepen political democracy; and to forge an independent foreign policy. As Manley himself explained:

> We began and ended with four basic commitments, each of which bears a relationship to and reinforces the other three. Firstly we wanted to create an economy that would be more independent of foreign control and more responsive to the needs of the majority of the people at home. Secondly we wanted to work for an egalitarian society both in terms of opportunity and also in the deeper sense of a society in which people felt that they were of equal worth and value. Thirdly we wanted to develop a truly democratic society in which democracy was more than the attempt to manipulate votes every five years. Finally, we wanted to help, indeed accelerate the process by which Jamaicans were retracing the steps of their history.[4]

Manley's overall effort was guided by the desire to find what he termed a 'third path'. As he put it, 'The PNP won a landslide victory in the general elections of February 1972. Before our eyes were these two models – Puerto Rico and Cuba. Surely there was another path, a third path. . . we were to spend the next eight and a half years in our periphery exploring that third path'.[5] It is in this context, therefore, of trying to discover and pursue a third path, that Manley's economic policies in Jamaica must be analysed. It is important to note from the outset that Manley was unaware of what that path was, but was none the less convinced of its existence.

He approached his first goal, which was to end foreign control over the economy, through a combination of two policies, namely selective nationalisation and the imposition of taxes on the bauxite-alumina industry at the very core of the country's economy. Selective nationalisation was directed to the public utilities, those parts of the sugar economy under foreign control, some textile operations, the flour-refining industry, some financial institutions and hotels in the tourist industry. These nationalisations reflected the wish to keep natural monopolies in state hands (public utilities) and to rescue ailing industries so as to minimise economic and social dislocation (hotels). They were also expected to increase the state sector's influence over the pace and direction of internal capital accumulation, so that other industries could be developed and forward and backward links within the national economy forged. It was on the basis of this rationale that the state decided to form agro-industrial enterprises and to increase public control over distribution by establishing a state trading entity and state importation of certain basic goods.

It is important to note that all the nationalisations of the Manley period were undertaken with prompt and adequate compensation. Manley himself described his government's attitude to capital as follows:

> We were determined to try to put the whole question of foreign investment on some kind of national basis. Make no mistake about it: we wanted foreign investment. . . but we were not willing to continue the approach to foreign investment of the Puerto Rican model type, where foreign investment is seen as the main engine of development with all policy being made to revolve around the entrenching of that element. We saw foreign capital as part of but not the whole of the development process.[6]

Manley's government often expressed its support for local

small business, which it undoubtedly hoped would counteract the entrenched influence of the famous 21 families. At the same time, however, the government's allies within these families were invited to play active roles in negotiating the nationalisation of foreign capital and in administering the state enterprises which were subsequently created.

Manley's bauxite policy was in many ways the most interesting of those initiated during his administration; although it fell short of nationalisation, it ironically provoked more protest from the companies than any of the nationalisations. Its declared aims were to secure a 'limited disengagement' of the country's most vital natural resource from North American ownership and control and to integrate this resource more closely into Jamaica's productive system.

The former was to be pursued through securing state participation in the ownership of the bauxite companies operating in Jamaica, through forming a world-wide cartel of bauxite-producing countries, through introducing a tax levy and through setting up a Jamaica Bauxite Institute. The latter was to be achieved through returning idle land owned by the bauxite companies to the local peasantry and, in association with Guyana, Trinidad-Tobago, Mexico and Venezuela, developing an aluminium-smelter complex. Over the period of Manley's government this complex secured 51 per cent of the local operation of the bauxite-mining companies and between 6 and 7 per cent of the companies producing bauxite-alumina. Although the purchase price was relatively low in relation to market prices or replacement costs and interest rates were attractive, the agreement none the less contained the management-contract clauses discussed in the previous chapter. The partial ownership and return of idle bauxite lands took several years to negotiate and was eventually achieved through the government buying up all the land and then reassigning to the companies what they needed to mine bauxite (with guaranteed access to ore reserves for the next 40 years).

As we noted earlier, the companies resisted the levy and took the issue for legal settlement. After strenuous effort the International Bauxite Association was formed, but without the teeth of OPEC. For one thing, Australia was a member and, as a developed capitalist country, did not have the same kind of interest as the oil producers had in disrupting the international economy. For another, the other Third World countries in the association showed little interest in asserting the association's monopoly power and all, in fact, tried to preserve their competitive advantage by imposing lower levies on their bauxite sales than Jamaica.

During the Manley period, bauxite-alumina sales were diversified to Eastern Europe but, by all accounts, the terms were not particularly concessionary price-wise. This diversification nevertheless opened up the possibility of stable long-term sales contracts, which must have constituted a major advantage in marketing the product in these countries. By 1980, Norway had signed a deal to establish an alumina plant in Jamaica, but this never materialised because Manley lost the election in that year. In like manner, Manley's efforts to persuade other countries in the region to pool their resources to establish a major alumina complex had not managed to get off the ground by 1980. The levy had none the less led to substantial growth in bauxite earnings. Government revenue from the industry increased from an average of US$30 million between 1970 and 1973, to an average of US$164 million between 1974 and 1977 and US$196 million for 1978/79. At the same time, however, Jamaica's share of world output was falling fast. This was due to three major factors, the rapid growth of the industries in Guinea, Australia and (later) Brazil; the policy adopted by the companies in Jamaica of cutting back production to reduce the impact of the levy on their global operations; and the general uncertainty created by the government's confrontation with the companies. With respect to the last of these factors, it should be noted that recorded foreign capital inflows through the bauxite-alumina sector in Jamaica dried up in the later years of Manley's rule. Also, mainly because of the concern the companies raised over the levy, insurance to Jamaica was suspended by the Overseas Private Investment Corporation.

In relation to land, the government implemented moderate land-reform based largely on a land-lease programme and the establishment of sugar cooperatives. The land-lease programme aimed 'to put idle lands into idle hands' and the scheme was modelled on one created by the bauxite companies to put idle bauxite lands into productive use through leasing them to small farmers. Basically, the programme required government to lease to small farmers its own lands as well as privately-owned lands which it acquired where holdings were in excess of 100 acres and were kept idle. In the first stage the leases were for a period of five to ten years, with the government providing credit for seed and other costs. A second stage was envisaged for the future with longer leases and a more cooperative structure.

The Manley government attempted several innovations in various important socio-cultural areas. It introduced legislation on a number of trade-union issues in need of attention, such as minimum wages for certain categories of workers, maximum working hours in some industries, severance pay, maternity leave and sickness benefits and also initiated some worker-participation programmes in the public sector. Considerable attention was paid to primary and secondary education, particularly to curricula reform, teacher training and the provision of improved physical amenities. Broad reforms were also attempted in the area of health with the government generally trying to make the social welfare services it provided sufficiently meaningful and effective to improve the situation for the mass of the impoverished population. It was with this in mind, that the government provided unemployment relief through a number of site-and-service work programmes, tried to upgrade the public media as fora for public education and even sought to improve the tax system by taking measures to counter the extensive tax evasion practised by the well-to-do.

In its external relations, efforts were made to diversify trade away from North America and the UK which, in the early 1970s, between them accounted for as much as 90 per cent of the country's trade. By 1980, this had been reduced to 60 per cent, with the CARICOM countries, Latin America, Japan and Europe (East and West) becoming more important as markets for Jamaican produce and as sources of imports, particularly oil. In this drive, Manley was exceedingly vocal in his support for a New International Economic Order. His most radical departures on the external economic front were probably the development of technical assistance, trade and other economic relations with Cuba and the formation of the International Bauxite Association, with its headquarters in Jamaica.

In an attempt to counteract the historic powerlessness of the masses, Manley's government advocated more popular forms of democracy than periodic national and local elections, including worker participation and community councils. The latter were promoted as a 'new arena for group cooperation and, consequently, a new focus for a sense of communal reality'.[7] They were to be set up in 'a defined geographical area in which residents share basic services and institutions, and where residents regard themselves as having common interests and needs. Examples of communities are villages, districts, housing schemes, neighbourhoods'.[8] These organisations, together with government and other nongovernmental agencies, were supposed to initiate, develop and implement plans and programmes for the community, to mobilise people to participate in community affairs, to disseminate public information and provide fora for community discussion and education on issues of importance to it, to represent communities in relation to other agencies and to coordinate their relationship to government agencies and non-governmental organisations.

Weaknesses

Over time, several weaknesses became apparent in the Manley government's programme. Some of these were intrinsic to the policies themselves, given the context in which they were being implemented, while others developed weaknesses through poor conceptualisation, articulation, implementation, or monitoring and evaluation.

Any society undergoing a fundamental transformation has difficulty achieving the correct blend of social reform and material progress. In societies such as Jamaica, with limited resources and a small economy, these difficulties are compounded. In both articulating and implementing its policies, Manley's government seems, at best, to have underestimated the importance of sustained income flows (particularly in the form of foreign exchange) in creating the social space required for social reforms. This is a complex issue which is partly linked to the expectations of the masses and the alternative experiences to which they are exposed through the media and partly to the degree to which political and social mobilisation is achieved. It is the latter, I believe, that ultimately determines the trade-off between present and future, or the extent of self-sacrifice the masses are prepared to accept. As a rule, they are more likely to put up with poverty if they believe their social power has increased to a point of no return and that they and their representatives are able to play a leading role in ensuring its permanent eradication.

How Manley and the People's National Party (PNP) articulated their plans is much clearer now than it was then. For most of the period, there was no comprehensive plan or framework to guide economic policy. The 1972-74 period thus differs significantly from the later period when the IMF became intimately involved and there were many starts and false starts. This is not intended to suggest that the PNP should have had a hard-and-fast plan to which it stuck through thick and thin, but merely to advance the view that the strategy emerged confusedly as events, which were more often than not unanticipated, bore down heavily on the government, forcing it to react. In other words, the strategy Manley employed was largely *ad hoc* and pragmatic, and it was only after the event that it was rationalised to fit into the government's ideology. It was because the ideology was phrased in radical terms that its downfall was predictable. As Barry *et al* put it: 'For all the criticism levelled at it by the United States, the Manley government was never a radical government with a plan for a substantial restructuring of the economy. The PNP had not formulated an overall plan to mobilise domestic agricultural and industrial workers. Consequently, it fell helplessly victim to international and local pressures'.[9]

The record suggests that many of the programmes the PNP implemented failed because of maladministration, a good example being the Community Enterprise Organisations which, although regarded as *the key element* in popular mobilisation, never really got off the ground. By December 1980, only 86 of these organisations had been financed at a total expenditure of only J$6.6 million, despite the 1978-82 Development Plan describing them in such exalted terms as 'a higher stage of development in socialist relations of

National Experiments: The Radical Options

production than the cooperative'[10] and arguing that they were 'ideally suited to undertake an integrated complex of socio-economic activities primarily oriented toward satisfying the basic needs of the community'.[11] Structurally these organis-ations were to have two transitional forms, the Pioneer Farms, where 'idle hands were put on idle lands' to work cooperatively and an urban unit, which would use idle build-ings, land, local materials, unemployed labour and various other facilities. Although the 1978-1982 Plan envisaged creating 300 farms employing 15,000 people, by the end of Manley's rule only a few existed. As for the urban units, it was not until 1979, which was two years after they were first announced, that the first one was established, but with its 'socialist content' watered down to the point of being unrecognisable.

Apart from their negligible quantitative impact, many of the community organisations were criticised for being cooperative in name only, with only a few living up to the high promises and expectations of the original concept. Many had no building of their own, nor even, in some instances, a permanent address. All seemed to have suffered from central government bureaucracy and disputes frequently arose over their relationships with the numerous government depart-ments with which they had to deal (agriculture, housing, regional affairs, youth, sports and community development, or local government). By the end of the Manley period, there were no truly mass or community-structured organisations in existence, for most of them had degenerated into partisan bodies in which only PNP supporters actively participated.

Similar problems arose in the sugar farm cooperatives, which not only were created when sugar prices were depressed, but also by the time they were established the sugar companies had largely run down their capital stock. Also, because the sugar factories were not integrated into the farms, the cooperatives were located in the least profitable segment of the industry. Many members of the government opposed the sugar cooperatives and this complicated their dealings with central government and the difficulties they had in acquiring resources to put the industry on a profitable footing.[12] As Kaufman observes: 'When all was said and done, there was one last set of problems key in limiting the

economic health of the coops – and in limiting the attractiveness of the coops as a model for other workers in Jamaica. . .
the farms were now worker-owned. . . but actual control
was not exercised by the average worker'.[13] He goes on to
point out that 'because the cane workers were not peasants
they had no entrepreneurial experience or orientation'[14]; there
was:

> . . . a lack of educational programmes, low levels of literacy,
> income inequalities, the maintenance of the pre-existing
> division of labour and actual social relations of production
> and the large size of the coop farms and the estates which
> prevented identification between individual workers and prob-
> lems of the coop. . . these problems were exacerbated by low
> self-esteem among a group that had been severely oppressed
> – socially, culturally and economically – for generations.[15]

This leads to the more general point that the expansion of
the state sector during the Manley period was at too high a
cost. Not only were nationalisations paid for promptly and
in full, but very often, to minimise social and economic
dislocation, the government purchased enterprises in danger
of economic collapse. This was the case with the sugar cooperatives. The general weaknesses inherent in this sort of state
expansion were accentuated by the severe shortage of trained
managers to ensure that the newly-acquired enterprises were
properly run. The inefficiencies of the sugar coops and
community-enterprise organisations therefore mirrored the
even greater inefficiency of an unplanned, uncoordinated, *ad
hoc* expansion of state property, which was hardly helped by
the government's own socialist propaganda.

Another critical weakness in the government's policy
was its failure to appreciate the crucial importance of foreign
exchange and, in particular, the need to maintain sufficient
inflows to service the economy it had inherited. It was the
drying up of these supplies which eventually forced Manley's
government into the hands of the IMF and laid the basis
for its eventual removal from office. Jamaica's balance-of-
payments difficulties reached a crisis point in 1976, when
foreign-exchange reserves fell from J$137 million in June
1975 to *minus* J$181 million in December 1976. In June 1977,
the government signed a Stand-by Agreement with the IMF,

but this was terminated in December 1977 when it failed to meet the net domestic assets test set by the IMF. After extensive discussions, an Extended Fund Facility was obtained in May 1978, which lasted until December 1979 when the Bank of Jamaica failed to meet the net international reserves test set by the IMF. Between December 1979 and March 1980, prolonged negotiations were held with the IMF but the National Executive Council of the PNP eventually decided to reject the IMF path. Two ministers of government resigned in protest. A new economic path was envisaged, but by then, it was too little, too late.

Underlying the foreign-exchange crisis was a rapid expansion of imports (126 per cent between 1972 and 1976), particularly oil imports which increased from J\$63 million worth in 1973 to J\$178 million worth in 1976. External-debt repayments also worsened, rising from J\$49 million in 1974 to J\$100 million in 1976 as the gross external debt increased from US\$195 million in December 1973 to US\$489 million in December 1976. The government's budget deficit had also grown from J\$67 million in the fiscal year 1972/73 to J\$278 million in the fiscal year 1975/76. Tourism receipts also fell by 13 per cent during 1974/75 and again by 10 per cent in 1976.

Much of this was due to the destabilisation measures pursued by the US administration, which was becoming increasingly hostile to Manley's foreign policy positions and increasingly supportive of Seaga, who seemed to offer the prospect of a good collaborator. The US was particularly concerned about Manley's position in the Socialist International, his friendship with Castro, the increasing contact between Cuba and Jamaica, Manley's support of Angola and Cuba's efforts to defend it and the formation of the International Bauxite Association. The result was that, in 1975, the USAID turned down Manley's request for aid and food grants unless the government changed its stance. The Export-Import Bank also reduced Jamaica's credit rating. Manley winning the elections in 1976 served only to harden positions on both sides and the US press campaign on violence in Jamaica continued unabated, fuelled by the loss of over 750 lives through the partisan struggles of the time.

During this period, Jamaica's share of total world

bauxite exports fell from 27 per cent in 1970 to 17 per cent in 1975. Capital inflows into Jamaica, which had averaged US$254 million in 1973 fell to US$115 million in 1975 and became negative (ie a net outflow) by 1976.

By the end of Manley's rule in 1980, there had been no real improvement in the economy. In fact it actually had increased its focus on a few key exports which made it even more vulnerable than before. Although trade with 'non-traditional' countries had grown from 10 to 40 per cent, commodity dependence on bauxite-alumina, sugar and bananas had also grown from 79 to 83 per cent between 1972 and 1980. Trade as a ratio of GDP had increased from 72 per cent in 1970 to 107 per cent in 1980, indicating a decreased self-sufficiency. The external indebtedness of the country had grown from $US370 million in 1972 to US$1,700 million in 1980. The debt service ratio in 1979 was 17 per cent of exports of goods and services. Capital flight out of Jamaica was extraordinarily high, prompting the formation of a special detection unit in the security services. All the public utilities were in a state of disrepair with massive investments required to upgrade their capacity and the quality of their services. The bauxite-alumina, sugar and tourist industries were all in a state of such crisis that between 1972 and 1980 real income decreased by 25 per cent. Recorded inflation in this period was 320 per cent. Efforts at diversification and import substitution of food were not significantly successful, for although food imports as a percentage of non-fuel imports fell from 14 to 10 per cent between 1973 and 1980, food shortages were a prominent feature of that year. An enormous amount of skilled people left the country, with an estimated 18,000 having gone to the US alone between 1976 and 1980. In one year (1978), 2,705 emigrants were in the category of managerial, administrative or technical.[16]

Assessment

In assessing this attempt to solve Jamaica's problems through recourse to a 'third path', it is important to try and gain insights that could be useful to any future social experiment along these lines in the region. I believe there is a need for a constructively critical approach and that, despite the contradictory evidence, the central figures behind the 'third-path' approach were, on balance, guided more by their concern for the poor and powerless than, as some have argued, by the social opportunism of their class. Also, I do not believe that the experiment's collapse into the conservatism of Seaga's government rules out future efforts along these lines by other political and social movements in the region. After all, there have been other instances when so-called 'confirmation' that reformist socialist change was impossible to achieve in the Third World, has been proved wrong.[17] Not only do memories fade in time but many political actors and theorists are attracted to the 'third path' in the belief that it is the only one to combine socialist and liberal democratic practice. This, however, is based on a false notion held by many socialists, Marxists and Marxist-Leninists that socialism and political democracy are contradictory and ultimately irreconcilable objectives in the transition to socialism. The weaknesses of this view have been explored elsewhere,[18] but the main point to grasp here is that the proponents of the 'third path' are usually criticised for trying to resolve the 'contradiction' between socialism and liberal political democracy by diluting socialism to its social democratic form.

Given its reformist goals, all 'third-path' options obviously carry in them the dangers of vacillation and the risk of government policy becoming 'caught between two stools' and ending up with the worst of all possible worlds. As events unfolded in Jamaica, the PNP was clearly caught between the demands of the upper classes and the lower classes. Constructed on the basis of and espousing an all-class alliance, the party strove with all its might to avoid establishing a clear priority in its class line. As economic disintegration continued and the pressures mounted the government ended up displeasing both sectors and alienating middle-class support. The lower classes resented the pressures on their living standards (which mounted rapidly after 1976) and the upper classes, through their terror of socialism, proceeded to pursue destabilisation, sabotage, the flight of capital and migration as their main social and political goals. While one can say that this development partly reflected the traditional vacillatory character of Jamaica's petty-bourgeoisie, more generally it also reflected the political underdevelopment of class in general and the division of the country's labour force into two rival trade union political groupings. The extraordinary premium this situation places on creative and constructive political mobilisation was something the Manley government did not fully appreciate.

Instead, a second weakness emerged which can best be described as a consistent underestimation of the impact of ideological rhetoric and foreign-policy stances in a period of acute cold-war rivalry on local politics. Such rhetoric served to 'over-ideologise' the domestic struggle and consequently to expose it to developments in the international arena with which it could not contend. Whilst no doubt those who used the rhetoric saw its internal mobilising appeal as a decisive factor in its favour, they clearly did not fully gauge the use to which persons hostile to the regime could put this same rhetoric in mobilising opposition to the regime. The US administration and media, in particular, skillfully used the rhetoric to whip up capital flight from the country, to deter tourists from visiting Jamaica and to swing opinion in such institutions as the IMF in its direction. The fact that the rhetoric belied the internal social reality was of little immediate concern to those who promoted it, or to those who reacted to it. Barry *et al* cite a statement attributed to Larry Burns of the Council on Hemispheric Affairs, who said that 'In the closing days of the Ford Administration, Kissinger had become almost manic about getting rid of Manley'.[19] Similarly, Stone makes the perceptive observation that:

> Mr Manley's radical foreign policy clothed his relatively moderate domestic economic and social policies in an aura of leftist radicalism far removed from the reality of what he attempted to implement. But the image of a radical, marxist orientation to domestic social policies was sharpened both by the leftist rhetoric of Mr Manley and his party spokesmen and by self-serving interpretations of what was happening in Jamaica promoted by the North American media and the Jamaican bourgeoisie.[20]

He goes on to state that these pronouncements 'panicked the local bourgeoisie who became convinced that Jamaica was heading towards communism. Washington made common cause with the Jamaican bourgeoisie in seeking to undermine Mr Manley's administration'.[21]

It is perhaps in its relationship with the IMF that many of the limitations of the third path pursued by the Manley administration are best expressed. Although Jamaica's foreign-exchange difficulty manifested itself dramatically in the last four years of Manley's rule (1977-80), its origins can be traced to the earlier decline of bauxite-alumina investments in Jamaica and the position of the industry globally, to import-price inflation occasioned by the oil-price shock of 1973/74, to declining export production as local industries such as sugar and bananas faced major structural constraints, to the high import-intensity of the manufacturing sector, to the failure to develop a significant export capability in manufacturing and to the reliance on tourism, which was very susceptible to adverse publicity generated in North America. The flight of capital, the migration of skilled people and the retaliation of the bauxite companies, were all important in the last four years and, in effect, compounded the existing structural difficulties.[22]

Bernal provides a good starting point for appreciating what is involved in relations with the IMF:

> All programs of balance of payments adjustment involve the manipulation of macroeconomic variables and, therefore, implicitly contain a specific strategy of economic development that takes effect during, and continues after, the adjustment period. The IMF's strategy. . . is derived from its role in the capitalist world economy. . . [its role] is to maintain an environment that facilitates the accumulation of capital on a world scale. This requires the complete international mobility of capital and commodities.[23]

The IMF's adjustment strategy for third world countries comprises a familiar package: deregulation (that is removal of price controls), subsidies, exchange controls and import licensing; devaluation of the currency; emphasis on the development of the private sector as a corrective to the 'inefficient' statist bias of the previous period; a reduced public sector; strict fiscal goals to be set in terms of the size of the government's deficit and the amount of borrowing permitted from the banking system; and wage controls. The objective of the package is to stimulate capitalist initiatives through the promotion of 'free markets' and the policy of rolling back the state serves as a means of stimulating exports and making the previously inefficient import-substitution sector competitive. At the same time, the growth of real wages and living standards is to be contained and, if necessary, reduced to a level compatible with import-expenditure levels the country can 'afford'. This reduction is achieved through a mix of cuts in social expenditure, retrenchment of public-sector employees, wage restraint, reduced government deficit and its associated tight monetary policies and the implementation of 'realistic rates of interest'. The policy differences between this approach and Manley's and their probable political impact has been neatly summarised in two tables prepared by Bernal.

Given the very different trajectories of these approaches and their varying political impacts, Manley's ultimate capitulation into seeking to preside over the imposition of the IMF solution on the Jamaican population could only have led to his party's removal from power. From the literature emerging since 1980, it is clear that as the struggle between the government and the IMF progressed, the IMF and its backers became more and more prepared to push for their view of how Jamaica should develop, even to the point of removing the government if necessary. At this juncture, Seaga's JLP provided the perfect ally for derailing the third path. In retrospect, the only viable option for Manley would have been to have qualitatively deepened the government's commitment to the poor and powerless at the outset. This would not of course have guaranteed success – in real life political certainties are rarely known in advance – but short of capitulation and certain downfall, it was the only option available. To have moved in this direction, however, would have required the political and social movement he headed to have made a qualitative leap. This, again in retrospect, does not seem to have been as impossible as some have argued. In the end, the crisis confronting the third path through the IMF permitted no third option or third solution, but it did not rule out a transformation of the political movement itself. The IMF wanted to reverse Manley's policies and

Table 11.1
Policy Differences Between the Manley Government and the IMF

Issue	Manley Government	IMF
Type of Society	Mixed	Dependent Capitalist
Dominant Sector	State	Capitalist
Ownership of the means of production	State/cooperatives/ capitalist	Capitalist
Allocation of resources	Planning/Market	Market
Openness	Reduced	Complete
Accumulation and distribution	State-directed capitalist/ cooperatives	*Laissez-faire* capitalist
Investment	State/cooperatives/ capitalist state to invest in production, distribution and infrastructure	Capitalist investment in production and distribution. State confined to infrastructure investment
Savings	Public and private	Emphasis on capitalist savings out of profit
Foreign capital	Aid, loans and regulated foreign investment	Direct foreign investment
Income distribution	Increase the share of labour	Increase the share accruing to capital
Economic management	Increased state intervention and planning	*Laissez-faire* with emphasis on monetary policy
Monetary policy	One of several policy instruments	The most important policy instrument
Fiscal	Expansionary	Contraction
Exchange rate	Dual exchange rate	Devaluation
Exchange controls	Yes, to effect foreign exchange budgeting	Elimination of controls

▶

Table 11.1—Continued

Issue	Manley Government	IMF
Trade	Import restrictions and licensing	Removal of import restrictions and licensing
Prices	Control and subsidies	Removal of controls and elimination of subsidies
Wages/Incomes	Increased; pegged to cost of living increases.	Decrease in real terms

Source: R Bernal, 'The IMF and Class Structure in Jamaica 1977–1980', *Latin American Perspectives*, Issue 42, vol. 11, no. 3, Summer 1984.

pursue the forms of dependent capitalist growth typified in the colonial and later nationalist period. The only way of avoiding this would have been to have secured a hegemonic position for the mass of the working people who had always opposed these strategies. While the class alliance supporting Manley and the PNP was in the end too fragile to pursue a third path successfully, there is no certainty that a progressive advancement of the interests of the working people in the coalition could not have been achieved on the basis of an early and resolute decision to pursue an economic programme that placed their interests first. But the regime vacillated and when in March 1980, after years of unsuccessfully trying to implement the IMF programme, it was decided to end all relations with the IMF, it was already too late.

These exciting events in Jamaica raise two further sets of issues of considerable importance. One is to what extent the defeat of the third path can be said to have been caused by the *specific conjuncture* of events in the capitalist world economy at that time. The other is how far the basic limitations of Caribbean societies prevent any sort of solution to the problems of poverty, powerlessness and underdevelopment. Although it is true that Manley's period in office coincided with a deep crisis in the capitalist world economy, there is no evidence to suggest that this crisis was sufficiently immutable to prevent any form of social or political advance.

Table 11.2
Political Impact of IMF Policies

IMF Policies	Economic Effect	Classes Affected
Devaluation	Increased cost of living by increasing the cost of imports	Reduce real income and standard of living of all classes except the capitalists and self-employed workers
Wage restraint policy	Reduce real income as the upper limit of wage increases was below the rate of inflation	Reduce the standard of living of workers, the salariat and state bureaucrats
Reduction in budget	Cutbacks in social programmes and shortages and delays in the state sector	All classes, especially the poor, severely affected
Increase indirect taxation – no taxes on profits and property	Reduce disposable income	Reduce the standard of living of all classes except capitalists and self-employed professionals
Incentives to capitalists including price increases to ensure 20% rate of profit	Capitalists accumulate profits but do not invest profits, often illegally smuggled out	Support capitalists at the expense of small business and wage earning classes
Reduction and elimination of subsidies provided by the budget	Price increases of all basic food items	Reduction in the standard of living of the poorest
Reduction in the state's borrowing from local and foreign sources	Leave loanable funds in the domestic banking system for capitalists. Capitalists do not respond, state expenditure restrained	Reduction in the ability of state and state enterprises to perform – all classes adversely affected
Restraint on direction and expansion of state enterprises	State prevented from assuming a dominant role in the economy	State impotent to meet demands of various classes

►

Table 11.2—Continued

IMF Policies	Economic Effect	Classes Affected
Debt repayment and repatriation of profits and royalties made the first charge on available foreign exchange	Service foreign capital at the expense of imports of food, raw materials and spare parts	Shortages of essential imports, especially food, hurt all classes and lead to price increases in the 'black market' and hoarding by capitalists and small businesses. Lack of spare parts and raw materials hampers production and distribution, resulting in layoffs and work stoppages. All classes hurt.
Unwritten demand for the government to adopt a pro-capitalist, pro-foreign investment posture	Reduces the government's ability to borrow from progressive oil-rich countries and to forge trade links with socialist countries	Failure to realise aid and trade benefits outside the capitalist orbit. Destroys the credibility of democratic socialism and the PNP, internationally and domestically. Intensifies differences between left and right in the PNP.

Source: R. Bernal, 'The IMF and Class Structure in Jamaica 1977–1980', *Latin American Perspectives*, Issue 42, no. 3, Summer 1984.

Indeed it could even be argued that, after 1974, the crisis was actually helpful worldwide in pushing political and social movements, including Manley and the PNP, in a radical direction and that it 'was the cumulative impact of this severe economic situation rather than political commitment *per se* which forced the Manley government to press ahead with the more radical of its proposed reforms'.[24]

One has to conclude that although the conjuncture of internal constraints and international crisis complicated events, they cannot fully explain the weaknesses of the third path. As Stephens and Stephens put it, a crucial issue to determine is 'whether idiosyncratic and country-specific features of the Jamaican experiences in the seventies were primarily responsible for the decline or whether it was due to the very characteristics of the path itself'.[25] While in their sympathetic review of the Manley period they conclude that the third path achieved more than it is usually given credit for, the point to emerge (and which is important for us here) is that commentators who have offered different judgements about how much was achieved during the Manley period still unite in rejecting a simple determinist interpretation of events. It is clear that this experience supports the view that, important as they are, neither international developments in relation to local societies nor country-specific limitations, are, in themselves, enough to rule out forever the prospect of meaningful social and political change in the region.

This is not meant to underestimate the negative impact of either of these factors in the struggle for change in the region. The internal constraints have often been underrated, but are particularly severe and wide ranging. They include small size, limited national resource endowment, population and markets; a geopolitical location in the 'back yard of imperialism', a limited capacity to manage radical social change or even broad-based reform programmes over a wide range of social life; a non-participatory political tradition; divided labour movements; pressing social problems (especially poverty and unemployment) which place a high premium on directing resources for their immediate relief; and the importance of foreign-exchange flows to the ongoing system of economic reproduction. In themselves, each of these constraints are serious, but when they are combined they become particularly daunting. That Cuba was able to make a revolution and survive against these odds is indeed heartening, even though the struggle for development still continues in Cuba. What is more, judging from the hostility exhibited by imperialism against even moderate social change in the region, it could be said that Cuba's existence has reduced the chances of other states following the same route.

Conservative Reaction

By 1980 Jamaica was in complete disarray. Political violence had left over 750 people dead; shortages of basic commodities were widespread; labour unrest was the order of the day; foreign-capital inflows had dried up (with the US government providing only US$56 million over the final years of Manley's administration); 28 per cent of the labour force were unemployed; between 1977 and 1980, GDP growth was negative and in 1980 alone it declined by nearly 6 per cent and manufacturing by 12 per cent. As we observed earlier, capital flight, migration of skilled personnel and inflammatory news reporting, all added to the feeling of crisis and collapse. Not surprisingly, the people rejected the Manley administration and voted in Seaga and the JLP with the largest electoral victory ever – 51 of the 60 seats in the national parliament.

Seaga's policies were diametrically opposed to those of Manley and the PNP. On the domestic front his administration advocated giving foreign investment (and not national ownership and state control) the leading role in promoting economic growth; divesting state enterprises in favour of privatising the economy; placing the major focus of economic activity on exports rather than on self reliance and import-substitution and, in this regard, readily embracing the IMF package for stabilising the economy in the hope that this would facilitate loans from the IMF itself, private commercial sources and, in particular, the US government; opening the economy to foreign expertise and skills in the belief that this was a necessary complement to the flow of foreign capital; and finally, as Stone put it, adopting a 'style of political management [in which] the PNP's emphasis on intense political mobilisation gave way to demobilisation and a technocratic managerial style'.[26]

On the external front, the Seaga administration presented itself as a willing collaborator to the right-wing Reagan administration, which won office in the USA at about the same time as Seaga did in Jamaica. Diplomatic ties with Cuba were cut, a strong attack was launched on the Bishop regime in Grenada and Seaga offered Jamaica's cooperation in promoting an anti-leftist, pro-US alliance in the region. The Seaga government thus played a leading role in both the invasion of Grenada and the formation of the Caribbean Basin Initiative[27] and was rewarded with a considerable inflow of foreign capital. It is estimated that between 1981 and 1984 Jamaica obtained (from all sources) nearly US$2,000 million of concessionary financing. From the US alone, the government received US$679 million of concessionary support for the fiscal years 1980/81 to 1984/85. On a per capita basis, the US gave more support to Jamaica than to any other country in the world barring Israel. These details are shown in Table 11.3.

Table 11.3
US Concessionary Support for Jamaica 1980/81 to 1984/85
(US$m)

US Fiscal Year *	Balance of Payments	Rejects	PL 480	Other Food	Housing Guarantee	Total
1980/81	47.7	13.9	17.1	–	–	78.7
1981/82	95.0	31.3	17.5	–	–	143.8
1982/83	54.4	27.2	20.0	–	15.0	116.6
1983/84	50.0	37.7	20.0	6.8	25.0	139.5
1984/85	99.5	29.4	40.0	16.0	15.0	199.9
	346.6	139.5	114.6	22.8	55.0	678.5

*The US Fiscal Year runs from 1 October to 30 September

Source: USAID Office, Kingston, Jamaica, cited in O. Davies, 'Socio-Economic Developments in Jamaica, 1980–1985', mimeo, 1985.

In addition, it is common knowledge that the Reagan administration used its influence to secure funds for Jamaica through multilateral institutions like the IMF, the World Bank and the Inter-American Development Bank. It also tried to cushion the impact of the world recession on Jamaica's bauxite by purchasing for the government's stockpile, even at a time when adequate stocks were on hand.

Despite the massive support by the US and other foreign capital of the Seaga administration and its full cooperation with the IMF stabilisation programmes in a free-enterprise strategy of recovery and growth, by the end of 1986 the economic and social situation in Jamaica was no better than it had been in 1980. The foreign-exchange and balance-of-payments crisis, which had precipitated Manley's downfall, continued unabated. The exchange rate continued to deteriorate to the detriment of the living standards of the poor. An experiment with a multiple exchange-rate system (introduced in January 1983 to give a formal recognition to the thriving black market in foreign currency which had developed by then) was abandoned in December 1983, when the exchange rate was unified and fixed at a par value of US$1 = J$3.30 and thereafter determined at a twice-weekly public auction. By the end of 1985 the rate had been reduced to US$1 = J$5.50. Such a large devaluation over so short a period had predictable inflationary effects. In one year (1984) the retail price index rose by 31.2 per cent and the GDP deflator by 36.3 per cent. Between December 1984 and December 1986 the retail price index rose by a further one-third. Seaga's import-liberalisation programme and the continuing decline in export earnings brought about by low output in the major industries, worsened the trade balance so dramatically that by 1984 the deficit was more than half the export earnings and in 1985 it was larger than export earnings. In 1986, although there was an improvement on 1985, the deficit was still nearly two-thirds the value of exports. The total value of exports in 1986 was 60 per cent of the value in 1980. (See Table 11.4 for more data). Net official reserves at the end of 1986 totalled *minus* US$680 million, that is, one-third worse than the negative value in 1980. The external debt had grown to US$3,500 million which was almost double the 1980 level. On a per capita basis this debt was twice that of Brazil, the third world's largest debtor country. This debt as a percentage of GDP stood at 170 in 1986, as compared with 82 in 1980. Finally, real output growth had stagnated with the GDP in real terms, with the 1986 level being 20 per cent below that of 1972 and less than 1980. While Seaga promised to reverse the increase in the public sector (where employment had doubled and public spending as a percentage of GDP had grown from 22 per cent in 1972 to 42 per cent in 1980, whereas private sector employment had fallen by 25 per cent), his programme of divestment achieved little in the way of positive results.

There were many social manifestations of this failure. The number of children under four years of age showing signs of malnutrition had increased from 38 per cent of the total in 1978 to 41 per cent in 1985. Children admitted to

Table 11.4
Jamaica: Selected Economic Indicators

Year	Exports (f.o.b.)[2]	Imports C.I.F.[2]	Trade Balance[2]	Unemployment (%)	Rate of Growth of GDP (%)	Changes in retail price index over year (%)	Net External[2] Debt	External[1] Debt/ GDF Ratio (%)	External Debt/ Exports of Goods and Services Ratio (%)
1978	782	865	−83	23.0	0.4	+49.4	–	–	–
1979	815	1,003	−188	24.4	−1.7	+19.4	–	–	–
1980	965	1,179	−214	27.9	−5.8	+29.0	1,734	82	122
1981	975	1,474	−499	26.2	2.5	+4.6	2,212	105	148
1982	768	1,382	−614	27.0	1.0	+6.5	2,690	129	193
1983	686	1,281	−595	25.8	2.0	+16.7	2,920	141	215
1984	702	1,183	−443	25.6	−0.4	+31.2	3,207	135	233
1985	569	1,144	−575	25.6	−3.7	+23.4	3,499	170	290
1986	598	976	−379	25.0	–	+10.4	3,500 (est)	–	–

Notes (1) disbursed debt medium-long term   (2) value in US$ million

Source. Bank of Jamaica (25th Anniversary publication) and Government of Jamaica Statistics.

the Bustamante Hospital for Children with malnutrition and malnutrition/gastro-enteritis as a percentage of total admissions increased from 3.5 per cent in 1978 to 8.5 per cent in 1985. The weekly cost of feeding a family of five increased from 92 per cent of the minimum wage in 1979 to 247 per cent in 1985. The pass rate of children at the CXC/GCE 'O' levels (secondary school leaving examinations) had declined from 58 per cent in 1976 to 34 per cent in 1985. All these data were publicised by the Roman Catholic Archbishop, Samuel E Carter, S J, in his pastoral letter to commemorate the 20th anniversary of Pope Paul VI's encyclical, 'The Development of Peoples' (Populorum Progressio).

Huge public demonstrations (with as many as 50,000 protesters) were mounted against the exchange-rate auction system; rioting and looting followed petrol-price increases in 1984; Manley's party abstained from the 1983 general election on the grounds that electoral changes which had been promised had not been implemented when the election was called. After that the Seaga administration functioned as a 'one-party state', despite persistent pressure to call fresh elections. The crime rate rose alarmingly, with a survey undertaken in 1981 showing that 'approximately 10 per cent of the total volume of produce and livestock on Jamaican farms was stolen by highly organised criminal gangs for sale in urban areas'[28] Crimes of violence increased from 13,000 in 1974 to 15,300 in 1981 and cases of theft increased by more than a third between 1974 and 1981. With this atmosphere of economic chaos, decline, crime and corruption, the sense of crisis which had helped bring the PNP to power in 1972 and the JLP in 1980 continued to pervade the society. As Stone comments:

> The revival of faith in the future aroused by the change of government in 1980 after the bitter disappointment with socialism in the 1970s had dissipated by mid-1982, to be replaced by a feeling of hopelessness as the Seaga government seemed unable either to solve the basic problems or to engineer the promised economic recovery. A mood of national desperation led to the embrace of any inflow of aid or any political or economic terms. A renewed and pervasive form of neocolonialism set in under the JLP as the country lost confidence in local initiatives and efforts as a means of pulling out of its deep economic problems. External influence . . . had now

taken over in a country that ten years earlier was boasting aggressively about taking on the multinationals and the world economic system, and breaking the cycle of dependency. The national mood had come full circle.[29]

Such then was the situation 40 years after the end of the Second World War and more than two decades after independence.

II: Non Capitalist Development/Socialist Orientation: Grenada

Background

As with Jamaica under Manley, Grenada during the period of the New Jewel Movement (1979-83) acquired an extraordinary reputation as a progressive social experiment. Fidel Castro once said that Grenada, along with Nicaragua and Cuba, were 'three giants rising up to defend their rights to independence, sovereignty and justice on the very threshold of imperialism'.[30] Ambursley and James comment on how:

> In four years. . . [Grenada] acquired an international status out of all proportion to the tiny size of the island. On account of [Prime Minister Maurice] Bishop's fervent and astute oratory, and the energy and originality devoted by the regime to Third World issues, Grenada emerged as a leading force in the non-aligned movement. The PRG [People's Revolutionary Government] consistently spoke out in support of national liberation movements throughout the world, and was audacious in its opposition to the aggressive designs of US imperialism in the Caribbean.[31]

Even in relation to Jamaica, where Manley's task of economic transformation was made so difficult because of the island's small size, Grenada is an extremely small microstate. With a population of only 110,000, an area of only 133 square miles and a GDP of only US$100 million on the assumption of power by Bishop's PRG, the pressures of the society's small scale were indeed awesome. Its tiny size and colonial history together produced a situation in the early 1970s in which over 90 per cent of GDP was derived from traded goods and services.

The island mainly depended on exporting three primary crops (bananas, cocoa and nutmeg), on tourism and on the wholesale and retail trade associated with it. Most of the manufacturing goods were imported – such as food, fuel, raw materials, equipment and machinery – and the local population also depended heavily on income remitted from relatives and friends living abroad. The small size of the economy also created severe diseconomies of scale in the provision of public services. This considerably raised the average per capita cost of any state venture with the result that (along with many of the other Leeward and Windward Islands) there was a historical reliance after the Second World War on grants-in-aid from the British Treasury to finance basic services. Agriculture contributed on average about one-third of the GDP over the two decades of the 1960s and 1970s. Over this same period the contribution of manufacturing never exceeded 4 per cent of GDP. Similarly, except when hotels were being built, construction activity was low, averaging less than 5 per cent in the five years before the PRG came to power. In 1979, when the PRG did eventually take over, the economy was in the midst of a severe depression, with per capita income lower than it had been at the beginning of the decade.

Although heavily dependent on agricultural production, extreme inequalities prevailed in the rural areas, with farms of up to five acres accounting for 89 per cent of total landholdings but only 45 per cent of cultivable acreage in 1972. Farms of 100 acres or more accounted for 0.5 per cent of total landholdings and 49 per cent of the cultivable acreage. To this can be added such features as the concentration of idle lands among the larger acreages, the extreme fragmentation of the smaller holdings and the concentration of better-quality lands among the large holdings.[32] Despite this, the peasantry produced two-thirds of the spices, half the cocoa, and about a third of the bananas. Processing, however, was not in the hands of the peasants and it has been estimated that as much as 90 cents in every dollar was assigned to processing their produce. Historically, the plantocracy dominated the three statutory agricultural export-marketing organisations which had the exclusive right to purchase the entire nutmeg, cocoa and banana crops. These organisations marketed the products overseas and, after deducting their commissions, paid the producers. Under Eric Gairy's rule, this group was replaced by his own political henchmen.

The drive to establish a tourist industry began in the 1960s and, as in other West Indian territories, it was mainly foreign owned with a sprinkling of local interest, particularly among planters who tended to move into this sphere of economic activity. An important offshoot of the tourist industry was that a significant number of foreigners built holiday and retirement homes in Grenada, which had a noticeable impact on the property market, causing much speculation and a considerable increase in the price of land. Outside tourism and farming, most of the capital was concentrated in the retail and distribution of vehicles, food, building materials and household appliances. In addition, some capital was attracted into areas such as local branches of insurance companies, shipping lines and tour operators.

Unlike other West Indian territories, however, Grenada had an unusually low rate of urbanisation, with net rural-urban migration recorded at only 0.6 per cent during the two censuses held in 1960 and 1970. At the end of the 1970s a high percentage of the rural youth were still living and working in the agricultural sector. This has been accredited to the combination of subsistence farming and the use of wage labour as a supplement to family labour on almost all Grenadian farms. Another of Grenada's features was that, in the absence of a significant manufacturing sector (3 per cent of GDP), the part of the labour force it employed (10 per cent) was confined to many small establishments; the largest manufacturing employer being the local brewery which offered only 76 permanent jobs. One consequence of this was that very little unionism developed in the country. The largest concentrations of the labour force were found on the docks and in the large agricultural estates.

Economic Policy

After many years of rigged elections, repression and terror, the Gairy government was forcibly overthrown in March 1979 and replaced by the PRG, which immediately proclaimed the start of revolutionary reconstruction of Gren-

adian society along a non-capitalist or socialist path. Its economic programme was derived from these principles and had
the following objectives: (1) to build an airport large enough
to land commercial passenger jets. It was anticipated that this
would lead to a very rapid expansion of the tourist industry;
(2) to construct a mixed economy based on three major
sectors – state, cooperative and private – with the state sector
playing the leading role; (3) to improve the quality of life of
the citizens through a comprehensive programme aimed at
upgrading social services and ensuring that basic needs were
met; and (4) to diversify overseas trade and sources of investment with a particular view to opening up links with the
socialist bloc and improving South-South cooperation. All
this was part of a broader strategy in support of international
efforts to create a new international economic order.

The absence of an airport with facilities to handle
modern passenger jet aircraft was an obvious weakness in the
Grenadian economy at the time of the PRG takeover, for it
severely impaired the growth of the country's tourist
industry. Without this facility tourists were having to be
brought in on smaller aircraft via other islands, and making
the connection invariably involved an overnight stay on
another island. It was a difficult project because with Grenada's mountainous terrain there was only one area large
enough and flat enough on which a runway of the right
length could be built at a tolerable cost and even this involved
filling in areas covered by the sea. Nevertheless the PRG was
firmly committed to this project. As Bishop himself put it,
the airport would be 'the gateway to our future. . . it is what
alone can give us the potential for economic takeoff. . . it
can help us to develop the tourist industry more. . . to
develop our agro industries more. . . to export our fresh
fruits and vegetables better'.[33]

The bulk of the capital, technical expertise, equipment
and machinery for the airport project was to be provided by
Cuba. It was projected that when the airport was completed
tourist arrivals would increase by nearly 60 per cent above the
prevailing level of about 32,000 tourists per annum (excluding
passengers on cruise liners. The increased number of tourists
was expected to lead to a tripling of gross tourist expenditure
on the island which, in turn, would stimulate development in

related industries, such as hotels and other services, domestic agriculture, food supplies, local crafts, clothing, footwear and furniture.

Unfortunately, things did not work out this way. When the PRG assumed power, tourist numbers dropped to a staggering low of about 23,000. The government's dreams of a 'new tourism' with foreign-owned hotels nationalised; a shift from luxury to more modest accommodation; new markets developed in Latin America, the rest of the Caribbean, Africa and among non-white North Americans; middle-class categories such as students, teachers and the higher-paid blue-collar workers attracted to the island; and local establishments serving locally-grown foods and menus, never really materialised. Although the Holiday Inn was acquired and added to the five other hotels the state had taken over from Gairy and his cronies, the state sector remained in a minority in the hotel industry which, in 1983, had 20 hotels and eight guest houses owned and operated by private local and foreign capital. All the state-owned hotels appeared to have functioned uneconomically as a result of the decline in the tourist trade and through factors such as overstaffing, weak management and an inexperienced work-force. Nothing was done in any systematic manner to promote Grenada in any of the new markets listed above. Indeed, as time progressed, even in the leaders' speeches, less and less emphasis was placed on this sort of reform. The PRG seemed to be growing increasingly aware of the inherent contradiction in a progressive government supporting tourism, especially given the industry's historical associations in the region. The government's strategy for a mixed economy envisaged the state controlling major areas such as agriculture, science and technology, public utilities, tourism, trade and finance; promoting cooperatives; and working together with private capital.

When the PRG was established, the state already controlled 30 estates totalling 4,200 acres, in other words approximately 9 per cent of the land under cultivation. In 1982, with the passing of the Land Utilisation Act, the state could compulsorily acquire ten-year leases on estates of over 100 acres and on idle and under-utilised lands. These would be handled through a National Land Reform Commission. Here again, things did not work out as planned and, although the centrepiece of the land-reform programme, very little happened under this Act. In 1983, when the revolution was overthrown, the agricultural sector was no differently organised in terms of resource ownership than it had been before. The state still owned less than 15 per cent of the arable land and even this was being badly managed. The PRG itself admitted in 1983 that only 37 per cent of the targeted output on these estates had been achieved, apparently because the estates were plagued with poor organisation and management, backward agricultural methods and an aged and inadequately-trained labour force. Levels of physical productivity were also reported as consistently low. There was no way in which these state-owned lands could be presented as models for other farmers to imitate as part of the PRG's modernisation drive. Yet this was what the PRG had hoped for at the time. The results were particularly disappointing given the prospect they offered of providing food supplies for the extra tourists the new airport was meant to bring; yet they were no doubt characteristic of the difficulties other socialist regimes have encountered with agriculture.

In addition to the land-reform measures, the state offered an array of other supports to agriculture, including upgraded extension services, more credit and better infrastructure by way of improved roads, water and electricity. The commodity boards, which had been in the hands of Gairy's henchmen, were returned to the farmers.

A state-owned marketing and import authority was created to promote trade. This provided farmers with agricultural inputs (such as fertilisers and implements) at subsidised prices, offered guaranteed markets for farmers' output and, at the same time, served as sole importer for such basic commodities as sugar, rice, cement and powdered milk. Part of the function of this authority was to stabilise prices, particularly through the purchase of local farmers' output. The authority was also expected to complement the work of the statutory export boards.

Although the PRG set up a state-owned bank in late 1979 (after purchasing a foreign-owned branch bank) and in 1983 acquired the shares of the local branch of the Royal Bank of Canada, foreign-owned commercial banks continued to dominate the financial sector. The eight life-insurance and

15 general-insurance companies operating in the country during the PRG's period of rule were entirely controlled by local and foreign private capital. In 1982, the government started a national-insurance scheme to provide sickness, work injury and maternity benefits. In that the PRG had singled out science and technology as crucial to Grenada's progress, much emphasis was laid on training, providing scholarships for Grenadians to study in Cuba and Eastern Europe, developing agricultural extension schemes and undertaking basic resource inventory tasks such as land capability surveys, particularly of idle land. Much attention was also paid to the existing public utilities (telephones, electricity) and concerted policies developed in relation to the public media, internal public transport and the airlines.

With respect to the cooperatives, there were several notable developments. A National Cooperative Development Agency was established and given responsibility for implementing the government's policy of providing 'idle lands for idle hands'. Fishing and handicraft cooperatives were also promoted. In general, however, it has been widely admitted that despite government efforts the cooperative movement grew slowly during the period of PRG rule. Young people preferred the glamour of 'jobs with the state', particularly in the security forces, which expanded rapidly after the revolution. In addition, the local peasantry, seemed to have had far too fierce a tradition of independence to go along with any ideas about forming cooperatives. In retrospect, however, it would seem that excessive outside leadership, particularly by the state, had once again, dampened local initiatives and stifled the self-reliant, self-help motivations of truly cooperative endeavours.

Because of the PRG's ideological position, it was especially sensitive on the issue of private capital, particularly foreign private capital. Its decision to adopt a mixed-economy approach reflected the existing dominance of private capital (local and foreign) in the economy and the need for the state to play a leading role in promoting development. In this scheme, the cooperatives were seen essentially as a transitional or intermediate arrangement. As the government stated:

> Our economy as a mixed economy will comprise the state sector, the private sector, and the cooperative sector. The dominant sector will be the state sector, which will lead the development process . . . we intend to provide assistance to the private sector wherever possible, whether it be local or foreign, or in partnership with the state or with other private individuals, so long as it is in keeping with the country's economic development.[34]

The key elements in the PRG's approach to foreign private capital consisted of retaining the incentives legislation in force at the time of the takeover and institutionalising an investment code (in 1983) as a further redefinition of its policy. The code stressed the essential role of private capital and identified manufacturing and tourism as important components of the private sector. It also said that local capital had a leading role in retail business, taxi services, garages, cinemas, travel, restaurants and food services. Meanwhile, public utilities, transport (including airlines), radio and television, finance and trading in strategic sectors were identified as important to the state sector. The PRG felt that foreign capital was required to facilitate the transfer of technology, to train local labour, to develop an export capability and to maximise the use of indigenous resources. Foreign capital's access to the local credit markets was restricted, but guarantees on profit repatriation were provided, along with various tax incentives (tax holidays, income-tax rebates, exemption from withholding taxes and accelerated depreciation allowances). The code also stipulated that nationalisation could occur only after due legal process and with fair and adequate compensation.

In seeking to improve the quality of life of the population and to meet its basic needs, much emphasis was placed on social services, particularly education and health. Free medical and dental care were provided, new health clinics were opened and existing ones upgraded and expanded. Given the dearth of local personnel, the vast majority of these were provided as part of Cuba's technical-assistance programme to Grenada. In the field of education, hundreds of scholarships were provided for study abroad, adult-education programmes were introduced and free text books, uniforms and lunches were offered in schools. As a result, an average of approximately one-third of the state's annual expenditure was in these two areas. Outside education and health, much attention was directed to housing (low-cost materials were provided to repair homes), women (legislation was passed to protect them at work and to provide maternity leave) and the provision of national insurance. A mass literacy campaign was organised through a Centre for Popular Education. Workers were encouraged to join trade unions and it has been claimed that, during the period of the PRG rule, union membership grew from 30 to 90 per cent of the labour force. Apart from the trade unions, other mass movements were established such as the local militia, as well as various national women, youth and student organisations. So-called organs of 'popular power' were also promoted through parish and local council meetings.

In Grenada's external economic relations a number of initiatives were taken. First, ties with Cuba were developed to the point of Cuba becoming the major aid donor, providing nearly US$60 million mainly through financial and material aid, to construct the airport. In addition, Cuban technical personnel played the leading external role in the health services, schools, army and fishing industry. The PRG's outspoken attacks on imperialism, calls for a New International Economic Order and denunciations of IMF policies formed part of a wider foreign and regional policy which stressed the right to self-determination of all people (particular emphasis being laid on surviving colonies in the region); respect for sovereignty, territorial integrity and the legal equality of all states; resistance to efforts to destabilise governments; and the region's right to exist as a zone of peace and to accept ideological pluralism as a basis for coexistence of states with different social systems. This line of argument brought Grenada into many confrontations (usually verbal) with other states in the region, especially Barbados. It is apposite to note here that, in response, the centrepiece of the PRG's economic strategy, the airport, was vigorously denounced by the Reagan administration as a future military base for Cuba and the Soviet Union which threatened vital Western interests and the security of other states in the Caribbean.

Evaluation

A common feature of the Grenadian and Jamaican experiences was that they confirmed that any attempt at radical social reorganisation in the region would be met by insistent efforts on the part of the US to destabilise the process (or worse), especially if the proposed reorganisation involved new options for foreign policy and external relations. Whether or not these countries are able to resist the pressure from the US ultimately depends on the extent of internal mobilisation in support of the process. Such mobilisation cannot be measured by rented crowds or staged assemblies in support of the government, however well intentioned, but must come from the consciousness of the major groups in the society that the process speaks to, their class and other interests. The degree of democratic expression and self-organisation practised by these groups is the key determinant of their mobilisation. Moreover, given the geopolitical context, every effort should be made to ensure that verbal ideological confrontations with imperialism do not run ahead of a real and developed capacity to resist destabilisation, no matter how tempting the mobilising appeal of this approach. Any gap between rhetoric and reality can and will be exploited by the enemies of the process.

In Grenada, not only did these unfortunate developments occur, but the implosion of the revolutionary process signalled the existence of a dangerous gap between the leadership and the led. Naive vanguardism and high-profile verbal anti-imperialism conspired to exploit weaknesses already inherent in the structure of the society and the regime in power. The development of mass organisations and organs of popular power (which the PRG offered as an *alternative* to the parliamentary traditions of political democracy and not as its *complement*) was rationalised on the grounds that political democracy was a bourgeois confidence trick. Socialism was therefore opposed to democracy and, in the process, the real historical experiences of the region were ignored.[35] The failure, therefore, of the PRG to hold national elections and, worse still, the tendency to deride elections publicly, constituted a crippling limitation which eventually produced Bishop's house arrest and execution, and the seizure of power by Bernard Coard's faction as a legitimate means of resolving political conflict among the left.

Judging from the Grenadian economy's performance over the period in question, the PRG's policies were largely unsuccessful, with the major weakness being in the decline of traditional agricultural exports (nutmeg, mace, bananas and cocoa) which, between 1979 and 1982, reduced agriculture's contribution to GDP by about 10 per cent. Domestic agriculture was not particularly successful either. Despite this poor agricultural performance, however, overall GDP grew by 2.1, 3, 3.4 and 4 per cent over the years between 1979 and 1982. This was mainly because of the rapid expansion of construction associated with building the airport, community projects, feeder roads and housing. Between 1979 and 1983 the value of construction in the GDP trebled. Investment as a percentage of GDP was high; in the years 1978 to 1982, it was 5.2, 13.6, 16.7, 30.1 and 36.1 per cent respectively and, over the years 1979 to 1982, the airport construction alone averaged 45 per cent of total construction investments. Unemployment fell from 50 per cent of the labour force to 12 per cent during the PRG's period in office. Inflation, which averaged 20 per cent in 1979, stood at an annual rate of 5 per cent in April 1983. Most of the capital expenditure was externally financed, mainly by Cuba, which in turn increased the destabilisation pressures directed at Grenada. In addition to Cuban support, however, the economy was also fairly heavily dependent on funds from multilateral sources such as the Inter-American Development Bank, the Caribbean Development Bank, and the European Development Fund. This overall dependence on foreign funding, although different in some ways from what had previously obtained, nevertheless indicated that the real movement of the economy away from its inherited characteristics was, by 1983, still only marginal. In all fairness though, four years is far too short a time to change centuries-old economic patterns.

While there were definite pragmatic reasons for building a new airport, its direct link with tourism meant that its longer-term benefits to the economy (once the construction phase was over) would depend on the capacity of other sectors in the economy to prevent the many leakages which characterise the tourist industry regionally. At the same time, getting rid of the negative socio-political aspects of tourism would, in the long run, depend on the government's ability to change the traditional character of tourism and to integrate it more meaningfully into the national way of life. The failure of domestic agriculture to expand and the absence of any plans for the 'new tourism' being implemented by 1983, when the airport was nearly completed, did not therefore augur well for these expectations. In fact the government probably realised this, as it became increasingly vague and ambiguous in its pronouncements on these issues. Prior to seizing power, the New Jewel Movement (out of which the PRG developed) had campaigned against the negative aspects of Grenadian tourism, thus raising the question of whether a left-wing Caribbean country really could use tourism to generate economic development and transformations. The answer, from the PRG's experience, must be a guarded 'no'. Apart from its historical legacy, which in itself is overwhelming, tourism is far too vulnerable to hostile external propaganda and therefore too easy a target for destabilisation, as both Manley and Bishop found to their cost. Also, to have supported a major thrust towards tourism would have required the PRG to 'make peace' with the countries supplying the tourists and to continue to expose the local population to life styles and levels of affluence it considered abhorrent.

The failure to transform agriculture not only weakened the potential impact of the airport/tourism strategy but also had further important implications. As we noted earlier, neither the state farms nor the cooperatives fared well. In the end, feeling that the only solution was to intensify private capitalist farming, the government procrastinated and, as a result, achieved little by 1983 in the most important sector of the national economy. As Mandle puts it:

> With cooperatives resisted, and with managerial incompetence hampering the state farms, the PRG decided to live with the status quo in the structure of the country's agriculture. It did so rather than adopt an agricultural reform strategy which would strengthen private farming. . . But the fact that the government did not adopt such proposals meant that as late

as 1983 the PRG had not found an acceptable means by which to break the deadlock in agriculture which it had inherited. [36]

The PRG's attempts to promote a good relationship with local private capital were rather unsuccessful and, throughout the period, there was no real expansion in the private sector. During 1979 to 1982, private sector investment as a percentage of GDP averaged 4 per cent. Except for 1980, when it reached 6.2 per cent, the percentage never exceeded 3.4. For the same period, public-sector investment grew from nearly 13 per cent in 1979 to about 35 per cent in 1982, for a four-year average of 23 per cent. Kirton, who was an economic advisor to the PRG and has since examined its policy in relation to private capital, concludes that:

> . . . despite the wide ranging attempts by the PRG to promote the 'confidence' of private capital and to improve the 'invest-ment climate', the dominant response of private capital was an unwillingness to operate beyond the performance of minimum tasks. From its own statements the private sector remained 'uncertain' and 'apprehensive' about future PRG policies citing 'government's ideological posture' and related implications as major deterrents. [37]

While bearing some similarity to the situation in Jamaica during the later years of the Manley administration, the more influential elements in the private sector did not and indeed could not play the same wide-ranging political role in Grenada as they did in Jamaica. To begin with, the PRG did not act in any way to support the institutionalisation of a multi-party political system or a range of different sources of public communication. To play a political role, therefore, private capital would have had to confront the government directly and in this confrontation it would necessarily have had to act outside the PRG's decreed legality. It is interesting to observe that, despite the weak political base of private capital at the time, it nevertheless maintained strong ideo-logical and other social connections with international capital.

The PRG's failure either to win or to bribe capital into supporting the process it directed indicates clearly that in any future efforts to transform Caribbean societies this issue will recur as a crucial one. Ultimately, it is a question of confi-dence, which stems from the consideration that basing the region's development in the past on the private-profit motive has helped to produce the very inequalities and poverty we have so frequently alluded to. To the poor and powerless, motivating the economy primarily on the basis of private gain would seem to imply the perpetuation of their inferior social status. The issue therefore then becomes one of determining how to move from private gain (as the major motivating factor) to social needs and benefits. What clearly emerges from the two cases examined so far is that this transition is long, slow and difficult. In fact it is as difficult as transforming these societies' economic structures, for without transformed structures the transition could never be sustained.

In conclusion, it is worth mentioning that, as in Jamaica, the whole process was dogged by a shortage of skills, but in Grenada this was even more acute than in Jamaica and, although the PRG made strenuous efforts to secure overseas training for Grenadians, very few had completed their courses by the time the regime ended. The government therefore had to acquire skilled labour from elsewhere, usually from within the Caribbean. Although only an interim measure and induced by a real shortage, it generated a certain amount of resentment among Grenadians, which was compounded by the PRG's natural inclination to place a premium on the ideological credentials of the personnel it recruited. The shortage of skills also brought about an inevitable dilution of tasks, with the result that the government ended up with a number of partial plans concerning issues such as investment, labour requirements, government revenue and expenditure policies, credit and agriculture. The failure to incorporate its plans into a general, aggregative macro-framework of national planning inevitably reduced planning efficiency and adversely affected all stages of planning, from analysis, through implementation, execution and monitoring, to post-implementation evaluation of performance.

III: Cooperative Socialism: Guyana[38]

Policy

While the social experiments in Jamaica under Manley and in Grenada under Bishop attracted considerable international and regional attention, they lacked the flavour of notoriety which surrounded the People's National Congress (PNC) in Guyana under Forbes Burnham and, since August 1985, under Desmond Hoyte. The reason for this notoriety was that few accepted the regime's claim to be motivated by concern for the poor and powerless as genuine, particularly since there was increasing evidence to support the widely-accepted view that the regime existed only through the combination of force and fraud it employed to rig the national elections of 1973, 1980 and 1985, and the national referendum in 1978, which led to changes in the constitution and the postponement, until 1980, of the elections due in that year.

On independence in 1966, the dominant structural relations of the Guyanese economy and the social form through which they were systematically reproduced, portrayed many of the classic features of underdevelopment/dependency relations. The principal products produced were sugar, bauxite-alumina and rice. Except for a small fraction of sugar-cane cultivation (less than 10 per cent), sugar was grown and processed by two foreign-owned plantations. Sugar was the dominant crop, accounting for the largest share of value added, employment, foreign-exchange earnings, capital accumulation, crop land and agricultural infrastructural resources. Rice, initially cultivated as a domestic staple, had grown into a significant export cash crop, with most of the sales to the Caribbean market. Bauxite-alumina production took place in two enclave mining areas under the control of two aluminum-producing TNCs – Alcan (based in Canada) and Reynolds (based in the US). The bulk of the production was under the control of the Canadian company. Export specialisation was complemented by extensive dependence on imported foodstuffs, manufactures, intermediate goods (particularly fuels and fertilisers) and capital equipment. Unemployment was estimated at nearly 20 per cent of the labour force, while the largest source of employed labour (sugar) operated on a seasonal basis.

In 1970, four years after independence, the ruling party declared Guyana a Cooperative (socialist) Republic. A number of factors promoted this particular development. To begin with, as in other territories in the region, while impressive rates of growth in per capita product were recorded in the 1960s, most of the acute problems of poverty and dispossession were still very much in evidence. Second, the broad mass of the population had had a particularly militant anti-colonial tradition. This militancy is reflected in the early maturing of relatively highly-developed trade-union structures in the country. Third, the tradition of militant anti-colonialism and the trade unionism was both product and producer of a situation in which large sections of the work force were influenced by Marxist ideas and functioned within organisations with Marxist-Leninist leaders. This is seen in the history and development of the People's Progressive Party (PPP) (the first Marxist party to win free and fair elections in the hemisphere) and of its associated trade union, the largest in the country and the one to have organised labour on the sugar plantations since the 1940s. Fourth, because the left of the political spectrum effectively opposed the PNC state, in order to use the state to transform itself into a national bourgeois class, the PNC had to adopt a popular socialist rhetoric acceptable to the masses.

The declaration of a cooperative socialist republic implied four major policy initiatives by the state. The first was to nationalise foreign property so that the government could assert more control over its own economy. By the mid-1970s, both the main producing sectors (sugar and bauxite-alumina), the import trade, public transport, alcohol and drug manufacturing, TNC-operated foundries and shipyards and significant sections of distribution and communications, had all been taken over by the state. With the nationalisation of sugar in 1976, the government boasted that it now 'owned and controlled 80 per cent of the economy of Guyana'. These nationalisations followed the usual pattern, namely they gave fair and adequate compensation, they took the initiative to nationalise when companies were in difficulties or threatened with closure and they provided post-nationalisation contracts to cover management, technology and licensing fees.

The second was an undertaking by the government to carry out a programme to feed, clothe and house the nation. Its aim was to substitute the private profit motive with the social goal of making 'the small man a real man'. This programme was embodied in the 1972-76 development programme and was, from the outset, heavily propagandistic. The development programme first appeared as a public document in draft form in July 1973. Since then it has never been revised or presented for public scrutiny. Moreover, the actual course of production bore little relationship to the programme's stated objective of 'feeding, clothing and housing the nation by 1976'.

The third was to ensure the cooperative sector's dominance, given the existence of a tri-sectoral (private, state and cooperative) national economic structure, for it was through cooperative ownership and control that the socialist foundations of the society were to be laid. As it turned out, Guyana's cooperative sector remained a miniscule part of the national economy. Institutions especially set up by the state as cooperatives, such as the Guyana National Cooperative Bank, did not operate on cooperative principles, whatever formal cooperative ownership structures they might have had. Many economically important cooperatives which had been set up by private initiative also operated along capitalist lines, often employing exploited wage labour. In fact enterprises frequently formed themselves into cooperatives to take advantage of tax concessions or to carry out limited objectives (such as acquiring a plot of land) and then dissolving the cooperative once it had served its purpose.

The fourth was the claim that the ruling party, the PNC, stood over all other parties and over the state itself. Since the government did not come to power either through free and fair elections or as the result of a popular social revolution, this was in effect a thinly-disguised proclamation of a dictatorship. The PNC's paramountcy was enshrined in the creation (in 1973/74) of a new government department, the Ministry of National Development and Office of the General Secretary of the PNC. As the name suggests, the PNC party office was merged into a department of the state and financed through public funds. The state thereafter rapidly proceeded to make it clear that there could be no legal or constitutional change of government. The rigged elections in 1973, the postponement of elections due in 1978 and the rigged elections in 1980, were indications of the extent to which state authoritarianism had become entrenched in Guyana.

These features of cooperative socialism were combined with certain foreign-policy initiatives by the state, which included recognition of Cuba, support for the Popular Movement for the Liberation of Angola (MPLA), militant anti-apartheid rhetoric, support for the Arab cause, support for a New International Economic Order and visits to and contacts with Eastern Europe and China. On close examination, however, it becomes evident that many of these were purely for the purposes of propaganda. For example, the Guyanese government only gave its support to the MPLA during the final stages of the war, having all along been behind the CIA-backed group, UNITA (the National Union for the Total Independence of Angola). Recognition of Cuba was also only undertaken as part of a broad-based Caribbean initiative to unite governments of differing outlooks in the interests of asserting an independent and separate indentity for the region.

Despite such reservations, however, in 1975 a number of theorists[39] joined with the PPP (which after the 1973 elections had launched a programme of passive resistance and civil disobedience) in adopting a policy of critical support for the government because of the radical turn it was taking.

The PPP's new position reflected its formal acceptance of the Havana Declaration of 1975, in which communist and workers' parties agreed to support the application of the 'non-capitalist thesis' of revolutionary democracy to the region.[40] An important point about this is that the so-called radicalisation of the state in Guyana was accompanied by such anti-democratic measures as rigged elections, the denial of basic human and trade-union rights and the suppression of the rule of law and the traditional independence of the judiciary. The theorists supporting the regime clearly did not associate radicalisation with increased opportunities for the working classes and peasants to develop their own democratic organisations through which to exercise their power. On the contrary, they saw radicalisation as consistent with reducing mass access to these rights and therefore directly opposed to democratic development. Another important point is that the Havana Declaration ignored the importance of the points discussed in Chapter 9 concerning internal class struggle and the role a state in the capitalist periphery must necessarily play in consolidating a hegemonic class.

As events have shown, nationalisation in Guyana aided the expansion of the state bureaucratically, ideologically and militarily and in so doing, increased the capacity of the ruling PNC to assert its various forms of authoritarian control over civil society. This process, however, required other accompanying developments however, and it is to these that we now turn.

Degeneration and Social Decay

Guyana has been in a state of continuous crisis since 1975. The numerous manifestations of this include a negative rate of growth of real product since 1975, with the result that per capita real income at the end of 1986 was less than that of 1970 and more than one-third below that of 1975; dramatic increases in malnutrition and deaths from deficient nutrition related illnesses, particularly in public institutions (hospitals, prisons and homes for the aged and disabled); widespread and endemic shortages of foods as well as other basic items of consumption; shortages of raw materials so severe that for the past decade industry has been utilising only 30 to 40 per cent of rated capacity. In addition, electricity cuts are common, with scheduled cuts in March 1986 averaging 36 hours per week for all districts in the country. Unscheduled interruptions also occurred; double figure inflation rates (between 1975 and 1985 the consumer price index had more than quadrupled); over half the labour force unemployed following large-scale public sector retrenchments; the virtual collapse of all public utilities to the point of constituting a major obstacle to production; the dramatic deterioration of social services; drastic increases in crime, corruption, clientilism, graft and nepotism in public and private life; a massive external debt in excess of US$700 million or three-and-a-half times the value of GDP, a rapidly deteriorating balance-of-payments deficit (in excess of one-quarter of GDP for the period 1976-84) and a deteriorating exchange rate; the growth of a huge black market for all items in the wake of acute foreign-exchange shortages and bureaucratic restraints on activity; and a migration rate conservatively estimated at over three-quarters the rate of natural increase of the population. Less conservatively, estimates indicate an absolute decline in the population since 1975.

An important feature of the crisis was the way in which the economic dislocation affected other areas of social life. For example, although the post-independence period witnessed a rapid expansion of state property and state intervention in economic life, the government that promoted these developments was brought to power through an Anglo-American manoeuvre in the 1960s and since then has held onto its power without holding proper elections. As a consequence, the regime has always lacked legitimacy. It is important to recognise that Guyana did not conform to the typical export-oriented Third World model, that the economic crisis was not caused predominantly by the world economic crisis and that the crisis in its export sector was not directly produced by shrinking export markets and falling prices. As the selected data in Tables 11.5 to 11.7 show, levels of output in the agricultural sector have been substantially below both rated capacity levels for these industries and peak output levels achieved many years earlier. Thus, while current annual output of sugar is under 250,000 tons, at the time of nationalisation the government placed the TNC's capacity at 450,000 tons. The peak output level of 374,000 tons was achieved as long ago as 1971. In the rice sector, annual output in 1986 was 180,000 tons, whereas the capacity of the industry was estimated at 250,000 tons with a peak output of 212,000 tons being achieved in 1977. In both these industries preferential contractual export markets paying premium prices have not been satisfied. Sugar obtains a quota and a premium price under the EEC-ACP Protocol, as well as for sales to the USA. In the case of rice, export markets in the CARICOM region are not serviced, although the industry receives a premium price currently in excess of two-thirds above the world level. In the bauxite industry, Guyana enjoyed a virtual monopoly in world sales of high-grade calcined ore. In the 1960s and early 1970s, output accounted for 90 per cent of the world market. By the mid-1980s, however, the industry could only supply between 40 and 50 per cent of the world demand; the output for 1986 (at 441,000 tonnes) being approximately 55 per cent of the peak level attained in 1975. Although the Guyanese product is superior to that of the Chinese with which it has been replaced, it has lost its position on the world market because of the unreliability of its supply. It should be noted that since 1983 the alumina plant has been closed down, while dried bauxite output is currently less than half that attained in the early 1970s. In the absence of any significant diversification in Guyana's production structure the decline in the basic industries has negatively influenced economic growth. For the period between 1970 and 1975, the real growth of GDP averaged 3.9 per cent, between 1975 and 1980 it averaged -0.7 per cent and for the years 1981 to 1986 the growth rates were -0.3, -10.4, -9.6, +2.5, +1.0 and +0.3. The data on growth of GDP are shown in Table 11.5.

Table 11.5
Guyana: Real Growth of GDP (Compound % per annum)

	1970–1975	1975–1980	1981	1982	1983	1984	1985	1986
Total GDP	3.9	−0.7	−0.3	−10.4	−9.6	2.5	1.0	0.3
Sugar	0.9	−1.3	10.9	−3.8	−12.6	−3.6	−	−
Rice	2.4	0.9	−2.2	15.6	−19.2	23.8	−	−
Mining	−2.3	−5.3	−11.4	−31.5	−22.4	47.0	−	−
Government	10.5	1.9	1.0	−7.7	−1.9	zero	−	−

The decline in the export sector has also been the main cause of the country's acute foreign-exchange and balance-of-payments difficulties. While other factors, such as reduced inflows of private investment capital (through lack of confidence in the economy) and compensation payments for nationalised enterprises are important, they are not decisive. The crisis is basically a *production crisis* in that output and productivity declines are directly linked to basic deficiencies in the structure of production and not to fewer opportunities for profitable external sales. The selected monetary and price data shown in Table 11.7 reveal a per capita external debt of

about US$900; per capita external arrears in excess of
US$1,000; a current-account balance-of-payments deficit in
excess of one-quarter of GDP for the years 1983 through
1986; large annual increases in money supply and a price
level in 1985 about four-and-a-half times higher than that of
a decade earlier and 145 per cent above that of 1980. A
similarly rapid expansion of the internal debt can be noted,
with a cumulative current-account balance-of-payments
deficit resulting in net international reserves (which peaked
in 1975) standing at minus US$554 million in September
1986.

Table 11.6
Guyana: Physical Output – Major Sectors 1970–86

Year	Population (Beginning of Year)	Output (in Thousands of Tons)				
	(In Thousands)	Sugar	Rice	Dried Bauxite	Calcined Bauxite	Alumina
1970	699	311	142	2,290	699	312
1971	704	369	120	2,108	700	305
1972	710	315	94	1,652	690	257
1973	716	266	110	1,665	637	234
1974	721	341	153	1,383	726	311
1975	727	300	175	1,350	778	294
1976	733	333	110	969	729	265
1977	739	242	212	879	709	273
1978	745	325	182	1,021	590	276
1979	750	298	142	1,059	589	171
1980	751	270	166	1,005	598	215
1981	763	301	163	982	513	170
1982	769	287	182	958	392	73
1983	777	252	149	761	315	nil
1984	782	238	181	823	517	nil
1985	788	243	154	1,096	478	nil
1986	793	245	180	1,036	441	nil

Source: Government of Guyana

Among the many causes of these basic differences are (i)
an unplanned, uncoordinated expansion of the state sector
(principally through nationalisation) between 1970 and 1976;

Table 11.7
Guyana: Monetary Indicators 1975–86

	Net International Reserves	National Debt		External Arrears	Balance of Payments	Government Finances (G$ million)			Money Supply	Consumer Price Index (Urban)
	US$ million	External US$ million disbursed. (end of year)	Internal G$ million (end of year)	US$ million	Current a/c G$ million	Total Revenue	Total Expenditure	Surplus (+) Deficit (−)	(G$ million)	1970=100 (Average)
1975	+77.4	295.5	399.2	n.a.	−35.2	497.7	638.8	−141.1	449.3	145
1976	−12.3	363.8	657.9	n.a.	−350.8	389.9	803.0	−413.0	491.5	158
1977	−39.3	404.3	853.9	n.a.	−251.1	355.1	543.6	−188.5	603.0	171
1978	−42.9	438.8	1035.2	n.a.	−72.3	365.8	542.2	−176.4	667.2	197
1979	−98.5	507.1	1312.5	n.a.	−208.1	412.2	690.7	−278.5	713.3	231
1980	−206.5	566.3	1650.8	45.4	−300.4	455.1	935.2	−480.1	850.4	264
1981	−267.4	660.0	1089.1	136.4	−475.8	578.9	1,205.7	−626.8	997.1	323
1982	−362.2	681.3	2775.7	249.5	−426.0	550.6	1,570.9	−1,020.3	1269.3	390
1983	−552.4	692.6	3820.8	450.6	−468.0	568.2	1,291.0	−722.8	1533.7	449
1984	−663.4	682.5	4544.0	595.5	−434.0	651.4	1,830.2	−1,178.8	1814.9	562
1985	−526.9	691.0	5425.7	771.9	−426.0	1,200.2	1,562.8	−362.6	2169.7	646
1986	−553.5(Sept.)	707.0	(Sept.)5399.3	897.5	−497.0	1,618.1	2,858.4	−1,240.3	2691.7	n.a.

Source: Government of Guyana.

(ii) the operation of political diktats in the state sector (in the narrow sense of state property being used to serve the interests of the ruling elites) which reduced efficiency and led to the nepotism, corruption and alienation mentioned earlier; (iii) the rapid emigration of skilled personnel at all levels leading to exceptionally high turnover rates; (iv) poor industrial relations with increasing numbers of employer/employee and government/worker conflicts; (v) acute foreign-exchange shortages which affected maintenance and delayed production; and (vi) inadequate monitoring of projects resulting in huge cost overruns and long delays in completing projects.

Although the tables show that production began to deteriorate with the expansion of the state sector in the early 1970s, this should not be taken to mean that state control *per se* is necessarily inefficient, but rather that the *specific* nature of the state and political configuration in Guyana since independence has been problematic.

For a start, the terms under which the regime came to power were based on the general exclusion of the then dominant PPP, which is important given the militant tradition of anti-colonialism among the Guyanese people and the PPP's Marxist-Leninist leadership.

In the light of the above and also because the political opposition was left-wing, the regime sought legitimacy by presenting itself as a radical, progressive, third world socialist regime. The high point of this propaganda was the formal declaration in 1970 of Guyana's intention to become a cooperative socialist republic.

The deteriorating productive system and severe decline in living standards accompanying nationalisation ruled out the possibility of achieving any basic needs goals and undermined the propaganda appeal of cooperative socialism. As a result, the regime had to resort to the systematic use of force and fraud to maintain its rule.

There are two other important aspects of the processes indicated above. One is that political power was used to convert the petty bourgeoisie (who wielded the power) into a big indigenous bourgeoisie. This occurred despite deteriorating living standards, principally through the appropriation of the relatively large amounts of monopoly rent present in a situation of such widespread shortages and scarcities of virtually all commodities. A substantial proportion of this wealth was converted into foreign assets as political uncertainty grew. The second aspect of this process was that the large state sector expanded the government's potential for nepotism as well as the scope for the intimidatory use of economic processes. Thus, not only are the faithful rewarded, but (and equally important) a host of administrative and economic mechanisms have been made available to control dissenters.

The expansion of state property was accompanied by increasing bureaucratisation of economic and civil life. In keeping with its claims, the party turned everything into ideology. For example, nationalisation of the public media was used to promote state ideology, to impose administrative restraints and to restrict publication of opposing or independent views. Another feature has been the rapid expansion of the country's security services, which on a per capita basis, became the largest in the hemisphere. There was also an increase in the number of armed groups attached to members of the party leadership, military training for young party activists and the training and arming of religious cults associated with the ruling party.

This preoccupation with security and increasingly partisan politicisation of economic functions meant that when the economic crisis first manifested itself in a major balance-of-payments crisis in the mid-1970s, the government lightly brushed it aside as opposition propaganda and proceeded to print money and expand state credit as if this were a temporary phenomenon. It also took the government many years to admit that its major propaganda plank of 'feeding, clothing and housing the nation by 1976' had been a failure.

The society seemed to contain within it a response/reaction mechanism (which I have described elsewhere as a *repressive escalator*) through which the ruling regime sought to solve its crises by repressing or rejecting political democracy. As a result, the economic/production crisis became generalised into a social and political crisis, thus calling into question the very character of the state. And since there was no legal or constitutional means of changing the government, the society was faced with a fundamental and inescapable dilemma.

There have been three main phases in the development of the state's 'repressive escalator', each of which has sharpened the divide between state oppression on the one hand and popular resistance and deteriorating living conditions on the other. In *Stage 1* the government's attempts between 1977 and 1979 to bring down real wages so as to reduce the demand for imports, to halt domestic inflation and to overcome the country's foreign-exchange and balance-of-payments difficulties in an effort to solve the production crisis were resisted by the workers and their organisations. This resistance was directed against the state which had become the major employer of wage labour. In turn, the state responded by trying to repress the discontent and to contain the rights workers had inherited under the prevailing system of industrial relations. During this stage, there were three main forms of repressive intervention. First, the *right to work* was undermined through political dismissals and victimisation of agitating workers. Second, the *right to strike* was undermined through invoking the notion of a political strike whereby any strike the government did not consider 'industrial' was deemed 'political' and, as such, treated as a 'subversive' activity. Third, the *corporatist* solution pursued in Latin America was adopted whereby the state, reinforced by its dominant employer status, intervened in selecting the executive and membership of the trade unions to determine the eventual composition of the national Trades Union Congress and other central decision-making bodies. As the central trade union council fell under state direction it was made more and more responsible for individual unions which were less amenable to corporatist solutions.

In *Stage 2* all citizens had their legal and human rights curtailed simply because it became impossible to separate trade union rights from the rights of any other citizens within a framework of justice. During this stage, the struggle was centred mainly in the courts and in various church, human rights and independent social organisations associated with workers' struggles. An important by-product of this stage was the blurring of traditional racial boundaries within the work force and a rise of worker solidarity, as revealed in several major industrial actions in 1977, 1978 and 1983.

In *Stage 3*, which began in the early 1980s, trade union, human rights and legal attacks became highly politicised as economic disintegration continued and the government grew increasingly unpopular. Repression was extended to all opposition, including independent social and political groups. To maintain its control, the state rapidly consolidated its authoritarianism and, in 1978, (instead of an election) held a referendum to decide whether or not to adopt a new constitution. This was 'approved' and the new constitution promulgated in 1980, thus giving legality to an even more dictatorial form of government.[41] During this stage, political assassinations and direct repression of any form of popular expression were routine and the security aparatuses almost totally politicised.

Parallelling this 'repressive escalator' have been a number of vicious circles operating both within and outside the sphere of production which have inhibited the restructuring of the country's productive base. Principal among these are (i) the decision to build up the security apparatuses when the state is least able to afford it, resulting in funds being diverted from the productive and social sectors; (ii) shortages of consumer goods through import restrictions, increasing inflationary pressure, reducing real wages and generally destabilising the structure of employment and industrial relations. Malnutrition, poor health care and inadequate public transport have in turn affected work force morale and productivity; (iii) restrictions on public sector borrowing (necessary for obtaining IMF/World Bank credit) intensified relations between the government and the IMF/World Bank Group between 1978 and 1981. The government's inability to meet the IMF/World Bank targets has subsequently resulted in the suspension of all these agreements. The consequent failure to obtain balance-of-payments support funds operates as a serious contraint on the flexibility of the state; (iv) as external indebtedness grows and arrears accumulate, the government's ability to borrow from abroad is further reduced. Crisis conditions at home are then worsened because the government cannot call on foreign savings to cushion declining domestic incomes. This then intensifies the external debt problems and reinforces the vicious circle; and

(v) because sources of government revenue dwindle when GDP falls, tax increases are imposed in an attempt to improve yields. This, however, further depresses economic activity and increases the tendency towards price inflation. The government is then forced to reduce its outlays and this in turn negatively affects output and incomes.

Vicious circles such as these show how the production crisis literally feeds on itself and in the process reinforces the 'repressive escalator' which, in turn, generalises the crisis. At this point also, instead of taking steps to solve the crisis, the government becomes a part of it and a major contributory factor in its continuation and worsening in the society.

The concept of a 'repressive escalator' should not be construed too mechanistically. The link between one stage and another, which reflects the unfolding dynamic of repression-resistance-repression, is a dialectical relationship and should not be seen as marking an automatic advance from one stage to another. Those who repress do not do so in anticipation of even more resistance: on the contrary they expect less. Similarly, those who resist are not trying to invite more repression. If indeed these things do occur, the determinants lie in the social relations prevailing at a particular juncture and not in the intentions of the various actors. The stages outlined are therefore not self-contained entities.

Neither can one presume an automatic link between the continuing impoverishment of the population and failure to overcome the economic crisis on the one hand and the willingness of the masses to revolt on the other. It would be disastrous for the organisers of resistance to make such an assumption, for the society's disintegration has inevitably affected the social psychology of the masses who already show a growing sense of resignation, helplessness, indifference (if not cynicism) to political struggle and extraordinarily high levels of migration.

The final conclusion to draw here is that, although wrapped in socialist/progressive rhetoric, by its systematic repression and denial of rights to the broad mass of the population, the Guyanese government has created a state that is antithetical to the interests of the poor and powerless. In this respect it differs from Grenada and Jamaica. Events in

Guyana have shown the West Indian people that despite the widespread ideological acceptance of 'Westminster parliamentarianism', the potential for authoritarian and fascist degeneration of the body politic clearly exists. When Grenada's experiences are also taken into account, it becomes obvious how important it is for the people in the region to lay singular emphasis on deepening the democratic political forms for which they fought in the past if they are to prevent future social experiments degenerating into dictatorship, whether of the right or the left. As the descendants of slaves and indentured servants, as a group they are as well placed as any other people on earth to appreciate the value of personal freedom. Their commitment to democracy can be second to none.[42]

12 *National Experiments: The Conservative Options*

I: Intensification of the Capital-Import Model: Barbados

Unlike Jamaica, Grenada and Guyana, no post-independence government in either Barbados or Trinidad-Tobago has ever advocated making a break with past policies or adopting a radical approach to the problems of underdevelopment. Instead they have tended to build on the capital-import strategy of development which evolved during the colonial and early nationalist periods evolved during the colonial and early nationalist periods after the Second World War.

Barbados has been widely proclaimed as the region's success story for it has largely escaped the economic crises which have gripped other West Indian territories since the mid-1970s. Despite the recession of 1981-83, it has been relatively free of the balance-of-payments, foreign-exchange, external-debt and inflationary problems with which the experiments discussed in the previous chapter were dogged. Since its independence in 1966, Barbados has managed to avoid becoming too dependent on the IMF for balance-of-payments support funds and, as a consequence, has not had to resort to any of the stringent deflationary and exchange-rate adjustment policies characteristic of this dependence. Its success in avoiding the acute manifestations of periodic and cyclical crises has not, however, been matched by any major structural changes in the economy and consequently the problems of poverty and powerlessness remain acute.

As the oldest British colony in the region, Barbados had an exceptionally large white resident planter group. Although always a minority of the population, by the 1930s this group controlled the dominant sugar industry and many of the distribution and service trades. As a result, instead of the classic imperial form of domination by international monopolies, which characterised colonial investments in this period, local capitalist monopolies prevailed.[1] The 1960s and early 1970s were periods of significant growth in the Barbadian economy. Between 1964 and 1971, according to Jainarain's estimates the annual growth rate was 11.5 per cent. For the longer period from 1956 until 1971, he estimates that the annual growth rate was as high as 9.5 per cent. Per capita national income in 1964 was about 60 per cent higher than it had been in 1956; while for the longer period between 1953 and 1971, Barbados had the highest per capital national income growth rate in the West Indies. By 1971 only Trinidad-Tobago, with its oil-based economy, had a higher per capita income than Barbados and even so it was less than 10 per cent higher.[2]

Underlying this growth in incomes were certain important changes in the industrial structure of Barbados. Whereas in 1956 sugar accounted for just over 26 per cent of the GDP and was the country's main industry, by 1971 it was contributing less than 8 per cent to GDP. During the same period, the manufacturing sector's share of GDP grew from slightly under 8 per cent to just over 12 per cent. Tourism also expanded rapidly, with the result that the contribution of services to GDP rose from just over 8 per cent in 1956 to just under 18 per cent in 1971. Over the years for which data were available, 1956-60, Jainarain estimates a gross investment ratio of nearly 33 per cent (somewhat in excess of the 25 per cent for the years 1960-64), of which 47 per cent was borrowed from abroad.[3]

Unemployment was the most serious indication that rapid growth had failed to deliver the all-round development the authorities had anticipated. The percentage of the labour force unemployed in 1960 and 1965 was just over 12 and 15 per cent respectively. In 1970 the figure was somewhat reduced, but was still quite high at 9 per cent. The dependence of the labour force on tourism and export agriculture for employment has produced large fluctuations in employment levels depending on agricultural cycles, crop failures, or other periodic factors which influence activity in these sectors.

Policy

The economic policies pursued in Barbados since independence have five major elements. First, they are wholly non-ideological – purely technocratic, pragmatic and rational. To combine ideology with economics is thought of by the country's ruling elites as a certain recipe for disaster. While this rejection of ideology is itself an ideological position, one of its consequences has been that although highly conservative in both outlook and implementation, successive Barbadian governments have never attempted to espouse the virtues of their economic approach in either regional or international debates. This low-key approach stands in contrast to Seaga's conservatism and has in many ways blended better with the technocratic image post-independence governments have sought to project.

Second, all the Barbadian post-independence governments have basically accepted the colonial and early nationalist strategies, with their outward orientation and heavy reliance on imported capital. The emphasis was mainly on how to make these received strategies more effective and in this regard, there have been three major developments since independence. These consist of (1) greater stress being placed on the importance of management for successful economic development. This has led to the provision of a number of training facilities within Barbados as well as many overseas scholarships and management training awards for Barbadian citizens; (2) providing for the systematic development of skills at all levels within the country at large, for which a number of measures have been taken to improve the training of operatives in all sectors of the economy; and (3) the studied cultivation of an outlook that constantly tries to anticipate global economic changes, particularly in the North American and European markets, which the country might exploit. Evidence of this outlook in Barbados is found in the country's timely development of off-shore banking, export-processing zones and tourist diversification both within the region (Venezuela) and in non-traditional European countries (West Germany and Scandinavia).

Third has been the promotion of political and social stability as a vital economic necessity. Although the social climate is in fact extremely hostile to radical ideas, there is still a strong appearance of democratic tolerance. Much emphasis is placed in Barbados on the virtues of their two-party system, its long parliamentary tradition (it is claimed to be the third-oldest parliamentary system of the former British empire), the absence of political violence and a respected judiciary and police force (which is seen as an indication that the rule of law prevails). Barbados has been successful in cultivating this image largely because both political parties, which are very similar in both ideology and social composition uphold and project it. As the Governor of the Central Bank aptly stated at a seminar in Jamaica in November 1985, 'the two parties manage conflict between each other and one would never push the other to the wall, unlike the situation which obtains in many other Caribbean territories, and that is a key to Barbados' success'. The formation of a Marxist party in 1985 marked the first overt departure from the middle ground the two major parties have traditionally occupied.

Fourth has been the introduction of measures to facilitate the inflow of foreign capital. These have already been examined in relation to tourism, manufacturing and off-shore finance. It is important only to recall here that Barbados placed much emphasis on the development of export-processing zones, (EPZs) especially in electronics, with the result that by 1984 the EPZs were providing almost 90 per cent of export earnings (see Table 12.1). Since much of this is the fabrication of imports in enclave areas, the net effect on foreign-exchange earnings and employment is less significant than it otherwise might have been. According to the Central Bank, six basic ingredients have contributed to the success of Barbados as an off-shore financial centre – a good record of political stability, a liberal and efficient public administration, a reliable judicial system, a well-developed infrastructure of public utilities, the availability of a suitable work force and a congenial social and cultural climate.[4]

And fifth has been the very careful attention all the post-independence governments in Barbados have paid to continually upgrading the infrastructure and basic services. As a result, Barbados probably has the best public utilities and most comprehensive social services in the West Indies. 'The quality of the island's roads, air and sea ports, housing stock, tourism plant, communication, education and health facilities, industry and its electronic sub-sector, non-sugar agriculture, the media and forms of entertainment have all undergone such transformation as to have placed Barbados high among the better-off countries of the Third World.'[5] That conservative governments have done so much to improve the quality of life of the citizenry at large, even though

Table 12.1
Barbados: Selected Economic Data

	Percentage Sugar exports as of domestic exports	Percentage Manufacturing exports as of domestic exports (1)	Imports of Food, beverages, feed, fats and other agricultural materials US$m	Wages Index	Unemployment Rate (%)	National Debt US$m	International Reserves US$m	Consumer Price Index (1980 = 100)
1965	69	15	19 (1966)	–	15	–	–	21
1970	47	35	29	32	9	–	–	27
1975	53	36	55	54	22	22	40	63
1980	32	64	96	100	11	82	81	100
1981	17	79	105	110	11	130	75	119
1982	17	80	94	122	13	143	97	131
1983	7	91	92	128	16	174	119	138
1984	10	88	98	141	18	183	111	144
1985	10	88	92	–	18	222	137	150

Source: Government of Barbados, various publications.

Notes: (1) includes rum.

motivated by the need to make Barbados an attractive investment location for foreigners, has gone a long way towards
defusing social tensions in the post-independence period.

As part of their open-economy policy since independence, successive Barbadian governments have encouraged
industry to become export-oriented, particularly within the
regional market, with the result that over the 1980-84 period,
as much as one-quarter of domestic exports were sent to
the CARICOM markets. Domestic exporters are encouraged
through a credit-insurance and guarantee scheme as well as
an export-promotion corporation which provides them with
technical and marketing assistance. There have, however,
been some serious difficulties in the operation of CARICOM
which have caused significant setbacks for Barbadian
manufacturers.

The Governor of the Central Bank believed it was fortu-
nate that:

> . . . in the 1960s and 1970s when the conventional wisdom in
> the Caribbean was towards closure of the system Barbados
> did not go in that direction. It is now evident that as a result
> of serious difficulties in recent years those who had sought to
> close off their economies are now turning around. Barbados
> has no need to reverse direction. Whereas others in emotional
> terms had deemed linkages with the outside world to be a
> terrible thing, Barbados has found such linkages very useful
> in practical terms. I think that the open system approach has
> helped this country considerably.[6]

With the coming to power of Bishop in Grenada, Seaga in
Jamaica and Reagan in the United States, in the early 1980s
there was considerable ideological tension in the region.
Despite the usual low-key style of successive post-independence governments in Barbados, the Adams administration
entered into heated arguments with Bishop in Grenada and
in so doing overtly projected US foreign-policy interests in
the region. This culminated in Barbados (along with Seaga's
Jamaica) playing a central role in the US-led invasion of
Grenada in 1983 and in subsequent efforts to militarise the
region. Once catapulted into abandoning its low-key profile
and becoming a leading critic of Marxist and radical political
formations in the region, it was not long before Barbados

began to extol the virtues of privatisation, democracy, 'our way of life' and Western, particularly American, values.

Evaluation

On the whole there has been considerable growth in real output in Barbados since 1970. While at current market prices its GDP stood at BDS$325 million in 1970, by 1975 this had risen to BDS$813 million and by 1984 to BDS$2,300 million. Per capita GDP in current prices stood at US$4,404 in 1985 (see Table 12.2). As noted, this growth was accompanied by a significant expansion of public utilities and basic social services, bringing considerable improvements in the general quality of life for large sections of the population since independence. Underlying this development has been a certain degree of diversification of the economy's industrial structure, especially noticeable in the robust expansion of manufacturing and tourism and in the continuing decline of sugar, which by 1986 was contributing less than 3 per cent to GDP and made up only 10 per cent of domestic exports. These changes are reflected in the economy's external sector, where manufactured exports as a percentage of domestic exports averaged 85 per cent between 1981 and 1985 (see Table 12.1). Between the end of the 1960s and 1980, manufacturing exports grew by over 28 per cent per annum. Most of this expansion has been in the enclave industries set up under various incentive schemes in which the fastest growth has been clothing, textiles, electronics and electrical equipment. By 1985, there were 23 enclave industries operating under the aegis of the Barbados industrial development authority. Meanwhile the number of tourists visiting the island had also grown rapidly, rising from over 220,000 in 1975 to nearly 370,000 in 1984, an increase of over two-thirds.

The wages index in Barbados also reveals vigorous expansion, increasing from 32 in 1970, to 100 in 1980 and 141 in 1984 (see Table 12.1). However, the retail price index rose by 42 per cent between 1980 and 1984 (which was about the same as the wages index), thus indicating no improvement in real wages. From as far back as 1970, the wages index has just kept ahead of the retail price index. While the growth of the index is therefore a 'money illusion' it nevertheless reflects an achievement unmatched anywhere else except Trinidad-Tobago, for most Caribbean people have experienced a definite fall in their real wages and standard of living since the 1980s.

Table 12.2
Barbados: GDP 1970–84

	Per Capita GDP (Current) Market Prices) US$	Sugar Contribution to GDP (%)	Manufacturing contribution to GDP (%)	Construction Contribution to GDP (%)
1970	678	14.5	. . .	9.9
1975	1,504	9.5	10.3	6.6
1984	4,109	2.8	12.7	6.3
1985	4,404	2.9	9.4	4.6

Source: Government statistics

Barbados's excellent record of rapid overall growth in national income and the positive changes introduced into its industrial structure have, however, to be viewed in relation to four major considerations. First, the diversification of the economy is more apparent than real, for the economy is basically incapable of generating autonomous growth or eradicating poverty permanently. The reason for this is that much of the expansion has been in tourism and in the EPZs, which are two particularly vulnerable sectors, not only in the region but also worldwide. Tourism is vulnerable to changes in taste, variations in levels of economic activity in North America and Europe, cross-currency rates (particularly the US dollar against European and Japanese currencies) and adverse media reports in Europe and North America. All these factors lead to considerable annual swings in the number of visitors and in how much they spend. The industries are vulnerable because of the enclave character of the EPZs, their limited internal links and the footloose nature of the firms established in the EPZs. Also, given the amount of capital restructuring taking place among the TNCs, these weaknesses are unlikely to lessen. The electronics industry has already been hard hit by these changes. Moreover, in both tourism and the EPZ industries, low Barbadian wages are an important factor in the decision of firms to locate there and this creates an inbuilt incentive to keep wage levels down.

Given the vulnerability of these new industries, it is important to realise that their expansion has not been accompanied by a deliberate reduction of sugar as the data may suggest. To the contrary, all the evidence suggests that the decline in the sugar industry was caused by the Caribbean-wide structural weaknesses of agriculture analysed in Chapter 7 and was not a result of deliberate choice. The economy's increased dependence on imported foods, beverages, fats, animal feeds and other agricultural materials can be seen in Table 12.1, which shows that the value of imports of these products trebled between 1970 and 1985, when it was averaging about US$93 million per annum.

Employment in these industries is characterised by marked seasonal and cyclical variations and these add to the social burden created by the all too familiar West Indian social sickness – persistently high levels of open unemployment. In 1984, 18 per cent of the labour force in Barbados was unemployed. In any context this would be a colossal social tragedy, but it is made worse by the absence of any significant unemployment relief. Successive governments have regarded unemployment, not as a temporary, transitional phenomenon but as a structural and endemic feature of the economic system, which makes unemployment relief unaffordable. Like other West Indian territories, Barbados has allowed employment/unemployment to take care of itself, to remain a by-product of the growth in incomes and output. No systematic attack on unemployment as a high priority social problem has ever been mounted.

Recognising the limitations of EPZ-style diversification and the structural factors behind the high levels of unemployment has meant that both the government and the opposition have tended to view the rapid rise in GDP with a certain amount of caution. This is evident in the government's widely-publicised resistance to the World Bank's attempts to change Barbados' status to that of 'least needy', on the grounds of its high level of per capita income. The government, however, have argued that because of the small size and openness of the economy and the fragility of tourism and EPZ industries, Barbados needs more time to build up the stock of social and human capital necessary to construct a qualitatively different kind of diversification. In particular, as the government was quick to point out, the 1981-83 international recession came close to bringing disaster to Barbados, for during that period tourism, agriculture, and EPZ activity all suffered significant declines. Indeed, in real terms, per capita GDP fell by 7 per cent between 1980 and 1983 and it was not until 1984, with the revival of economic activity in Europe and North America, that a real growth of over 3 per cent was achieved.

The open strategy adopted in Barbados since the Second World War and intensified by successive governments since independence is the product of a particular set of social circumstances. For 350 years (until 1966) Barbados, unlike all the other West Indian territories, was ruled solely by the British. This, along with a substantial resident planter class, created structures in which 'white' capital (in other words that of the descendants of the original planter class) became economically dominant in the country although the vast majority of the population was black. Thus, whereas in the early 19th century 20 per cent of the population was white, by 1970 the white elite constituted only 4 per cent of the population, (and the 'mixed' group a further 4 per cent). As a result, class, racial inequality and white domination were integrally built into the society's economic structures. Hence a popular consciousness which prides itself in describing Barbados as 'Little England' and in which imitation of British traditions, customs and practices have been particularly important to the dominant elites.

If there is any strong resistance to this cultural and ideological domination among the underclasses, it has certainly never been articulated. This is especially lamentable considering that in a country in which 96 per cent of the population are the descendants of slaves and 4 per cent of slave owners, the local press should have considered it necessary to run a series of debates in 1985 over whether Barbados should join the other West Indian territories in celebrating the 150th anniversary of the abolition of slavery. Most of the letters opposed the celebration on the grounds that there was 'no point in looking back to the past, since all Barbadians are now equal' and that to talk of the slave past was to stir up racial hatred. Indeed, it is this kind of logic, a logic that effectively denies Barbadians their own history, which allows for this peculiar blend of seemingly democratic tolerance to coexist in Barbados with a virulent hostility towards any radical ideas. Gomes sums this up well in citing the President of the Employers' Federation in Barbados, who, in response to the upsurge of black power sweeping the region in 1970, argued that:

> . . . events have made us focus our attention on the serious state of affairs of unrest which exists in the area. While all eyes are on Trinidad-Tobago, there cannot be any doubt that many of the Caribbean territories harbour the same explosive elements. Nor can there be any doubt that many of those who are currently championing the cause of the underprivileged, who claim to represent the interest of Black dignity in their struggle against past oppression, imagined or real, are preaching a philosophy which is very akin both in content and in its terminology to that preached by communist revolutionaries as exemplified by the late Che Guevara. If we do not know what motivates such a movement, we must find out how to counter it; because we do know that the result of it, if successful, is the end of democracy.

The statement thus not only refers to 'past oppression, imagined or real' but clearly adopts the cold war position of regarding claims 'to represent black dignity' as communistic and anti-democratic.[7]

As in other Caribbean states, one of the most notable features of post-independence policy has been its promotion of a local bourgeoisie linked to the growth of a domestic manufacturing sector. Although there are no firm data on this, the expansion seems to have favoured the already dominant elements of 'white capital' which have diversified into these areas. In addition, a group of mixed and black businessmen has been formed around these new activities. Lawyers, accountants, engineers and economists have also done quite well out of this expansion. These elements of local capital none the less remain junior to the larger structure of international capital, which continues to provide the economy with its main momentum. In reality, those in the political ruling class are the managers or house-slaves of the system. And, in terms of the overall economic, political and cultural objectives of the model, they have done better in Barbados than in any other Caribbean state.

The broad mass of the population appears to believe that progress is being made and to accept the cultural forms that go with it. Resistance is still isolated despite the formation of a Marxist party. Increasingly, however, political debate will have to encompass a much wider range of opinion and, out of this, the repressed consciousness of the mass of the population will eventually reassert itself. It is my prediction that this development will occur irrespective of the actual course of economic events. The chances are that any model of expansion and accumulation as contingent as this is on accumulation elsewhere, will expose the economy to severe shock and disruption.

II: Oil Boom and Bust: Trinidad-Tobago

Background

Between its independence in 1962 and 1986, Trinidad-Tobago was under the political rule of one party, the People's National Movement (PNM) and, until his death in 1981, Eric Williams led the party and headed the government. Unlike Guyana, however, which also had uninterrupted rule by one party, Trinidad-Tobago always held free and fair national elections as required by its Constitution. Except for a nearly successful coup in 1970 (when the black power protests in the region reached their apogee) and the subsequent boycott of the elections by the opposition parties in 1971, the two-party parliamentary system of politics has worked well.

Trinidad-Tobago is the only West Indian country with a substantial petroleum sector and, not surprisingly, the central feature of the development model pursued since the 1970s has been the use and misuse of the completely unanticipated windfall gains produced by the Arab oil embargo and the 'good oil years' which followed. It has been estimated that between 1974 and 1983, Trinidad-Tobago received a total of US$10,000 million in windfall oil revenues and nearly US$17,000 million in overall oil revenues. Subsequent developments in the world petroleum industry have, however, shaken the foundations of the economy and revealed yet another instance of a Caribbean economy following the boom and bust of a product cycle. In the midst of the prosperity of a product-cycle boom, it is easy to forget its inherent transitoriness and for those who control the windfall to assume that it will last forever. As Eric St Cyr observes:

> Caribbean countries have never failed to generate sizeable economic surpluses, as the fortunes of 'King Sugar' in the 18th century must attest, and more recently the post war bauxite boom in Jamaica and the massive oil booms in Trinidad & Tobago . . . our problem is that institutional and structural factors have combined to see it expatriated or less than optimally deployed at home.[8]

Despite its petroleum base, however, the economy of Trinidad-Tobago did not fare too well in the years preceding the dramatic rise in oil prices. Although growth in real terms was of the order of 10 per cent per annum for the period between 1955 and 1961, between 1962 and 1965 there was virtually no growth at all. The years 1966–68 saw a slight improvement, but by 1969/1970 the slide had set in once again, with unemployment in 1970 running at 12.5 per cent of the labour force.

As we saw in Chapters 5 and 6, the PNM strongly favoured a policy of 'industrialisation by invitation' from the mid-1950s onwards. The high capital intensity of the import-substituting industries which were actually established and the relatively small-scale nature of their operations, however, resulted in very little net labour absorption. In fact the sector as a whole employed only about three-quarters of the 25,000 people employed in the traditional sugar industry. Between 1958 and 1973 the government published three national plans. The first, which covered the period between 1958 and 1962, was known as the 'People's Charter for Economic and Social Development', and was prepared principally by Sir Arthur Lewis. Although Lewis usually advocated a combination of import substitution and export-promoting industrialisation as the major thrust for West Indian economies, in this case the structure of incentives was heavily focused on the local market. In the second plan (1964–68) state intervention in economic life featured more prominently than ever before. This resulted in the introduction of a number of institutions and laws to encourage local and foreign private investment, to provide the infrastructure for industrial and agricultural development and to improve basic social services especially in health and education. In addition, the state took over a number of commercial activities, including sugar, oil and certain selected enterprises in the import-substitution manu-facturing sector. By 1972 the state owned 21 enterprises and employed about 30 per cent of the labour force. It was often stressed at the time that, although the government was conservative and pro-capital in outlook, it was sufficiently nationalist and pragmatic to have created in Trinidad-Tobago in the early 1970s, the largest state-owned sector in the whole of the Caribbean apart from Cuba and without any recourse to labels such as 'taking the commanding heights of the economy' or 'expropriating the expropriators'.

The PNM's policies towards the major sectors of the economy (manufacturing, agriculture, tourism and other services) were so much like those of the other Caribbean territories that there is no need to discuss them here. What is important, however, is that by the time of the third five-year plan (1969–73) the import-substitution model was showing signs of rapid exhaustion and the plan strongly recommended regional integration as the best way out of the impasse the industrialisation experience of the past had created. With real incomes falling and signs of deep social unrest, the oil boom of the early 1970s came as a completely unanticipated blessing to established political and economic interests in the territory. As Farrell notes:

> The economic policies of its government, centering initially on attracting investment and subsequently on import substi-tution, failed either to generate genuine industrialisation and transformation, or to deal with the problem of growing unem-ployment. The result was the 1970 Black Power rebellion which shook the nation to its foundations and threatened at one time to topple the government. Eric William's adminis-tration managed to weather that storm, but between 1970 and 1973 the economy continued to decline . . . and Eric Williams announced his imminent retirement from the Prime Minis-tership and political life. Then came the Arab oil embargo and

the quadrupling of oil prices. These events, with generous assistance from expanded oil and gas production based on new reserves ushered in a decade of the long oil boom.[9]

Policy

At the macro political-economy level of formulation, the development strategies and policies pursued by the PNM government in Trinidad-Tobago after the 1970s differed little in their main essentials from those pursued in many other parts of the region. The effective differences, where they do exist, derive principally from the huge economic windfall oil generated in this period and which was of course, specific to Trinidad-Tobago. As in other countries of the region, control over the machinery of state in Trinidad-Tobago has resided in the hands of a favoured section of the petty bourgeoisie, which has sought to use this control to pursue the wider class project of creating a large indigenous bourgeoisie in the country. Everywhere this process has been facilitated by historical circumstances, particularly those that permitted the post-colonial state to play 'exceptional roles' in West Indian social life. The marked expansion in the state-owned sector of Trinidad-Tobago, which preceded the oil boom, is but one indicator of this. In Trinidad-Tobago the period after the 1970s witnessed the use of state power by these elements to reinforce capitalist relations within the national economy and to promote the continued integration of the country into the international system of capitalist accumulation and reproduction. The windfall gains were used to promote this project. Such an overall policy thrust, however, could only have been predicated on the continued capacity of the ruling strata to demobilise and de-politicise the masses and so contain the development of alternative pathways. Their demonstrated capacity in this direction has been striking, particularly since its chief architect, Eric Williams, as both historian and anti-colonial politician, had done much to stir the consciousness of the poor and powerless, not only in Trinidad-Tobago, but farther afield in the wider Caribbean area.

It is from this background that the policies developed to utilise the windfall oil gains are best understood. As it emerged, *five* major thrusts were developed by successive PNM administrations in the wake of the oil boom. *First*, the already vigorous role the state had been playing in economic affairs since independence was considerably intensified. This time, however, the principal orientation was not towards import-substituting industrialisation (although this continued) but towards the state's utilisation of oil revenues to create large-scale resource-intensive export industries. Because the oil boom happened to coincide with the discovery of huge natural gas reserves, the energy intensive export industries tended to be favoured. *Second*, the mechanisms used to bring this new sector into existence were centred on collaborative arrangements between the state and the TNCs. A wide array of arrangements was set up, ranging from traditional joint ventures at all levels (exploration, production, technology and marketing) to using TNCs as project managers, contractors, consultants and suppliers of technical services. There were also the usual marketing and management contract arrangements, especially joint arrangements for approaching bank consortia to raise loan finance. The boom in oil revenues gave Trinidad-Tobago an edge over other countries in this regard – a factor the TNCs were quick to exploit – with the result that the new enterprises averaged a loan-finance/equity ratio of 3:1.

The new activities, which were centred on fertilisers, chemicals and iron and steel, were located in a huge industrial complex in the south of Trinidad at a place called Point Lisas. The idea for this development did not originate with the government, but first surfaced as a proposal by businessmen active in the South Trinidad Chamber of Commerce who were eager to stimulate port development and heavy industry in the South. The government's first involvement was indirect and in a sense unintentional. At the height of the black power protests in 1970, the government acquired majority shares in the Caroni sugar estates – the largest agricultural enterprise and largest employer of labour in the country. The remainder of the shares were acquired in 1975. As it turned out, Caroni had acquired shares in the Point Lisas development company (formed by the southern businessmen) in exchange for the land it had ceded to the company for the port development and proposed industrial complex. With the sudden rise in oil revenues and discovery of huge natural gas reserves, the government decided to back this proposal as a way of monetising the natural gas reserves. The Point Lisas project subsequently became the main pivot for its development and the largest outlet for state capital expenditures during that period.

There are three major activities located in the Point Lisas complex – an industrial estate; a chemical fertiliser industry; and an iron and steel works. The industrial estate not only provides excellent transport, power, telecommunications and infrastructural facilities, but also contains an enormous new port (Point Lisas) capable of handling huge volumes of trade. The chemical fertiliser industry, which is based on the country's natural gas reserves, has several major components. One of these is Federation Chemicals (a subsidiary of Grace) which first came to Trinidad in the late 1950s when Grace set up a subsidiary to manufacture nitrogenous fertilisers. The original intention was to exploit the regional market created by the short-lived West Indian Federation, but when this collapsed in 1962 its focus shifted to exports in the world market. With the discovery of natural gas, large-scale fertiliser production operations commenced in its plant in the 1970s. Another component of the chemical fertiliser industry consists of two state/TNC joint-venture operations, *Tringen* (in which the TNC is Grace) and *Fertrin* (in which the TNC is Amoco, itself a subsidiary of Standard Oil). By 1981, Trinidad-Tobago was already one of the world's largest producers of fertilisers with a capacity in excess of 1.2 million tons per annum. Then, in 1984 the government set up an operation of its own to produce fertilisers and methanol. Between 1980 and 1984, the capacity of the chemical fertiliser sector grew by a factor of 2.6. With export earnings at nearly TT\$ 440 million, this sector was bringing in more than seven times as much revenue as sugar, although only a tenth of the value of oil exports.

The government-owned iron and steel works (ISCOTT) produces sponge iron, billets and rods from imported lump ores and pellets. Although the company was originally intended to have foreign partners, for a multitude of reasons these backed off as economic problems with the venture loomed large. In 1986 it was reportedly making a daily loss of half-a-million dollars and the government was still assiduously trying to find a suitable TNC to manage the enterprise and, hopefully, to acquire equity in it as well. It has been estimated that about US$1,600 million have been invested by the state in the Point Lisas complex. While the above constitutes the preponderant activities of the complex, a number of minor industries have developed around it.

While these state activities overshadowed the traditional import-substituting manufacturing (favoured before the oil boom) and the EPZ-type investments (which became fashionable later), the *third* policy thrust was towards developing these two subsectors as an ancillary to large-scale, export-oriented, resource-intensive investments. Between 1959 and 1980, over 700 establishments employing approximately 20,000 people were created in the traditional import-substituting areas. Some of these establishments produce cement, household appliances, radios, televisions and motor vehicles. The result of this has been the emergence of a significant indigenous bourgeoisie centred in these operations and located in four large economic groupings:

—   *Neal and Massey Group* (motor vehicles, building materials, machinery distribution, real estate and finance. It also owns a number of subsidiaries elsewhere in the region and is reputed to be the largest indigenous economic grouping in the West Indies).
—   *McEnearney Alstons Group* (motor vehicles, building materials, engineering services, publishing, finance, supermarkets and other retail and wholesale outlets. It also has Caribbean subsidiaries).
—   *Geddes Grant Group* (principally trading. This group is the most international of the four in that it operates in Britain as well as in six West Indian countries. About half its trading, which accounts for nearly 90 per cent of its turnover, takes place outside Trinidad-Tobago).
—   *Kirpalanis Group* (a private company owned by one family, unlike the others which are public concerns. Its main activities are department stores, light manufacturing, principally footwear and textiles, and some finance).

285

Sandoval estimates that for the period 1979-81, the combined sales of these groups 'listed above in descending order of economic importance) averaged about one-sixth of the non-oil GDP.[10]

The PNM's *fourth* policy thrust followed from the consideration that one of the immediate consequences of increased petroleum prices was a rapid expansion of central government revenues from this source. This peaked at over two-thirds of all government revenues collected. Apart from financing the capital budget, a significant proportion of this was diverted into providing transfers and subsidies. Together these exceeded 40 per cent of the government expenditure (one-tenth of GDP at current market prices) in the 1980s, as compared with 16 per cent in 1953, 17 per cent in 1963 and 27 per cent in 1973. A levy (which was introduced in response to local protests in the 1970s to finance unemployment relief works) raised over TT$400 million in 1980, of which over three-quarters came from the oil sector alone.

The *fifth* and final policy thrust involved using the surpluses generated by oil to improve the basic services provided by the state. Telephones and telecommunications were completely refurbished, roads were constructed to cope with traffic congestion, water and electricity supplies were improved, along with public transport, postal services, public warehousing, docks and airport facilities. Despite the considerable investment of public funds, however, these improvements failed to keep pace with the pressures created by the growth in incomes and the population's expectations. As a result, the congestion on the roads and the overloading of public facilities continued. There were also some major investments in social areas, particularly in education, health, recreation and housing. Among the more impressive of these were the Mount Hope medical complex, advertised as one of the best in the hemisphere, a modern sports and recreation stadium, which has attracted several world-class events, as well as many housing complexes, even although the housing shortage continues and land and house prices steadily increase. The emphasis has tended to be on large building projects which have physically transformed the landscapes of many of the country's neighbourhoods.

Evaluation

As a result of the oil boom and the construction activity associated with the new enterprises considered above, between 1974 and 1982 total GDP in Trinidad-Tobago (measured at factor cost in current prices) grew by a factor of nearly 5, that is from TT$4,000 million to over TT$19,000 million. Over the same period, per capita incomes (in current prices) grew from TT$3,937 to TT$19,682. Almost all the expansion centred on the performance of the oil sector. Excluding some smaller companies, each producing less than 1 per cent of total output, Trinidad-Tobago housed four major oil companies. Until 1985, two of these (Texaco Trinidad and Amoco) were TNC subsidiaries, but in 1985 the government purchased a significant share of Texaco's operations. The third company, a joint venture between the state and Tesoro of Texas, was formed in 1969 after BP pulled out of Trinidad. As with Caroni, the government intervened at the time to protect the employment of BP's 1,500 workers and, when all else failed, eventually bought BP's assets. The fourth major company came into existence after the government took over Shell and created its first wholly-owned oil company, Trintoc, in 1974. In addition, Texaco, Tesoro and Trintoc became equal partners in an offshore oil venture, Trinmar, with the distribution in the production of domestic crude as follows: Texaco 8 per cent, Amoco 51 per cent, Tesoro 13 per cent, Trintoc 5 per cent and Trinmar 22 per cent. Amoco, which became the largest producer of local crude in 1977, had (unlike the other TNCs) entered Trinidad-Tobago in 1968 in search of crude, of which it was short for its world-wide operations. Texaco, which produces less than one-tenth of the local crude, came there mainly to refine imported crude. In 1986 approximately three-quarters of the domestic crude was being produced in offshore fields.

Although domestic crude is produced, the traditional focus of the oil industry in Trinidad-Tobago has been its role as an offshore refining centre. The TNCs undertaking these investments were originally attracted by the lower processing costs, the political stability of the country (which was presumed to stem from the fact that it was still a colony) and its geographical proximity to the east coast of the US where most of the oil (residual fuel) was consumed. Initially, most of the imported crude came from Venezuela, but with larger tankers and the consequent decline in freight rates, crude was brought in from the Middle East, Africa and Asia for refining. Crude imports peaked in the early 1970s at over 290,000 barrels per day (bpd), but by 1978, had fallen to 230,000 bpd and by 1985, to between 160,000 and 170,000 bpd. In 1984, there was a small 6 per cent increase in output over 1983 and in 1985 a 4 per cent increase over 1984, but this was the first time any increase had been recorded since 1978. In 1986, domestic production of crude was less than three-tenths of 1 per cent of world output.

The structure of the industry is such that the country both produces and exports crude, while at the same time also importing crude for processing. This has developed because of specific company interests. Most of the oil refined and exported is residual fuel, whereas most of the local production comes from offshore fields.

The contribution of oil to GDP peaked at 48 per cent, averaging 44 per cent for the period 1974–77. Thereafter there was a decline and it was not until 1980 that the figure once again exceeded 40 per cent. Petroleum also dominated the export trade, accounting for over 90 per cent of export earnings. In 1982, however, the oil economy began to stagnate and in 1986 its prospects were still exceedingly depressing. Since 1982, the economy has had negative rates of growth of GDP in real terms, with the decline in 1983–85 being −3.8, −6.3, and −10.8 per cent respectively. Foreign-exchange reserves peaked in 1981 at over US$3,200 million, in other words about four times the value at the end of 1975, but by the end of 1985 this total was down to US$1,000 million. The external debt, although not as economically significant as in other West Indian territories, stood at US$1,000 million at the end of 1985, about double the debt at the end of 1982. Foreign-debt servicing, which cost only 2.5 per cent of exports of goods and services between 1970 and 1983, has since trebled. Government fiscal operations, which showed huge surpluses on current account (averaging 50 per cent of current revenue in the year 1980/81) declined substantially after that period, resulting in an overall deficit on current and capital account for the first time since the oil boom began. For the year 1982/83, this overall deficit averaged 13 per cent of GDP at current market prices. By 1984, this was reduced to under 7 per cent GDP as government tightened its fiscal operations. Oil's contribution to government revenues has declined rapidly since 1980/81 when it averaged about two-thirds of total revenue. Over the period 1983–85, this averaged 40 per cent of total revenues. Total exports, which peaked at nearly TT$10,000 million in 1980, had declined to TT$5,300 million by 1985. Oil exports at over TT$9,000 million in 1980 were less than half that amount in 1985 (TT$4,200 million) and as a percentage of total exports had fallen from 93 per cent in 1980 to 80 per cent in 1984. Selected data for the years 1980–85, are shown in Tables 12.3 and 12.4.

Data on crude and refining throughput in Trinidad-Tobago (shown in Table 12.4) indicate the domestic falls in refining-throughput levels, as well as the decline in domestic crude, as the petroleum market has weakened. Currently, the refining capacity of the local industry is several times larger than the local crude available and, with a dramatically softened oil market, the effects on the local industry have been disastrous. In evaluating the experience of Trinidad-Tobago it is important to recognise that declining output in the oil industry reflects a number of basic changes taking place within the structure of the industry at both the international and local level. First, there is the obviously important softening of the petroleum market, which has created the bust in oil prices. Second, the high price structure created by OPEC in the 1970s and again in 1980/81 resulted in concerted efforts by the US to reduce its dependence on imported residual fuels for its public utilities by encouraging a switch to coal. The reduced demand led to significant over capacity in the region's refining sector, which was oriented towards serving this market. Third, the traditional specialisation of the region on residual fuel is a specialisation on the cheap end of the oil barrel and not the more expensive end of the distillates and lighter fuels such as gasolene. As a result, this subsector of the region's operations has been less resilient to the adverse effects of collapsing oil prices. Finally, the whole development of the oil sector in the country has been

Table 12.3
Trinidad–Tobago: Selected Economic Data

		1980	1981	1982	1983	1984	1985
Trade TT$ 000 m	Exports	9.8	9.0	7.4	5.6	5.2	5.3
	Total Imports	7.6	7.5	8.9	6.2	4.6	3.7
	Mineral/fuel lubricants Exports	9.2	8.1	6.5	4.7	4.2	4.2
	Fertiliser Exports	0.16	0.13	0.28	0.41	0.44	–
	Food Imports	0.6	0.7	0.8	0.8	0.8	0.7
Government Finances	Central Government Current Revenues TT$ 000 m	6.4	6.8	6.8	6.4	6.5	6.3
	Oil Revenues TT$ 000 m	4.1	4.2	3.3	2.5	2.8	2.5
	Total Expenditure TT$ 000 m	5.5	6.7	9.5	8.8	8.3	7.5
	External Debt US$ m	437	448	558	644	829	1000
	Net Foreign Reserves US$ m	2640	3203	2983	2083	1181	1001
GDP	Changes in *Real* GDP on previous Year (%)	3.5	2.4	0.5	–3.8	–10.8	–6.3
	Oil as percentage of GDP (*current* prices)	42.0	36.0	26.9	23.4	24.9	23.5
Prices	Retail Prices 1982 = 100	78.5	89.8	100	115.2	130.5	140.5

Table 12.4
Trinidad–Tobago: Output of Selected Products

		1980	1981	1982	1983	1984	1985
Domestic Manufacturing *(units)*	TVs	12,779	13,266	18.222	21,217	19,150	20,200
	Radios	8,387	8,521	8,331	6,948	2,194	3,300
	Gas Cookers	23,386	15,265	22,779	18,313	20,320	19,300
	Fridges	27,550	14,865	28,387	19,952	21,803	6,400
	Cars	11,852	13,436	15,026	20,677	22,753	11,900
	Cement ('000) kg.	186	139	189	390	405	329
Petroleum '000 Cubic Meters	Crude Output	12,341	10,989	10,274	9,275	9,841	10,232
	Crude Exports	7024	5978	5275	4769	5170	5912
	Crude Imports	8345	6139	3719	–	–	–
	Refinery Through-put	13,455	9,913	8,761	4,321	4,475	4,460
	Refinery Through-put as a % of capacity	47	38	47	23	23	23
Agriculture	Sugar '000 tonnes	112.7	92.6	78.7	77.2	64.7	81.0
	Coffee '000 kg	2,239	2,433	1,794	1,388	853	2,135
	Cocoa '000 kg	2,381	3,145	2,246	1,717	1,560	1,307
Fertilisers '000 tonnes	*Output*	687	555	940	1,274	1,458	1,664
	Exports	614	494	851	1,214	1,282	1,460
Heavy Industry	Natural gas million cubic metres	5601	5604	6916	6318	7229	7573
	Methanol '000 tonnes	–	–	–	–	180.9	358.2
Iron & Steel '000 tonnes	Direct reduced Iron	21.5	179.5	217.9	302.3	239.0	243.2
	Billets	3.2	53.1	179.2	209.6	198.6	166.9
	Wire Rods	–	29.1	115.5	164.2	134.7	102.9

made subservient to the TNC logic of global profit maximis-
ation and balancing strategic interests. At the moment, this
is undergoing a major restructuring in which the original
attractions of the region do not command the same premium.

The fortunes of the large natural gas/fertiliser enterprises have, on the whole, been mixed in recent years. When,
in 1981, the country had an output capacity of over 1.2
million tons per year of ammonia, it was the world's largest
exporter of the product. With cheap natural gas and a world
hungry for food, this appeared to be a strategic cornering of
a major market and encouraged the more than doubling of
capacity since then. The industry has, however, encountered
some protectionism in the metropolitan markets which has
aggravated recessionary declines in fertiliser imports. In
addition, although the country is still a major supplier of
fertilisers and methanol to the US, competition has emerged
from new sources, mainly Mexico, the USSR and the Middle
East. Finally, there is a long-term threat to synthetically-
derived fertilisers posed by scientific discoveries in the field
of direct nitrogen fixation. These threaten to have the same
disruptive effect that oil-based fertilisers had on guano
production in South America. Because the industry is highly
capital intensive (about US$2.5–US$3.0 million per job),
highly protected/subsidised and of an enclave export nature,
domestic returns in the form of employment, tax yields and
internal linkages are low. It has been estimated that domestic
value added in this sector is as low as 13 per cent and direct
employment less than 0.30 per cent of the respective totals
for the country.[11]

This rapid development of the new energy-intensive
export sector is not only inherently limited by these
marketing and other technological threats, but is also too
small to make up for declining oil production and prices,
the neglect of domestic agriculture and the limitations of a
manufacturing sector so highly dependent on external sources
for raw materials, capital inputs, spares, licences, patents,
know-how and privileged access to protected local and
regional markets. Moreover, there are significant income and
foreign-exchange leaks from the new energy-intensive sector
because foreign contractors, skilled personnel, hardware and
software were used to set it up in the first instance and also

because the sector has had to resort quite extensively to loan financing in the international market which has helped to increase the country's external indebtedness. The TNCs have encouraged this development as a partial hedge against risk, for they know from experience that Third World countries find it easier to nationalise foreign equity represented in local facilities than to default to loans.

In the wake of negative developments in the mid-1980s, the government adopted the classic pattern followed by other Third World oil producers, namely to cut public expenditure, restrict imports, lay off or retrench employees in the state sector, remove subsidies, tighten bank credit and introduce a more active system of foreign-exchange management. As Tables 12.3 and 12.4 reveal, oil revenues declined by nearly one-third between 1980 and 1985 and total revenue, which averaged TT$6,600 million in 1981/82, was down to TT$6,400 million in 1984/85. State expenditures declined from a peak of TT$9,500 million in 1982 to TT$7,500 million in 1985. Most of the cuts were in capital expenditure, which had increased at an annual rate of over 40 per cent between 1974 and 1981 and declined by over 50 per cent for the two years of 1983 and 1984. In addition, subsidies to a wide range of enterprises and activities fell in 1984 after increasing at an annual rate of over 50 per cent between 1979 and 1982. Oil exports were more than halved between 1980 and 1985 and, to offset this, imports were reduced by about 40 per cent over the same period. Foreign-exchange control mechanisms were put in place and, towards the end of 1985, the exchange rate was placed on a dual-rate system and devalued by 50 per cent for most imported commodities. Many of these policies, particularly attempts to tighten up on non-essential imports, capital flight and luxury consumption at home, came too late, since most of the losses had already been incurred at the height of the oil boom when, as one calypsonian put it, Trinidad-Tobago was a place where 'capitalism gone mad'.

Despite the massive windfall gains, unemployment in 1985 stood at 15 per cent of the labour force, with the huge investments at Point Lisas yielding less than 1 per cent of total employment. In that unemployment was still one of the major social illnesses, and was not being treated directly as a problem in itself, but left to solve itself as a by-product of

growth in exports and incomes, the situation in Trinidad-
Tobago was no different from that of the rest of the Caribbean. The neglect of domestic agriculture and the traditional
export staples are reflected in the output figures in Table
12.4. Between 1980 and 1984, the output of sugar fell by
over 40 per cent to an all-time low of 65,000 tons. The output
in 1984 was just over one-quarter of output levels achieved
since the Second World War. As with other sugar-producing
territories in the region, this decline did not reflect a phased
withdrawal from sugar but the mismanagement and poor
organisation of the industry at all levels. Cocoa production
at 1,307 metric tonnes in 1985 was also less than one-third
of the 1975 output, while in the same year coffee fell to about
one-half of its 1975 output. Citrus production also showed
a decline.

The overall result of all this was that, by 1985, per capita
consumption of imported foods was estimated to be as high
as US$800 per annum – a reverse of the situation 20 years
earlier when the country was a net exporter of food. In 1986
the domestic food supply was estimated at less than one-
third of domestic consumption. Meanwhile the TNCs have
secured strategic control of the country's food-processing
sector and have generally prospered, particularly in such areas
as dairy milk (Borden and Nestlé), feeds and grain (Central
Soya, Pillsbury and International Multifoods), juices,
biscuits, preserves and concentrates (Unilever and Nabisco),
beer (Guinness and Heineken), soft drinks (Pepsi-Cola and
Coca-Cola) and fast-foods outlets (Pizza Hut and Kentucky
Fried Chicken).

In the case of the domestic assembly/manufacturing
sector, output performance since 1980 has been mixed despite
the state's protection. This is partly due to the recession and
partly to the failure of these products to capture significant
shares of the regional market. For example, as Table 12.4
shows, far fewer radios were produced in 1985 than in 1980,
whereas television production was up by over a half. Gas
cookers were about one-seventh below their 1980 output,
but the production of motor vehicles grew substantially from
under 12,000 in 1980 to nearly 23,000 in 1984, only to fall
by nearly a half in 1985. Domestic cement output expanded
so significantly since 1980 that by 1984 the product was no

longer being imported. It has frequently been claimed that one of the major factors affecting the regional export capability of the manufacturing assembly sector in Trinidad-Tobago has been the high wage/high cost inflationary economy which materialised with the oil boom. This factor is also blamed for the weak performances of the traditional export crops, although there is ample evidence that other circumstances may be of at least equal importance. The 50 per cent devaluation introduced in 1985 was mainly designed to rectify the situation produced by inflationary wage increases and an overvalued exchange rate.

In evaluating the PNM's policies, it is also important to look at the nature of the relationships which have developed between political leaders, top state employees and the TNC's corporate leadership, for a considerable amount of evidence has been unearthed over the years of bribery, corruption, nepotism and criminal negligence in the disbursement of public funds.

A number of scandals have been reported in the press involving the purchase of aircraft for the national airline, the proposed construction of a horse-racing complex, ISCOTT, the handling of import licences, foreign-exchange remittances and customs administration at ports of entry, to name but a few. One source estimates that as much as one-quarter of the windfall oil revenues has been wasted through corruption and negligence. If to this we add the gross inefficiencies which have been disclosed in project preparation and feasibility analysis, the social cost of the investments has been unbelievably high. To cite just one example, the final cost of installing ISCOTT was nearly two-thirds higher than the original estimate.

To conclude, there seem to be four major lessons to learn from Trinidad-Tobago's experiences. First, even with windfalls of the magnitude obtained by Trinidad-Tobago, economic transformation in the region is no easy task. The intractable nature of the economic and social elements of the system should never be underestimated, for the historical tendency to reproduce discrepancies between resource use, production, consumption and the basic needs of the broad mass of the region's population has been formed by centuries of slave and colonial domination. Difficulties of this magnitude do not simply disappear with an abundance of foreign exchange, or, for that matter, of any other resource. The pro-capital conservative policies adopted during the oil boom masked rather than removed the economy's basic structural weakness.

Second, responsibility for the use (or misuse) of resources during a windfall ultimately lies with the classes, strata and groups who control the state and who own and control the means of production. The link between these various social elements is what keeps the momentum of the system going. The petty bourgeoisie pioneered the drive for energy-intensive industries and it is important to recognise that, although this was presented as an attempt to transform the economy and the society as a whole, it was actually designed to transform the country's petty bourgeoisie into a big industrial bourgeoisie. It is therefore no coincidence that the Point Lisas proposals originated from a group of ambitious businessmen and that it was only with the oil boom that the initiative was taken over by the state. As it has turned out, the massive investments in this sector not only led to a substantial siphoning off of public funds into the private hands of corrupt leaders, but also brought prosperity to a range of increasingly important local petty-bourgeois interests (subcontractors, engineers, architects, financiers, accountants, estate agents and property developers) who turned the services they offered into lucrative business ventures. It is also not surprising that many of the financiers associated with the Point Lisas project's scandals and 'rip-offs' were also heavily involved in dubious deposit-raising and loan schemes. The dominant local classes, however, were prepared to accept their junior status in the system of international capitalism. Throughout the period they vigorously pursued links with the TNCs and welcomed state initiatives in this direction. Since these groups had many links with the US and Europe, they staunchly supported an 'open system', for it protected their assets and offered them unrestricted access to foreign exchange with which to finance their personal travel abroad and their conspicuous consumption at home. The end result was a colossal social waste of resources.

Third, because of Trinidad-Tobago's abundant supply of natural gas (it is among the ten leading countries in the world), energy-intensive industrialisation is bound to play a part (despite the disappointments it has brought) in any foreseeable transformation of Trinidad-Tobago's economy. Opponents of this strategy argue that a country should exploit the resources the world needs rather than the resources it has and that the energy-intensive industries of the sort being promoted in Trinidad-Tobago (especially iron and steel) are in structural decline and should therefore not be developed. As Farrell argues:

> The essential conception behind Point Lisas was not only seductive but intuitively seems both logical and correct. The basic idea was that Trinidad and Tobago was rich in natural gas and that it should make maximum use of this abundant and cheap resource. More specifically, it should go into industries which were energy intensive and gas intensive. Trinidad and Tobago would have a natural comparative advantage in such industries. . . this notion which seems intuitively correct is exactly of a piece with several other famous examples of notions which seem intuitively correct, but are in fact false. . . the truth about industrialisation and what industries a country should get into is. . . counterintuitive. The truth is that for a small country which has to export, the first criterion in the list needed for deciding on what to get into has to be what is in demand. In what areas is demand on a secular upswing. Those are the commodities to try to get into. Your cheap and abundant resource may or may not be relevant to such areas. If it is, great, if it is not, then that cheap and abundant resource is not as valuable as you might intuitively think it is. It is important not to confuse the usefulness of something with its value.[12]

The flaw in this reasoning, however, is that the world economy is replete with examples of countries discovering an abundant resource for which they then create a world demand through skillful development, promotion and marketing. There is no reason why the Caribbean should not do the same. Rather than making the energy-intensive sector the central pivot for development, it would surely be prefer-able to use the sector exclusively for extending the foreign-exchange earning potential of Trinidad-Tobago's resources. What *form* of development the natural gas takes could then be determined in the light of what plans are being developed for the effective use of the foreign exchange. These criteria were given insufficient attention in the initial feasibility studies for the project, which laid far more emphasis on projected industrial diversification than on net foreign-exchange earnings. Consequently, as with the processing of sugar or production of alumina, this type of industrial development is not geared to the needs of local and regional people but seems to be directed abroad, much as any other typical third world export industry based on an abundant natural resource.

The fourth and final lesson to be learned is that promoting economies vulnerable to adverse shifts in world demand of this magnitude is particularly disadvantageous to the poor and powerless. This is because in the downward adjustments of economic activity and decline in real incomes (which are then deemed necessary) they will be forced to carry a disproportionate burden. Retrenchment, state cuts in social expenditure, the withdrawal of subsidies and consequent increases in domestic prices and devaluation, with its impact on prices, have always placed the heaviest burden on the society's underclasses. The effect is all the more significant given that, despite the focus on the social sector and public utilities during the boom years, there was little improvement in the distribution of income. According to Barry *et al*, in 1975/76 the top 10 per cent of households received one-third of the income, while the bottom 40 per cent received only 10 per cent and, on the basis of the 1980 census, Ramsaran concludes that 'there is no reason to believe that the situation has improved significantly since'.[13] The decline in incomes is likely, given other circumstances, to bring with it an increase in social tensions, particularly as many hold the view that the past ability of the ruling classes to maintain their rule has depended on the rapid growth in wealth of the ruling classes in the country to the point where enough crumbs have fallen to the poor, thus relieving them of the need to implement major measures in this area. As Sandoval points out, 'the triumvirate formed by the state, the local and foreign bourgeoisie has evolved without major friction up to 1981. Each part has found room to manoeuvre at the economic level. This has been possible because of the availability of economic surplus which has so far remained buoyant in terms of volume and value'. He then goes on to warn than 'the prospects for continued buoyancy are, however, not clear'.[14]

13 *Small Countries in a Big World: Metropolitan Versus Caribbean Integration*

I: Introduction

The Caribbean Sea embraces the world's largest concentration of small and mini-states. This balkanisation of the region is a direct outgrowth of the pattern of penetration, conquest and settlement outlined in Part I. Apart from a few minor European possessions (such as those of Denmark), four major European empires have historically operated in the region, each promoting its own exclusive monopoly zones through exercising tight control over metropole/colonial relations. The frequent changes in possessions occasioned by the constant European wars of rivalry created a bewildering array of small islands, which spoke different languages, practised different religions and developed different customs depending on which particular metropolitan power's influence happened to prevail. With the introduction up until the end of the 19th century of European settlers, African slaves and Asian indentured labourers, by the 20th century the region contained a large number of ethnic groups, including Africans, Indians, Chinese, Europeans, indigenous Amerindians and various Semitic and Hispanic peoples. And, with considerable racial intermingling taking place, a strong Creole group also emerged. The movement for independence in the 19th and 20th centuries resulted in a number of independent states being formed, but although this considerably weakened the European imperial powers' influence in the region, it has been substituted by US imperialism. Through its colonial possessions (Puerto Rico and the US Virgin Islands) and various cold war dealings in the region (mainly in Cuba and Grenada), the US has sharpened the region's historical divisions.

Despite imperial policy, ethnicity, religion, class and culture fostering obsessive individualism and deep divisions among Caribbean peoples, there has, paradoxically, long been a recognition that considerable benefits could derive from economic cooperation in the region. As Gordon Lewis points out, 'the recognition of the seminal truth that only a unified Caribbean, economically and politically, can save the region from its fatal particularism is at least a century old'[1] and derives from the view that, despite its legacy of divisions

302

and diversity, the region did once have a unified history and culture. The yearning for unity, which is strongest among the very small countries (or mini-states as they are now termed) comes from the feeling that each unit's capacity to survive and perhaps even to protect or promote its interests in the wider world is enhanced by operating as a group. Historically, a wide variety of interests, ranging from colonial officials (even the Colonial Office itself from time to time), to individual planters, writers and even some early labour leaders in the region, have recognised the potential for economic cooperation. Cipriani of Trinidad-Tobago, for example, introduced a resolution in support of economic union at the 1926 Regional Labour Conference, which was passed with only the delegates from Guyana (British Guiana) expressing reservations.

In recognising the 'seminal truth', as Gordon Lewis terms it, it should also be recognised that in their promotion of integration there was considerable inconsistency in both form and content among these various sectors. For example, the 1897 Royal Commission proposed a federation of Barbados and the Windward Islands, whereas the Closer Union Committee of 1932 had been working towards a 'loose grouping of the Leeward and Windward Islands. Again, the 1882 Royal Commission had proposed the 'ultimate federation' of the region, but the 1897 Royal Commission opposed such 'strong unity' and indeed voiced its objection to the earlier proposal of a unified civil service. The 1938 Caribbean Labour Congress supported integration and included the Bahamas, Belize and Guyana in its proposals, whereas the Moyne Commission of the same period saw integration as a far-off ideal and made a point of stressing how difficult it would be to make provisions over such a wide area for the cheap and effective transport and communications necessary to make economic union meaningful. It is also significant that all the proposals of this period were confined to British possessions.[2]

II: West Indian Federation: The Colonial Initiative

The end result of all this was the formation in 1958 (under the British government's urgings, guidance and tutelage) of a federation of ten West Indian islands, which was formally dissolved four years later in 1962. The birth and demise of this short-lived experiment in integration is instructive in two major respects. First, it shows that plans to integrate the region from above, particularly if they involve creating a new administrative agreement among existing governments are bound to fail. To pursue ruling-class interests without taking into account those of the masses within the context of the region's historical divisions is a certain recipe for disaster. The 1958 federation was promoted as an administrative convenience for the imperial power which was finding it burdensome to deal with so many small states as independence approached. As Gordon Lewis puts it:

> British opinion . . . throughout viewed federation, not as a vehicle for West Indian self-government, but, overwhelmingly, as a problem of colonial administrative convenience. Examination of the voluminous documentation of that opinion in Westminster debates, royal commission reports, Colonial Office memoranda and the published correspondence between the Colonial Secretary and individual West Indian governors shows that the most persistently recurring reason evoked in support of federation was the greater economy and the improved administrative efficiency it was supposed federation would bring about.[3]

Important as administrative economies may be in a unified (as distinct from fragmented) region of small states, in retrospect, it is clear that this could hardly sustain a social project of this magnitude.

Second, although integration may be expressed legally (through treaties, agreements, institutions and laws) whether or not it can be sustained depends on the extent to which *internal* social forces are in favour of it. In the West Indies, the best measure of this is in the nature and extent of the involvement of the poor and traditionally powerless in the process. Integration is not about institutional mechanisms, however important these are to its eventual success. For example, the British empire brought a number of different territories together under one Crown and subjected them to common legal, commercial and financial arrangements, but this is regarded as integration only in the most institutional of senses. During the struggle for independence, both the ruling classes in the region and the more enlightened sections of the British ruling classes recognised that the dismemberment of the empire was a necessary prelude to progress in the direction of genuine unity and integration. Similar reasoning applies to the neo-colonial world of today in which the TNCs spread across the region have achieved considerable *de facto* control and integration of resources, yet if the development of the region is subjected to the logic of the TNCs' corporate interests in the region, then further disintegration and disunity would in fact prevail.

The root of the argument therefore is that the best approach to evaluating the process of regional integration is through an analysis of the social (class) content of the process. In other words, it is necessary to ask such questions as whose class interests does the integration movement advance? Does it alleviate unemployment, redress social inequities in income and wealth, or do its benefits mainly swell the profits of the TNCs? Does it struggle against dependency, distorted production structures and the region's peripheralisation in the global process of accumulation, or does it reinforce the absence of autonomous and internally articulated sources of expansion? Does it bring an end to uneven capitalist development and polarised growth? And whose interests are best served by the expansion of intraregional trade and investment?

The federal experiment foundered in 1961 when Norman Manley, then Prime Minister of Jamaica, decided to hold a referendum to determine whether Jamaica should continue to participate. Among the many reasons for this development was the alienation of the Jamaican people (as indeed the rest of the West Indian masses) from the negotiations which were taking place at the top. This enabled the opposition to suggest that Jamaica was being forced to carry the burden of the smaller, poorer states and that Britain was merely off-loading its responsibilities for these other countries onto them. If this occurred, it was argued, the benefits of Jamaica's new-found wealth (bauxite-alumina and tourism) would be diverted away from the mass of Jamaican people and used to subsidise the poorer islands. Another objection derived from the fact that industrialisation by invitation was gaining considerable momentum in Jamaica and it was argued in business and political circles at the time that although a strong federation would provide the framework for an even larger market, its policies might negate the advantages the Jamaican government had already secured in dealing with foreign capital. Similar anxieties were being expressed in Trinidad-Tobago. The then Secretary of the Caribbean Labour Congress believed that the:

> . . . reason for this change of policy was that Mr Manley's whole conception of how to industrialise had changed. He now saw industrialisation not as a process to take place under local ownership and against the interests of imperialism, but as a process actually to be performed by foreign investors . . . He therefore no longer wanted a strong federal government with power to control investment in the entire area. Instead he wanted a weak central government, so that he would have the right to pursue an independent policy of attracting foreign capital by tax and other incentives to Jamaica.[4]

When Jamaica withdrew after the referendum, Eric Williams, on behalf of Trinidad-Tobago, made his famous pronouncement that 'one from ten leaves nought'.

The local political elites' ability to change positions derived from the fact that, by 1959, both Jamaica and Trinidad-Tobago had received internal self-government from Britain and no longer saw federation as a *necessary* route to independence. Britain was clearly exhausted by war and a rapidly disintegrating empire. Independence for the West Indies, except possibly for Guyana where a strong Marxist-led party had emerged, was more or less there for the taking. I have argued elsewhere that:

> . . . when these lessons are put together what we find emerging as a fundamental conclusion is that the West Indian Federation collapsed because it was conceived essentially as a colonial arrangement to protect colonial interests. This however, was introduced at a time when the masses were on a strong offensive against colonialism and the petty-bourgeois leadership of the period had already been committed to the struggle for constitutional independence. This . . . did not imply by any means a fundamental breach between the interests of imperialism and the nationalist interests of the ruling political elites. On the contrary . . . to the extent that the petty-bourgeois leadership represented the interests of

national capital, they were against colonialism and colonial arrangements.[5]

It is somewhat ironic that the pro-integrationist, William Demas, who was Secretary-General of CARICOM before becoming head of the Caribbean Development Bank, tried as late as 1974 to revive the view that integration provided a route to independence. He argued that 'the best way for the non-independent countries to sever their constitutional links with the United Kingdom would seem to be either through the creation of an independent state taking the form of political union among the Leeward and Windward Islands, or, preferably, a political union embracing all the English-speaking countries in the Eastern Caribbean'.[6] By this time, however, it was too late for imperial wishes and bureaucratic goadings to have their way.

III: From CARIFTA to CARICOM

After the federation collapsed, the heads of government held annual meetings to try and preserve areas of cooperation, some of which (such as the University of the West Indies), had in fact preceded the federation, as well as to explore the possibilities of other areas of cooperation outside a formal federation structure. By December 1965, the governments of Antigua, Barbados and Guyana had agreed to form a modest three-country Caribbean and Free Trade Association (CARIFTA). Three years later, on 1 May 1968, the Treaty came into force and, within three months, was expanded to permit the participation of the federation's original ten plus Guyana. Later Belize (1974) and the Bahamas (1983) joined.

Two factors favoured this development. One was that the Burnham government in Guyana saw in the Caribbean the possibility of a population counterweight to the East Indian ethnic advantage he presumed Cheddi Jagan and his party held in Guyana. Integration was therefore seen as an alternative to the rigged elections which were to follow. The second factor was that Britain was about to join the EEC, which would mean that the preferential status the region enjoyed in the UK market, as well as any moral claims to her resources, would be placed in severe jeopardy. This therefore prompted a collective effort to put political pressure on

Britain to settle with the region as a condition of entry to the EEC.

The CARIFTA arrangement, which came into force in 1968, represented a minimum degree of integration in that its principal integrative mechanism was the phased freeing of intraregional trade. It did not, however, require the region to have uniform external trade arrangements and did not promote a common market for the other productive factors, labour and capital. In other words, CARIFTA was neither a customs union nor a common market, but merely a free-trade zone. In addition, the arrangement did not include any compensatory mechanisms to cater for the maldistributional effects freer trade within the region was likely to have on the smaller and poorer territories. Although the Caribbean Development Bank was established in this period (1970) it was not formally part of the integration structure and was seen solely as a device for raising cheap capital outside the region.

Because all the territories' production structures were oriented to export sales in metropolitan markets, it was correctly anticipated that competition under a system of free trade would yield few gains to the region. The decision was then taken to promote competition artificially within the region by including a long list of commodities not produced in the region among those eligible for free-trade concessions. This provision was taken over by CARIFTA's successor, CARICOM, and was not abandoned until 1981.

CARIFTA's architects did not have to be very astute to realise that, as it stood, the agreement could not have survived for long. Shortly afterwards, therefore, it was replaced by a new arrangement which the signatories to the Treaty of Chaguaramas set up in 1973 when they established CARICOM – heralded as a 'deepening of the integration process' and, unlike its predecessor, based on three pillars. These comprised (i) a common market for the purposes of trade and economic cooperation, based not only on free trade as in the earlier agreement, but with a common external tariff, the commitment to the progressive removal of non-tariff barriers to trade, harmonised fiscal incentives and free intra-regional movements of capital. No explicit provisions were made for the free movement of labour. In practice, the customs tariffs of Belize and Montserrat continue to exist as anomalies in relation to this general rule, while Article 28 of the Annex of the treaty contains a provision which allows countries to reverse these mechanisms and to impose restrictions on trade and capital movements if there are serious balance-of-payments difficulties. Furthermore, CARICOM's uniform external tariff coexists with a common external tariff arrangement among the subgrouping of the smaller countries (the Leeward and Windward Islands) which operate in the larger body through a joint initiative in the form of the Eastern Caribbean Common Market (ECCM); (ii) functional areas of cooperation based on a number of inter-ministerial committees in matters such as health, education, labour, finance, agriculture, industry, transport, energy, mining and natural resources, science and technology, as well as agreed programmes to develop production and distribution structures for food and industry, along with cooperation in the development of a communications and transport infrastructure to service the region. In addition to these, there is provision for *ad hoc* cooperation in such areas as the law, information and women's affairs; and (iii) the coordination of foreign policies. This provision is unique in integration arrangements, for although EEC treaties contain provisions for political cooperation through foreign policy cooperation, this is the only integration treaty that formally incorporates a specific requirement to coordinate foreign policies.[7]

The CARICOM agreement operates through two principal organs and a number of institutions, associated institutions and subsidiary committees and agencies. The two principal organs are the Heads of Government Conferences (although supposed to be held annually, only eight meetings were convened between 1973 and 1987) and the Common Market Council of Ministers. The former has overall responsibility for the development of the integration movement and is the highest decision-making authority; the latter has general responsibility for supervising the operations and development of the common market areas of the agreement. CARICOM's main institutions comprise a number of Permanent Standing Committees of Ministers, each of which is charged with the responsibility of formulating policies and performing all the necessary functions required to achieve CARICOM's objectives in its respective sphere of competence. In addition to these institutions, there are a number of regional bodies with associate status. These include the Caribbean Development Bank, the Caribbean Examinations Council, the Council of Legal Education, the University of Guyana, the University of the West Indies, the Caribbean Meterological Organisation and the West Indian Shipping Corporation. A number of permanent subsidiary committees have also been created in areas such as customs administration, statistical services, air transport, airfares and rates, tax administration, national planning, agricultural marketing and the production and sale of oils and fats. Finally, there is the sub-regional grouping of the smaller states forming the Organisation of Eastern Caribbean States (OECS), which was established in 1981 and was predated by the ECCM (which was formed in 1968). Both CARICOM and the OECS have secretariats, the former's being located in Guyana and the latter's in Antigua.

IV: Performance

Trade

Despite all its complex and far-ranging associations, the common market arrangements still form the core of the CARICOM agreement. While the move from a free-trade zone to a common market was designed to deepen the process of integration between 1973 and 1985, intra-CARICOM trade in fact never rose above the 9–10 per cent of total trade established during the CARIFTA years. In absolute terms, however, this trade has grown from US$47 million in imports in 1967 (the year before CARIFTA came into force) to approximately US$330 million by 1984. As the data in Table 13.1 show, there were annual fluctuations in the ratio of intraregional imports to total imports, the figures ranging from 7.5 per cent to 9.8 per cent between 1973 and 1984. For domestic exports the range for the same period was larger, 8.1 to 13.1 per cent.

Table 13.1
CARICOM Trade as a Percentage of Total Regional Trade
(Selected Years)

Imports		Domestic Exports	
Year	%	Year	%
1967	5.0	1967	6.3
1973	7.5	1973	10.3
1974	7.1	1974	7.3
1975	8.6	1975	8.3
1976	7.6	1976	8.8
1977	7.8	1977	8.1
1978	8.0	1978	8.6
1979	9.3	1979	9.2
1980	9.8	1980	8.7
1981	9.6	1981	9.9
1982	8.9	1982	12.0
1983	9.2	1983	13.1
1984	9.8	1984	11.7

Source: CARICOM Bulletin and CARICOM Perspectives (Various Issues)

As one might expect, the trading pattern that emerged among CARICOM members reflected those of the regional economy. The main traded commodity thus consisted of Trinidad-Tobago's oil exports, which accounted for about 40 per cent of regional trade and 75 per cent of the country's exports to the region. Trinidad-Tobago's prosperity also resulted in the growth of its import market from about one-seventh of total regional imports in 1973 to about one-third in the 1980s. Indeed, if petroleum is excluded, Trinidad-Tobago accounted for about half the region's imports in the 1980s. Rice is still the main agricultural item traded in the region, although declining production in Guyana has seen dramatic falls in recent years. Between 1981 and 1982, rice sales fell from about US$27 million (or 8 per cent of total imports) to US$15 million. Although the value of intraregional imports of agricultural products quadrupled between 1970–73 and 1984–85 (from US$14 million to US$45 million), as a percentage of total food imported into the region there was a fall from 11.3 per cent to 10.7 per cent. In recent years, intraregional import of fruit and vegetables has been the significant growing category. It presently accounts for more than one-third of intraregional agricultural trade as against 13 per cent in the years 1970–73. Yet another feature is the growth of intraregional trade in goods produced by the new import-substitution sectors. There are two aspects to this, namely a significant increase in trade among the larger and more industrially-developed territories (Jamaica, Trinidad-Tobago and Barbados) and the import-substitution activities some TNCs have set up in the smaller OECS states. The result has been that while the larger states accounted for about 80 per cent of intraregional trade, the regional market for the exports of the OECS countries increased from 11 per cent of its total exports in 1973 to over 40 per cent in the 1980s. Most of this was in manufactured goods and non-traditional agricultural crops.

Although Trinidad-Tobago's market is the largest in the region, it shows a marked asymmetry in that its domestic exports to the region were only 7–11 per cent of its total exports between 1973 and 1985. For Barbados, the regional market was more significant, representing 24–28 per cent of its total domestic exports between 1973 and 1980 (except for one unusual year, 1975, when it was only 18 per cent). Over the year 1981/82 the figure averaged 31 per cent, but in 1983 there was a drastic decline to 21 per cent. Between 1973 and 1981 Jamaica's exports in the region averaged only 4–7 per cent of its domestic exports, but rose to 12 per cent in 1981/82 partly because of the drop in bauxite-alumina exports to the US. For the years 1984 and 1985 the ratio was 7 per cent. In Guyana the ratio of regional exports to total exports between 1973 and 1982 was in the range of 13–18 per cent, although it should be borne in mind that the significance of these figures is distorted by the country's protracted economic distress.

The 1980s has seen a marked decline in intraregional trade. Between 1981 and 1984 the value of intraregional imports fell from US$456 million to US$335 million, a decline of over one-quarter. Several factors are responsible for this.

First, the exchange rates in Jamaica and Guyana depreciated as their economic difficulties increased. Jamaica introduced a system of multiple rates and devalued its currency; between 1977 and 1984 its exchange rate fell from J$1=US$1.1 to J$1=US$0.20 and at one weekly auction in 1985, it even fell as low as US$0.15. The Guyanese dollar fell from US$0.39 in 1980 to US$0.24 in 1984. These developments had the effect of seriously dislocating intraregional trade.

Second, in the wake of their respective economic crises, Jamaica and Guyana imposed severe restrictions on both global and CARICOM imports. When between 1981 and 1984 Jamaica halved its imports from CARICOM countries, Barbados and Trinidad-Tobago retaliated by imposing restrictions on CARICOM's imports into their own more successful markets. Trinidad-Tobago introduced a system of import licensing whereby exchange approval was required for all foreign transactions, including those within CARICOM. In Barbados, the government allowed its currency to float against the Jamaican dollar as a response to what it terms Jamaica's 'discriminatory treatment' of its exports to that country.

Also, as economic difficulties began to manifest themselves in Trinidad-Tobago and Barbados (although to a far lesser extent than in Guyana and Jamaica) protectionist sentiment grew with the result that intraregional trade was considerably reduced. To make matters worse, the community's sole trade-facilitating mechanism, the Community Multilateral Clearing Facility (CMCF), collapsed in 1983 as it reached the US$100 million limit to its credit-granting powers. At that point, Guyana alone was indebted to over US$96 million and owed Barbados US$60 million. As this debt was never repaid, the community decided to function on the basis of more or less strictly balanced trade, particularly in relation to trade with Guyana. Since that country's difficulties are reflected in an inability to produce, however, this has acted as a strong downward drag on intraregional trade.

While each of these factors has had an adverse effect on intraregional trade, the problem has been the continued weakness and vulnerability of the region's economy. One difficulty is that national policies have produced considerable duplication of protected, high-cost, import-substitution enterprises, each of which seeks to exploit the regional market so as to benefit from any possible economies of scale. When difficulties occur, the resort to protection by individual governments seems to them the only logical recourse if these inefficient local producers are to survive. Moreover, in so far as this type of structure of production is generally very import intensive, it is highly vulnerable to external shocks. Consequently, given these inherited production structures, there are severe limits to the benefits to be derived from trade and market-oriented cooperation in the region.

The rules governing CARICOM's trade arrangements from the beginning favoured protecting each national economy's newly-created manufacturing sector. The principal device for doing this was through the creation of an origin system based on the 'value-added criterion' whereby if 50 per cent of a product's value was created in the region, then it qualified to be treated as a local product. This was then followed by a long list of basic materials which existed in the CARIFTA agreement and which made exceptions to this criterion.

> Both in its implementation and conception (and here a close study of the Treaty is relevant), recent integration efforts have sought consistently to underwrite, protect, and advance the positions of the MNCs in the region. Thus Schedule II (Appendix of the Treaty) gives a list of products which are always to be treated as having been produced in the region, irrespective of where in fact they have been actually produced: 'These materials may always be regarded as originating wholly within the Common Market when used in the state described in this list in a process of production within the Common Market'. This is then followed by twelve foolscap pages listing products ranging through apples, grapes, rye, barley, oats, semolina, linseed, wheat, paper, silk, wool, iron, steel in all forms, copper, nickel, tungsten, zinc, printing and writing paper etc. Some of the items are so general as to include hundreds of sub-categories, one example being the item: 'all other non-ferrous base metals, whether wrought or unwrought'.[8]

After much criticism, this system was modified in 1981. The

list of exempted materials was reduced and its use restricted to the smaller territories of the OECS subgrouping. Preferential treatment was given to the natural produce of the region and to products produced exclusively from these, for example, minerals, agricultural goods, livestock and marine products. The criterion was introduced whereby a product had to be 'substantially transformed' to qualify for CARICOM benefits. Measures for this were specified either in certain processes or in the product moving from one level of classification in the Customs Cooperation Council Nomenclature to another. That these regulations have failed to threaten any significant producers trading under the old rules is an indication that no substantial transformation of requirements under the rules of origin has actually taken place. Once again there is talk in business and government circles about the need for further improvements in this area.

Functional Cooperation

There has been functional cooperation in many fields, some of which have resulted in important new regional institutions or initiatives. These include the formation of a regional secondary school examination system, a regional news network (CANA), a technical-assistance programme to help the smaller states, cooperation in health training and the institutionalisation of a regional creative arts festival. Without doubt, however, the major target area for regional cooperation has been production and here the focus has been on the development of a coordinated regional programme for food and industrial production. In the area of food production, however, although there have been limited joint efforts in training, human resource development, research and intraregional marketing, the main hope of building up a regional capacity to replace imported food is far from being realised. As the Secretary-General of CARICOM observes:

> Several reviews of various sub-sector needs have been undertaken and efforts made to build up institutional arrangements, essentially in the form of the Caribbean Food Corporation, to intervene directly in the food production situation. Much of this had its impetus in the resolve, during the first half of the 1970s, to make the Region more self-sufficient in food

and thus reduce the regional food import bill. Regrettably, however, the first twelve years of CARICOM have not produced any serious dent in the overall food import bill, and if anything. . . it has been increasing.[9]

He is similarly frank about cooperation in industrial programming: 'In the area of industrial programming, the first twelve years of CARICOM have come and gone without seeing the first formally recognised regional industries going into production.'[10] A position echoed by the Group of Experts CARICOM appointed to deliberate on its future: 'Efforts to programme industrial production on a regional basis have been slow and disappointing.'[11]

The real significance of the observations cited above stems from the consideration that efforts in these directions are seen by its proponents in the integration movement as *fundamental corrections* to the inherited patterns of regional production and consumption, as well as the limitations of post-war industrial experience and the neglect of agriculture. In this view, regional industrial programming is intended to promote the development of basic industries, foster the growth of a capital-goods sector, generate technological development and the spread of skills and, in so doing, provide the basis for an integrated, autonomous system of regional production. Such a regional approach is expected, not only to draw upon the benefits of a wider regional market, but also, through regional planning, to provide a larger catchment area for natural resources and skills. In other words, the proponents of this view have seen in this effort an attempt to approach the earlier position advocated by Brewster and Thomas that integration 'should not be limited to those conditions which govern the exchange of goods, but should also include in its perspective the integrated production of goods'.[12] In Brewster and Thomas's formulation, integration could not be judged (nor should it be) primarily by the extent to which previous imported manufactures were produced in the region, but instead by the extent to which it harnessed basic resource inputs and developed the requisite skills and technology to meet the needs of the Caribbean people and so reduce the wide disparity between the inherited structures of domestic demand and domestic resource use which was systematically reproducing itself through time, on an extended scale.

It is significant that the Group of Experts who deliberated on CARICOM's future come to the conclusion that industrial production (and employment) is *key* to the success of CARICOM. As they put it, 'to a very considerable extent the success of CARICOM hinges on the extent to which the operation of the CARICOM arrangements leads to increased industrial production and employment in the countries of the region'.[13] In similar vein, proponents of agricultural programming within the integration movement have seen this as a transformation device, in other words a means of implementing a regional food and nutrition plan targeted at achieving a regional production of a minimum of 80 per cent of the energy and 60 per cent of the protein consumed in the region and making available, along with imports, on a daily basis the minimum recommended per capita dietary allowances of protein and energy for the region's population as a whole. This would be achieved through restructuring regional output and demand and through collective efforts at greater regional self-sufficiency. These, in turn would require an increased output of food and other agricultural products for the local and export market, a marked reduction of post-harvest losses, adequate marketing and improved food processing. The supports for all of these would be provided through a massive collective effort to achieve self-reliant research, training, storage, transport, land reform, credit and vital inputs.

CARICOM's failure to achieve any of the major objectives of the food and nutrition plan, combined with its equal failure to achieve anything significant in the area of industrial programming, has meant that, so far, it has been unable to function as a medium for transforming the regional economy, even from the standpoint of its own principal architects.

Coordination of Foreign Policy

The idea of making the coordination of foreign policies a specific feature of the CARICOM treaty is believed to have grown out of the region's earlier experiences of negotiating with the EEC. This led to the formation of the African-

Caribbean-Pacific Group, the region's negotiations with Canada for a successor arrangement to the Canada-West Indies Agreement of 1925 and the Law of the Sea negotiations, which were of particular importance to the island territories of the region. These experiences showed that a collective voice carried more weight than a series of single ones and enabled the four independent territories to take joint action in 1972 to assert the region's independence and right to pursue a Caribbean identity through fraternal relations with *all* Caribbean states thereby breaking the US's isolation of Cuba in the region.

Since CARICOM's formation in 1973, the main areas in which foreign policies have been coordinated are in (i) joint work in promoting the interests of small island states and in protecting them in the international community, especially from the threat of 'private mercenary invasion'; (ii) a joint call to declare the Caribbean a 'zone of peace'; (iii) regional support for the view that ideological pluralism is an irreversible fact of international relations and should not therefore constitute a barrier to strengthening CARICOM (Declaration of the Fifth Meeting of the Standing Committee of Foreign Ministers, St Lucia); (iv) regional support for Guyana and Belize in their territorial disputes with Venezuela and Guatemala respectively; (v) a joint statement condemning destabilisation, which, it was alleged, was being directed against Manley in Jamaica and Burnham in Guyana; and (vi) a unified reaction of a somewhat critical nature to the limited perspective of Reagan's Caribbean Basin Initiative.

The combination of heightened cold-war pressures following Reagan's election to the presidency, the clash of ideologies which surfaced in the region at the time of the Grenada invasion, the US-supported attacks on Nicaragua and the practically simultaneous rise to power of Reagan and Seaga have, however, served to undermine any progressive orientation or regional concensus. As a result, Heads of Government Conferences held since the invasion of Grenada have carefully avoided discussing any controversial foreign-policy issues.

It should be noted, however, that unlike other functional inter-ministerial committees, the Standing Committee of Foreign Ministers (which is responsible for coordinating foreign policy) has no decision-making authority. This is partly through fear of giving CARICOM a supranational status for, along with most other Third World countries, members of CARICOM see their independent relations with other states in the world as the highest expression of their sovereignty. This position is reinforced by the treaty stipulating that any changes in its provisions, must be on the basis of a unanimous decision by all the participating countries.

V: Evaluation

Since economic integration involves more than the simple coming together of a group of countries, the process is never neutral. All actions in the pursuit of integration are directly or indirectly linked to one or other set of social (class) interests. It was because the West Indies Federation sought to advance the class interests of the old colonial order at a time when these had already been defeated by the rise of anti-colonial and nationalist movements that it did not and could not have survived. Existing integration arrangements similarly express the class interests of the region's contemporary political leadership, of the emerging national bourgeoisies its manufacturing policies have helped to found and of the TNCs which have dominated the area's economic structure. Thus, although ostensibly supposed to promote integration, the move from CARIFTA to CARICOM has actually, through the pursuit of two economic objectives, been designed to consolidate at a regional level the capitalist framework and market relations developed in the individual territories. In a nutshell, these objectives are (i) to liberalise trade, harmonise incentives and finance intraregional transport and communications with the aim of providing a uniform market at the regional level for the emerging local bourgeoisies and their TNC counterparts to exploit; and (ii) to harmonise the interests of the various national bourgeoisies in the hopes of gaining their support for a regional programme of providing the larger market with incentives to induce government and TNC participation, not only in the final-touch assembly industries where these may become necessary, but also and especially in the intermediate and capital-goods sector.

The pursuit of these twin objectives has been far from easy. Indeed CARICOM itself has emerged as an arena in which struggles for sectional economic interests are fought. The contradictory coexistence in the arrangement of harmonising and contending interests is not, however, unusual; it characterises all capitalist endeavours. The most likely outcome would be for the indigenous capitalists of the territories where capitalism is already most advanced to become dominant in the integration movement, yet remain subordinate to transnational capital. This means that the integration process will yield uneven development, polarised growth, an inequitable distribution of the costs and benefits of such growth and conflicts between local, regional and transnational capital. Something of this sort was no doubt anticipated, which is why the agreement contains compensatory mechanisms to encourage OECS participation. These mechanisms include priority access to soft loans provided by the Caribbean Development Bank (CDB), a technical-assistance programme focused specifically on their needs and longer time frames for implementing the treaty's various harmonising arrangements, such as the common external tariff.

Sectional economic interests within CARICOM, which present the integration movement with considerable difficulties, consist either of disagreements *among* various sections of national capital or disagreements *between* regional capital and the region's political establishments. Examples of the former are to be found in the many protectionist, beggarthy-neighbour and retaliatory measures which were introduced as the economic crisis worsened. These peaked in 1985 when the Trinidad-Tobago's Manufacturers' Association (TTMA), the dominant economic group in CARICOM, called for the suspension of CARICOM trading arrangements and its replacement with a system of bilateral arrangements:

> The TTMA has been advocating for two and a half years the temporary suspension of the trading arrangements of the CARICOM Treaty in order to enable a review of these arrangements to take place, since current economic conditions in the region are significantly different from those obtaining in 1973 at the formation of CARICOM. The instruments of trade liberalisation in the CARICOM Treaty are totally

inadequate to meet current conditions. The TTMA's position is certainly not one of panic but derives from a through examination of the trading situation. . . The multilateral nature of the treaty prohibits effective measures. . . action is therefore being taken on a bilateral basis.[14]

There is little doubt that, given the weight of Trinidad-Tobago's market in CARICOM, bilateral arrangements could hardly do less than enhance that country's position in the region and advance the position of the dominant economic groups.

One example of the disagreement between regional capital and the political establishment surfaced when, in his address to the Jamaica Exporters Association in June 1985, the President of the Caribbean Association of Industry and Commerce (CAIC) complained that at 'every Heads of Government and CARICOM Ministerial meeting several decisions are taken re the improvement of intra-CARICOM trade and trading relationships. Yet very few, if any, of these decisions are implemented at the national level'. After citing examples from the Nassau Summit in 1985, he concludes that 'this is a serious indictment of our political leaders and suggests very strongly that at the political level, CARICOM faces serious problems which necessarily impact on intra-CARICOM trade. These problems include: lack of communication, lack of unity, lack of commitment on the part of some leaders, too much self-interest, and the power of national sovereignty over regional decisions'.[15]

The factional economic interests which have hampered CARICOM's development are paralleled by similar factionalism in the political sphere. At a time of nation state consolidation the region's ruling classes have operated on the basis of two sets of rules. One is to foster economic integration to the extent that it serves their wider class project, while at the same time minimising the threat of the emergence of any supranational authorities; the other is to cooperate as much as possible in both political and security terms so as to protect the political *status quo*, including the *traditional* positions of opposition parties.[16] With such rules in operation the CARICOM treaty could hardly represent more than a minimal form of agreement, certainly when judged by the historical imperatives which lie behind the need to integrate.

Consequently the treaty contains legal provisions to make it compatible with a wide range of external economic and political relations. Several countries unabashedly advertise their client-state relations with US imperialism, while at the same time representing CARICOM as a serious attempt to achieve the collective self-reliance, economic independence, diversification and structural transformation of the region's economy and wider society. As the cold war has intensified and Reaganism has aggressively moved into the area, we find that the earlier positions on pluralism and on the Caribbean as a 'zone of peace', have been more or less silently abandoned.

Any evaluation of CARICOM should recognise that the economic crisis facing the region has produced a considerable amount of political fallout, particularly in the growth of beggar-thy-neighbour policies of protectionism and retaliation. Certain economic disparities within the region underlie this development. They include the skewed population distribution in favour of Jamaica, the skewed resource availability situation (oil) in favour of Trinidad-Tobago and the long-term resource advantages possessed by Guyana. Unless the region's ruling classes and strata can at the very least act in consonance with the long-term 'nationalist' interest of the area, these disparities will continue to predispose the integration process to conflict.

With about half the region's population, Jamaica has always (ever since the days of the West Indies federation) been sceptical of the benefits of regional integration. Manley was clearly more interested in South-South cooperation and Seaga quite definitely sees North-South cooperation as the most strategic economic imperative. Trinidad-Tobago, with its new-found oil wealth, felt that having paid the piper, it should call the tune, which was why the CARICOM Heads of Government failed to meet for seven years between 1976 and 1982. This had quite a lot to do with Eric William's pique over the fact that, despite Trinidad-Tobago's generosity to the region, other states were pursuing policies detrimental to its interests. He made no effort to hide his displeasure at the region's unwillingness to support BWIA as the regional airline and was clearly disappointed by his inability to set up a joint aluminum project with Guyana and Jamaica, using their bauxite resources and his own country's natural gas. To him, the final straw was when, in the midst of protracted discussions on the regional aluminum project, Jamaica announced it was in the process of negotiating a similar arrangement with Mexico.

In evaluating CARICOM it is important to remember that it came into existence in the midst of the global crisis of capitalism when the shock of high oil prices was most acute. Such timing was indeed inopportune, especially since the treaty left the region unduly susceptible to these external shocks, for there were no provisions within it for dealing with recessionary conditions in world trade. Ultimately, however:

> . . . the weaknesses of CARICOM are the weaknesses of the nation states which have created it. If at a national level the TNCs dominate, at a regional level they cannot but do otherwise. . . the fact of operating regionally cannot by itself resolve the basic national issues of ownership and control by the people over the means of production, of the struggle to develop a just, humane, and socialist society, or the need to effectively secure the development of social and political life. In other words, regionalism does not do away with classes and the historical-materialist base of social development.[17]

Dr Eric Williams, who was one of the key architects of the system, was even more pessimistic when he argued that 'it is now clear beyond any possibility of doubt that Caribbean integration will not be achieved in the forseeable future and that the reality is continued Caribbean disunity and even perhaps the reaffirmation of colonialism'.[18] This was, however, clearly an expression of the frustration he felt over having his attempts to promote unity thwarted.

Although regional integration is essential if there is to be any permanent eradication of the systemic reproduction of poverty and powerlessness, CARICOM's efforts in this direction have been disappointing. Without far-reaching and effective policy coordination in critical areas of production, the movement of labour, consumption and exchange currency rates, foreign-reserve management and monetary and fiscal policies, any benefits that might derive from integration would be quite minimal and would flow mainly into the pockets of the region's ruling minorities. At the present historical conjuncture, certain limited forms of supranationalism, such as a regional parliament and courts, a human rights commission, common codes of labour and employment practices and progressive freedom of movement within the area would also be necessary. Since there is no immediate prospect of any of this happening, any moves towards greater integration would have to come from bodies, outside the established power structures, such as the Caribbean Conference of Churches, the Caribbean Congress of Labour and the regional committees of intellectual workers, as well as through the contacts and relationships being developed among trade unions, cooperatives, political parties (of the right and the left) and voluntary professional and trade associations.

These factors, combined with the practice of legal and illegal inter-island migration for work, education and pleasure, the family ties that already exist and develop with each new wave of contact, as well as the shared elements of culture in such areas as calypso, theatre and literature, are essential for cultivating a consciousness, not only about the vital importance of unity to the region, but also about its nature and the role it must play in transforming the region's economy and society. At the moment, the penetration of North American ideology, particularly through the electronics media, press and school system, is taking the lead in the region's cultural 'development' in much the same ways as the TNCs, with their dogmas about the efficiency of the market place and the private pursuit of private gain, are taking the lead in the region's economic 'development'. A balkanised region is unfortunately easy prey to these new forms of dependency. As an institution of the past rather than of a new Caribbean society, CARICOM, as it is presently structured, offers no alternative.

14 *Crisis, Reaction, Response: The Caribbean in the Late 1980s*

I: Crisis

Throughout the Caribbean, 'crisis' is the term most widely used by all social groups to describe the prevailing economic conditions. This acknowledgement of the crisis, however, should not be taken to mean that there is agreement over its nature, root causes and the best remedies for solving it. At one level of social reality the crisis has been portrayed as reflecting internal and external monetary imbalances and here stress is placed on such variables as the rate of inflation, government budgetary imbalances, balance-of-payments difficulties, lack of foreign reserves, currency overvaluation and external indebtedness. Evidence to support this interpretation comes from the fact that, for the CARICOM region, the combined balance-of-payments deficit on current account (including unrequited transfers) was nearly US$1,500 million at the end of 1986; with the foreign debt being over US$9,000 million, that is, over US$1,800 per head. The growth in debt has been accompanied by huge losses in foreign reserves, particularly in Trinidad-Tobago, the region's largest holder, while the chronically ill economies of Jamaica and Guyana have in recent years been effectively bankrupted by their mammoth accumulated arrears. In some countries double figure inflation rates have occurred since the early 1980s; the overvaluation of local currencies has forced several devaluations, produced a variety of experiments in multiple exchange-rate systems and led to stringent controls on foreign-exchange movement. With declining incomes, government budgetary deficits have also climbed rapidly and these have fuelled inflationary pressures while inflation, in turn, has discouraged local savings, encouraged capital flight and set in train pressures for higher wage settlements which have encouraged the wage-price inflationary spiral.

While there is a great deal of truth in the above description, it clearly does not go far enough. To begin with, it fails to recognise the extent to which internal and external monetary imbalances in the regional economies reflect a deeper crisis of growth and development which, in turn, means that effective analysis of the crisis has to be situated in a wider socio-political framework. These imbalances become even more significant when it is taken into account that for most of the region real rates of growth since the 1970s have been negative or very modest. For the region as a whole, per capita real income in 1986 was no higher than it was in 1970 and, for some economies such as Guyana's, it is estimated to be as much as 60 per cent lower. Furthermore, over this period the regional economies have become no less vulnerable than they were before; their failure to diversify being partly due to rising protectionism in the north and partly to the continued internal misdirection of savings and resources. The narrow productive base of the region's economy, the internal disarticulation of its production structures, its small size, openness and dependence on foreign capital, technology and skills, ensure that monetary imbalances will always have a special significance which the standard North American or European textbook-type discussions are unlikely to capture because they confine the analysis to these monetary phenomena.

In seeking to gain a broader or deeper understanding of the crisis in the region, it is important to make a distinction between *permanent or ongoing crisis* and a *periodic crisis*. The former, which is made up of the basic elements of the socio-economic structure and their historical form and motion, can become accentuated at certain historical conjunctures. This is often manifested by periodic interruptions in the process of capital accumulation, when profits drop, overseas markets contract, disproportions endemic to the consumption/production structure become more acute and internal demand and confidence in the economy decline. These points of accentuation are what produce the periodic crisis; the acute monetary imbalances are but a surface manifestation of it. At the same time, however, it should be recognised that from time to time the conflation of internal and external social processes create the possibility (and only the *possibility*) of a qualitatively deeper entrenchment of the old order, on the one hand, or of a radical (even revolutionary) rupture with the past on the other. These conjunctures constitute periods of *general crisis*, the best-known examples being the collapse of the slave system in the region, the collapse of indenture in Guyana and Trinidad-Tobago and the widespread crisis of the 1930s. It is my belief that the current crisis has this general character to it, but whether it will yield important socio-economic changes or reconfirm the existing neo-colonial order, is far from predictable.[1]

Included among the many and varied manifestations of the crisis are (i) the 'scissors squeeze' on land brought about by the disintegration of domestic food systems and difficulties with traditional export crops, on the one hand, and the rapid rise of TNC agro-processing industries based on imported inputs, on the other; (ii) a worsening distribution of income, wealth and access to productive resources, especially in those countries where structural adjustment policies have been introduced; (iii) massive, persistent and increasing unemployment (estimated at between 15 and 50 per cent of the region's labour force) and growing under-employment; (iv) woefully inadequate social security provisions for the unemployed, aged and infirm; (v) high rates of emigration among skilled workers; (vi) the growth of huge underground/parallel/informal sectors, which divert entrepreneurial talent and allocate much of the available foreign exchange to their own priorities; (vii) an increase in corruption, nepotism and clientilism, evident in the heavy penetration of drug dealers and traffickers into the highest political circles in the Bahamas, Jamaica, Turks and Caicos, the Cayman Islands, Barbados, St Kitts-Nevis and Trinidad-Tobago, to name a few; (viii) massive flight of capital and high turnover of assets in the region; (ix) a weakened trade union movement in the face of increasing unemployment, declining living standards and widespread poverty; (x) the penetration of foreign media, values and culture into the region, symbolised by the 'satellite dish' culture found in every island, no matter how small; (xi) the systematisation of repression and political murder as techniques of social control; (xii) the institutionalisation of fradulent and rigged elections in some countries; (xiii) accelerated foreign control of domestic resources, despite the localisation and nationalisation programmes pursued by several governments; (xiv) the impact of the war in Nicaragua and the invasion of Grenada, seen particularly in the increasing militarisation of the region; and (xv) the failure of the Caribbean 'right' and private sector to solve the problems of poverty and powerlessness.

It is important to recognise that no automatic link is intended between the deepening of the crisis identified here and the willingness or not of the people to revolt against their worsening circumstances. Indeed it would be a mistake for those who play a leading role in the struggles for a new Caribbean society and in organising resistance to declining living standards to make such a link, for social disintegration invariably has a negative affect on the social psychology of the masses. This is evident in Grenada, where the post-invasion trauma has immobilised a number of people who traditionally supported the left. In the recent past, signals that the region's peoples are wanting change have emerged in the sweeping victories of the opposition parties in Barbados and Trinidad-Tobago, and the narrow victory of the ruling party in St Lucia. These opposition advances have, however, been confined to the 'established' parties and have not favoured those who advocate radical alternatives. Many people now turn to migration as a solution to poverty at home and there is certainly a growing indifference, if not cynicism in some quarters, towards political efforts to challenge the *status quo*. The US's perceptions of the crisis (and the solutions it has offered to it) have played a particularly pernicious role in this respect.

II: Reaction/Responses

There have been five major responses to the crisis, each of which will be examined in turn. These are: (A) structural adjustment; (B) privatisation; (C) the search for new external sources of trade and aid to replace the thrust towards privatisation; (D) militarisation; and (E) ideologisation, or, in other words, the acceptance of an ideology that presents the solution in terms of a *de facto* recolonisation of the region by the US.

A. Structural Adjustment

We have already considered, in some detail, the stabilisation measures and structural policies of the IMF and World Bank and their roles in Jamaica (under Manley and Seaga) and Guyana. Here it is necessary only to stress that these policies are based on an interpretation of the crisis which confines it to the level of internal and external monetary imbalances, with, at best, token recognition of the causes of these difficulties. It is for this reason that the standard package of policies is always prescribed: wage restraint, devaluation, tight money supply and restrictive credit, reduced government deficits, removal of subsidies and reduction of social expenditure by the state, deregulation of the economy and primary emphasis on the role of market prices, privatisation of economic activity and the wooing of foreign capital. It is also for this reason that these policies have failed everywhere in the region, even in Jamaica, which is supposed to be the third world model of successful Reaganomics.

The impact of the IMF, World Bank and various regional institutions on the development of stabilisation policies as a solution to the crisis should not be underestimated. By mid-1985, the World Bank had loaned the region over US$1,100 million, while the IMF had several stand-by and extended-fund arrangements operating in the region, although some of these had been cancelled because of failure to meet targets. The IMF's impact on regional policy derives from its wide-ranging responsibilities for promoting exchange-rate stability, international trade and monetary cooperation, along with its short-term support programmes for balance-of-payments correction. The World Bank's influence is also considerable, since it presently chairs the important Caribbean Group for Cooperation in Economic Development (CGED). In this capacity it coordinates assistance among aid donors, the multilateral institutions and 20 Caribbean countries. In addition, the Caribbean Development Bank (CDB) and the Inter-American Development Bank (IDB) have also provided resources for the region. The CDB has loaned about US$600 million, more than three-quarters of which has been raised from outside the region, while the IDB has, in the four-year period between 1981 and 1984, loaned the five CARICOM members nearly US$350 million and provided US$30 million to the CDB for further on-lending. On average more than two thirds of the current external indebtedness of the region (US$6,000 million) is owed to non-commercial bilateral and multilateral aid donors and lending institutions. This ratio of commercial to non-commercial debt (1:2) distinguishes the region from other

Third World countries, where the ratio is the exact reverse (2:1). This greatly reduces the scope for strategies of debt amelioration which involve an element of default as the 'risk' commercial lenders should carry when seeking profit.

The impact of these various institutions on attempts to solve the crisis cannot be assessed solely in terms of how much money they disburse, for in other ways (especially through their perspective on development) they play an important part in reinforcing capital-import dependency. As far as can be discerned, the differences between their approach and that of most regional governments is largely one of emphasis and tactics. The latter, in so far as they may have to face the electorate, are usually eager to temporise on the harsher prescriptions of the stabilisation solutions – even if they are convinced of the logic behind it. In this symbiotic relationship, politicians increasingly try to use these multilateral institutions as the whipping-boy, in other words, they present themselves to the public as hapless victims of IMF and World Bank pressure. The failure of the stabilisation measures has led to a search for means of promoting growth rather than restricting economic activity in the effort to correct internal and external monetary balances and it is out of this that the privatisation thrust and the growth of EPZs have been spawned.

B. Privatisation

As noted in Chapter 9, governments were subjected to strong social pressures to expand the role of the state in the region's economy. This is reflected in the growth of state ownership, in the proliferation of institutions, laws and regulations governing economic activity and in the elaboration of strategies and models of development which lay primary responsibility on the state. The Reagan administration believes that the underdevelopment is largely attributable to the limited role of the private sector in the region's economic activities and has consequently decided to exercise its considerable influence to organise the region's bourgeoisie under US leadership. For this purpose, the promise of large inflows of capital, skills and technology from the US private sector has been used as a carrot to encourage the flow of resources from international institutions and friendly governments into the region's private sector. Organisationally, this effort has been focused on two institutions, the Caribbean-Central American Action (CCAA) and the Caribbean Association of Industry and Commerce (CAIC).

The CCAA, originally established in April 1980, was one of President Carter's initiatives for dealing with the Caribbean/Central American crisis and the negative effect it was having on US relations in the region. Privately funded from corporate and individual sources, it grew out of the earlier Committee for the Caribbean, headed by Robert West Jr, Chairman of the Board of Tesoro Petroleum and Mervyn Dymally (originally from Trinidad-Tobago, but at the time Lieutenant-Governor of California). In 1983, it affiliated with the Americas Society, a New York based group composed of several private organisations concerned about US relations in the hemisphere. The Chairman of the Americas Society, David Rockefeller, was elected chairman of the CCAA in 1983. The group's main objective is to encourage the private sector in the US to help promote a vibrant private sector in Central America and the Caribbean.

The CCAA's promotional activities include organising conferences and sending trade and investment missions from the US into the region; fostering links between private organisations in the region (such as chambers of commerce, manufacturing associations and trade groups) and similar institutions in the US. For example, it twins US and regional chambers of commerce and, in the first year of operation (1981), 25 of these were put into effect; sponsoring the famous Miami Conferences in the Caribbean, considered to be 'by any yardstick the most important regular gathering of businessmen, bureaucrats, government leaders and academics from the Caribbean Basin, the US and beyond'.[2] Several heads of governments in the region attend these annual gatherings; creating the Caribbean Basin Information Network (CBIN), which is a data base on exporters, importers, investment opportunities and joint venture schemes. The CBIN has accesss to Control Data Corporation's data sources; sponsoring the CBI; and, finally, playing a major role in revitalising the CAIC.

The CAIC, which was 'founded with high hopes in

1963, has had a chequered history. Always hamstrung by chronic underfunding and its effectiveness impaired by the lack of a Secretariat, it struggled as best as it could, depending upon who was President and how much time could be spared from personal interests'.[3] By 1980, it was indeed a moribund institution, but, under CCAA auspices, it was revitalised in 1981 and a Secretariat created in Barbados. The CAIC's main functions are to build institutions in the region; to sponsor the training of private-sector executives (mainly through USAID and in cooperation with the US Chamber of Commerce Institute); to promote privatisation, sponsor seminars and become an effective lobby; and to undertake selective research on regional economic matters. In addition, the CAIC helped to form the Caribbean Financial Services Corporation, a private financial institution designed to promote the private sector. One-third of its US\$2.3 million equity is held by leading Caribbean industries and the remainder is provided by commercial banks. USAID has provided long-term funds to the tune of US\$12 million and US\$0.4 million in loans and technical assistance. The CAIC has formed close links with the CDB and the Caribbean Project Development Facility (CPDF). The latter was established in 1981 under the auspices of the United Nations Development Programme (UNDP). It is managed by the International Finance Corporation with a mandate to assist businessmen in the region to raise money for new productive investments in the range of US\$0.5 million to US\$5 million. This came out of a recommendation of a Task Force on Private Sector Activities sponsored by IDB, USAID, CDB, the Netherlands Government and the Canadian International Development Agency (CIDA).

In a short space of time these institutions have become powerful arbiters of Caribbean development. Their ambitions seem to lie in creating a congenial neo-colonial climate in which to help the North American TNCs, restructuring global capital and advancing the US government's conception of the area's strategic significance during the present phase of imperialism's development. As Peter Johnson of CCAA sees it, these 'places can't get along without outside investment, outside technology. Alone they are not viable; they will in the end have to become something like *offshore states of the United States'*.[4]

But, whatever the limitations of public sector development, historically the private sector's record on the poor and powerless is no better. This holds true for both the US and the West Indies. Without making any direct reference to the historical role of the US in the development and continued colonisation of the region, Dymally, one of the co-founders of the CCAA, could himself observe that:

> . . . what is happening in the US under the present administration . . . [is] diabolical. I cannot think of a stronger word to express my feelings . . . and this is the cup of milk that the US would offer you. In the past five years the Reagan administration has come very close to pulling down upon the heads of the American people the social systems so painstakingly erected over the previous fifty years.[5]

He also pointed out that 'an administration that has shown no compassion for its own poor and dispossessed cannot fool the Caribbean people that it intends to help the poor and disinherited of another region'.[6] Having given the context of US governmental actions in the region he argues that:

> . . . what the White House believes is most threatened – and what must be protected at all costs – are US business investments . . . and this private sector, this monied, elite group of people who oppose humanitarian concerns in favour of the military, in order to resist the Communists and thereby safeguard their economic interests, – this same private sector, you say, is going to help 'stabilise democracy'. Now, I ask you: Is a pervasive military presence conducive to stability? Is that the hallmark of democracy?
>
> Do you think US soldiers are playing war games in the Eastern Caribbean because of a commitment to domestic tranquility? . . . I would suggest to you that the private sector is suspect as a partner. It is suspect because the private sector, by-and-large, is the problem. It has been the problem throughout our turbulent history in these islands. Three hundred years of racism and greed have now brought the world to the brink of fiscal and nuclear disaster. Still, some of us are willing to look to these same sources for our salvation.[7]

I have quoted Dymally at some length, not only because he is a congressman and has played a role in the development of the CCAA, but also because no other representative of the private sector in the region has ever been as frank or forthrightly self-critical in public, especially in his open admission of the link between developing the private sector and the US's military and security interests in the region.

C. Trade and Aid: the CBI, CARIBCAN and Lomé

The CBI

Because the US government views the economies of the region as too small to achieve self-sustaining growth, it has all along recognised that exports would be the key to their long-term viability. In the spring of 1982, President Reagan proposed a package of aid, trade and investment incentives, which, after a turbulent passage through Congress, finally became law in July 1983, (the Caribbean Basin Recovery Act of 1983, popularly known as the Caribbean Basin Initiative or CBI).

The original package contained three components: (i) one-way duty-free entry to the US market for Caribbean-made products for a period of 12 years with certain key exceptions (textiles and clothing, footwear and leather goods, canned tuna, petroleum and petroleum-derived products). Various stipulations defined whether or not the products were Caribbean-made; (ii) tax credits to encourage US businesses to invest in the Caribbean and, to bring tourism to the region, the granting of credits for the use of CBI-designated convention sites; and (iii) supplementary aid (put at US$350 million for the first fiscal year).

In addition, the CBI aimed to ensure that the beneficiaries cooperated with the US government in controlling narcotics trafficking, in fair compensation for expropriated US property, in setting up an extradition treaty between the US and CBI-designated countries and in negotiating bilateral investment treaties with the US. The Act did not, however, provide for tax credit for new investment in the region, but in its final stage increased the duty-free access of the region by about 8–15 per cent over the existing US Generalised Scheme of Preferences. Significantly, trade in sugar was excluded from the agreement and when the US government subsequently reduced the sugar quotas, the loss from this alone exceeded the gains derived from the new access under the CBI. Since the inception of the CBI, the decline in the trade of traditional items (sugar, bauxite and petroleum) which accounted for 85 per cent of the region's exports to the USA, has outweighed the gains (or potential gains) of expanded exports from non-traditional items. The value of CARICOM-eligible CBI countries' exports to the US in 1985 was US$2,600 million, that is only 70 per cent of the value of this trade in 1983 (US$3,700 million) and only two-thirds of the value of the 1981 trade (US$4,100 million). When we examine their exports of CBI eligible non-traditional products, we see an increase from US$451 million in 1981 to US$596 million in 1983 (the year CBI started) to US$687 million in 1985. This increase did not compensate for the massive decline in traditional exports. The aid provision of US$350 million is also small in relation to the CARICOM region's current balance-of-payments deficit of US$1,500 million and its estimated need for external financing for the period 1982–86 of nearly US$5,000 million.[8] Yet this provision is expected to provide aid for 27 Caribbean and Central American countries, with more than half (US$190 million) going to four Central American countries and about one-third of the remainder to Jamaica alone.

Because the CBI is the main economic tool in the US government's approach to solving the region's crisis, it is important that certain aspects of this strategy are recognised. First, in contrast to the obvious need to promote cooperation in the region, the CBI operates on a bilateral basis and creates the opportunity for playing off one Caribbean country against another. It bypasses all the established regional institutions (CARICOM, CDB, IDB, OECS) and, unlike other sister arrangements such as Lomé, makes no provision for creating an institutional framework for its administration. In this regard the CBI also fails to give even token acknowledgement to the idea of equality among partners. Second, its divisiveness is reinforced by the exclusion of countries such as Cuba and Nicaragua on political grounds; the test of ideological acceptability being determined exclusively by the US. Third, it makes no concessions to the different levels of development in the region and consequently unlike other trade and aid arrangements, offers no special mechanisms for attending to the problem of the least developed states. And fourth, the CBI has to be seen in the context of its special emphasis on privatising economic activity (which the Reagan administration propagates) and of widening the scope for the penetration of US private capital into the region. EPZ-type activity and the Puerto Rican proposals on production sharing and twinning arrangements are examples of the sorts of development envisaged by US capital. The stress on privatisation may also account for the fact that the CBI effectively disregards the issue of social infrastructure and societal support structures in the region, presumably on the grounds that these are a government's responsibility.

The most disturbing aspect of the CBI, however, is its link with the US government's military and security interests and the fact that, like the Alliance for Progress in Latin America in the 1960s, it was prompted by cold-war consider-ations. George Shultz more or less admitted this in a speech in 1984 when he said that when 'President Reagan first proposed the CBI three years ago, he had in mind more than a partnership between the US and the Caribbean Basin to promote trade and investment. His was a broader vision of a peaceful and prosperous Caribbean in which people could realise their aspirations and build better societies for them-selves and their children'.[9] And then, after expressing these lofty sentiments, Shultz went on to say that from 'the US point of view, the CBI's underlying premise is that the Carib-bean Basin is vital to our security and to our social and economic well-being. It is indeed, our third border. Econ-omic, social and political events in the Basin have a direct and significant impact in the United States'.[10]

Shultz was in fact echoing President Reagan's speech in February 1982 to the Organisation of American States in which he declared that the Caribbean Basin was 'a vital stra-tegic and commercial artery for the US' and that nearly half the US's trade, two-third of its imported oil and over half its imported strategic minerals pass through the region encompassing the Panama Canal and the Gulf of Mexico. Statements such as these, coming from the highest level of decision-making in the US, are a strong indication that the CBI is more likely to remain an extension of the US's Monroe Doctrine/Manifest Destiny style imperialism of the past than to usher in a new order or show a new way forward. Thus, as with previous arrangements, the CBI places US interests at the top of the agenda and, propaganda notwith-standing, will contribute little, if anything to the poor and powerless. And, as the region becomes even more integrated into the orbit of US capitalism, the interests of the minority are likely to become even more deeply entrenched.

CARIBCAN

Disappointment over the CBI has been widespread in the region, even though there has been much publicity on such proposals as the export of winter vegetables and sugar-cane based ethanol. This has led government officials to turn to Canada for improved access to its market and, out of this, came the establishment of CARIBCAN in 1986. The arrange-ment basically introduces (i) preferential one-way duty-free trade for products defined as Caribbean-made with a limited number of exceptions. It is proposed to cover nearly all Canadian imports from the English-speaking Caribbean, which in addition to the CARICOM countries includes Anguilla, Bermuda, the British Virgin Islands, the Cayman Islands and the Turks and Caicos; and (ii) doubling Canadian aid between 1982 and 1987 (from approximately US$28.5 million to US$57 million). Trade in textiles, clothing, foot-wear, luggage, handbags, leather garments, lubricating oils and methanol is considered 'sensitive' and is therefore subject to certain escape clauses.

In mid-1986, the Canadian government held a series of seminars in the region to brief businessmen on the potential of the proposed scheme. Judging from the response, CARIBCAN is likely to be better received than the CBI, for Canada has a lower profile in the region and therefore arouses fewer fears in government circles about its big-power ambitions; also the scheme is tailor made for the English-speaking Caribbean. When Prime Minister Trudeau promised the initiative to West Indian leaders at a summit in 1983, he had reassured them that 'Canada has consistently chosen to address hemispheric tensions from their economic and social causes, being equipped neither by ambition nor by capacity to pursue military solutions or grand strategic designs'.[11] He might have added that over a century ago in 1884, the local

legislatures of Barbados, Jamaica and the Leeward Islands
had taken steps to unify their territories with Canada; that
later on the Bahamas had proposed itself as part of the
Canadian Confederation and that, as recently as 1974, the
State Council of the Turks and Caicos Islands had asked that
their territory be annexed by Canada. There is little doubt
that Canadian political liberalism, combined with its middle-
power status, make it appear less threatening to the region.
There is, however, on the part of the Canadian ruling class,
as indeed among its population at large, much ambiguity in
its attitude to the region. Should it be a junior partner of the
US in the region? Is it Britain's surrogate following the
collapse of empire? Should relations be primarily economic
given that an opportunity exists for easier Canadian access
to the region's markets and resources than either the US or
the UK enjoys? Or is there, in any meaningful sense, a special
historical relationship? Whatever primary considerations
eventuate, the Canadian economic presence in the region has
been quite substantial: mining, tourism, forestry, transport,
manufacturing, finance and consultancy services. Even here,
however, there is an underlying ambiguity in that some
important Canadian companies in the region are themselves
either subsidiaries of US companies (Commonwealth
Holiday Inns) or include large amounts of US capital (Alcan)
and, as such, reflect the branch-plant character of the
Canadian economy and its junior role in the circuit of US
capital. What is more, under the Mulroney government,
Canadian foreign policy is increasingly subsuming a gamut
of international relations beneath bilateral US/Canadian ties.

These considerations apart and even assuming the best
of intentions, it is difficult to see how CARIBCAN will, in
the foreseeable future, be able to contribute significantly to
the transformation of the region's economy. Indeed, it will
have achieved much if, in the light of the growing protectionism in the north, it does not, like the CBI or the Lomé
convention, become riddled with so many exceptions that the
export possibilities of the region are significantly retarded.

The Lomé Convention

The belief that incentive packages of trade, aid and investment
can cure poverty and underdevelopment in the Caribbean is

as old as the region's European empires and is nowhere more clearly expressed than in the Lomé Convention. The Convention, which is a direct descendant of the mercantilist arrangement of empire, came into effect in 1975 to unite the EEC and the ACP in an agreement, which also included trade preferences and aid. It developed out of an EEC decision in 1957 to set up a European Development Fund to encourage development in its then predominantly African colonial territories. After independence, the arrangements were formalised at the Yaoundé Convention in 1963. By 1973, however, Britain had become a member of the EEC and its ex-empire territories wanted to join the Convention. In the course of negotiations the ex-colonies realised that they could improve their bargaining positions if they operated as a unit and, as a result, they formed the ACP grouping. A new five-year Convention was signed at Lomé (Togo) in 1975; it has been renewed twice (in 1980 and 1985) and the number of ACP countries participating in it has grown from 46 in 1975 to 66 in 1986.

The EEC has somewhat ambitiously promoted the Lomé Convention as an attempt to redress the colonial exploitation of these territories in the past and boasts of it being the only agreement to bring the industrialised countries of the north and the poor countries of the south together as equal partners in the quest for a New International Economic Order. The main provisions of the Conventions which, like the CBI, are based on the conviction that expanded trade can solve the region's problems, centre on two features, namely one-way duty-free access to the EEC of ACP-made products (although there are certain exceptions such as sugar, rum, bananas, rice and beef to which special regulations apply); and aid, which has increased from ECU3,500 million (European Currency Units) in 1975 to ECU8,500 million for the period 1985-89.

This aid package includes two innovatory mechanisms, Stabex and Sysmin, which together dispense about one-sixth of the resources. Stabex provides compensation under certain criteria for loss of earnings from exports to the EEC and, in certain cases, to the rest of the world. To qualify, the product(s) involved must represent at least 6 per cent of the claiming country's exports and earnings must also fall by at least 6 per cent, both occurring during the claim year. The figure is reduced to 1.5 per cent for landlocked, island and least developed countries and some Caribbean countries benefit from this provision. Sysmin provides aid where there is a fall in the capacity of ACP states to export copper, cobalt, phosphates, manganese, bauxite-alumina, tin, or iron ore. To qualify, 15 per cent of total export earnings should be derived from the mineral concerned, with a special arrangement of 10 per cent for landlocked, island and least developed countries. About half the total aid is in the form of grants to individual ACP states and there has been much disputation over the terms and conditions under which it has been granted, as both the ACP states and the EEC struggle to influence the uses to which these funds should be put.

Despite these innovatory mechanisms, however, successive Lomé Conventions have so far failed either to deal effectively with the region's periodic crises or to make any noticeable dent in the poverty and underdevelopment underlying these crises. As one commentator graphically puts it, 'ten years after Lomé, it is now patently clear that the Lomé process is a falling curve with the break-even point out at the end of each successor agreement coming to represent a new *status quo* that is considered satisfactory mainly from the standpoint of declining development commitment and a world economic situation not supportive of development'.[12] This view is echoed in the regional trade union movement's 1986 policy proposals, which state that in 'spite of some ambitious features, the record of the Convention in several areas has been a disappointment. Unfortunately, the implementation of Lomé coincided with the start of the world economic recession and has not proved to be the hoped for engines of development'.[13]

There is little doubt that the record is disheartening. To begin with, EEC assistance has fallen in real per capita terms. Trade between the EEC and the ACP show a decline from 6.3 to 4.5 per cent between 1976 and 1983 for EEC imports from these states as a percentage of its total imports. Moreover, despite the preferences, over the years the EEC's ACP imports have remained stable at 19 per cent of its total imports from all developing countries. At the same time, the EEC's balance-of-trade surplus with the ACP states has grown from ECU3,500 million to ECU4,400 million between 1976 and 1983. Stabex has also suffered from insufficient funds, a situation worsened by declining prices in recent years. These have been further compounded by the failure to establish effective international commodity arrangements. Concern has also been expressed about the restrictive product coverage of Stabex, the EEC's huge agricultural surpluses, the disincentives which exist in its special arrangements for products such as sugar and bananas (which are crucial to the Caribbean), its restrictive use of the rules-of-origin yardstick to determine ACP-made products and the existence of safeguard clauses with which the EEC can suspend the Convention to protect a threatened activity.

Successive Lomé Conventions have generally been unable to counteract the north's deep-seated and growing protectionism and the promise of easy access to the EEC's market has remained illusory. The claim that Lomé would usher in a new era of partnership in development can hardly be sustained. Anyone following the regular rounds of negotiations between the EEC and the ACP and who has seen how the various funds are dispensed, would quickly realise that the usual donor-recipient relationship which characterises other aid institutions prevails. The ACP countries, and for our particular purpose the Caribbean states among them, can expect from these arrangements no quick fix or easy solution to their problems. Even in the most propitious circumstances, external arrangements can only assist an internal programme of economic and social transformation. By themselves they cannot generate the social momentum needed to remove internal constraints and to liberate the poor and powerless. In a world system structured as ours is, historical redress begins at home when the priorities of the historically dispossessed take precedence over all others.

D. Militarisation

If trade preferences, aid and the special facilities of CBI, CARIBCAN and ACP are the carrot with which to draw the region into particular north-south axes, western geostrategic interests and those of the US in particular require that the military stick should also be used. Although security concerns about the region were prominent in the US's external policies ever since the Cuban revolution in 1959, in the closing years of the Carter administration these concerns began to turn into a US military offensive. This was prompted by the advances of popular forces in Nicaragua and Grenada, the breakdown in Cuba's isolation and, further afield, the events in Iran, Angola and Afghanistan. In 1979, the Caribbean Contingency Joint Task Force was formed and headquartered at Key West. In 1980, the US navy made 129 visits to 29 Caribbean ports. In 1981, the Defence Department reorganised and upgraded its regional defences into a single US Forces Caribbean Command (bringing together the Caribbean Contingency Joint Task Force and the Antilles Defence Command in Puerto Rico) and put it on the same footing as one of three full-scale NATO Atlantic Commands. Routine training of the Atlantic Fleet was also located in the Caribbean. An exercise called Ocean Venture, reputed to be the largest peace-time naval manoeuvre since the Second World War, was held in 1982 and since then, repeated several times, with the 1986 exercise being based partly in Grenada. By 1984 the Caribbean Basin contained 21 US military installations and a troop strength of close to 30,000 with an additional 9-10,000 ship-borne troops.

Although this new show of military strength is linked to developments in Grenada and Nicaragua, it is important to realise that the US has a long-established tradition of using force in the region to pursue its geo-strategic interests. Prior to the Cuban revolution, the US government had already made 47 military interventions against Central America and the Caribbean, of which 38 pre-dated the Russian revolution. The expansionist designs of the Monroe Doctrine and the Manifest Destiny conceptions of US foreign policy were not therefore born of the anti-communism of today's rhetoric. The importance of the Basin in the movement of strategic materials into the US, its role as a vital link in the US's North and South Atlantic fleets, as well as Cuba's rapidly-growing military capability and links with the Soviet Union are all responsible for the huge military presence of the US in the Caribbean theatre. The US no doubt intends to encircle Cuba with a string of military bases (which it has more or less already achieved) in the expectation that a strong military presence, combined with demonstrations of its capability, would contain the left and prevent any social upheavals that might challenge US interests. Given the position of the US in the world, all these objectives are best served with an 'economy of power'.

The US invasion of Grenada, which Jamaica, Barbados and all but three of the OECS states supported,[14] was a critical turning point in the US's militarisation of the region. Prior to 1980, only Jamaica was a significant recipient of US military aid, but after the Grenadian revolution it was stepped up everywhere, with Barbados receiving 98 per cent of all the military aid it had ever received from the US in the years 1980-83 and several islands receiving military aid in 1981 for the first time in their histories. Whereas only US$0.2 million was recorded for the fiscal year of 1981 for military sales, assistance and training programmes, by 1986 this had grown to nearly US$19 million, of which about US$8 million went to Jamaica. The total US military assistance to the Eastern Caribbean is now thought to be running at about US$30 million annually, and in Jamaica at about US$80 million. Much of this was spent on training special service units in the various islands' police forces (there are 80 permanent members on each island) and commando groups in the standing armies of Barbados and Jamaica to cope with insurgencies. This arrangement was formalised with the formation of an Eastern Caribbean Security System and, in September 1985, military exercises were held to test its readiness to stave off threats from 'externally backed forces'. US, British, Jamaican and Barbadian forces participated in these exercises alongside the OECS states, which were operating in the framework of the Defence and Security Committee of their treaty. Exercises were again held in 1987.

Although these developments have emanated from US global strategic concerns, the ambitions of the regional leaders to use these forces against internal enemies has been barely disguised. Thus Vere Bird, the Premier of Antigua, on the occasion of signing a Memorandum of Understanding in 1982 with Barbados, St Vincent, St Lucia and Dominica to form a Regional Defence Force, stated that 'the whole idea behind the defence force is that if you get through today on your own island, don't forget there will be forces in all the other islands and you will have to answer them'. A month later he added that 'in this region we cannot afford to have another Cuba or another Grenada'.[15] After the invasion of Grenada in 1983, St Kitts-Nevis and Grenada itself also joined the Regional Defence Force, thereby facilitating the incorporation of these arrangements with the Eastern Caribbean Security System.

This concern with internal insurrection was picked up by Adams, the then Prime Minister of Barbados, who called for a standing army of 1,500 people to strengthen existing arrangements and, as he put it, to protect the region from 'external aggression and domestic revolution'.[16] Coming from Adams this was indeed a dangerous call, for not only had he led Barbados into playing the principal proxy role for US military interests in the Eastern Caribbean, but he had also already set a precedent by sending Barbadian troops to St Vincent in 1979 to help the government over a domestic dispute and to Dominica in 1981 to prevent a coup, as well as stationing forces off the island of St Lucia during its troublesome elections in 1982. Fortunately his proposals stirred up so many hornets' nests that his benefactors in Washington decided to ignore it.

According to Tiryakian, the 'various US security related actions in the Caribbean during the 1980s indicate a clear pattern of militarisation. Washington's conduct reveals that in the economic sphere its words have spoken louder than its actions while militarily its actions have undoubtedly spoken louder than words. Thus the US seems to be offering baby carrots and wielding a big stick'.[17] The regional leaders have not yet fully appreciated quite how much their attempts to use the US's security ambitions to serve their own interests to contain internal revolts, particularly on the left, are elevating the role and status of the military in their societies. It is naive to assume that with its new-found strength the military will be content simply to pride itself as a defender of the system. Experience elsewhere suggests that it will become increasingly impatient with what it sees as the politicians' incompetence to resolve social and economic problems peacefully and will want to resort to more 'disciplined' measures. With sometimes fragile party systems, short-lived popular institutions and a long tradition of colonial authoritarianism, this appeal can easily lead to direct intervention, despite the popularity of liberal democratic institutions in the English-speaking Caribbean. Furthermore, in countries with few options for pursuing social and economic advancement, a potential incentive exists for middle-class officers to exercise their military muscle. To make matters worse, the collusion of political leaders with questionable military and police practices (usually associated with the drugs trade and repressing dissent) only exacerbates the growth of militarism. The solution that militarism seems to offer, namely the containment of social conflict, may well generate an entirely new range of problems, witnessed for example, in the military's role in supporting corrupt authoritarianism in Guyana.

If the CBI's 'bilateral' carrot, seems to play one country off against another, then with its 'multilateral' stick militarisation has used a regional approach recognising implicitly the limitations of going it alone.

E. The Role of Ideology

Ideology has always been used to win people over to certain positions or world views of social reality and, in times of crisis, helps define the range of permissible options and the preferred solution. In this regard the Caribbean is no different; it has always been a battleground of world views. The struggles of the slaves for their personal freedom were not only social, political and economic, but also enjoined strong contestation about the very definition of man as a political and social being. Similarly, there is a link between the US's military and economic solutions and its ideological initiatives in the region. This is seen, for example, in the relationship between privatisation as an ideology and the CBI proposals, or between anti-communism and the mobilising of regimes to arm themselves (with US support) to counter the 'totalitarian alien threat of communism' or to rationalise destabilisation and covert actions against 'unfriendly' governments. The chorus of negative publicity about Bishop's Grenada and Manley's Jamaica was thus pivotal in disrupting these countries' tourist economies and bringing pressure to bear on their governments. The naval manoeuvres and bellicose statements about Soviet/Cuban bases have also been similarly shrouded in cold-war ideological rhetoric.

Ideology is not, however, confined to overt propaganda, but is also conveyed through cultural, educational and other socialising mechanisms. It is through these that the considerable influence of the US is most strongly felt in the region, particularly in the field of labour and through the media. The American Institute for Free Labour Development (AIFLD), which is tied to both the AFL-CIO and the CIA, trains 20 unionists a year in the US and through holding seminars and courses in the region has contributed to the training of over 25,000 West Indian trade unionists. The AIFLD, which was formed in 1961, receives 95 per cent of its funding from USAID and is conceived of as a tripartite venture between government, labour and big business, which is why only a limited range of societal options are deemed acceptable by 'free' trade unionism. The AIFLD replaced the Caribbean Labour Congress when the latter broke up after a split in WFTU and the formation of the explicitly anti-communist ICFTU, which for much of its history has been the standard bearer in 'labour's struggle against communism' in the West.

The effect of this largely US-influenced organisation structure has been to narrow the range of actions and interests to which regional trade unionists are exposed. Any communist ideas are automatically branded as hostile to free trade unionism and democracy; any radical or progressive tendencies in the labour movement that fail to find full expression within the existing framework are considered communist and, as such, antithetical to free and democratic processes. Fortunately, the effect of this line of reasoning has been less monolithic than expected and there is still considerable concern for the poor and powerless among both the rank and file and the leadership of the region's trade union movement. This has encouraged a constructively critical approach to other social systems, especially the social successes of Cuba, which have had a considerable influence despite the continuous barrage of negative propaganda.

In the media the penetration of US ideas is more complete. Cable News Network is regularly available on a number of local television stations (which is particularly significant given that most countries only have one station of their own) and numerous satellite-dish owners and private companies pirate US channels for local redistribution.[18] Several islands claim to be able to tune into as many as 13 channels from the US. Indeed, it is unlikely that any other part of the world is as heavily penetrated by foreign media. People often know more about the squabbles in the US Congress or the latest hailstorm in Kansas than they do about developments in their own country, let alone those of their closest neighbours. To strengthen this already strong grip, the Voice of America Caribbean Basin Project plans to spend US$50 million on 11 more transmitters in the Caribbean Basin and to add medium wave (FM) to its existing short-wave broadcasts. In addition to this penetration of the regional media, ownership in all the territories is highly centralised. Guyana's national daily newspaper is a government and party organ, the Jamaican *Gleaner* belongs to one of the 'famous 21 families' in control of the economy and Trinidad-Tobago's two dailies, the *Guardian* and the *Express* are separately owned by the country's two leading conglomerates. These locally-owned media are usually conservative and anti-socialist, often presenting hostile images of socialism by associating it with shortages (Manley's Jamaica, Guyana), corrupt authoritarianism (Guyana) and domination (Cuba) and thereby helping to contain the range of options available through which to express social discontent. If to these are added the fare provided by local cinemas and weekly news magazines, such as *Newsweek* and *Time*, then exposure to the US's interpretation of the world is indeed very great.

By straightjacketing regional perceptions into a cold-war context, this ideology has helped sustain the retreat from an acceptance of ideological pluralism and a tolerant liberal view of the region as a 'zone of peace'. It has hampered the growth of a truly Caribbean perception of the region's identity and of what social tasks need to be undertaken. It has also tempted some of the region's leaders into becoming spokespersons on the global confrontation of ideas and systems and has thereby raised the region's profile in the arena of world politics. At this stage, this reinforces the likelihood of the region becoming incorporated into a new US empire, based on a system of off-shore manufacturing to replace the Far East, as many argue the CBI intended.

The formation in 1986 of the Caribbean Democratic Union (the regional arm of the International Democratic Union) is the most recent indication of just how much US ideology has permeated the region. This grouping, whose original signatories were the leaders of the ruling parties in Jamaica, Dominica, Grenada, Montserrat, Belize, St Kitts-Nevis, St Lucia and St Vincent, is seen as a political wedge against communism and a defender of 'democracy' in the region. The most striking features about it are its cold-war origins, its ties with the two main political parties in the US and that it makes no secret of the fact that it regards the social-democratic parties' international organisation (the Socialist International) as 'too soft on communism'. Given that some parties in the region (including some that have formed governments) belong to the Socialist International, the conservatism of the Caribbean Democratic Union threatens to be very strident indeed and, in effect, begins to cast doubt on the legitimacy of the party system, on the ways in which policies are negotiated and on the kinds of political options that have been available over the past few decades. One provision worth noting is that the signatories have introduced the concept of mutual assistance for members facing elections. A precedent in this regard had already been set in Grenada (1984), Dominica (1985) and St Lucia (1987) when the conservative parties threw their weight behind Blaize, Charles and Compton. The prospect of open interference in the internal affairs of member states seems to be lurking behind this new development. Here again the thrust is towards using ideology to define the crisis in such narrow terms that the masses are unable to conceive of development in any way other than through the maintenance of the *status quo*.[19]

15 *Conclusion: Another Development?*

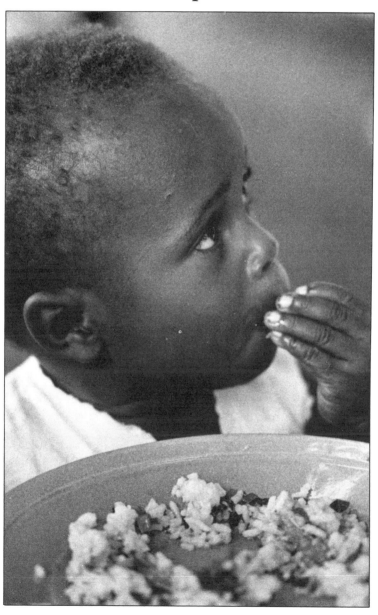

I: Development: Meaning and Purpose

I conclude this book by outlining an alternative conception of development in the region. Before commencing, however, a word of caution is required. It would be unwise (and probably impossible) for any one individual, no matter how well-intentioned, to compile recipes for the future. One of the points I hope that this book has made is that development is about people, about the concrete context of their existence, and that this is largely influenced by the social conditions they inherit and the movements and rhythms underlying them. Even although people make history with their daily lives, they do not and indeed cannot expect to start with a clean slate. But if development and change are about people, then it is they who should ultimately choose what path they wish to pursue. Individuals and groups can offer ideas, suggestions and leadership, but the ultimate test of their efficacy lies in the willingness of the people to adopt them as part of their daily existence. What I offer here, therefore, is no more than a tentative starting point for a pathway to be carved out by the willing actions of the people themselves, working as much in concert as is socially and politically possible at a given time.

It is important to remember that the pattern and rhythm of growth the region has inherited is also the point of departure for constructing a new economy and society and that if new economic and social foundations are to be built, the old ones must be pulled down. Consequently, any plans or programmes that act outside the historical possibilities of these inheritances and the radical (revolutionising) zeal of the people are bound to be frustrated. It is also important not to underestimate just how depressing daily life is for the broad mass of Caribbean people who are poor and powerless and how stark the contrast between their life styles and those of the small minority who make up the rich and powerful. The existence of this inequality is a clear reminder of how easy it has been for social forces of underdevelopment and dependency to reproduce themselves and how, under conditions of negative real growth and declining per capita real incomes, a minority can still prosper. The mushrooming of black-market goods and foreign currency in Jamaica and

Guyana show that even in the context of widespread depri-
vation and shortages, a small minority has been able to
'capture' supplies for themselves and to monopolise the
scarcity values these commodities generate in the market
place.

The region's economic policies are still largely based on
the assumption that development and a satisfactory growth
rate of per capita product are one and the same thing, with
the main constraint to its achievement (maintaining a balance-
of-payments equilibrium) being externally induced and
internal imbalances (such as unemployment and domestic
inflation) holding far less significance. While a number of
different opinions have been espoused on what constitutes a
satisfactory rate of growth, it is only recently that popular
forces have sought to challenge this line of argument with a
double line of attack.

The first advances the view that, although perhaps
willing to agree on what constitutes an acceptable rate of
growth, it is important to know whether the chosen rate can
be *sustained* before deciding whether or not development is
taking place. Posing the issue in this way raises some ancillary
questions.[1] For example, is the rate of increase of per capita
national product brought about by the existence in the
country of some non-renewable resource for which there
happens to be a world demand, such as oil in Trinidad-
Tobago or bauxite in Jamaica and Guyana? If so, what are
the reserves of these resources and their current and projected
rates of exploitation? How far into the future can favourable
demand conditions be projected? Does the satisfactory rate
of increase depend on foreign borrowing? If so, what are the
prospects of it continuing? Is per capita national product
increasing because of reduced population pressure brought
about by the mass emigration which has taken place since
the Second World War? If so, what are the prospects of
the political and social conditions that make this possible
continuing?

The second line of attack argues that such a formulation
of development ignores the region's internal problems, such
as growing unemployment, the worsening distribution of
income and wealth and the persistence of poverty. This criticism was particularly marked during the unprecedented rates

of increase of per capita national product in the 1950s and 1960s in the region as a whole and in the 1970s and early 1980s in Trinidad-Tobago.

Liberal tendencies among the ruling strata have responded to these challenges by introducing social and political considerations into the development analysis, but these usually remain somewhat incidental to the interpretation of development and the debate continues to be conducted at an institutional level, at best. The approach adopted in this book, however, differs from the liberal approach in that it expressly includes class and social relations as integral dimensions of development. The liberals never ask for whom the development is supposed to take place, but it is important to recognise early on that how development is interpreted, defined and measured goes a long way towards determining what development path is pursued. Asking who the development is for also helps determine the criteria for future development strategies and policies.

Our *first task*, therefore, is to identify the essential rhythms of underdevelopment in the region so that *strategic* choices can be made about how these rhythms should be altered. Thereafter, the development of lines of production, consumption and social organisation can be deduced.

As I have repeatedly argued throughout this book, development in the Caribbean cannot be studied in isolation. The question of alternative paths of development has to be raised within the historical context of the concrete manifestation *on a world scale* of a group of countries described as 'underdeveloped' (as distinct from undeveloped which might have been the condition of Europe before the development of capitalism). For our purpose, this underdevelopment (when used to describe the condition of the region) refers to the consequences of the long period (16th-18th century) during which capitalism became an international system of production and created a world market. During this process of internationalisation, two important divergences emerged in the way in which the material conditions of social life in the Caribbean were reproduced.

The first was that as market relations became more and more generalised and entrenched in the regional economy, a systemic divergence occurred between the pattern of resource use and the demand structure. This happened because European conquest and settlement destroyed the communal and other pre-capitalist production relations which prevailed at that time in the Caribbean. Thereafter, domestic resources were systematically garnered to service overseas markets in Europe and elsewhere. The development of tropical export cash crops (sugar, cotton, spices, cocoa and coffee), mineral production for export (oil and bauxite), services (offshore finance and tourism) and even the recent wave of export-processing firms operating from regional enclaves, are all reflections of this orientation.

The second was that the export sector became highly specialised in producing and selling what is still essentially a very narrow range of products to one or two major capitalist markets. Even now, when there is so much talk about revitalising the region's agriculture, the focus is either on non-traditional exports (such as exotic flowers) to special access markets (CBI), or on reviving dying speciality crops (such as sea-island cotton and arrowroot). The internal regional market is thus neglected at a time when masses of small farmers are living in poverty and over US$1,000 million is spent on food imports from outside the region. This divergence developed as the market economy spread and the ability to purchase (to command money incomes) became the principal determinant of consumption. As a result, ever since colonisation, the needs of the broad mass of poor people have played virtually no part in directing the course of production, for, apart from a few residual subsistence sectors in some territories, commodities from both local production and imports are allocated on the basis of purchasing power. In the context of widespread poverty and unemployment, this has resulted in a systemic bias in favour of servicing the needs of the relatively better off. Even where commodities have become popular consumer items (for example, poultry and consumer durables such as radios, televisions and cookers), their import content remains high (over 80 per cent in several territories for the above items) with the result that domestic production of these products has become a thinly-disguised form of importation.

If this is the dynamic for reproducing the material needs of the society as a whole, then it follows that the complex set of political, social and legal relations (patterns of owner-ship of productive factors); institutions, organisations and other decision-making structures; and ideas and ideologies have grown out of and dialectically interact with this rhythm of production. It is therefore only through understanding this expression of the condition of underdevelopment that we can begin to understand what constitutes development.

The *second task*, therefore, is to indicate what develop-ment (as the negation of underdevelopment) means in the Caribbean context. Eight points seem critical. In the first instance, and in direct contrast to what prevails, development requires a system of ownership, control and production oriented towards satisfying the basic needs of the masses. By the masses is simply meant all those who are poor and 'who do not have any power in society derived from property, wealth, religion, caste, expertise or other sources not widely shared',[2] including political party affiliation. This definition recognises that, in the past, property relations and production have benefited too few at the expense of too many. It explicitly states that redistribution, social equality and a parti-cipatory political process should be the cornerstone of another kind of development in which the concerns of the poor and powerless are central rather than incidental items on an agenda for some other disembodied abstraction, such as export competitiveness, building an industrial sector, or developing a new and appropriate technology. In other words, production aimed at providing for the basic needs of the masses, in the first instance, implies a systematic, conscious, deliberate and planned attack on poverty. Elimin-ating poverty should not be treated merely as a possible or desirable consequence of production, which is what happens when profit is the main determinant of output.

The basic needs of the masses are either personal (food, clothing, housing) or public/collective (health, sanitation, education, culture, recreation), or seen differently, both material (food, clothing, housing) and non-material (health, education). During the heyday of Bishop's rule in Grenada, Burnham's in Guyana and Manley's in Jamaica, there was much talk of a 'basic needs' approach to development, but in practice such programmes failed to reorient the system of production, although they probably did in some instances heighten concern about social equality. In Guyana, the basic needs programme coincided with a period in which the real incomes of the masses actually fell. In fact Cuba is the only territory in the region where redistributive ideals and popular enhancement of the status of the masses is a motive force in economic production. The effects of this are particularly obvious in areas such as health care, recreation, sport and education. Apart from this, there are only a few isolated examples of communities where this conception of the purpose and meaning of social production is accepted, although during the Second World War (when access to the UK and the US was considerably curtailed) there was some production along these lines in the region. This was a period when, of all things, colonial propaganda spoke of the advantages of eating local foods and encouraged some forms of domestic industry.

Second, there can only be real development in the region if these basic needs are satisfied through planned and effective implementation of the right to work. This implies not only that all those who want jobs have them, but that they also have (i) the right to a job without coercion as to place and type of work (given their particular skills); (ii) a framework of industrial relations that permits free collective bargaining and effective (as distinct from nominal) representation within bargaining units; (iii) a work process that allows for effective worker involvement and control; (iv) health protection and guaranteed education and training for the tasks they are engaged in; and (v) an end to discrimination based on sex, colour, ethnicity, age or physical disability.

The objective is to situate work within a process of self-realisation, so that for West Indians work is both an end in itself and a means of development. The persistence of high levels of unemployment (ranging from 18 to 40 per cent and more in some instances) is an unacceptable social scourge which will not simply 'disappear' as per capita incomes grow. It has to be tackled as a separate objective. The stress on making work more meaningful is to counteract the humiliating and degrading practice sometimes employed by governments in the region of paying a limited number of people to perform meaningless tasks for brief and uncertain periods of time to 'ease the unemployment problem'. Not surprisingly, this has often degenerated into a form of political patronage. It is also to restrain progressive forces from directing labour from above as a short-cut to development and full employment, a practice which, as experience in Guyana has shown, can degenerate into enforced labour, often requiring state employees to abandon their rights to choose a job without coercion or to select the place of their employment.

Third, to reverse the region's authoritarian tradition, the material conditions of life should be reproduced within a self-reliant and endogenous pattern of growth. This is in fact the only sustainable pattern of growth given the particular historical formation of underdevelopment (with its resultant pattern of producing what is not consumed locally and consuming what is not produced locally) and the widespread foreign ownership and domination of production in the region. It is premised on the need to reverse dependency relations and to situate development in the Caribbean in the context of the capacity of people of all regions to develop themselves. Various forms of cooperation and self-organisation, such as the community councils in Jamaica, the sousou land societies in Trinidad-Tobago, the agricultural cooperative movement in Dominica and the activities of the Caribbean Conference of Churches should be encouraged and regarded as mainstays in the organisation of economic activity. Fortunately, a regional research project is being launched to study these phenomena in Guyana, Grenada, Jamaica, Belize, Cuba and Nicaragua.

Fourth, development also implies that work, politics and social organisations are based on democratising power in society and on the effective (as opposed to nominal) exercise of fundamental rights, such as those to free expression and organisation, respect of an individual's privacy and the abolition of repression and torture. The democratisation of power also implies the democratisation of all the decision-making structures in the society, from the level of the workplace and community right through to central government. An equitable distribution of wealth and income, equitable access to the use and management of society's resources and equitable access to information are, of course, necessary requirements for achieving this objective. Being in full possession of all the necessary information is absolutely vital if sound decisions are to be made, if control from below is to be assured and if popular participation in development is to be socially efficient.

This point explicitly seeks to negate certain aspects of social life in the Caribbean. One of these is the somewhat authoritarian view (held on the right and the left) that direct democracy can act as a substitute for the political democracy embodied in representative political institutions. In other words, direct democracy should complement rather than replace political democracy. Another is to conceive of political democracy as a colonial or local ruling-class 'trick'. Rights of representation and political forms of democracy do exist in the region (they were won through the heroic struggles of the masses), but are limited because they exist within a social context in which inequalities of income and wealth are systematically reproduced. Thus, as far as practical considerations go, they are severely constrained. The task in hand is to secure economic and social rights so as to negate these limiting considerations and not to reduce their significance by caricaturing them as a 'longing for British parliamentarianism', as certain left circles in the region are wont to do.

Fifth, development also implies preserving the stability of the environment and putting an end to the degradation it has suffered through the growth of national production in Caribbean societies. This is a simple and straightforward point which merely seeks to situate the region's development within the context of an unequivocal acceptance of our universal responsibility to protect the environment and sustain life.

Sixth, it is important to recognise that because of the polarity between the state and private sector, the state would have to play an important part in the development of the region, but only within the context of a participatory political process in which the ordinary West Indian's status as a citizen, producer and consumer of wealth was enhanced. To achieve this, the economic process would have to be based on workers having strong organisational and representational roles in their places of work. There is no doubt that, even when it has ostensibly been pursuing the public good, the West Indian state has revealed many weaknesses, which advocates of privatisation have successfully exploited (often through the use of Reaganite propaganda) in moulding the consciousness of the West Indian masses. So successful have they been that it is not generally recognised quite how frequently they turn to the state for help in promoting their own interests, in negotiating with foreign agencies and countries when they have difficulties gaining access for their products (often because of high local costs), or for providing domestic protection when competition from abroad adversely affects their operations.

The truth of the matter is that the private sector (the local capitalist class) in the region is incapable of directing a process of economic development that could ensure a sustained increase in the living standards of the broad mass of the population, reduce unemployment to the barest minimum and achieve an acceptable degree of social and political equality. The local capitalist class is limited in its vision (it does not even advocate the kinds of reforms many metropolitan capitalists uphold) and this is particularly evident in periods of crisis. Whereas Colonial Office officials looked inward for solutions during the Depression in the 1930s and the Second World War, all the solutions to the crisis of the 1980s are looked for outside the region, through measures such as more aid or better access for traditional crops. In Jamaica under Seaga, for example, recourse to the CBI and the development of non-traditional exports are the two most frequently relied on strategies for trying to solve the country's economic impasse. Yet, despite the publicity, Jamaica's exports to the US have declined by 27 per cent since 1984. Bank credit to the much touted manufacturing sector declined by 64 per cent between 1983 and 1985 and imports of industrial raw materials fell by 19 per cent over the same period. The high rate of growth in non-traditional non-CARICOM exports has in reality meant an expansion from US$0.45 million in 1980 to US$0.88 million in 1986 – a pitiful amount in absolute values.

The new manufacturing bourgeoisie in the region operates much like the absentee planter class of old. Most of its members live in two societies, with assets in each, the local ones always hedged by foreign ones. Levels of inefficiency and corruption are high. On the Jamaican stock-market insider trading and conflicts of interest are rife. On 8 May 1987 the *Financial Gleaner* wrote of one stockbroker on the Jamaican stock-exchange who was 'in the invidious position of also being a director of a listed company. He is literally being forced to be tempted to be an insider'. The same issue of the *Financial Gleaner* reported how 'investment advisers guiding institutional investors and portfolios also act as financial journalists and economic commentators in the news media. Some even act as unregistered stockbrokers positioning stocks for clients who then have registered stockbrokers execute the transaction'. Often financial journalists write under different names in different media creating the deception that different (and independent) persons are commenting on the same stock. At the time of this report, only two of the 22 companies listed on the Jamaican stock-exchange had met the 31 March 1987 deadline for publishing their financial results and only one other had done so by 1 May 1987.

Whether or not the government intervenes *per se* is neither here nor there. What is significant, however, is the purpose of the government intervention and what class and social interests it serves or seeks to serve. It is pure fantasy to believe that political freedom in the region can be reduced to, or is in some way dependent on, the operation of unrestrained market forces.[3] The interpretation of development advanced here is intended to subject the functioning of the state, as well as the development of the society as a whole, to what has been aptly termed the 'logic of the majority'. As Xavier Gorostiaga succinctly puts it, 'economic and political transformation cannot be carried out *for* the majority unless it is part of a project implemented *by* the majority. . . the majority must be the subject and not the object of their own history'.[4] In other words, given the authoritarian traditions of colonial and plantation autocracies in the region, alienation is a characteristic feature of life for large sections of the population, particularly the poor and powerless. It is therefore important to avoid reinforcing this alienation by uncritically accepting vague notions of development that seek to galvanise people into projects which then substantively marginalise them by turning them into the objects of the project.

Seventh, a realistic approach to development in the region must begin by recognising the stark reality of the hostile environment created by living in imperialism's backyard:

> Whatever may be the economic logic of US policies towards Central America and the Caribbean, it is clear that geopolitical considerations predominate. Historically, the region has always been considered 'America's backyard'. So long as the area was thought to be secure, the US could afford to ignore it; but any threat to the status quo has always triggered an immediate response. US military intervention in the region has been more frequent than in any other part of the world. . . the underlying assumption of US policy towards the region appears to be that its own geopolitical interests are incompatible with the emergence of genuinely independent states.[5]

Given this incompatibility, the future scope for development in the region is ultimately bound up with the survival and eventual success of the region's two major social experiments, Cuba and Nicaragua. It is important to recognise that this view does not imply that Cuba, Nicaragua, or even a combination of the two, have to be accepted as future models for the poor and powerless to adopt, but rather that the survival of the *very notion of experimenting to build new Caribbean societies is indissolubly linked to the survival of the only two surviving experiments*. It provides, as it were, a regional alternative and, as such, must remain a high priority in any development thrust. Given the historical circumstances, an effective regional alternative must at all times and in all situations seek to challenge the mechanisms that facilitate the absorption of the region into the US. And it must do so especially at this critical time when the US is pursuing the larger projects of engulfing Canada and Mexico and securing the submission of Central America through undeclared war against the region's popular forces.

And eighth, the criticisms mounted against Lomé, CARIBCAN and the CBI in the previous chapter should not be taken to mean that the external context is irrelevant to the region's successful development. On the contrary, the chosen path of development cannot realistically be separated from the outside world. The interface between internal class struggle and the international operation of capitalism is a crucially important consideration to take into account and it is for this reason that proposals designed to offer a 'global challenge' to existing structures are, I believe, of some importance.[6] If multilateralism could be restored, prices and incomes of primary commodities stabilised and clear controls over the TNCs instituted, improvements would follow. Similarly, if disarmament were to take place and the saved resources then spent on redistributing and restructuring the world's production and consumption structures and if 'better-my-neighbour' policies were to replace 'beggar-your-neighbour' ones, the world would be a better place and development that much easier. The sad reality, however, is that multilateralism is in retreat and unilateralism is dominant; protectionism in the north is the order of the day, while monetarism and *laissez-faire* policies are prevalent in both the north and the south. In this context, therefore, it is all the more important to successful development that accumulation should take place within national boundaries, but given how small most of the region's economies are and the high social costs of small size, the only realistic solution is to develop a regional alternative as an essential part of the process of national transformation.

II: Accumulation: Basic Goods and Basic Needs

In outlining an alternative conception of development, the *third task* is to tackle three key problems identified above. These are (i) that the pattern of consumption in the region fails to satisfy the basic needs of the broad mass of the population (it instead reflects the unequal distribution of wealth and income, disparities in urban and rural development and the poverty and dispossession of large social groups, particularly the peasants and urban poor); (ii) that because imperatives for bringing resources into production in the past derived largely from the needs of international capitalist expansion, the pattern of resource use and resource endowment are improperly reconciled; and (iii) reflecting the situation in 1 and 2 above, the pattern of property ownership and the social relations centring on this, show sharp and worsening inequalities both at the national/international level and within each national territory. Because of the systemic nature of these problems, it follows that the configurations of a transformed regional economy must be based on the *construction of a process of accumulation founded on the priorities required to ensure the eventual reversal of these divergences.* In other words, accumulation has to be founded on the logic of a dynamic convergence between social needs and the use of domestic resources.

In the past, even in revolutionary Cuba, this was taken to mean a simple sequence of import substitution. Beginning with the products in greatest demand, attempts were made through limiting imports to foster the development of local or joint-venture enterprises to produce these products. As my earlier critique of the industrialisation process showed, this pattern of industrialisation not only takes import demand (and hence the prevailing pattern of consumption) as desirable, but more often than not results in assembly and fabricating concerns with very little domestic value added and a very high import content. Its main weakness is its failure to grasp the source of the divergences. That source lies in the inability of the productive factors (as they currently exist) to produce the commodities used directly or indirectly in the production of all other commodities. The region's development strategies should at the very least aim to develop a domestic capability in this regard. Goods used directly and indirectly in the production of all other goods can be termed 'basic goods'.[7]

It is often claimed that starting import-substitution industrialisation with the final goods will, in the long run, create market incentives strong enough to produce backward linkages so that more and more inputs into the final process are attained. Nowhere, however, have market forces successfully induced this backward expansion. The USSR and other eastern European socialist countries are the only places in recent times to have bypassed market inducements in their attempts to plan or force economic transformation. They set about this task by developing an agricultural system that deliberately aimed to supply domestic food and raw material needs and by building up a heavy capital-goods industry. (The latter is known as Department I in the Marxian scheme of extended material production.) Once accomplished, this gave them the capacity not only to produce the basic goods or commodities used in producing all other commodities as identified above, but also and more importantly, the factories and scientific/technological infrastructure required to produce these commodities.

In the Caribbean, however, with its smallness and qualitatively different pattern and degree of integration into the international economy, the Eastern European model is not feasible. The Department I conception of Marx's scheme of extended reproduction is neither appropriate nor adequate for the task at hand. A far more suitable alternative would be to create a basic goods sector.[8] This approach is supported by a survey of world consumption patterns and their basic material input requirements, which shows that of the millions of products currently consumed around the world, only a dozen raw materials (iron and steel, cement, rubber, textiles, glass, leather, paper, plastics, industrial chemicals, aluminum, wood and fuels) account for more than 90 per cent of all the basic materials used in manufacturing. The list of basic foods is similarly short and the pattern is revealed in both capitalist and socialist economies.

The conclusion of all this is that for the region to embark on another development, three priorities have to be taken into account in the process of accumulation. These form the strategic choices or options to be pursued and it is from them that detailed programmes, sub-programmes and specific production activities should be based. They are (i) agricultural production oriented towards supplying the needs of the population in the *first instance* and with export specialisation following on as an extension of this. (The population's needs include food as well as raw materials. This reorientation would require major social changes, including radical land reform, a generally enhanced social status for traditional small farmers and a scientific and technological capability in these domestically-consumed crops); (ii) developing a capacity to produce basic materials as a key element in the industrialisation strategy. (Industrialisation would be limited to manufacturing in the traditional sense, but would include agroprocessing and the provision of services); and (iii) raising the level of economic and technical competence, although not necessarily increasing output, in the entrenched mineral and agro-exporting sector. (This is necessary to lower costs and enhance foreign-exchange inflows, to support the process of diversification, to extend the use of an internally developed scientific production capacity and to exploit the scope for innovation leading not only to lower costs but also to new products based on old lines of production.)⁹ Colonial policies and the downgrading of the region's technological capacity are not wholly responsible for the low level of technical competence in the traditional export sector. Petroleum was produced in Trinidad-Tobago for almost 80 years before a national research initiative was undertaken (nearly two decades after independence) in 1982, and here the focus of research has been on enhanced recovery methods.

It should be borne in mind that accumulation must be subordinated to socio-political priorities if it is to be interiorised in the society. Unless this happens, the material base of Caribbean social life will not complement the indispensable prerequisite of the move towards political and social change being generated from within the society. In the region, neither political nor economic decisions revolve around the issues of the society. This does not derive solely from its openness, as some presume, but essentially from the general marginalisation of the masses from social life. It is this marginalisation that allows the present ruling class to treat their hard-won independence (after centuries of slavery and exploitation) so carelessly.

Because the region is so open and vulnerable in the present world context, the approach outlined here encourages, but does not guarantee, its participation in the world system in such a manner that it does not automatically become a hapless victim of the system's systematic reproduction of inequalities. It is evident from the protectionism in the north, from the foreign-exchange and development pressures in the south (which are imposing more and more restrictions on imports), from the secular decline in primary commodity prices, from the former consumers of West Indian exports themselves becoming exporters of the same products (sugar from the EEC, oil from Britain and rice from Indonesia) and from the technological changes which are undermining the region as an export-processing zone, that the traditional exports and the new exports from the EPZs cannot constitute an 'engine for the region's growth'. By creating both a *social base* (with the orientation towards needs) and a *material base* (with the emphasis on domestic resources) for the development of a scientific and techno-logical capability in the region, this difficulty is overcome. One of the striking characteristics of the region is that even in its area of specialisation and comparative advantage in the world economy, it does not have highly-developed technical or scientific competences. An essential task of economic construction must be to create them, but this can only be done from a material base and within a logic of accumulation that explicitly promotes and accommodates it.

It is clear from the above that since size imposes an important constraint on the region's development, a reversal of its present balkanisation is essential to the task of success-fully pursuing the path of another development. The resolute and relentless pursuit of the interests of the poor and power-less requires an equally resolute and relentless pursuit of regional unity. Indeed, in a real sense, neither is achievable by itself.

Given the nature of the Caribbean economies, transfor-ming them will inevitably be an extended social project. Nevertheless, it is still necessary (as part of the mobilising effort of the society) to incorporate, as early in the process as possible, a more or less definite *conception* of the main economic configurations of the economy the society is working to construct. Moreover, this conception should be elevated to the level of a *popular conception*, rather than simply remaining the possession of the economy's political leadership, technocrats and managers. Rooting the project in the popular culture is the only way of ensuring its success, of organising and promoting the development of a new social order.

Another reason for having a clear idea of the configur-ations of the economy under construction is that it provides a point of reference with which *to test and measure its performance and development. This is important since there are no purely technical tests of a process as profound as the transformation of an economy.*[10] The crisis in the region accentuates the importance of this point, for there is an ever-present danger that, unless the popular consciousness embraces the vision of another development, the many 'quick-fix' solutions being offered and attempted will take on an impetus of their own and, in the process, become the end product of development itself.

The issue of property and social relations is central to the re-direction of the accumulation process. Contrary to popular left orthodoxy in the region, at this conjuncture the formulation presented here neither implies nor requires extensive state ownership, nor that the process be centrally planned and directed. On the contrary, it seeks to promote development from below, so that the vision of popular participation in a political democracy is translated into popular and participatory forms of ownership as well as economic policies and activities. In fact, at the present stage in the region's development, many factors work against extensive state enterprise and the possibility of being able to direct centrally planned economic change. These include a shortage of skills, lack of data and information, the instability of the region's price-formation process, the heterogeneity of production and the entrenchment of corruption and bureau-cratisation in central government. The new development, however, envisages a different conjunction of state-society relations as the social complement to policies of economic transformation. As Fagen, Deere and Corragio put it, the emphasis is on 'the reconstitution of state-society relations such that the 'popular classes' have a high degree of partici-pation in determining public policy at all levels' and go on to add that the goal is to end 'class, gender, racial, ethnic and other forms of privilege in access to 'valued goods' such as income, culture, justice and recreation'.[11]

Views, popularly regarded as progressive in the past, which equate state ownership of the productive factors and state direction of the economy with the transition to a higher order of economic, social and political organisation are, in my view, dangerous and are consequently rejected in my formulation, as are those which equate the entrenchment of democratic social forms with the entrenchment of a state elite and/or vanguard group 'chosen' by the people to give leadership to the 'immense majority' – the poor and the powerless.

In conclusion, it should be stated that, at the philosophical level, this formulation, along with the critical analysis of economic policy which had preceded it, seeks to do two things. One is to challenge the traditional ways of perceiving the operation of economic processes in the region, and hopefully in other countries of the third world where the basic conditions are sufficiently similar. The other is to dramatise the 'poverty of the received doctrines' in which economic policy is more often than not framed. The 'poverty' is clearly revealed in the many 'irrationalities' and paradoxes which prevail within the economic order and which, as we have shown, public policy systematically reinforces. Thus we find that despite the widespread under- and unemployment of the labour force and the absence of any form of institution-alised unemployment relief, public policy continues to direct a high proportion of the region's resources into subsidising foreign capital, with little or no challenge. Similarly, one would imagine that a rational system would require a society to treat its people and its land as its premier resources. Yet with all the poverty and unemployment in the region, its small size, and the dearth of resources available to its poor and powerless, both land and labour continues to be system-atically under- and unutilised.

This sort of paradox or irrationality is also observed in the present regional situation where the external debt continues to be posed as a critical element of the crisis, and to which governments have invariably responded by repressing the living standards of the poor. At the same time there is a substantial haemorrhage, as the reverse flow of foreign exchange has reached a stage where the region's econ-omic and political elites probably possess more overseas assets than the value of the public external debt. In the face of this, the current real wage of the poorest sections of the population in many countries (which include all those on the minimum wage or less and the unemployed) cannot purchase at today's prices the rations of protein (salted fish and beef), carbohydrates (corn, flour and cassava), shelter, wood fuel, working implements etc, allocated to the typical slave more than a century ago.

The prevalence of the 'black market', 'informal', 'under-ground' sector in some of the region's economies has reached a stage where in at least two territories (Guyana and Jamaica) it accounts for a substantial share of employment, importation of basic goods, ownership of financial assets, 'illegal' exports and earnings of foreign exchange. It includes the well-known marijuana trade and the not so well-known illegal export of precious metals from Guyana. Despite the importance of this sector, in neither of these territories has there been a serious and sustained attempt to collect and order the available data for use in public policy.

Perhaps the ultimate symbolic manifestation of these paradoxes is revealed in the appeal of the Prime Minister of St Vincent in his opening address to the CARICOM Heads of Government Conference, held in July 1987:

> Let us invite Canada, the United States and those countries of Europe which have historical links to the Caribbean to put together a development plan for this region to be called the Columbus Plan, to be launched on the anniversary date of the first landing of Christopher Columbus in this hemisphere.

As that event sparked the wanton slaughter of the region's indigenous peoples and the later enslavement of millions of Africans and Asians, it stands in cruel paradox to all our aspirations to sovereignty, independence and self-worth. It is, in other words, the very negation of the idea of a free West Indian people.

Notes

Chapter 1

1. Lewis, G. K. 1968 and 1983.
2. Mintz 1971: 36.
3. Parry and Sherlock 1971: 93–4.
4. Williams 1970: 148.
5. Moyne Commission 1945: 4.
6. Thomas 1984: Chapter 1.
7. *Ibid*: 11.
8. Colonial Office 1949: 10.
9. Patterson 1971: 66.
10. Adamson 1972: 183.
11. Thomas 1974.

Chapter 2

1. Fraginals 1984: 2.
2. Williams 1970: 293.
3. Adamson 1972: 34–41 and Farley 1954.

Chapter 3

1. Wong 1984: 125–40.
2. Smith 1976: 141.
3. Marx 1974: 751.
4. Beaud 1983: 121.
5. Moyne Commission 1945: 37, 38–39.
6. *Ibid*: 24.
7. *Ibid*: 92.
8. *Ibid*: 99.
9. *Ibid*: 174.
10. *Ibid*: 215–216.
11. *Ibid*: 195.

Chapter 4

1. Caribbean Commission 1948: 116.
2. Thomas 1980.
3. Moyne Commission 1945, Report on Agriculture, Fisheries, Forestry and Veterinary Matters.
4. Thomas 1974: 59.
5. Thomas 1980: 6.
6. Thomas 1984.

Chapter 5

1. West India Royal Commission 1897: 2.
2. Moyne Commission 1945: 443.
3. Lewis, W. A. 1977: 44; Caribbean Commission 1951.
4. Portojas García 1984: 12.
5. *Ibid*: 13.
6. *Ibid*.
7. Ayub 1981: 3–15, 30–56.
8. *Ibid*: 10.
9. *Ibid*: 12.
10. St Cyr 1982: 1–2.
11. Jefferson 1971: 109–20.
12. Carrington 1971.
13. Ayub 1981: 13.
14. Barry *et al* 1984: 13–26, 55–74.
15. Long 1985: 56–7.
16. Barry *et al* 1984: 65.
17. *Ibid*: 60.
18. Brewster and Thomas 1967.
19. Payne 1984: 145.
20. Group of Experts 1981: 50.
21. Brewster and Thomas 1967: 60.
22. McIntyre 1984: 3.

Chapter 7

1. Thorne 1971: 38.
2. Marshall 1968; Mintz 1974; Frucht 1967; Lewis, W A 1936; Sebastian 1980.
3. Moyne Commission 1945: 8.
4. Redwood 1967: 117.
5. *Ibid.*
6. Inter-American Development Bank, 1981: 21.
7. Barry *et al* 1984: 51.
8. Group of Experts 1981: 44.
9. Long 1985: 32.
10. *Ibid*: 35 (emphasis added).
11. *Caribbean Farm News* 1985: 1.
12. *Ibid: 4.*

Chapter 8

1. Barry *et al* 1984: 77.
2. *Ibid*: 78.
3. Bell 1983.
4. *Ibid.*
5. Taylor 1984: (i).
6. Government of Jamaica 1984: 13.1.
7. *Ibid.*
8. *Ibid.*
9. Kaufman 1985: 36.
10. Barry *et al* 1984: 130.
11. *Ibid*: 131.
12. *Ibid*: 131.

Chapter 9

1. Thomas 1974: 13–122; Thomas 1984a: Part I.
2. Thomas 1974: 87.

Chapter 10

1. Thomas 1984a: 49–66.
2. Shivji 1976; Thomas 1984a.

3. *Ibid*: 61–3.
4. PAHO/WHO 1976; Standing 1979.
5. PAHO/WHO 1976: 32.
6. Kaufman 1985; Stone 1980.
7. Stone 1980: 57–7; Nutrition Advisory Council 1975; Jamaica National Planning Agency 1982: xiv-xv; Kaufman 1985.
8. Thomas 1974: 88–96.
9. Thomas 1973: 358–9.
10. Thomas 1984b.
11. Thomas 1984: 145–62; Girvan 1976; Girvan 1975; Girvan 1978: 92–129; Girvan 1971: 217–40.

Chapter 11

1. Ambursley 1983: 72.
2. Payne 1984: 18.
3. Reid 1977; Beckford and Witter 1982; Ambursley 1981: 76–87.
4. Manley 1982: 39.
5. *Ibid*: 38.
6. *Ibid*: 41–2.
7. *Ibid*: 83.
8. Jamaica Social Development Commission 1979, cited in Kaufman 1985: 155.
9. Barry *et al* 1984: 344.
10. Jamaica National Planning Agency 1978: 86.
11. *Ibid*: 86.
12. Kaufman 1985: 169–72.
13. *Ibid*: 171.
14. *Ibid*: 171.
15. *Ibid*: 172; Fever 1983.
16. Stephens and Stephens 1983; 1983a.; 1984; Ambursley 1983.

17. Stephens and Stephens 1983: 373; Lewis, A. 1982; Ambursley 1981; Thomas 1977; 10–28.
18. Thomas 1984a; Kaufman 1985.
19. Barry *et al* 1984: 342.
20. Stone 1985: 288.
21. *Ibid*: 288.
22. Girvan, Bernal and Hughes 1980: 113–55.
23. Bernal 1984: 53.
24. Payne 1984a: 27.
25. Stephens and Stephens 1984: 2.
26. Stone 1985: 294.
27. These are discussed more fully in Part 5.
28. Stone 1985: 309.
29. *Ibid*: 295.
30. Clark 1983: xi.
31. Ambursley and James 1983.
32. Size holdings in the category 0.4–6.0 hectares comprised on average 2.38 fragments. The 1961 agricultural census suggested that 50 per cent of the land in the size group 500+ acres was idle despite the prevailing land shortage and land hunger.
33. Marcus and Taber 1983: 30 (emphasis added).
34. Grenada Deputy Prime Minister, and Minister of Planning, Finance and Trade, People's Revolutionary Government 1981: 64.
35. Thomas 1985; 1977; 1984a; Thorndike 1985.
36. Mandle 1986: 14; Thomson 1983.
37. Kirton 1985: 32.
38. Thomas 1983; 1984b; 1984c; 1984d; Committee of Concerned Citizens 1978; International Team of Observers at the Elections in Guyana 1980; Parliamentary Human Rights Group, London and Americas Watch 1985; 1985a; Guyana Human Rights Association, n.d.
39. Mandle 1976: 37–50; Mars 1978: 71–106.
40. Thomas 1976: Struggle for Socialism in Guyana, *Monthly Review* 23–5.
41. James and Lutchman 1985.
42. Interested readers may follow the further analysis of the themes in this chapter in Thomas 1987a.

Chapter 12

1. Gomes 1980; Karch 1977; Parris 1974.
2. Jainarain 1976: 205–29.
3. *Ibid*: 209–10.
4. Blackman 1982: 60.
5. Caribbean Development Bank 1985: 4.
6. *Ibid*: 7–8.
7. Gomes 1980: 42.
8. St Cyr 1982: 11. For estimate on windfall gains see Farrell 1986: 8.
9. Farrell 1986: 8.
10. Sandoval 1983: 247–68.
11. Parsan 1981; Long 1985.
12. Farrell 1986.
13. Barry *et al* 1984: 364;

quoted from Ramsaran
1984: 5.
14. Sandoval 1983: 266.

Chapter 13

1. Lewis, G. K. 1968: 343;
   Viner 1950; Meade 1953;
   Meade 1955.
2. Lewis, G. K. 1968:
   343–67.
3. Lewis, G. K. 1968: 345;
   Thomas 1979: 284–99;
   Thomas 1978: 59–71;
   Brewster and Thomas
   1967.
4. Hart 1982: 89.
5. Thomas 1979: 285.
6. Demas 1974: 37.
7. Searwar 1984.
8. Thomas 1979: 289–90.
9. Rainford 1985: 5.
10. *Ibid*: 5.
11. CARICOM Secretariat
    1981: 50.
12. Brewster and Thomas
    1967: 19.
13. CARICOM Secretariat
    1981: 50.
14. *Sunday Express* 3 March
    1985: 19.
15. Kelseck 1985: 12.
16. Note the emphasis.
    Although in Guyana
    rigged elections have
    traditionally excluded the
    opposition from this
    process, the situation is
    tolerated. Bishop's
    disruptive rise to power in
    Grenada posed severe
    problems, and it was no
    surprise that some
    CARICOM states were US

allies in the military
invasion of that country.
17. Thomas 1979: 298–9.
18. Williams 1979: 298.

Chapter 14

1. Thomas 1984d.
2. *Caribbean Business News*
   n.d.: 1.
3. *Caribbean Business News*
   1981/82: 10.
4. Black 1985: 35 (emphasis
   added).
5. Dymally 1985: 8–9.
6. *Ibid*.
7. *Ibid*.
8. Sunshine 1985: 120.
9. Shultz 1985: 6.
10. *Ibid*.
11. *Caribbean West Indies
    Chronicle* 1984: 8.
12. Gonzales 1985: 16.
13. ICFTU/CCL 1986: 24.
14. The three states which did
    not participate are
    Montserrat (still a colony),
    St Kitts-Nevis and Grenada
    itself.
15. NACLA 1985: 33.
16. *The Nation* 1984: 1;
    Caribbean Contact 1982:
    9.
17. Tiryakian 1984: 48.
18. Significantly, the US
    restrictions on TV piracy
    which is encapsulated in
    the CBI proposals apply
    only to government-owned
    stations and not private
    ones.
19. Dosman 1985.

Chapter 15

1. Thomas 1982: 1–20.
2. Thomas 1982: 8; Haque *et al* 1977: 46.
3. Thomas 1987.
4. Irvin and Gorostiaga 1985: 28.
5. *Ibid*: 17.
6. Manley 1985.
7. Thomas 1974.
8. *Ibid*
9. Thomas 1985a.
10. Thomas 1974.
11. Fagen *et al* 1986: 10.

Acronyms

ACP	African/Caribbean/Pacific
AFL-CIO	American Federation of Labor-Congress of Industrial Organisations
AIFLD	American Institute for Free Labor Development
BP	British Petroleum
BWIA	British West Indian Airlines
CADEC	Caribbean Conference of Churches' development agency
CAIC	Caribbean Association of Industry and Commerce
CANA	Caribbean News Agency
CARIBCAN	Caribbean/Canadian trade agreement
CARICOM	Caribbean Community and Common Market
CARIFTA	Caribbean Free Trade Association
CBI	Caribbean Basin Initiative
CBIN	Caribbean Basin Information Network
CCAA	Caribbean-Central American Action
CCL	Caribbean Conference of Labour
CDB	Caribbean Development Bank
CGED	Caribbean Group for Cooperation in Economic Development
CIA	Central Intelligence Agency (US)
CIDA	Canadian International Development Agency
CMCF	Community Multilateral Clearing Facility
CPDF	Caribbean Project Development Facility
CTA	Caribbean Tourist Association
CTRC	Caribbean Tourism Research Centre
DOM	Département Outre-Mer (France)
ECCM	Eastern Caribbean Common Market
ECU	European Currency Unit
EEC	European Economic Community
EPICA	Ecumenical Program for Interamerican Communication and Action
EPZ	Export Processing Zone
FOMENTO	Puerto Rican Economic Development Administration
GDP	Gross Domestic Product

HMSO	His/Her Majesty's Stationery Office
ICFTU	International Confederation of Free Trade Unions
IDB	Inter-American Development Bank
IDC	Industrial Development Corporation
IDS	Institute of Development Studies (Guyana)
IDS	Institute of Development Studies (Sussex)
ILO	International Labour Organisation (Geneva)
IMF	International Monetary Fund
ISCOTT	Iron and Steel Company of Trinidad-Tobago
ISER	Institute for Social and Economic Research (UWI)
ITT	International Telegraphs and Telecommunications
JLP	Jamaica Labour Party
MNC	Multinational Corporation
MNE	Multinational Enterprise
MPLA	Popular Movement for the Liberation of Angola
NACLA	North American Congress on Latin America
NATO	North Atlantic Treaty Organisation
OECS	Organisation of Eastern Caribbean States
OPEC	Organisation of Petroleum Exporting Countries
PAHO	Pan-American Health Organisation
PNC	People's National Congress (Guyana)
PNM	People's National Movement (Trinidad-Tobago)
PNP	People's National Party (Jamaica)
PPP	People's Progressive Party (Guyana)
PRG	People's Revolutionary Government (Grenada)
TNC	Transnational Corporation
TTMA	Trinidad-Tobago Marketing Association
TWA	Trans World Airlines
UNDP	United Nations Development Programme
UNECLAC	United Nations Economic Commission for Latin America and the Caribbean
UNICA	Association of Caribbean Universities
UNIDO	United Nations Industrial Development Organisation
UNITA	National Union for the Total Independence of Angola
USAID	United States Agency for International Development
UWI	University of the West Indies

| WFTU | World Federation of Trade Unions |
| WHO | World Health Organisation |

Bibliography

Adamson, A. *Sugar Without Slaves*. Yale University Press, New Haven, 1972.

Ambursley, F. 'Jamaica: The Demise of "Democratic Socialism" ', *New Left Review*, no. 128, July-August 1981, pp. 76-87.

Ambursley, F. 'Jamaica: From Michael Manley to Edward Seaga' in Ambursley, F. and Cohen, R. (eds). *Crisis in the Caribbean*. Monthly Review Press/Heinemann, London and New York, 1983.

Ambursley, F. and Cohen R. (eds). *Crisis in the Caribbean*. Monthly Review Press/Heinemann, London and New York, 1983.

Ambursley, F. and James, W. 'Maurice Bishop and the New Jewel Revolution in Grenada', *New Left Review*, no. 142, November-December 1983.

Ayub, M.A. 'Made in Jamaica: The Development of the Manufacturing Sector', *World Bank Staff Occasional Papers*, no. 33, 1981.

Barry, T., Wood, B. and Preusch, D. *The Other Side of Paradise: Foreign Control in the Caribbean*. Grove Press Inc, New York, 1984.

Beaud, Michel. *A History of Capitalism*, 1500-1980. Monthly Review Press, New York, 1983.

Beckford, G. (ed). *Caribbean Economy*. ISER, University of the West Indies, Jamaica, 1978.

Beckford, G. and Witter, M. *Small Garden, Bitter Weed: Struggle and Change in Jamaica*. 2nd edition, Zed Press, London, 1982.

Bell, J. 'The Operational Constraints Facing Caribbean Tourism Establishments and the Resulting Impact on their Financial Viability', Caribbean Hotel Association, Document no. CTMC/6, December 1983.

Bernal, R.L. 'The IMF and Class Struggle in Jamaica 1977-1980', *Latin American Perspectives*, issue 42, vol.11, no. 3, Summer 1984.

Best, L. 'International Cooperation in the Industrialisation Process: The Case of Trinidad-Tobago', in UNIDO, *Industry 2000 – New Perspective*, Collected Background Papers, UNIDO/10D337, October 1980.

Black, G. 'Laboratory Conditions', in *NACLA Report on the Americas*, July/August, 1985.

Blackman, C. *The Practice of Persuasion*. Cedar Press, Barbados, 1982.

Brewster, Havelock and Thomas, Clive Y. *The Dynamics of West Indian Economic Integration*. ISER, University of the West Indies, Jamaica, 1967.

Caribbean Business News, Special Report, 'Caribbean Central American Action', n.d.

Caribbean Business News, vol. XII, no. 1, 1981/82.

Caribbean Commission, 'Industrial Development in the Caribbean', Report prepared by the British member of the Industrial Survey Panel, vol. 1, 1948. Reprinted in *Caribbean Economic Review*, 1951.

Caribbean Contact, December 1982.

Caribbean Contact, December 1985.

Caribbean Development Bank, *Caribbean Development Bank News*. April-June 1985.

Caribbean Farm News, vol. 1, no. 1, March 1985.

Caribbean West Indies Chronicle, August/September, 1984.

CARICOM Secretariat, 'The Caribbean Community in the 1980s', Report by a Group of Experts, CARICOM Secretariat, Guyana, 1981.

Carrington, E. 'Industrialisation by Invitation in Trinidad since 1950', in Girvan, N. and Jefferson, O. (eds). *Readings in the Political Economy of the Caribbean*. New World Group, Trinidad, January 1971.

Central Bank of Trinidad-Tobago, *Annual Reports and Statistical Bulletin*. various issues.

Clark, S. 'Introduction' in Marcus, B. and Taber, M. (eds). *Maurice Bishop Speaks: The Grenada Revolution 1979-1983*. Pathfinder Press, New York, 1983.

Colonial Office. *Report of a Commission of Inquiry into the Sugar Industry of British Guiana*. HMSO, London, 1949.

Committee of Concerned Citizens. 'A Report on the Referendum held in Guyana, 16 July 1978', Guyana, 1978.

Craig, Susan (ed). *Contemporary Caribbean: A Sociological Reader*. vol. 2, Trinidad, 1982.

Demas, W. 'West Indian Nationhood and Caribbean Integration', Caribbean Conference of Churches, Barbados, 1974.

Dosman, E.J. 'Latin America and the Caribbean: The Strategic Framework – A Canadian Perspective', Extra-Mural Paper No. 31, Operational Research and Analysis Establishment, Department of National Defence, Ottawa, Canada, 1985.

Dymally, M. Speech to a public-private sector cooperation conference on sustaining stable democracies, sponsored by the National Democratic Institute and the Centre for International Private

Enterprises, Barbados 1985. Text reproduced in *Caribbean Contact*, December 1985.

Erisman, M. (ed). *The Caribbean Challenge: US Policy in a Volatile Region*. Boulder, Westview Press, 1984.

Fagen, R.R., Deere, Carmen Diana and Coraggio, J.L. (eds). *Transition and Development*. Monthly Review Press, New York, 1986.

Farley, R.E.G. 'The Rise of the Peasantry in British Guiana', *Social and Economic Studies*, no. 2, 1954.

Farrell, T. 'Why a Trinidad and Tobago Crisis?', *Caribbean Contact*, February 1986.

Feuer, Carl. 'Jamaica and Sugar Workers Cooperatives: The Politics of Reform', Ph.D. thesis, Cornell University, 1983.

Fraginals, M.M. 'Caribbean Sugar Plantations: their Past and their Probable Future', Mimeographed paper presented to a conference on *New Perspectives on the Caribbean: Towards the 21st Century*, Hunter College and Research Institute for the Study of Man, New York, August 1984.

Frucht, R. 'A Caribbean Social Type: Neither a 'Peasant' nor 'Proletarian', *Social and Economic Studies*, vol. 16, no. 3, 1967.

Girvan, N. 'Why We Need to Nationalise Bauxite and How' in. Girvan, N. and Jefferson, O. (eds). *Readings in the Political Economy of the Caribbean*. New World Group, Trinidad, January 1971.

Girvan, N. 'Economic Nationalists vs Multinational Corporations: Revolutionary or Evolutionary Change?' in. Widstrand, C. (ed). *Multinational Corporations in Africa*. Uppsala, Sweden, 1975.

Girvan, N. *Corporate Imperialism, Conflict and Expropriation*. Monthly Review Press, New York, 1976.

Girvan, N. 'Caribbean Mineral Economy' in Beckford, G. (ed) *Caribbean Economy*. ISER, University of the West Indies, Jamaica, 1978.

Girvan, N., Bernal, R. and Hughes, W. 'The IMF and the Third World: The Case of Jamaica, 1974-1980', *Development Dialogue*, vol. 2, 1980, pp. 113-55.

Girvan, N. and Jefferson, O. (eds). *Readings in the Political Economy of the Caribbean*. New World Group, Trinidad, January 1971.

Gomes, P.I. 'Barbados: The Post-Independence Period, 1966-1976', Working Papers Series A, no. 3, Department of Sociology, University of the West Indies, Trinidad, 1980.

Gonzales, A.P. 'The End of ACP/EEC Negotiations: Lomé

Cooperation Rides Again', *CARICOM Perspective*, January-February, 1985.

Grenada, Deputy Prime Minister and Minister of Planning, Finance and Trade, People's Revolutionary Government. *Report on the National Economy for 1981 and the Prospects for 1982*. Grenada, 1981.

Group of Experts, Report of. *The Caribbean Community in the 1980s*. CARICOM Secretariat, Guyana, 1981.

Guyana Human Rights Association. 'Annual Human Rights Reports', Georgetown, Guyana, n.d.

Haque, W. *et al.* 'Towards a Theory of Rural Development', *Development Dialogue*, no. 2, 1977.

Hart, R. 'Trade Unionism in the English-Speaking Caribbean: The Formative Years and the Caribbean Labour Congress' in Craig, Susan (ed). *Contemporary Caribbean: A Sociological Reader*. vol. 2, Trinidad, 1982.

Horowitz, M.M. (ed). *Peoples and Cultures of the Caribbean: An Anthropological Reader*. Natural History Press for the American Museum of Natural History, New York, 1971.

ICFTU/CCL. 'An Economic Policy for the Caribbean', Barbados, 1986.

Ince, B. (ed). *Contemporary International Relations in the Caribbean*. Institute of International Relations, Trinidad, 1979.

Inter-American Development Bank. *Annual Report* 1980-81, 1981.

International Team of Observers at the Elections in Guyana. 'Something to Remember', December 1980, London, Parliamentary Human Rights Group, House of Commons. (Reprinted by the Guyana Human Rights Association 1981).

Irwin, G. and Gorostiaga, X. *Towards an Alternative for Central America and the Caribbean*. George Allen & Unwin, London, 1985.

Jainarain, I. *Trade and Underdevelopment: A Study of the Small Caribbean Countries and Large Multinational Corporations*. IDS, University of Guyana, 1976.

Jamaica, Government of. *Economic and Social Survey*. 1984.

Jamaica, National Planning Agency. *Five Year Development Plan, 1978-1982*. Government of Jamaica, 1978.

Jamaica, Social Development Commission. 'Guidelines on the Structure and Role of Community Councils', Social Development Commission 1979, cited in Kaufman, M. *Jamaica under Manley: Dilemmas of Socialism and Democracy*. Zed Books Ltd and Lawrence Hill & Co., London, Toronto and Westport, Connecticut, 1985.

James, R.W. and Lutchman, H.A. *Law and the Political Environment in Guyana*. Institute of Development Studies, University of Guyana, 1985.

Jefferson, O. 'Jamaica Post-War Economic Development', in N. Girvan and O. Jefferson (eds), *Readings in the Political Economy of the Caribbean*. New World Group, Trinidad, 1971.

Karch, C. 'Changes in the Barbadian Social Structure, 1860-1937', Seminar Paper, ISER, University of the West Indies, Barbados, 1977.

Kaufman, M. *Jamaica under Manley: Dilemmas of Socialism and Democracy*. Zed Books Ltd and Lawrence Hill & Co., London, Toronto and Westport, Connecticut, 1985.

Kelseck, W. in *CAIC Calling the Caribbean*, vol. 5, no. 3, July-September 1985.

Kirton, C.D. 'Public Policy and Private Capital in the Transition to Socialism: Grenada 1979-1983', mimeo, 1985.

Lamming, G. (ed). *Reader in Caribbean Development*. Department of Economics, University of the West Indies, Jamaica and Freiderich Ebert Stiftung Foundation, 1987.

Lewis, A. 'The Fall of Michael Manley: A Case Study of the Failure of Reform Socialism', *Monthly Review*, February 1982.

Lewis, G.K. *The Growth of the Modern West Indies*. Macgibbon & Kee, London, 1968.

Lewis, G.K. *Main Currents in Caribbean Thought*. Johns Hopkins University Press and Heinemann, Jamaica and Baltimore, Maryland, 1983.

Lewis, W.A. 'The Evolution of the Peasantry in the British West Indies: An Essay', *West Indies and South American Pamphlets*, vol. 15, no. 656, 30 June 1936.

Lewis, W.A. *Labour in the West Indies: The Birth of the Workers' Movement*. Fabian Society, London, 1939. Republished by New Beacon Books, London, 1977.

Long, F. 'Employment Effects of Multinational Enterprises in Export Processing Zones in the Caribbean', mimeo, 1985.

Long, F. 'How the Caribbean's Food Production Plans Went Awry', *CERES*, vol. 18, no. 4, July-August 1985a.

Lowenthal, D. and Comitas, L. (eds). *The Aftermath of Sovereignty*. Doubleday, New York, 1973.

McIntyre, R.S. 'The Failure of Corporate Tax Incentives', Citizens for Tax Justice, Washington, 1984, and excerpted under the same title *in Multinational Monitor*, vol. 5, nos. 10 & 11, October-November, 1984.

Mandle, J.M. 'Continuity and Change in Guyanese Underdevelopment', *Monthly Review*, vol. 28, no. 4, 1976, pp. 37-50.

Mandle, J.M. 'Economic Development in Grenada under the Provisional Revolutionary Government', *Transition*, no. 14, 1986.

Manley, M. *Jamaica: Struggle in the Periphery*. Third World Media Ltd, London, 1982.

Manley, M., Report of International Committee chaired by. *Global Challenge: From Crisis to Cooperation: Breaking the North-South Stalemate*. Pan Books, London, 1985.

Marcus, B. and Taber, M. (eds). *Maurice Bishop Speaks: The Grenada Revolution 1979-1983*. Pathfinder Press, New York, 1983.

Mars, P. 'Cooperative Socialism and Marxist Scientific Theory', *Caribbean Issues*, vol. 4, no. 2, 1978, pp. 71-106.

Marshall, W.K. 'Notes on Peasant Development in the West Indies since 1838', *Social and Economic Studies*, vol. 17, no. 3. 1968.

Marx, Karl. *Capital*. vol. 1, International Publishers, New York, 1974.

Meade, J. *Problems of Economic Union*. University of Chicago Press, Chicago, 1953.

Meade, J. *The Theory of Customs Unions*. North Holland Publishing Company, Amsterdam, 1955.

Mintz, Sidney W. 'The Caribbean as a Socio-Cultural Area' in Horowitz, M.M. (ed) *Peoples and Cultures of the Caribbean: An Anthropological Reader*. Natural History Press for the American Museum of Natural History, New York, 1971.

Mintz, S. *Caribbean Transformation*. Aldine Publishing Company, Chicago, 1974.

Moyne Commission. See West India Royal Commission.

NACLA, 'Reagan's Mediterranean', *NACLA Report on the Americas*, vol. 19, no. 4, July/August 1985.

Nation, The, Barbados, 23 January 1984.

Nutrition Advisory Council, 'A Food and Nutrition Policy for Jamaica,' mimeo, Jamaica, 1975.

PAHO/WHO. *The National Food and Nutrition Survey of Guyana*. Scientific Publication no. 323, Washington DC, 1976.

Parliamentary Human Rights Group, London and Americas Watch. 'Interim Report', 1985.

Parliamentary Human Rights Group, London and Americas Watch. 'Final Report on Electoral Law and Practice in Guyana, 1985', 1985a.

Parris, R.G. 'Race, Inequality and Underdevelopment in Barbados', Ph.D. thesis, Yale University, 1974.

Parry, J.H. and Sherlock, P. *A Short History of the West Indies*. Macmillan Press, London, 1971.

Parsan, E. 'An Evaluation of the Organization and Development of the Fertilizer Industry in Trinidad and Tobago', M.Sc. thesis, University of the West Indies, St Augustine, Trinidad, 1981.

Patterson, H.O. 'Contribution on the Symposium on Sugar and Change' in N. Girvan and O. Jefferson (eds), *Readings in the Political Economy of the Caribbean*. New World Group, January 1971.

Payne, A. 'Regional Industrial Programming in CARICOM', in Payne, A. and Sutton, P. (eds). *Overcoming Dependence: The Political Economy of the Commonwealth Caribbean*. Manchester University Press, Manchester, 1984.

Payne, A. 'Jamaica: The 'Democratic Socialist' Experiment of Michael Manley', in Payne, A. and Sutton, P. (eds). *Overcoming Dependence: The Political Economy of the Commonwealth Caribbean*. Manchester University Press, Manchester, 1984a.

Payne, A. and Sutton, P. (eds). *Overcoming Dependence: The Political Economy of the Commonwealth Caribbean*. Manchester University Press, Manchester, 1984.

Portojas García, Emilio. 'Puerto Rico: The Making of a Corporate Paradise', *Multinational Monitor*, vol. 5, nos. 10 & 11, October/November 1984.

Rainford, R. 'The Caribbean Community and Common Market: The Next Twelve Years', *Regional Cooperation Recent Developments*, Report No. 9, January-September, Economic Affairs Division, Commonwealth Secretariat, London, 1985.

Ramsaran, R. 'The Growth and Pattern of Government Expenditure in Trinidad and Tobago, 1963-1983', Paper presented to the Sixteenth Annual Conference of the Regional Monetary Studies Programme, Jamaica, 1984.

Redwood, P. 'Statistical Survey of Land Settlements in Jamaica: 1929-1949', cited in Brewster, Havelock and Thomas, Clive Y. *Dynamics of West Indian Economic Integration*. ISER, University of the West Indies, Jamaica 1967.

Reid, S. 'An Introductory Approach to the Concentration of Power in the Jamaican Corporate Economy and Notes on its Origin', in Stone, C. and Brown, A. (eds). *Essays on Power and Change in Jamaica*. ISER, University of the West Indies, Jamaica, 1977.

St Cyr, Eric. 'Towards a Long-Term Strategy for Trinidad-Tobago: Some Alternative Perspectives', University of West Indies, mimeo, 1982.

Sandoval, J.M. 'State Capitalism in a Petroleum-Based Economy:

The Case of Trinidad and Tobago' in Ambursley, F. and Cohen, R. (eds). *Crisis in the Caribbean*. Monthly Review Press/Heinemann, London and New York, 1983.

Seawar, L. 'Joint Conduct of External Political Relations and its Effect on the Integration Process', Paper presented to the Seminar sponsored by the Inter-American Bank held in Barbados, 1983, on the theme *Ten Years of CARICOM*, published by the IDB, Washington, DC, 1984.

Sebastian, R. 'A Typology of Caribbean Peasantry: The Development of the Peasantry in Trinidad and Tobago 1845-1917', *Social and Economic Studies*, vol. 29, nos. 2 & 3, June/September 1980.

Shivji, I. *Class Struggle in Tanzania*. Monthly Review Press, New York and London, 1976.

Shultz, G.P. Speech to '8th Annual Conference on Trade, Investment and Development in the Caribbean Basin', Miami, Florida, 6 December 1984, in *CAIC: Calling the Caribbean*, January-March, 1985.

Smith, Adam. *An Inquiry into the Nature and Causes of the Wealth of Nations*. vol. 2, University of Chicago Press, Chicago, 1976.

Standing, G. 'Socialism and Basic Needs in Guyana' in Standing, G. and Szal, R. (eds). *Poverty and Basic Needs*. ILO, Geneva, 1979.

Standing, G. and Szal, R. (eds). *Poverty and Basic Needs*. ILO, Geneva, 1979.

Stephens, E.H. and Stephens, J.D. 'Democratic Socialism and Dependent Capitalism: An Analysis of the Manley Government in Jamaica', *Politics and Society*, vol. 12, no. 3, 1983, pp. 373-411.

Stephens, E.H. and Stephens, J.D. 'Democratic Socialism and the Capitalist Class: An Analysis of the Relation between Jamaican Business and the PNP Government', Universidad Interamericana de Puerto Rico, working paper no. 8, 1983a.

Stephens, E.H. and Stephens, J.D. 'Jamaica's Democratic Socialist Path: An Evaluation', Latin American Program, The Wilson Center, Working Papers, 1984.

Stone, C. *Democracy and Clientilism in Jamaica*. Transaction Books, New Brunswick, New Jersey, 1980.

Stone, C. 'Jamaica in Crisis: From Socialist to Capitalist Management', *International Journal*, no. XL, Spring 1985.

Stone, C. 'Jamaica in Crisis: From Socialist to Capitalist Management', *International Journal*, Spring 1985.

Stone, C. and Brown, A. (eds). *Essays on Power and Change in Jamaica*. ISER, University of the West Indies, Jamaica, 1977.

Sunday Express, Trinidad-Tobago, 3 March 1985.

Sunshine, C.A. *The Caribbean: Survival, Struggle and Sovereignty.* EPICA Publication, Washington DC, 1985.

Taylor, J. 'How Clean is the Caribbean?', Monitor Section, *Caribbean and West Indies Chronicle*, February/March 1984.

Thomas, Clive Y. 'Meaningful Participation: The Fraud of It', in Lowenthal, D. and Comitas, L. (eds). *The Aftermath of Sovereignty.* Doubleday, New York, 1973.

Thomas, Clive Y. *Dependence and Transformation: The Economics of the Transition to Socialism.* Monthly Review Press, New York and London, 1974.

Thomas, Clive Y. 'Bread and Justice: The Struggle for Socialism in Guyana', *Monthly Review*, vol. 28, no. 4, 1975, pp. 23-5.

Thomas, Clive Y. 'The Non Capitalist Path as Theory and Practice of De-Colonization and Socialist Transformation', *Latin American Perspectives*, no. 17, 1977, pp. 10-28.

Thomas, Clive Y. 'On Formulating a Marxist Theory of Economic Integration', *Transition*, vol. 1, no. 1, 1978, pp.59-71.

Thomas, Clive Y. 'Neo-Colonialism and Caribbean Integration', in Ince, B. (ed). *Contemporary International Relations in the Caribbean.* Institute of International Relations, Trinidad, 1979.

Thomas, Clive Y. 'From Colony to State Capitalism: Alternative Paths of Development in the Caribbean', *Transition*, no. 5, 1980.

Thomas, Clive Y. 'State Capitalism in Guyana: An Assessment of Burnham's Cooperative Socialist Republic' in Ambursley, F. and Cohen, R. (eds). *Crisis in the Caribbean* Monthly Review Press/Heinemann, London and New York, 1983.

Thomas, Clive Y. *Plantation, Peasants and State.* University of California, Los Angeles, and ISER, University of the West Indies, Jamaica, 1984.

Thomas, Clive Y. *The Rise of the Authoritarian State in Peripheral Societies.* Monthly Review Press/Heinemann, New York and London, 1984a.

Thomas, Clive Y. 'Guyana: The Rise and Fall of "Cooperative Socialism" ' in Payne, A. and Sutton, P. (eds). *Overcoming Dependence: The Political Economy of the Commonwealth Caribbean.* Manchester University Press, Manchester 1984b.

Thomas, Clive Y. 'Guyana: Crisis, Reaction and Response', Paper presented to the Conference entitled *New Perspectives on Caribbean Studies: Towards the 21st Century.* Hunter College, 1984c.

Thomas, Clive Y. 'The Grenadian Crisis and the Caribbean Left', IDS Bulletin, Guyana, April 1985.

Thomas, Clive Y. *Sugar: An Assessment of the Impact of Technological Developments in the High Fructose Corn Syrup and Sucro-*

chemicals. International Development Research Centre, Ottawa, 1985a.

Thomas, Clive Y. 'Caribbean State as Agent of Social Change', in Lamming, G. (ed). *Reader in Caribbean Development*. Department of Economics, University of the West Indies, Jamaica and Friederich Ebert Stiftung Foundation, 1987.

Thomas, Clive Y. 'The Next Time Around: Radical Options and Caribbean Economy', Paper presented to the first conference of the Association of Caribbean Economists, Jamaica, 1987a.

Thomson, R. 'The Potential and Limits of Agricultural Self-Reliance in Grenada', M.A. Thesis, Carleton University, Ottawa, 1983.

Thorne, A.P. 'Comments on a Monograph on Exploitation and Some Relevant Reminiscences', *Caribbean Studies*, vol. 11, no. 3, July 1971.

Thorndike, Tony. *Grenada: Politics, Economics and Society*. Frances Pinter, London 1985.

Tiryakian, J.C. 'Military and Security Dimensions of US-Caribbean Policy', in Erisman, M. (ed). *The Caribbean Challenge: US Policy in a Volatile Region*. Boulder, Westview Press, 1984.

Trinidad-Tobago, Government of. *Review of the Economy*. 1985.

UNIDO, *Industry 2000 – New Perspective*, Collected Background Papers, UNIDO/10D337, October 1980.

Viner, J. *The Customs Union Issue*. Carnegie Endowment for International Peace, New York, 1950.

West India Royal Commission. *Report of West India Royal Commission*. HMSO, CMD 8655, 1897.

West India Royal Commission. *Report of West India Royal Commission, appointed 1938*. HMSO, CMD 6607, 6608, 1945. (Usually referred to as the Moyne Commission Report).

Widstrand, C. (ed). *Multinational Corporations in Africa*. Uppsala, Sweden, 1975.

Williams, Eric. *From Columbus to Castro: The History of the Caribbean, 1492-1969*, Andre Deutsch, London, 1970.

Williams, Eric. 'Speech to the 15th Annual Convention of the PNM', cited in Thomas, Clive Y. 'Neo-Colonialism and Caribbean Integration', in Ince, B. (ed). *Contemporary International Relations in the Caribbean*. Institute of International Relations, Trinidad, 1979.

Wong, D.C. 'A Review of Caribbean Political Economy', *Latin American Perspectives*, 42, vol. 2, no. 3, Summer 1984.

Index